Whatever Happened to An.................

'The contemporary debate about antisemitism is both incoherent and appalling. It's incoherent because there's no consensus definition about what antisemitism is. It's appalling because the definition employed by many influential Jewish organizations and Western politicians label virtually anyone with a genuine commitment to Palestinian freedom a Jew hater. Faced with this hot mess, Antony Lerman offers a cool, well-reasoned, deeply learned and morally courageous meditation on what antisemitism is and isn't. An urgently needed book.'
—Peter Beinart, editor-at-large at *Jewish Currents*

'Nobody unpacks the confusions currently circulating around antisemitism, nor the complexities of Jewish identity, better than Antony Lerman. This elegantly written, erudite book is essential reading for all of us, whatever our identifications.'
—Lynne Segal, author of *Radical Happiness: Moments of Collective Joy*

'This important, essential book by a leading expert on antisemitism offers a nuanced and insightful history of the use and abuse of the fight against the world's oldest hatred. It powerfully unmasks the so-far very successful effort to twist the battle against antisemitism into a defence of the indefensible: Israel's subjugation of millions of people on the basis of their national and ethnic identity.'
—Nathan Thrall, author of *The Only Language They Understand*

'This is the best book I have read on why anti-Zionism has been equated with antisemitism and how the "new antisemitism" has been mobilised for political gain in a variety of arenas. Coming from one of the world's leading experts, Antony Lerman's incisive analysis will undoubtedly serve as the major reference for both pundits and novices for many years to come. I, for one, have learned a great deal from it.'
—Neve Gordon, co-author of *The Human Right to Dominate*

'We desperately need this book – and I can't imagine anyone better than Tony Lerman to write it. An essential tool to understand the weaponisation of antisemitism and its dangerous impact on free speech, Palestinian rights, and the very real threat of actual antisemitism.'
—Rebecca Vilkomerson, former Executive Director of Jewish Voice for Peace

Whatever Happened to Antisemitism?

Redefinition and the Myth of the 'Collective Jew'

Antony Lerman

PLUTO PRESS

First published 2022 by Pluto Press
New Wing, Somerset House, Strand, London WC2R 1LA

www.plutobooks.com

British Library Cataloguing in Publication Data
A catalogue record for this book is available from the British Library

ISBN 978 0 7453 3879 8   Hardback
ISBN 978 0 7453 3877 4   Paperback
ISBN 978 1 786806 29 1   PDF
ISBN 978 1 786806 30 7   EPUB

This book is printed on paper suitable for recycling and made from fully managed and
sustained forest sources. Logging, pulping and manufacturing processes are expected to
conform to the environmental standards of the country of origin.

Typeset by Stanford DTP Services, Northampton, England

Simultaneously printed in the United Kingdom and United States of America

for
Kathy

Contents

Acknowledgements

I have been intending to write this book for longer than I care to remember. It draws on so many things I have learnt from the work and advice of other people over a 40-year period that this short thank you note can never do them justice. Some are no longer with us, but I particularly miss the sage and clear thinking about antisemitism generously dispensed by the late Lukasz Hirszowicz, an expert on modern Russian Jewish history and so much more, with whom I worked at the Institute of Jewish Affairs in London in the 1980s and 1990s.

My longest continuing conversation about antisemitism has been with Brian Klug. It began around the turn of the century and was only partially disrupted during the COVID-19 pandemic. His seminal 2003 article, 'The collective Jew: Israel and the new antisemitism', did all the heavy lifting in debunking 'new antisemitism' and the false equivalence between anti-Zionism and antisemitism. It profoundly influenced my thinking, as has so much of his other writing in this area. It has been a tremendously rewarding dialogue and friendship, both when we agreed and when we disagreed, and long may it continue.

The dispassionate study of antisemitism has not been easy to maintain in the last 20 years, but someone who has done much to develop and sustain it is David Feldman. The seminars, lectures and workshops organized by his research institute at Birkbeck London University have shown the value of keeping open a space for discussion between people of very different views, however difficult that has been to execute. David's own work on the meanings of antisemitism played a key role in getting me started on this book.

The issue of antisemitism and other forms of racism was central to a five-year project, The Vienna Conversations, hosted by The Bruno Kreisky Forum for International Dialogue in Vienna and expertly led by its charismatic and indefatigable director, Gertraud Auer Borea. I had the good fortune to participate in most of the discussions and, here too, freedom to speak one's mind helped me greatly to develop my thoughts about current antisemitism within the context of understanding the seriousness of the problem of racisms in general in Europe. I am enormously grateful to Gertraud for inviting me to be part of this very rewarding project and subsequently honouring me with a Senior Fellowship.

I am also indebted to Richard Kuper for the work he did on exposing what we both knew to be the fundamental political nature of the creation of the European Union Monitoring Centre (EUMC) 'working definition' of antisemitism, and its reincarnation as the International Holocaust Remembrance

Alliance (IHRA) 'working definition'. On the IHRA version and the politicisation of antisemitism, Jamie Stern-Weiner has generously shared with me his deep and expanding knowledge. Collaborating with him has been enormously helpful both in getting details right and in clarifying the significance of key events in the 'redefinition' saga.

Jamie was one of four unbelievably kind friends, colleagues and academic experts who read my entire manuscript and gave me the most incisive, crucial and constructive feedback on every level, from my treatment of the book's key arguments to the smallest points of fact. Two have written essential books and articles illuminating the complexities of attitudes to Jews, both hostile and affirmative, in various historical contexts. Steven Beller is the author of many highly regarded books on Austrian, Jewish and Central European history. Adam Sutcliffe's most recent book, *What Are Jews For? History, Peoplehood and Purpose*, yielded many insights of great value to me in the latter stages of writing the book. The hours they spent reading the text, flagging issues for me to consider and then discussing them with me went above and beyond any call of duty. I am of course solely responsible for what I have written.

The fourth reader is Barbara Rosenbaum, Editor of *Patterns of Prejudice*, with whom I have been discussing the subject matter of this book in numerous London cafes for many years. As a brilliant editor and scourge of woolly thinking, she has constantly challenged me to clarify and sharpen-up my ideas. I am so grateful to her for keeping me on the right track.

Others, too, have contributed to this book in a variety of ways. Benjamin Ross very kindly took time out from film-making and scriptwriting to read early versions of the first five chapters, and gave me much food for thought. I owe a lot to a long lunch conversation with novelist and polymath Zia Haider Rahman at a time when I was finding it very difficult to continue working on the book. The advice he gave me unlocked the door to the eventual completion of the project. A thank you, too, to Chad McDonald for helping me so much in obtaining key research articles that I needed over the last two years.

Without the constant encouragement of my commissioning editor at Pluto, David Shulman, there would be no book. He tolerated missed deadlines and changing conceptions of the book's focus, and he never lost faith in my ability to deliver. His enthusiasm for the final result made it all worthwhile. My thanks go to him and all the other Pluto staff for shepherding the manuscript through to printing and publication.

Finally, my partner Kathy has calmly helped me get through the difficult moments, when writing seemed an impossible task, and shared with me the better moments when I was making progress and needed some celebratory back-patting. As an historian of modern Europe, she too read the entire manuscript and made many valuable suggestions for honing my arguments and breaking up my ridiculously long sentences full of embedded sub-clauses. I'm sure some slipped through the net though. My loving thanks to her for helping me through these last three years of work on the book, and for so much more that I cannot put into words.

Abbreviations and Acronyms

ACRI	Association for Civil Rights in Israel
ADL	Anti-Defamation League
AHR	American Historical Review
AIPAC	American Israel Public Affairs Committee
AJC	American Jewish Committee
AJCongress	American Jewish Congress
APPGA	All Party Parliamentary Group Against Antisemitism
AWR	*Antisemitism World Report*
BDS	Boycott, Divestment and Sanctions movement
BICOM	Britain Israel Communications and Research Centre
BIPAC	Britain Israel Public Affairs Committee
BoD	Board of Deputies of British Jews
CAMERA	Committee for Accuracy in Middle East Reporting in America
CFCA	Coordination Forum for Countering Antisemitism
CST	Community Security Trust
DM	Direct message (Twitter)
ECJC	European Council of Jewish Communities
ECRI	European Commission Against Racism and Intolerance
EHRC	Equalities and Human Rights Commission
EJC	European Jewish Congress
EUMC	European Union Monitoring Centre on Racism and Xenophobia
FRA	Fundamental Rights Agency
GFCA	Global Forum for Combatting Antisemitism
GRET	Group Relations Education Trust
HRW	Human Rights Watch
ICC	International Criminal Court
ICCA	International Commission to Combat Antisemitism
ICRAR	International Consortium for Research on Antisemitism and Racism
IHRA	International Holocaust Remembrance Alliance
IJA	Institute of Jewish Affairs
ISGAP	Institute for the Study of Global Antisemitism and Policy
ITF	Task Force for International Cooperation on Holocaust Remembrance and Research
JDC	American Jewish Joint Distribution Committee
JJP	Jews for Justice for Palestinians (formerly JfJfP)

JPPI	Jewish People Policy Institute
JPR	Institute for Jewish Policy Research
LFI	Labour Friends of Israel
LFP	Labour Friends of Palestine
MFA	Ministry of Foreign Affairs Israel
MSA	Ministry of Strategic Affairs Israel
NCC	National Constitutional Committee of the Labour Party
NEC	National Executive Committee of the Labour Party
NFP	National Focal Point
NUS	National Union of Students
ODIHR	OSCE Office for Democratic Institutions and Human Rights
OSCE	Organization for Security and Cooperation in Europe
PCAA	Parliamentary Committee Against Antisemitism
PSC	Palestine Solidarity Campaign
RJC	Republican Jewish Coalition
RWCHR	Raoul Wallenberg Centre for Human Rights
SICSA	Sassoon International Centre for the Study of Antisemitism
SWC	Simon Wiesenthal Center
UJS	Union of Jewish Students
UNESCO	United Nations Education, Scientific and Cultural Organization
UNGA	United Nations General Assembly
UNHRC	United Nations Human Rights Council
UNWRA	United Nations Relief and Works Agency
USHMM	United States Holocaust Memorial Museum
WJC	World Jewish Congress
WZO	World Zionist Organisation
YIISA	Yale Initiative for the Interdisciplinary Study of Antisemitism

Introduction

Warnings about the threat posed by antisemitism* today are as dramatic, extreme, apocalyptic and frightening as they have ever been since the end of the Second World War. For example, in an article for *Haaretz* in July 2021, Yair Lapid, Israel's foreign minister, wrote: 'Reports gauging hatred of the Jews in the world are unprecedented and horrifying'.[1] The Simon Wiesenthal Center (SWC), the high-profile Los Angeles-based, organisation dedicated to confronting antisemitism worldwide, reported on 28 December 2021 that 'There is no greater existential threat to the Jewish people than the growing nuclear threat from the antisemitic, Holocaust-denying, terrorist-sponsoring, human rights-abusing Iranian regime. In November, a bill was presented to the Iranian parliament obliging the country to "destroy" Israel by 2041'.[2] In January 2020, Walter Reich, former Director of the United States Holocaust Memorial Museum, wrote: 'I watch antisemitism's global resurgence, so soon after the Holocaust, with alarm and foreboding. Could murderous antisemitism, on a large scale, resume in our time? Could "never again," vowed so solemnly and so repeatedly after the Holocaust, revert to "yet again"?'[3]

At the same time, and set against the same 75-year period, confusion and disagreement have never been greater about who is antisemitic, what antisemitism is today, what its sources are, how it manifests itself, who is responsible for it and what to do about it. In 2017, Professor David Feldman, director of the Birkbeck Institute for the Study of Antisemitism, London University, one of the world's leading academic antisemitism research bodies, began a lecture on 'The Meanings of Antisemitism' saying:

> The starting point … is our present confusion over what antisemitism is … When it comes to antisemitism many of us literally don't know what we're talking about and are happy to admit it. And as for the rest of us who think we *do* know what antisemitism is, we are congenitally unable to agree among ourselves.[4]

---

* It is increasingly common practice to abandon 'anti-Semitism' spellings and use only 'antisemitism' – no hyphen and no upper case 'S'. The meaning is the same however it is spelt. And spelling it only one way avoids confusing the reader. I have therefore used 'antisemitism', 'antisemitic' and 'antisemite' throughout the book, no matter how it was spelt in the original or any quoted text.

The dissonance between the first two and the third statements about antisemitism is stark. If the current state of affairs in the third statement is accurately described, on what grounds can those who issue dire warnings like those in the first two statements, be so certain about their judgements? Is there some way of explaining these incompatibilities? Furthermore, can they be resolved?

There can be no doubt that forms of hatred, vilification, demonisation and dehumanisation of Jews are alive and well, and closer to you, wherever you are in the world, than you might imagine or ever wish to know. Spend a minute or two searching 'antisemitism' on the web and the most vile, dehumanising and vicious antisemitic conspiracy theories about Jews' nefarious control of the world, disgusting and sinister hook-nosed caricatures, blood libel accusations, Holocaust denial screeds and white supremacist Jew-hate is in your face, on your screen, in seconds. These are what most people who know anything about Jew-hatred would regard as classic expressions and manifestations of antisemitism.

And it is likely that many of the same people would include in this antisemitic horror show what they regard as wholly new: hatred of Israel, the Jewish state; a post-Second World War, and now very familiar modern form of antisemitism. This is often presented as synonymous with 'anti-Zionism', which could loosely be described as opposition to the political ideology upon which the state of Israel is based, but is also commonly known as 'new antisemitism'. At the core of this notion is the claim that 'Israel is the (persecuted) "collective Jew" among the nations'.[5] In other words, it is argued that classic or pre-Israel antisemitism was hatred, discrimination, ostracisation from society and ultimately mass murder directed at Jews. Since the establishment of the Jewish state, antisemitism has taken the form of hatred, discrimination, ostracisation from the community of nations and, ultimately, plans for the destruction of Israel. Expressions of this are said to include: the Boycott, Divestment and Sanctions (BDS) movement; accusations that Israel, as a Jewish state, is a racist endeavour; arguing that Israel has no right to exist; proposing that the entire area of what was Mandate Palestine from the Mediterranean to the Jordan River should become one single, democratic, secular state; charging Israel with responsibility for the *naqba*, the ethnic cleansing of Palestinians from their homes in the 1948 war and subsequent wars; singling out Israel for criticism in a manner that would never apply to other states; and holding all Jews responsible for acts of military aggression undertaken by Israel.

This alleged antisemitism is undoubtedly 'new', at least in the sense that it could only have arisen after the establishment of Israel in 1948. But it is probably accurate to say that for almost all who define such discourse about Israel as antisemitic, 'new antisemitism' has not *replaced* the old antisemitism. They also subscribe to the eternalist understanding of antisemitism: that a continuity of Jew-hatred has characterised more than two millennia of Jewish history.

For Jonathan Greenblatt, head of the Anti-Defamation League (ADL), America's leading Jewish defence organisation, and for many others, it is very simple: 'the reality [is] that anti-Zionism *is* antisemitism'.[6] But in truth, whether or not they are the same is a matter of the most extreme controversy and bitter argument, which is at the very heart of the confusion and disagreement about antisemitism that I referred to in the opening paragraph of this introduction.

There are also many other ways in which Palestine–Israel and antisemitism interact and confuse in modes that have highly significant political implications. At the top of such a list would likely be the fact that former US President Donald Trump claimed to love Israel and support Zionism, but allied himself with overt antisemites, sometimes using blatantly antisemitic images and ideas. But many Jews overlooked this or were untroubled by the implication that a case could therefore be made for a 'legitimate' antisemitism that is compatible with love of or support for Israel. Can such antisemitism ever really be justified?

Closely following the Trump example, like a reverse mirror image, is that of Jeremy Corbyn, the former leader of the British Labour Party, the largest social democratic party in Europe. A long-standing advocate of the rights of the Palestinians, Corbyn also has a long track record of supporting the safety and security of Jewish communities in the UK and joining protests when Jews have been subject to antisemitic harassment. He has also maintained very good relations with both secular and orthodox Jewish communities in his constituency, including very friendly relations with dozens of Jewish members of Islington North CLP. Nonetheless, no sooner was he elected leader than he came under unprecedented attack for his long-held, pro-Palestinian views and was branded an antisemite. In August 2018, the president of the Board of Deputies of British Jews (BoD) accused him of 'declaring war on the Jews', a hyperbolic claim, typical of many, and part of a sustained campaign that played a significant role in the Labour Party losing the 2019 general election.[7] The only person called to mind by such an extreme statement is Hitler. This sets up a patently irrational and absurd comparison, one that was not only a gross insult to the Labour leader but also trivialised the mass murder of Jews for which the Nazi dictator was responsible. Nevertheless, saying it is absurd does not explain why apparently rational individuals can play fast and loose with antisemitism, politicising it in this fashion and draining the word of any useful meaning.

As testified by the existence of differing views about its sources, salience, impact and potential threat, antisemitism today is a political phenomenon of some complexity. But if these differences are so unbridgeable that no consensus exists about what it is that needs to be fought; and that measures to combat it are radically different or even contradictory depending on what the threat is said to be, the danger is that either the phenomenon escapes being dealt with or that measures to tackle it will impact negatively and unnecessarily on human rights, including free speech, as well as Jews' religious and cultural aspirations to freely practice their religion, or maintain and develop their cultural activities; chill free speech; and have negative connotations for the promotion and maintenance of human rights.

And there can be no doubt that the differences are indeed stark. As Professor Jonathan Judaken, the Spence L. Wilson Chair in Humanities, Rhodes College, puts it: 'Like so much else in politics today, the debate about contemporary antisemitism is a dialogue of the deaf waged as a battle to the death. Both sides are correct about a number of their claims, but neither can hear the truths of the other'.[8] As a result, whatever you say or write on this subject, whether in a scholarly article, a lecture, a serious op-ed or a series of tweets, it is now perfectly normal to be subjected to abuse from some quarter or other. Rather than expect firm but respectful challenge that could lead to a constructive dialogue, one must prepare for bitter, abusive and wounding ad hominem attacks on social media.

An extraordinarily high proportion of these exchanges takes place between Jews. And this intra-Jewish conflict over antisemitism is overwhelmingly hateful and bitter. Some Jews seem to believe that there is a special place in hell reserved for other Jews who question the existence of a 'new antisemitism'. Jews who do not go along with the mantra that anti-Zionism is antisemitism are singled out for special vilification, being labelled as 'antisemitic', 'self-hating' or, at the very least, 'fellow travellers' of antisemitism, whose 'contributions to antisemitism are significant', in the words of Anthony Julius.[9] Criticise the ethno-nationalist basis of the Jewish state and/or its discriminatory policies towards its Palestinian citizens and the Palestinians it controls in the West Bank and Gaza, and suggest that these features of Jewish nationalism and Israeli government policies contribute to antisemitism, and you are marked out as completely beyond the pale. Even being professionally engaged in Jewish communal life for decades, or heading a university antisemitism research institute provides no protection against such accusations.

It must be understood that the degraded discourse around current antisemitism not only entrenches a simplistic conflation of antisemitism and anti-Zionism, and normalises the indiscriminate branding of anti-Zionist, non-Zionist or determinedly unclassifiable Jews as 'self-hating', or as 'kapos'. This trend, which has been gaining pace since the late 1970s, has lodged itself permanently in public debate about antisemitism, and shows no sign of abating. It connects with, draws on and mutually reinforces deeper social, cultural and political fractures, which characterise a world where 'post-truth', 'fake news' and 'alternative facts' undermine the values of trust, integrity and critical discourse.

Anyone seeking to understand, and choosing to write about, the controversies and battles that are so central to what has happened to antisemitism from a perspective not based on some or all aspects of the notion of the 'new anti-semitism' is stepping into a minefield. The mines have been laid, as it were, by those who have helped shape and/or adhere to the dominant narrative which, *inter alia*, takes popular assessments of the dire dangers of current antisemitism for granted, sees most of that antisemitism manifested in demonisation and vil-ification of Israel as the 'collective Jew' among the nations, lays the blame for it on left-wing groups whose solidarity with the oppressed allegedly leads them to justify hostility and hatred towards Zionist Jews, affirms that anti-Zionism is antisemitism and regards Zionism as integral to Judaism and Jewish faith.

This dominant narrative has been strongly reinforced in the UK over the last five years as a result of the furore over antisemitism in the Labour Party, and the pressure exerted by government and other bodies for all kinds of institutions, including universities and local councils, to adopt the 'working definition' of antisemitism of the International Holocaust Remembrance Alliance (IHRA).[10] There are those who go against this grain; writers who are sceptical about, or fundamentally reject, the dominant narrative based on their recognition and exploration of the complexity of the subject. This approach is regularly brushed aside as if it were a form of antisemitism denial. It is no such thing.

In this book, I offer a combination of ways of exploring what happened to antisemitism, drawing on my own work and that of other scholars, research-ers and informed commentators in this field. I try to bring some new analytical approaches to the question and reach conclusions that lead to a new under-standing of why we are where we are.

To grasp the significance of the fragmentation of popular belief and academic exchange about antisemitism, we have to be able to look beyond the day-to-day controversies, and take into account the wider context—historical, political, cultural, social, institutional, psychological—in which the antisemitism story unfolds. We should add to this the consideration of geopolitical realities and the careful scrutiny of the actions and motives of individual actors in this drama, even if the relevance of the former may suggest contextual overreach and the latter may appear too speculative because the analyst wants only to engage with intellectual history, the interplay of theories, arguments and trends and not the business of human agency.

But in the age of the internet and social media, when the dissemination and transmission of racist propaganda, abuse, incitement, imagery, tropes and so on, are not held in check by any physical borders, it is inevitable that geopoliti-cal factors, magnified through globalisation, will exert an influence on our sense of the shape, extent, impact and salience of antisemitism. These changes in the means of communication and dissemination of hate have turned upside down and completely disrupted our ability to assess the danger of Jew-hatred today. Traditional methods of monitoring, reporting and analysing the antisemitism

Jews experience and how they feel about it are deeply flawed. Nevertheless, such methods persist.

These realities, coupled with the fact that antisemitism's tragic twentieth-century historical consequences inescapably make confronting the problem a highly charged affair, present us with a difficult challenge: to find a way into explaining how we got to where we are. We cannot ignore the emotion, existential fear, moral panic, group claims of harm and fragile sense of security that weigh so heavily whenever antisemitism is discussed, but we also cannot be constrained by these factors.

In seeking such a pathway, I eventually settled on the perhaps unusual, and even somewhat ambiguous question, *Whatever Happened to Antisemitism?* as the title of this book. The combination of unprecedented attention being paid to antisemitism and the equally unprecedented level of confusion and bitter and confrontational argument about it, makes absolutely essential the creative framing of the kind of questions that can cut through to an explanation that rises above the endless, unresolvable cycle of proof and refutation to which every alleged incident of antisemitism is subjected.

The book's subtitle—*Redefinition and the Myth of the 'Collective Jew'*—is intended to alert the reader to the two principal overarching factors explored in attempting to answer the question in the first part of the title.

In respect of unique influences that have shaped my approach in this book, I wish to single out and acknowledge three sources.

The special issue of the *American Historical Review* (*AHR*), published in October 2018, was devoted to an *AHR*–International Consortium for Research on Antisemitism and Racism (ICRAR) roundtable on 'Antisemitism in historical perspective'. The papers reflected what the editor Alex Lichtenstein described as 'the ICRAR's ongoing effort to overcome the isolation and politicization of the study of antisemitism'.[11] The round table was initiated by Jonathan Judaken, and is an extraordinarily rich and stimulating collection of essays.[12] Although each of the eight scholars focuses on a different aspect of the study of antisemitism, they stand together on some fundamental principles and approaches, which are summarised by Judaken in his introduction and precis of the essays.

[V]exed and fundamental questions about antisemitism remain unresolved … [and] difficult to answer because they are straitjacketed twice over: first by the history of the Holocaust and its memory complex, and the way this often imposes an exceptionalist, transhistorical, teleological narrative on studies of antisemitism, but also by the politics of the Israeli-Palestinian conflict, which often turns discussions of antisemitism into fodder for debates about the Middle East or apologetics for the actions of either side.

6

He acknowledges that 'the Israeli-Palestinian question is a hot global debate, and how one understands antisemitism is now thoroughly wound into the dispute'[13]—so much so that 'Contemporary discussions about antisemitism have consequently become a battlefield, with scholarship caught in the crossfire'.[14] 'In short', Judaken states, 'we argue against exceptionalism, eternalism, teleology, apologetics, and theoretical naivety in how scholars approach antisemitism. We call instead for an entangled history of antisemitism'.

This means four things: 'Antisemitism has meant different things to different people at different times'; 'the oft-claimed uniqueness of antisemitism must cede to comparative frames, and ultimately to a history of interlaced pasts'; 'the concept of the Jew shapeshifts. These shifts help explain how myths about Jews have had different meanings at different moments or have signified differently to different people in the same era'; that studies of antisemitism 'more deeply engage the theoretical and methodological considerations that have character-ised work in cognate areas. Theory provides a language, ways of thinking, and methods that permit historians to reflect at the meta-level on precisely the kind of impasses that define the study of antisemitism at present'.[15] Nonetheless, the influence of partisan political considerations cannot be ignored.

Although Judaken speaks for the other contributors on fundamental prin-ciples and conclusions, he speaks for himself in calling for retiring the term antisemitism and replacing it, or at the very least delimiting its use, with the word 'Judeophobia'. He puts forward a strong case for this, arguing that the word antisemitism does not fully reflect the complex variety of attitudes to Jews. None-theless, my view is that at this point in the antisemitism battles, to make such a wholesale change would only confuse matters further, especially in a book such as this one, which is not written exclusively for an academic audience.

Judaken's analysis of antisemitism, together with the analyses of the other contributors, has had a major influence on my thinking, but I do not mean to imply that these scholars would agree with my own analysis. The views I express in this book, the conclusions I reach, are mine alone.

In a far more specific sense, two seminal articles by Gil Anidjar, Professor (and Chair) of Religion, Comparative Literature, and Middle Eastern, South Asian, and African studies at Columbia University, published in 2007[16] and 2017,[17] have shaped my approach to understanding antisemitism today by opening up a range of key questions about the phenomenon that no other scholar has been asking.

Anidjar writes about antisemitism as 'one of those who struggle against [it]'.

I tend to think about it a lot. I read and reflect ... I take action when I can. I even formulated some ideas, a theory of sorts, playing my part, adding my bit to the growing number of accounts of it. You could say that I have been moved, nay, mobilised to criticise antisemitism, to fight against it. I am no imaginary Jew, I do not think.[18]

However, Anidjar persists in asking and re-asking, what is this fight exactly? '[Am I participating] in a collective endeavour? Is there at all an organised movement against antisemitism? Should there be one? And if so, what kind of movement would it be? A religious, a social or a political movement?'[19] If it is one of these, can there be such

> a movement, a collective or social movement, that does not know itself? ... Is there a war against antisemitism? And if there is, what precisely am I in this fight? What kind of actor does it make me? Am I a rebel or a nonconformist? Am I an intellectual, an activist or a foot soldier? What exactly is it that I have joined?[20]

These quotations are from Anidjar's 2017 article, but they are substantially the same as questions he posed in 2007. I repeat them essentially because neither Anidjar himself, nor anyone else, he would contend, has provided satisfactory answers.

> Is there or is there not a war on antisemitism? To the extent that there are signs of a struggle, the question warrants an answer. None has been forthcoming ... There is, as it were, no 'grammar of a discourse', much less a portrait, of the anti-antisemite. Nor is there a description or an account of the struggle against antisemitism, whether there is such, in its social and institutional, cultural and political sweep, nor of its rate of success (including a measure of its failures).[21]

Anidjar does acknowledge that, to some degree at least, he has found tentative answers to some of his questions. '[T]here is a war on antisemitism ... (I now know that I am in fact part of something larger, a social movement of sorts)',[22] and yet, almost every such progression is then subject to further questions, throwing doubt on the idea that there has been anything that Anidjar himself would acknowledge as 'progress'. He remains sceptical about the nature of the 'movement'; he confesses to 'know little of what happens overseas'; he remains uncertain about what it means to be an anti-antisemite—'does that make me a "strategic dupe"?' he asks.[23]

Anidjar only provides answers to some of the questions he poses. To some of these unanswered questions, I supply my own answers. And as for the answers he does give, as I make clear later in the book, I do not agree with all of them.

Some may wish to mock Anidjar for his talmudic-like quest or criticise him for not answering all the questions he asks, and thus dismiss his concerns, but they would be very wrong to do so. So much is taken for granted in this field, both at the academic level and at the level of public debate; so many assumptions are made about antisemitism upon which dubious strategies to combat it are based, without those assumptions being subjected to rigorous scrutiny—a state of affairs that makes Anidjar's questions precisely the kind that need to be asked if we are to understand what has happened to antisemitism.

However, I detect another layer to Anidjar's interrogatory method. He is leaving it to the reader to draw conclusions about his own views from the very manner in which he poses the questions.

Finally, given that this book will show that over the last 40 years or so, a host of organisations, from small research units to major, globally significant intergovernmental institutions, have come into being or been partially re-purposed to fight antisemitism, particularly 'new antisemitism', key questions must be asked about what they represent, how they relate to each other, what functions they fulfil, whether they further values-based goals and so on. Anidjar raises some of these questions, but again answers them only obliquely, or rather, in the manner which I have suggested above.

A scholar who adopts a complementary approach to dealing with this issue is Esther Romeyn, Senior Lecturer at the Center for European Studies in the College for Liberal Sciences at the University of Florida. She frames this as

> a cast of actors—global governance actors, such as the United Nations, UNESCO, the Organisation for Security and Co-Operation in Europe, the European Commission, non-governmental organisations, experts and scholars, and politicians—[who] set out to define, invent measuring tools and technologies, analyse, formulate policy statements and programmes, and develop 'interventions' to address and redress ('fight') the 'problem' [of new antisemitism].[24]

She sees 'new antisemitism' emerging as a transnational field of governance, and particularly as a field of racial governance' acting as a 'power-knowledge field' controlled by 'institutional and human 'actors'.

Romeyn's hypothesis rings true, but needs testing against the empirical data about the 'actors', how they came into being, what is represented by the notion of the 'new antisemitism' as this transnational field by way of political values, the role assigned to those allegedly adhering to and spreading 'new antisemitism' and whether it 'erects an interior frontier around culture/religion that effectively externalizes and racializes antisemitism'. I therefore use Romeyn's concept of the transnational field of racial governance as a possible way of establishing the significance of the range of global actors populating this landscape over the last 40 years.

* * *

It might be suggested that Jewish researchers, academics and commentators would be more inclined to be extremely sensitive about the state of antisemitism than non-Jews—a justified sensitivity, many would say, when we reflect soberly on Jewish experience. But despite the very high proportion of Jewish individuals and institutions active in studying, monitoring, researching and combatting antisemitism, when surveying the broad range of voices from all backgrounds, extreme sensitivity is by no means confined just to Jews.

Nevertheless—and speaking from personal experience—I do think it reasonable to ask whether there is a problem facing Jews who purport to be objective observers and analysts of the racism they experience. The sociologist Zygmunt Bauman, who was Jewish, seemed to think so. When asked why he wrote so little about current antisemitism he is said to have replied: 'You cannot be a bird and an ornithologist at the same time'.[25] While I do not fully endorse this sentiment, I think there is still something in it that rings true and, at the very least, we Jews who write about antisemitism should bear it in mind, regarding it as a warning always to be conscious of how easy it is to allow emotional factors to become a barrier to a sober examination of the facts. Like all 'hot' subjects, antisemitism requires 'cool' handling. This is certainly not an endorsement of the criticism often levelled at anti-Zionist or non-Zionist left-wing Jews that their posture of writing or engaging in political activity critical of Israel 'as a Jew' is bogus and hypocritical because it is only when unfairly criticising Israel that they display their Jewishness.[26] Not only is this a groundless arrogation of the right and authority to make judgements about the authenticity of the Jewishness of others, and to essentialise what it is to be a Jew, but what's more, only a startling lack of moral self-awareness can make such an accuser think that they would escape from being charged with exactly the same thing.

* * *

I hope it is clear by now that the methodology I will employ in this book draws on more than one discipline. In tracing political developments and the building and re-purposing of institutions and organisations over time, I am writing history and following a chronological thread starting in the 1970s and ending in the present.

In tracing the development of the concept of 'new antisemitism'—and the discourse used to disseminate that concept—at the heart of which is the notion of 'Israel as the "collective Jew" among the nations', while there is change over time, tracing that cannot be undertaken by always weaving it into the chapters on political and institutional history. I show how discussion and debate on antisemitism, Zionism and anti-Zionism progressed partly by surveying expressions of opinion in conference or seminar settings, partly by quoting from journals, magazines and newspapers, and partly by focusing on the thinking of a few people whose teaching, writing and interventions in public debates were especially influential and emblematic of the way that the 'new antisemitism' and 'collective Jew' discourse became dominant. The historical and conceptual chapters are, of course, interrelated. Historical developments influence the discourse, and the discourse influences historical developments, and I endeavour to demonstrate this as the book progresses. But a consequence of this is that the book may occasionally appear to be repeating itself chronologically, when in fact the repetition occurs because the mode of the subject matter changes from historical to conceptual and vice versa. By flagging this here, I hope to help the reader avoid being confused by the book's structure.

Chapter 1 is a survey of the various ways in which confusion about what is antisemitism manifests itself. Jews are deeply divided about it. Polling the general public about the issue reveals much ignorance as to what the word refers to. Disinformation in the media leads to false claims presented as fact, while defence bodies often exaggerate the degree to which antisemitism is a serious current danger even when this conflicts with everyday experience.

I devote the whole of Chapter 2 to one particular area of confusion, the use and abuse of antisemitic stereotypes and tropes. This has figured as an important factor in some of the key controversial incidents of alleged antisemitism in recent years, especially in relation to the former leader of the Labour Party, Jeremy Corbyn. Everyone seems to think they know what a trope is, but this is far from the truth.

The confusion around tropes and what people understand by the term antisemitism is closely linked to the question of the relationship between antisemitism and anti-Zionism, which itself is central to one of the key themes of the book: interrogating the notion of the 'new antisemitism'. Chapter 3 therefore examines how the idea developed from the 1970s and the adoption of UN General Assembly Resolution 3379, which determined that 'Zionism is a form of racism and racial discrimination', to 1989, when communism collapsed and new freedoms brought a significant diminution in antisemitism for some, and a resurgence of it for others. Chapter 4 takes the story up to the turn of the century, by which time 'new antisemitism' was well on the way to becoming the 'orthodox' understanding of antisemitism. Chapter 5 turns to the parallel development of an institutional infrastructure, which encompassed bodies working to combat antisemitism, and was partly organic and partly by design. It shows how those embracing 'new antisemitism' theory came to dominate the field.

The central tenet of 'new antisemitism'—Israel as 'the persecuted "collective Jew" among the nations'—though contested throughout the two decades

11

prior to the beginning of the third millennium, and beyond, ultimately became, through pressure from institutions, academics and activists, the main plank of the dominant discourse about antisemitism. But the key turning point was 9/11. Chapter 6 explores this crucial phase, as the opening of the new millennium saw 'new antisemitism' discourse became ever-more dominant, and was reflected especially in Israel in a reconfiguration and status upgrade of institutions dealing with antisemitism at the governmental level. This sets the scene for the decisive step change discussed in Chapter 7: the codification of 'new antisemitism' in the 'working definition' of antisemitism published on the website of the European Union Monitoring Centre on Racism and Xenophobia (EUMC) in 2005. The chapter explores how this came about, establishing quite clearly that it was the result of a political project, not a response to widespread demands for a new definition. There were no such demands.

Chapter 8 returns to the development of an institutional infrastructure which, from the turn of the century, was decisively aligned with the increasing dominance of 'new antisemitism' discourse. Newspapers, magazines and websites were giving wide coverage of apocalyptic warnings of a dramatic rise in 'global antisemitism' after 9/11. Much of this was generated and amplified by new anti-antisemitism think tanks, research bodies, Israel lobby organisations in America, Europe and Israel. In a very significant move in the first decade of the new millennium, Israel abandoned its inconsistent engagement with antisemitism and decided to fully occupy the leadership role in the fight against the 'new antisemitism'. By the early 2010s, government and state institutions and agencies were contributing decisively to coordinating anti-antisemitism activity in many countries, further populating the field of transnational racial governance.

In Chapter 9 I turn to deconstructing the narrative of the redefinition project in the light of the adoption of a slightly modified EUMC 'working definition' by the IHRA. The EUMC 'working definition' had achieved significant international attention and approbation, but the organisation's successor, the Fundamental Rights Agency (FRA), distanced itself from the text. Reintroduced into the public domain by the IHRA in 2016, the 'working definition', assiduously disseminated by IHRA officials, but particularly by major Jewish organisations, quickly attracted very favourable international attention. At the heart of the 'working definition' is the notion of 'Israel, the persecuted "collective Jew" among the nations'.

The following two chapters flesh out two aspects of 'new antisemitism' that became especially significant from the early 2000s onwards. First, in Chapter 10, I cover the central role of the attack by Jewish groups on human rights culture and organisations for being an alleged antisemitic conspiracy against the Jewish state. In Chapter 11, I show how Israel's very favourable geopolitical situation allows it to use its status as probably the leading military and economic power in the region to normalise relations with some Arab states, and maintain fruitful relations with Russia, China and India, but also to get these states to acquiesce in accepting Israel's portrayal of itself as under attack from viral anti-semitic delegitimisation.

A feature of anti-antisemitism discourse is to refer to anti-antisemitism activity as a 'war', even though you cannot fight a war against an abstract noun. In Chapter 12, I argue that it is not enough to defend its use because it is 'only' a metaphor; it dangerously raises unrealistic expectations as to what can be achieved. Moreover, the use of the word reveals much about the problematic nature of anti-antisemitism activity. As I go on to demonstrate, even the generals waging the 'war' acknowledge that it is not being won, yet they successfully portray failure as success by in effect, saying there is no alternative.

In Chapter 13, I explore three highly problematic features of anti-antisemitism discourse that are common to expositions of 'new antisemitism', although all three were present in discussions of antisemitism before 'new antisemitism' theory became popular. They are: the use of medical analogies to describe antisemitism and promote forms of 'cure'; the insistence that only the 'eradication', 'elimination', or 'rooting out' of antisemitism are acceptable strategies for dealing with the problem; the conviction that any use of the word 'power' in relation to Jews or Israel is an antisemitic trope. All three bolster the rigidity of 'new antisemitism' theory and serve to shore up the central idea of Israel as the 'collective Jew' among the nations.

Medical analogies turn antisemites into victims. We may yearn for 'the end of antisemitism', but, like any racism, its eradication is impossible. The assumption that whenever the word 'power' is paired with 'Jew', it is an antisemitic trope ignores the fact that Zionism aimed to and did achieve the emergence of Jews from powerlessness, in the form of a state, the power of which Israeli governments have no compunction in celebrating.

In Chapter 14 I discuss the way key theorists and promoters of 'new antisemitism' use apocalyptic language in their warnings of imminent dire catastrophe from rampant antisemitism directed at the Jewish state, a discourse they repeat again and again over decades. Like true believers in end-of-the-world prophesy, they never admit that they might be wrong. The pronouncements of such figures often attract wide media coverage, which, when surveyed over 25 years, shows the same warnings of extreme threat time and again. And no one asks any searching questions about how these warnings can be justified. These regular manifestations of shock and fear have all the hallmarks of moral panics.

In the final chapter (Chapter 15) I recap the narrative of the book before summarising the key conclusions I have already reached and adding some further overarching ones that can now be made by dint of reaching the end point of this particular journey. By falsely conflating anti-Zionism—a form of legitimate political discourse and belief—and antisemitism—a form of ethnoracial hostility and hatred—and calling it 'new antisemitism', and codifying it in the form of the IHRA 'working definition' of antisemitism, antisemitism has been redefined to be what it is not.

The conflation is false because, first, the root concept of 'new antisemitism', that Israel is the 'collective Jew' among the nations, is a myth—a state cannot have the attributes of a human being. Second, it is a heretical corruption of Judaism because it entails an idolatrous deification and worship of the state. Third, it is an antisemitic construct, because it treats being Jewish as a singularity: 'all Jews are the same'.

Conceived of and presented as a 'war' of eradication, the struggle against antisemitism is destined to fail. You cannot wage war on an abstract noun. This does not mean that the anti-'new antisemitism' activity is a chimaera. Rather that the primary focus of attack is on freedom of speech. And waging war on freedom of speech is bread and butter to authoritarian regimes and their supporters. Moreover, while the attack on freedom of speech is undoubtedly achieving some success—and the Palestinians' public political struggle for justice, equal rights, an end to occupation, the right of return and so on, through advocating such means as boycott, divestment and sanctions, demanding Israel be investigated for war crimes by the International Criminal Court (ICC), and censuring by the UN Security Council, is simultaneously demonised, ignored, delegitimised and falls victim to double standards—it is also a war that can never be won. The cause of the Palestinians is a just one. The 'cause' of antisemitism is not.

* * *

As a Jew who has experienced antisemitism since childhood and whose commitment to Zionism in the 1960s led me to emigrate to Israel and become an Israeli citizen (I returned to the UK in 1972), I am very conscious of the need to bear in mind Bauman's observation. Antisemitism is a highly emotive subject and there is a close relationship between the personal and the political. But, in pursuing an answer to the question posed by this book, I bring more than my Jewish identity to the table. I have worked in the field of contemporary antisemitism and racism studies for over 40 years, witnessing and charting the significant developments and changes over this period. Moreover, my career took me from researching, writing and teaching about antisemitism to heading a widely respected international Jewish research institute with legitimate claim that its work should influence and inform public policy affecting the welfare of Jews worldwide. I thus became an active participant in aspects of the history I will be discussing in this book, above all the marked politicisation and instrumentalisation of antisemitism since the 1980s.

I first studied European antisemitism as part of a history degree course at Sussex University in the 1970s, but it was only when I joined the Institute of Jewish Affairs (IJA) in London as a research officer in 1979 that I expanded my knowledge and understanding of the subject in its contemporary context. As the research arm of the World Jewish Congress (WJC), the international political body, then based in Geneva that represented the interests of organised Jewish communities around the world, the IJA conducted, sponsored and published research, in association with the WJC, on the social, political, cultural and economic conditions of Jewish populations worldwide. It took a special interest in current antisemitism, monitoring, analysing and assessing it in the context of racism in general. The results of this work were disseminated through the IJA's own academic journals and research reports.

I was soon appointed assistant editor of *Patterns of Prejudice*, the IJA's international journal on antisemitism and racism, which the IJA founded in 1967 and published with the WJC. After becoming its editor in 1986, I transformed it into an academic, peer-reviewed quarterly, enlisting two academic experts on antisemitism, Professors David Cesarani (London) and Tony Kushner (Southampton), as my co-editors.

While continuing to engage with the subject of antisemitism at the IJA, I was also appointed editor of the *Jewish Quarterly* in the mid-1980s, a 30-year old magazine, which focused on politics, art, literature and Jewish culture. It was in this extra-curricular role that I first came face to face with the communal politics of antisemitism and the political arguments over the best way the Jewish community should deal with the problem. In 1985 I wrote an editorial entitled 'The politics of antisemitism', which criticised communal policy and the growing tendency to treat Arab opposition to Israel as antisemitic. The editorial sparked a furore and the affair dominated the letter pages of the *Jewish Chronicle* newspaper for seven weeks. There were calls for me to be sacked from my IJA position and I was vilified as an anti-Zionist (which I was not) and a 'self-hating Jew'. In the end, I resigned from the *Jewish Quarterly* editorship in order to keep my job at the IJA, but the affair marked for me the beginning of a more critical approach to the study of contemporary antisemitism, which I have followed to this day.

With the collapse of communism in Eastern and Central Europe in 1989–1990, and the resurgence of antisemitism in the former communist states, I expanded my activity as a writer and speaker on the subject of antisemitism. After I became Director of the IJA in 1991, I made contemporary antisemitism central to its work by founding *Antisemitism World Report*, the first-ever country-by-country, human rights style, annual report on antisemitism. (The *Report* was printed from 1992 to 1998, then published and updated online.) From the Report's inception, there was intense pressure on the IJA to collaborate with a new, Mossad-funded Project for the Study of Antisemitism at Tel Aviv University in the production of a joint Report. The IJA strongly resisted this proposal, already doubting the objectivity of this kind of Israeli involvement and concerned that the Report could be used to further the state's Zionist objectives.

While international Jewish interest in antisemitism increased in the 1990s, I remained firmly committed to the application of a rigorous methodology to the analysis of antisemitism, one that involved high-quality evidence-based research and was not politically motivated. This meant that the IJA, which I relaunched as the Institute for Jewish Policy Research (JPR) in 1996, frequently clashed with US and Israeli political and research organisations that prioritised Zionist and pro-Israel objectives. I left JPR in 1999 to set up a grant-making foundation supporting Jewish life in Europe, but I continued to write and speak publicly about antisemitism and returned to head JPR again in 2006. By this time, however, I was coming under attack from UK communal leaders and Jewish leaders elsewhere in Europe and Israel for my views on antisemitism, my personal rejection of Zionism and my publicly expressed conclusions that all in Israel–Palestine should have equal rights. I resigned from my post in 2009, convinced that I could only write and speak freely on these subjects without organisational constraints.

1

Varieties of Confusion in Understandings of Antisemitism

Consider what people understand by the term antisemitism. On the face of it, very many examples of visual, verbal and violent expressions of Jew-hatred could be said to be instantly recognisable. So how does that square with the far more complicated and rather puzzling evidence that there is deep and wide-spread confusion about what constitutes antisemitism today?

In *Antisemitism: A Very Short Introduction*, the historian Steven Beller writes: 'Some concepts, such as communism, while complicated to explain, are fairly simple to define and identify as an ideology and political movement, and just that. Antisemitism, in contrast, is a highly ambivalent, even multivalent term, which can cause great confusion'.[1] Kenneth L. Marcus, in his *The Definition of Antisemitism*, asserts that 'We do not have a shared definition of [the concept of] antisemitism ... the question of definition is now more unsettled than at any previous time. Indeed, the definitional issue has arisen as the central issue in the contemporary study of antisemitism'.[2] While Beller and Marcus are here addressing the vagaries of the academic study of antisemitism, they are also acknowledging the confusion that prevails, even among Jews, in naming and understanding antisemitism today.

The journalist Allison Kaplan Sommer sees this very clearly in the United States:

> In today's charged environment, the American Jewish community is often too divided to define what antisemitism is—making it impossible to combat it in a unified fashion. Nearly all Jews can call out an antisemite sporting a Nazi uniform or a Klan robe. But without clear visual cues, antisemitism is too often in the eye of the beholder.[3]

More specifically, Andrew Silow-Carroll, Editor-in-Chief of the Jewish Telegraphic Agency, locates confusion in the context of right–left divides in Jewish communal politics over who is antisemitic and how antisemitism should be combatted. 'Once upon a time', he writes,

> the Jews' antagonists were obvious: Louis Farrakhan, David Duke, Hamas, the UN General Assembly, neo-Nazis here and in Europe. They haven't

gone away, but now the Jewish left accuses the Jewish right of downplaying the dangers of the 'alt-right'. The Jewish right says the real threat to Jews is not from pro-Trump internet trolls but from progressive campus groups, including Jews on the far left, who condemn Israel but really mean 'the Jews'. The left thinks it a vital Jewish mission to enter into social justice coalitions with other minorities, including Muslims; the right says Black Lives Matter lost all moral authority when it joined the pro-Palestinian cause.[4]

Professor Dov Waxman acknowledges that there are difficulties in identifying the 'enemy', but is not optimistic about resolving the problem: 'The difficulty with defining antisemitism today does not mean that we should stop trying. To combat antisemitism, we have to agree on what constitutes it. But perhaps this has simply become impossible in our increasingly polarized times'.[5]

It should not really come as a surprise that political factors affect our understanding of antisemitism. After all, antisemitism is a political phenomenon. Like all forms of racial hatred, ethnic hostility and group prejudice, it finds its outlet in political action, the achievement of political objectives, propagating a political theory narrowly defining, on the grounds of national myth, who belongs; and its consequences are felt at the political level in terms of action taken to combat it, and the uses to which it is put at election times in some countries. Of course, antisemitism is other things too, not least what a Jewish person experiences when verbally or physically assaulted and, in its most extreme form, when Jewish people are collectively demonised and herded together for the purposes of mass murder, as they were during the Holocaust.

How can we bracket together antisemitism as a form of politics with antisemitism as a form of mass murder—politics as the 'ordinary', mass murder as the 'extraordinary'? And how can we make sense of antisemitism as a form of politics which divides Jews themselves? Would not the inevitably coarse, disrespectful, adversarial, crude, intemperate and ugly nature of political exchange result in a trivialisation of the Holocaust? With so much attention being paid to Holocaust memorialisation, education and the constant emphasis on 'learning the lessons' of this unprecedented Jewish tragedy, all in order to combat antisemitism today, how is it that so many voices are telling us that the problem is serious and getting worse? It may be hard to confront these questions, but they cannot be ignored. And even if we do come to terms with the political nature of the issue, the idea that we might reach some deeper understanding of what we are experiencing through an exclusively political approach—whether that be political analysis, history, or debate—is out of the question.

The picture looks no clearer at the broader societal level. In a 13 February 2017 lecture titled 'The Meanings of Antisemitism', David Feldman said the following:

The starting point … is our present confusion over what antisemitism is … When it comes to antisemitism many of us literally don't know what we're talking about and are happy to admit it. And as for the rest of us who think we *do* know what antisemitism is, we are congenitally unable to agree among ourselves.[6]

Feldman cited survey data on general public views and specifically Jewish views in the UK in support of his assertions.

In a 2015 Populus survey,[7] 45 per cent of respondents were not confident that they could explain to someone else what antisemitism means. Among respondents aged between 18 and 34, more than 60 per cent felt unable to explain what antisemitism is.

Moving from the general to the particular, we find opinion not merely uncertain but divided. Another Populus survey in 2016[8] revealed wide disagreement about the relationship between antisemitism, anti-Zionism and 'hatred of Israel'. Forty-eight per cent were confident that hating Israel and questioning its right to exist is antisemitic, which means that more than half disagreed. In 20 per cent of cases respondents thought the opposite, that 'hating Israel' and questioning its right to exist was not antisemitic.

Opinion among Jews shows even greater division. In a Jewish Policy Research (JPR) and IPSOS-MORI poll in 2013 for the Fundamental Rights Agency (FRA) of the EU,[9] when Jews were asked whether they believed that antisemitism was a problem in the UK, respondents were split. Forty-eight per cent reported that antisemitism was 'a fairly big problem' or a 'big problem', but a small majority said it was 'not a very big problem', or 'not a problem at all'. One reasonable explanation for this is that among respondents, there were widely divergent opinions on what antisemitism is.

A follow-up survey in 2018 showed that 85 per cent of Jews surveyed across the twelve countries considered antisemitism to be either a 'very big' or 'fairly big' problem in their country.[10] Although these results indicate a greater consensus among respondents that antisemitism had become more serious, there were considerable differences as to what was considered antisemitic from country to country. (This is confirmed in other research. Doerte Letzmann, studying conceptualisation of antisemitism in Germany and Britain, concluded: 'The main finding is that although antisemitism is a global phenomenon, it is understood very differently in different contexts'.[11]) Moreover, as the JPR commentary on the data acknowledged,

the results reflect the opinions of Jews who are engaged in Jewish community life, as well as those who have some degree of connection with a Jewish organisation, however fluid and irregular. The attitudes of self-identifying Jews who have no connection with any part of the Jewish community in their countries are likely to be relatively underrepresented in the findings.[12]

Such self-identifying Jews can constitute 40 per cent or more of a country's Jewish population.

At the height of the antisemitism furore in the Labour Party in March 2019 in the UK, Deltapoll carried out a survey for the *Jewish Chronicle*, which revealed that 40 per cent of British adults said they did not know what the term meant, rising to more than half among under 25s.[13] Speaking from her own perspective as a Holocaust educator in Britain, Dame Helen Hyde, a Trustee of the National Holocaust Centre and Museum and Vice-President of the Jewish Leadership Council (JLC), made a telling acknowledgement of this confusion around what antisemitism is when she suggested using the term 'anti-Jewish racism' instead of antisemitism, because 'students do not know what antisemitism means'.[14]

A further, if somewhat more oblique, indication of public confusion was evident in the results of a nationwide Survation survey, conducted for the Glasgow University Media Group in March 2019, looking at the state of public belief about antisemitism in the Labour Party.[15] When asked 'From what you have seen or heard, what percentage of Labour Party members do you think have had complaints of antisemitism made against them?', of the 70 per cent who expressed an opinion, the belief was that, on average, the figure was 34 per cent. Just 14 per cent of the sample believed that the number who had been complained about was below 10 per cent. The actual figure at the time was less than 0.1 per cent of members.

A JPR report published in January 2019 explored the 'connection between extreme hostility towards Israel and more traditional forms of antipathy towards Jews', focusing specifically on 'two particularly prevalent ideas that are often experienced by Jews as antisemitic: the contention that Israel is "an apartheid state" and that it should be subjected to a boycott'.[16] Although the report claims that there is a clear connection, it states that:

> In the first instance, the study finds that large proportions of people actually have no view at all on these ideas, either because they do not know anything about the issues, or because they are simply unsure of where they stand on them. This is particularly the case for young people and women—knowledge levels improve and opinions sharpen the older people are, and, as has been found in numerous other studies, women tend to be less opinionated than men on these types of political issues.

Once again, ignorance of matters relating to negative views of Jews and Israel, as well as uncertainty, is shown to be typical of public opinion.

So, what might have led to this glaring gap between perception and reality? The Birkbeck College London and Media Reform Coalition Research Project into press reporting on antisemitism concluded in September 2018 that British media reporting of allegations of antisemitism in the Labour Party had involved: 'a persistent subversion of conventional news values'.[17] Researchers identified 'myriad inaccuracies and distortions in online and television news including marked skews in sourcing, omission of essential context or right of reply, mis-quotation, and false assertions made either by journalists themselves or sources whose contentious claims were neither challenged nor countered. Overall, our findings were consistent with a disinformation paradigm'. In particular, 'completely false claims were presented as fact, often without even the most basic challenge'. The BBC is singled out as one of the *very* worst offenders.

Exaggerated perceptions of the state of antisemitism are also evident in the US. On 29 January 2020, the Anti-Defamation League (ADL) released a new study on antisemitic attitudes among Americans.[18] The study found that only 11 per cent of American adults believed in six or more of the eleven stereotypes about Jews tested. This figure is the lowest percentage ADL's periodic survey has ever recorded. Compare this to the 29 per cent who believed in six or more of the eleven stereotypes in 1964, the first year the ADL undertook this study. And yet, ADL head Jonathan Greenblatt claims that 'anti-Jewish hatred in America is worse than at any point since the 1930s'.[19]

It cannot help public understanding of antisemitism if there is discrepancy between standard methods of measuring antisemitic attitudes and pronouncements made by influential opinion formers, especially those representing well-known Jewish organisations that the public expect—rightly or wrongly—to know what they are talking about. Moreover, those who are the targets of antisemitism may find that their own experience differs from what the stats convey—feeling that the situation is worse than presented or that the picture exaggerates—and/or do not chime with statements of nationally known figures like Greenblatt. With the internet now a primary source of expressions of anti-semitism, yet not uniformly accessed by members of groups on the receiving end of hate speech, divergent perceptions of the seriousness of the problem are even more likely to prevail. Before the internet became such a significant, ubiquitous and variegated source of news, most people would learn about the state of antisemitism, in so far as incidents of it were reported, from a limited number of sources—newspaper headlines, radio and television news—and therefore a more even public perception—in so far as there was any perception at all—of antisemitism existed. In fact, the way in which social media-based anti-Jewish hate speech has thrown into doubt the value of standard procedures for monitoring antisemitic incidents employed by such bodies as the ADL in the US and the Community Security Trust (CST) in the UK, and the process of producing yearly reports on their data, is neither fully acknowledged, nor has it led to a significant revision of incident assessing methodology. An attack on a synagogue resulting in serious casualties is one incident. But is one person's antisemitic tweet retweeted a few times or thousands of times, or a Facebook post liked by hundreds, one incident or more? And who is likely to investigate the extent to which multiple Twitter and Facebook accounts are run by the same person? With our tendencies to live increasingly in bubbles of the like-minded, the information we receive and how we process it makes it even more likely that confusion about antisemitism's meaning will prevail.

Over the last 30 years, growing intervention by Israeli governmental institutions, civil society actors and politicians has confused matters even more. In 2018, CNN released the results of a September poll of adults in seven European countries, which they claimed 'reveals the depth of antisemitism in Europe'.[20] 'The poll uncovered complicated, contrasting and sometimes disturbing attitudes about Jews, and some startling ignorance', CNN said, with highlighted areas of concern being: belief that Jews have too much power and influence in finance and politics, and over wars and conflicts; vastly exaggerated estimates of Jewish populations in the countries concerned; blaming Jews and Israel for the antisemitism that exists, saying it is a response to the everyday behaviour of Jewish people; one in 20 had never heard of the Holocaust. However, questions to do with Israel did not seem to elicit very much that could be considered antisemitic. But when presented with the evidence from the CNN poll, Prime Minister Netanyahu's response was that 'anti-Israeli policies, the idea that the Jewish people don't have the right to a state, that's the ultimate antisemitism of today'.[21] This downplaying of, or at best token concern for, diaspora experience of antisemitism while declaring criticism of Israel as emblematic of what real antisemitism is today is not only a matter of orchestrated Israeli government policy; it also reflects widespread opinion among Jewish Israelis. Even an atrocity so unambiguously rooted in events and atmosphere prevailing in the United States as the Pittsburgh synagogue massacre of eleven people was shamelessly equated with Israeli experience by the then Diaspora Affairs Minister Naftali Bennett when he said the day after the shooting: 'From Sderot to Pittsburgh, the hand that fires missiles is the same hand that shoots worshippers'.[22] In fact, the motivation of the Pittsburgh shooter was totally unrelated to Israel. He was attacking Jews because he perceived them as pro-immigration. Moreover, the hand that kills Palestinians in Gaza is an Israeli hand, while Pittsburgh synagogue members killed no one. For Israel, being the principal target of antisemitic hate is presented as an existential matter. So, 'it's not just that for Israelis, anti-Zionism is also antisemitic. It's that it's the only version of antisemitism they now recognize'.[23]

Differences between Jewish Israelis and diaspora Jews are undoubtedly uncomfortable for diaspora Jews who call themselves Zionists or who identify very closely with Israel. They are unlikely to draw much attention to these divisions. Nevertheless, they cannot be swept under the carpet since survey evidence suggests that the divide is definitional: 'Put simply, American and Israeli Jews no longer agree on what it means to be "Jewish"'.[24] '[I]n Israel, being "Jewish" is correlated mainly with nationalist and right-wing values and views'. But 'Liberal American Jews identify being "Jewish" with having a set of liberal orientations and values'. If you believe Judaism is nationalism, opposing the Jewish state is no different from opposing Judaism. By this logic, anti-Zionism is therefore antisemitism. As the 'Judaism = nationalism' sensibility strengthens, the liberal model of Jewish identity—embracing equal rights for all, identifying with other minorities including Muslims, combatting antisemitism as part of the wider struggle against racism—which exists in the US and, although not so strongly, in the UK, partly because of the dominance of conservative religious and representative bodies, is increasingly under pressure. Even so, given that ethno-nationalism is an unending project of purifying the tribe, Zionists equating their nationalism with Judaism are attacking the liberal model with increasing severity. And integral to that attack is to label liberal Jews who are critical of Israel as 'self-hating' and 'antisemitic'.

This internal Jewish conflict over who or what is a Jew, which further complicates our understanding of what antisemitism is today, resonates in the public space in a very significant way. Non-Jewish commentators now have no compunction in making judgements about who is and who is not an 'authentic Jew', reinforcing the spurious 'good Jew/bad Jew' dichotomy. A notorious example of this in the UK was the *Daily Mail* columnist Dan Hodges, who in 2015 was habitually attacking left-wing Jewish supporters of Jeremy Corbyn. Responding to this tweet from @hapoelorient: 'hi Dan, cud u stop using Jews as a political football. some Jews, including supporters of Corbyn don't appreciate ur comments', Hodges tweeted: '… if you want to be Jeremy Corbyn's useful Jewish idiot, you go right along …'[25]

More troubling is the behaviour of the person appointed in September 2019 by Prime Minister Boris Johnson to be its 'Antisemitism Tsar'—an upgrade on Theresa May's naming of him as her advisor on antisemitism, in one of her last decisions as the previous prime minister—the former Labour MP John Mann, who was elevated to the peerage at the same time.[26] (The irony in the Tsar appellation seems to have escaped both government officials and the advisor himself.) When the renowned children's author Michael Rosen, who is a member of the anti-Zionist/non-Zionist Jewish Socialists' Group, has written about his family's experience of antisemitism and the Holocaust and often tweets about antisemitism in public life, wrote to Lord Mann about investigating antisemitism in the Tory Party, Mann replied with a DM saying he wasn't responding to cases as they came up (though he was), and then with a further DM: 'Troll. Shifted from muted to blocked'.[27] Mann is one among many people who fully subscribe to the view that Jews are the only ones who can define their own oppression, but it turns out that it's only favoured Jews, Jews who avowedly support Israel, who are allowed to do this.

It was not Corbyn and the antisemitism crisis in the Labour Party that was responsible for provoking this. It reflects a more fundamental development in both the symbolic image of the 'Jew' and the way Western governments relate to what they see as Jewish concerns or what they understand the status of Jews should be. No matter that in Europe in the 1990s Jewish populations were increasingly defining themselves in the multicultural terms common in the United States, stressing their own diversity as part of the recognition of the value of diversity across the continent. At the same time, Israel was taking a more hegemonic role in delimiting the boundaries of Jewishness to shore up core support from diaspora Jews as part of its response to the failure of the Oslo peace process and mounting international pressure on it for its military interventions in Lebanon and Gaza. After the assassination of Israeli Prime Minister Yitzhak Rabin in 1995, Israeli governments increasingly laid claim not only to be the centre of the Jewish world, but also to be leading the Jewish world and acting on behalf of all Jews—effectively tying the fate of diaspora Jewry to that of the political ideology and policy decisions of the Israeli state. The erosion of Jews as symbols of liberal ideas as in America, of democracy as in France and as the 'real Europeans' as in the EU, and the loosening of the power of Zionism as a unifying concept and identity tying Jews to Israel and together, led to the increasing deployment of the concept of 'peoplehood'. Noam Pianko argues:

> At the start of the twenty-first century, Jewish peoplehood (the abstract noun variant of the Jewish people) has eclipsed religion (as well as ethnicity and nationality) as the conceptual vocabulary for defining what it means to be a Jew, and the group category that captures the ties that bind Jews from around the globe to one another.[28]

Although in a sense a reaction to the problematic nature of the term Zionism, peoplehood was not promoted by Jewish institutions critical of Zionism, but rather by those working in the engine room of the Zionist movement, in particular the Jewish Agency. The dominant right-wing political forces in Israel actually adopted rather late the discourse of peoplehood, but it flowed logically from the state's efforts to marshal Jewish diaspora support and to reinforce the image of Israel as responsible for all Jews, for the 'Jewish people'.[29]

Parallel to peoplehood, and a second major influence on the changing symbolic image of the Jew, has been the changing relationship between Israel and Zionism as a political ideology and the Holocaust. In the early years of the state, Israel avoided making Jewish suffering and the near annihilation of European Jewry an organising paradigm for the country's identity. Israel represented the overcoming of the forces that produced Auschwitz. It was the only place where Jews from the Displaced Persons' camps would be welcomed. And after 1948, wherever Jews were still considered by the Zionist movement and the government as the 'other'—predominantly in Arab and Muslim countries—Israel offered them a home. Or at least this was the story Israel wanted to tell. In reality, Holocaust survivors had to face a hostile or indifferent atmosphere, and Jews emigrating from Arab countries were subjected to racism, treated as second class citizens and were forced to abandon their Arab-Jewish culture. Antisemitism was a 'disease' afflicting diaspora Jewry and in so far as it continued to exist, fighting it was not something that the state should treat as a national objective. [30]

Apart from building and strengthening the state, the country's foreign policy was focused on managing what was then framed as the 'Arab–Israeli conflict', a national-political struggle. But after 1967, to deflect growing international criticism, Israel reframed its conflict with the Palestinians, no longer portraying it as a national-political one but rather as a threat to Israel's existence from 'antisemitic anti-Zionism', which had direct links with the antisemitism that led to the Holocaust and that also reflected current far-left and Islamic hostility to Jews. Israel was now no longer deliberately distancing itself from treating the Holocaust and antisemitism as integral to the national story. On the contrary, Auschwitz, symbolising the Holocaust, figured increasingly in Israel's presentation of its national identity, and particularly as a 'template for Jewish life'.[31]

There are many manifestations of this, but it reached a high point on the 75th anniversary of the liberation of Auschwitz, which was marked on 27 January 2020 by the largest gathering of political leaders ever to take place in Israel. And this was initiated by a close ally of President Putin, Moshe Kantor, the president of the principal body representing the interests of official national Jewish representative organisations in Europe, the European Jewish Congress (EJC). To put it simply, by laying proprietorial claim to owning Holocaust memory, styling itself as leader of the Jewish people, the embodiment of Jewish peoplehood—in effect, of Zionism—and leading the fight against the alleged main expression of antisemitism today—anti-Zionism—Israel has succeeded in essentialising the meaning of what it is to be a Jew, reducing it to a static embodiment of eternalised antisemitism and a conflation of Zionism and Judaism, whose fate is inextricably linked to the existence of Israel, which is under mortal threat from 'antisemitic anti-Zionism'. As we see from the UK context this translates into an image of the Jew, embraced and promoted by government, and by UK Jewish establishment organisations, as uniquely vulnerable.

At the same time, these very organisations are proud of their access to government, and to the police and security agencies, and their ability to put the case for Israel in the political arena. And by any socio-economic measure, the Jewish minority must be regarded as successful, well-integrated and secure. The Tory government's awareness of this emerged in an interview the then Party Chairman James Cleverly gave to the *Sunday Telegraph* in November 2019, just prior to the general election. Jewish 'individuals and groups, including entrepreneurs and other business figures', he said, people he had known 'much of my life', were planning to leave the country if Labour won the forthcoming general election.[32] Already well-primed to accept the alarmist narrative about 'Jewish flight', the media concurred, rather than expressing reasoned scepticism. The paper's front-page editors didn't hesitate before turning the people Cleverly knows into an unlimited number in their banner headline: 'Jews will leave if Corbyn wins'—a statement that, given the paper's leading role in fanning the flames of a nasty English nationalism, could easily be read as assuming that those clever, rootless cosmopolitans, interested only in turning a profit for themselves, can shift their assets and homes around the globe at will.

For all practical purposes, it is an essentialised, one-dimensional Jew that our political culture and decision-makers understand to be, and are happy to promote as '*the* Jew', whereas at the popular level, given that so many people never encounter a Jew, there is a mixture of images—ranging from common and crude antisemitic tropes to an exaggerated philosemitism,[33] which places 'good' Jews on a pedestal that endangers them more than obvious expressions of antisemitism—very few of which are informed by an understanding of the reality of Jewish diversity. It seems that Zygmunt Bauman was right, and a term is needed that goes beyond the simple dichotomy of antisemitism versus philosemitism. He suggested 'allosemitism', a term coined by Polish Jewish literary critic Artur Sandauer that reflects 'a radically ambivalent attitude' encompassing both philosemitism and antisemitism,[34] associated with the 'Jew';

> an apprehension and vexation related not to something or someone disquieting through otherness and unfamiliarity, but to something or someone that does not fit the structure of the orderly world, does not fall easily into any of the established categories … [but] tend[s] to sit astride all the usual divides and elide all the criteria normally deployed to draw them.

Bryan Cheyette describes this as 'a radically re-conceptualized account of antisemitism':[35]

> This was summed up in a later essay where [Bauman] argues that the terms 'antisemitism' and 'philosemitism', which focus on either hostility or sympathy toward 'the Jews', are two relatively distinct aspects of a much broader history of differentiating Jews from other human beings. The danger, for Bauman,

is that the communal account of antisemitism essentializes Jews as uniquely timeless, unchanging victims and thereby positions the history of antisemitism outside social, political and historical processes which gave rise to this history in the first place.

If the 'Jew' escapes consensual definition, both when Jews themselves seek to determine who is and who isn't one, and when non-Jews are asked what is one, it's hardly surprising, given such fertile ground, that confusion abounds as to what a Jew experiences in their interaction with others in society. And that when described using the word 'antisemitism', it can mean so many different and contradictory things.

* * *

Up to a point, Judaken is quite right to say that 'Contemporary discussions about antisemitism have consequently become a battlefield, with scholarship caught in the crossfire'.[36] However, this seems to imply that scholars are innocent victims in this battle, when that is by no means the case. From my remarks in the Introduction, it should be clear that I do not exempt the academic study of contemporary antisemitism from being afflicted by and contributing to the state of confusion around understandings of antisemitism, validating the image of the essentialised, one-dimensional Jew—albeit in its self-hating, anti-semitism-propagating form—and reducing all criticism of Israel to antisemitic anti-Zionism.

Among leading academics responsible for prosecuting this case over the last 25 years is Professor Alvin Rosenfeld, director of the Institute for the Study of Contemporary Antisemitism at Indiana University, Bloomington, whose pamphlet *Progressive Jewish Thought and the New Antisemitism*, published by the American Jewish Committee (AJC) in 2006, was very influential in shaping discussion of the issue.[37] In his introduction to *Anti-Zionism and Antisemitism: The Dynamics of Delegitimization* he quotes Frans Timmermans, first vice-president of the European Commission, who said on 1 October 2015: far from having been eradicated, 'antisemitism is still a reality, and … it is in fact on the rise—old antisemitism that we have known for centuries, and [a] new antisemitism that sometimes tries to hide itself behind anti-Zionism'.[38] However bad it was then, Rosenfeld, writing in 2018, believed it had become worse on various fronts:

> In both its older and newer forms, a resurgent antisemitism has come powerfully to the fore and is now widespread. That is especially so with regard to hostility to Israel, which, in its most extreme forms, impels its adherents to denounce the Jewish state as a criminal entity and to vilify and attack those identified with it.

'[S]even decades after Israel's establishment', Rosenfeld claims,

> public calls for its end are becoming more prevalent. Those who align them-
> selves with radical anti-Zionist agendas frequently advance the goal of
> delegitimization. And the ultimate end point of delegitimization is the dis-
> solution of Israel as a sovereign state and, for some, the nullification of the
> Jewish people as such.

'Those who hold these aggressive views may … hide behind the façade of
anti-Zionism', a label considered 'safe enough cover … to distance them from
any embarrassing connection to the older forms of Jew hatred'. Israel is routinely
charged with 'the worst of sins—among them, racism, apartheid, crimes against
humanity, ethnic cleansing, and even genocide. The ritual repetition of these
accusations', Rosenfeld argues, 'has developed into an emotionally charged
litany that demonizes the Jewish state and its supporters in ways that may recall
the antisemitism that preceded the persecution and destruction of the Jews
during World War II'.[39]

Many who view Israel in this way have often expressed support for the International Holocaust Remembrance Alliance (IHRA) 'working definition' of
antisemitism. For example, in February 2021, the Britain Israel Communications
and Research Centre (BICOM) online journal *Fathom* published a collection of
pieces defending the 'working definition', some written by a number of its most
vocal supporters. In his introduction to the collection, *Fathom*'s editor, Alan
Johnson, observed that antisemitism had taken on radically different forms
throughout history, with endless variations on a core demonology. 'Today, there
is a new antisemitism focused on a demonology of the Jewish state and those
who support its right to exist, "the Zionists" or "Zios"'.[40] Johnson's implication
here is that if you are a critic of Israel and call its supporters what they call themselves, 'Zionists', this is antisemitism.

In a review of *The War of a Million Cuts: The Struggle against the Delegitimization of Israel and the Jews, and the Growth of New Antisemitism*,[41] a 2017 book by
the prolific writer on contemporary antisemitism Manfred Gerstenfeld, Richard
Landes, former Professor of History at Boston University, explicitly spelt out the
bad faith that Johnson and others quoted above only implied:

> [M]any Europeans and Americans are not aware of the fact that important
> academics, NGO researchers, policy pundits and experts systematically
> abuse their professional principles in order to contribute to the million cuts
> that vilify Israel. In order to overcome the massive inertia of this assault
> on Israel and to wean Westerners from antisemitism disguised as progres-
> sive anti-Zionism, one must want to know the truth. This will happen only

when the public realizes the destructive nature of this campaign not only for Israel and for Palestinians who want peace but also for the important institutions created by the post-Holocaust global community. The latter have been corrupted by their blind adherence to the Palestinian cause. These organizations include: the UN and its various agencies, such as UNRWA, UNESCO and the UNHRC; the ICC; and the plethora of NGOs that deal with human rights that contribute to the 'decay and disintegration of large segments of European society'.

Academics who confront these claims do so in different ways. Scott Ury, head of the Stephen Roth Institute for the Study of Contemporary Antisemitism and Racism at Tel Aviv University, considered what motivates those who feel no compunction in accusing critics of Israel and anti-Zionists of bad faith or evil intent by contextualising the overall nature of their project.[42] He pointed to

one of the biggest problems facing the study of antisemitism today: its ongoing, seemingly inescapable connection to public affairs and the extent to which contemporary political concerns, in particular those regarding Zionism and the state of Israel, influence and shape the way that many scholars frame, interpret, and research antisemitism. While no academic field is free of contemporary social or political considerations, the study of antisemitism has a long, tension-filled, and problematic history of attempting to serve simultaneously two distinct albeit related masters. Over time, antisemitism's curious dual role—as both the topic of heated public debates and the subject of ostensibly neutral academic research—has repeatedly influenced the various and changing conceptualizations, definitions, and understandings of the phenomenon, as well as the contentious nature of the field today and potential plans for resolving the current academic and intellectual impasse.

The influential historian Shmuel Ettinger (1919–1988) held the view that hostility toward Israel on the European left was proof of the long, irrepressible, and potentially indelible nature of antisemitism, as well as the collapse of European liberalism. But it was the prolific late Robert Wistrich (1944–2015) who fleshed out and popularised this thesis, influencing an extensive cohort of historians and antisemitism researchers in the process. Undoubtedly driven by 'visceral anger at the betrayal of the left … [m]ore than any other scholar', according to Ury, 'Wistrich has helped move the study of antisemitism away from the contextual or comparative framework advocated by [Hannah] Arendt and [Salo] Baron and return it to a more traditional Zionist interpretation of Jewish history, society, and fate'.[43]

While many claim that warnings of a resurgence of antisemitism today are warranted in the wake of violent and at times deadly attacks against Jewish institutions and individuals in Paris, Brussels and elsewhere, others, Ury points out, will highlight the 'politically motivated endeavours' of frameworks such as the Israeli Ministry of Foreign Affairs' Global Forum for Combating Antisemitism (GFCA) 'that blur (both purposefully and accidentally) the ostensibly sacrosanct boundaries between the scholarly and the political realms'.[44]

The competition—often conflict—between the two means of understanding antisemitism has led academic research on it over three decades 'to become increasingly conflated with, and in many cases overshadowed by, heated debates about Israel'. Exchanges over 'new antisemitism', Ury continues, often seem like 'little more than surrogates for ongoing political conflicts, and that the underlying diffusion and confusion between political and scholarly approaches to the study of antisemitism leave little room for ostensibly neutral, potentially objective, and fundamentally apolitical interpretations of the phenomenon'. 'Is the reemergence of the traditional Zionist interpretation of antisemitism', Ury asks, 'a reflection of empirical findings, a by-product of deeply embedded political and ideological predispositions, or an unhealthy mixture of both?' If so, does this not mean that 'the boundary separating (and also protecting) academic freedom from political pressures [is being transgressed]?' Ury is clear as to how this can be overcome, but more than a little tentative about success: '[S]tudying antisemitism in comparison to or alongside other forms of prejudice and racism may provide the key to overcoming the biggest problem facing the study of anti-Jewish animus today: the constant intersection and seemingly unavoidable interference between political efforts to combat antisemitism and academic research on the phenomenon'. This 'would problematize, if not destabilize, prevailing assumptions regarding the ostensibly unique nature of antisemitism'.[45]

Judaken addresses the political in his contributions as initiator of the 2018 round table, but he had already in 2008 pointed to key factors influencing increasing politicisation of the subject. He singled out a key area of change as the role of technologies and the geo-global context in which they function, both facilitating the dissemination of antisemitism and furnishing new means to combat it. 'At bottom', he writes, 'this electronic warfare is both a symptom and cause of the global forces at work in antisemitism today'.[46] The internet-fuelled pursuit of the 'enemy' with detailed rebuttals of books, articles, etc., helps spur sales, further internet and blog coverage, the only thing people have read, adding to a 'media-driven frenzied war of words'. Global flows and mobilisation create unlikely virtual alliances, generating funding for the 'next skirmish'. 'All this leads to little more than the propagation of the "ticket thinking" that is the very source of the Judeophobic imagination'.[47] In his *AHR* contribution he draws attention to the 'powerful watchdog organizations that monitor these turf wars, and off-campus agitators who aid and abet the combatants on both sides'.[48]

It is very useful to have a sense of the mechanics that drive and reinforce the extreme polarisation within the academy and of the extent to which almost all public debate among academics, as well as their academic output, has, whether intended or not, a political dimension. But awareness and acknowledgement of this has not led to any amelioration of the damage being done to public understanding of antisemitism, or of the confusion about the entanglement between anti-Zionism and antisemitism. Moreover, it is impossible to ignore the fact that, while not exclusively an intra-Jewish confrontation, trading of some of the most extreme, vilifying language goes on between Jewish academics.

For example, in response to a Jews for Justice for Palestinians (JfJfP[49]) letter to the press protesting Israel's summer 2006 Lebanon war, three academics linked to the Engageonline website—Professor Shlomo Lappin, Dr Eve Garrard and Norman Geras—wrote:

> We are confident that when the history of this period is written and the widespread loss of political reason that characterizes our age is finally recognized, your group will be properly consigned to a footnote in the long and dishonourable tradition of Jewish sycophancy and collaboration with hostility that has polluted the margins of European Jewry over the generations.

This accusation that JfJfP, which counted many academics among its prominent signatories, was essentially a traitor to European Jewry, was ostensibly triggered by a misreading of wording in the letter that the Engage three took to mean that antisemitic statements by Hamas and Hezbollah were excusable. The JfJfP organisers quickly clarified that no such excuse for antisemitism was either suggested or implied. But as usually happens when such accusations are made, they have an extraordinarily long half-life.

Much of this kind of attack is relentlessly *ad hominem*. Returning to Rosenfeld, whose exposition of genocidal anti-Zionism I quoted at the beginning of this section, we find that in this intra-Jewish confrontation he, like many others, is quick to go for the jugular. Criticising the book *The Question of Zion* by Professor Jacqueline Rose in the *Progressive Jewish Thought and the New Antisemitism* pamphlet, he wrote: 'Rose typifies the most distressing features of the new antisemitism—namely, the participation of Jews alongside it, especially in its anti-Zionist expression'.[50] 'Nothing in her book expresses any genuine concern for the Jews as a people'.[51] 'She comes uncomfortably close ... to equating Zionism with German antisemitism at its worst ... [S]uch poisonous linkages reveal nothing about the reality of Zionism, but a great deal about the author's uneasy identity as an anti-Zionist Jew facing the reality of the Jewish state'.[52] Rosenfeld makes no attempt to engage with Rose's arguments, preferring to play the amateur psychologist and see Rose facing an 'identity' crisis because Israel's existence challenges her values as a progressive Jew. Quick to endorse Rosenfeld's approach, Professor Shulamit Reinharz baldly stated: 'Most [progressive Jews] would say that they are anti-Zionists, not antisemites. But I disagree, because in a world where there is only one Jewish state, to oppose it vehemently is to endanger Jews ... Jewish antisemitism/Zionism has major mouthpieces in England (Jacqueline Rose).'[53] It needs to be said that Rose never responded in kind to such criticism.

There is *some* clear and rigorous thinking about antisemitism in the academy, but to the interested layperson, identifying it, separating it out from the mountains of sub-standard text on the subject, academic in form only, is daunting. Nevertheless, it is important that we do not surrender either to taking sides purely on the basis of conviction or to distancing ourselves entirely from the issue.

2

The Use and Abuse of Antisemitic Stereotypes and Tropes

In February 2019, Andrew Silow-Carroll, Editor of the *Jewish Telegraphic Agency* (JTA), wrote:

> This has been the era of the antisemitic 'trope', with the word popping up in hundreds of news stories since the 2016 [US presidential] campaign. In short, tropes are phrases or images that evoke classic antisemitic ideas rather than state them explicitly. It's a long list: the dual loyalty trope, the blood libel, the clannishness charge, the global conspiracy motif and the control-the-media mantras (to name a few).[1]

Much the same could be said of the UK. While the phrase 'antisemitic trope' would previously have been common in discourse on antisemitism largely among scholars, following the election of Jeremy Corbyn as leader of the Labour Party in 2015, it seems that everyone who comments publicly on current antisemitism—journalists, opinion writers, politicians, anti-antisemitism campaigners, religious leaders—freely bases their judgement about an individual's antisemitism on identifying what they have said or written as an antisemitic trope.

Discussing antisemitism has relied heavily on references to the demonising literary and visual imagery used to isolate or 'other' the mythical Jew. The most useful amplifications of definitions of antisemitism provide baseline examples of the phenomenon. For example, Brian Klug fleshes out the imagined 'Jew' as the antisemite would see them in this way:

> The Jew belongs to a sinister people set apart from all others, not merely by its customs but by a collective character: arrogant yet obsequious; legalistic yet corrupt; flamboyant yet secretive. Always looking to turn a profit, Jews are as ruthless as they are tricky. Loyal only to their own, wherever they go they form a state within a state, preying upon the societies in whose midst they dwell. Their hidden hand controls the banks, the markets and the media. And when revolutions occur or nations go to war, it's the Jews—cohesive,

powerful, clever and stubborn—who invariably pull the strings and reap the rewards.[2]

Nothing exemplifies better some of the imagery Klug refers to than the visual tropes found in German Nazi antisemitic publications, particularly *Der Stürmer*, published from 1923 to 1945. However, examples of contemporary tropes do not have to look so gross, violent and malevolent to be obviously identifiable as tropes. One living figure commonly pictured in America and Europe in such a way as to suggest nefarious Jewish financial and political control of countries and markets is George Soros, the Hungarian-born financier and philanthropist. In the final days of the 2016 US presidential election campaign, Donald Trump ran an ad prominently featuring pictures of Soros with two other American Jewish finance leaders, Janet Yellin, chair of the Federal Reserve, and Lloyd Blankfein, CEO of Goldman Sachs, as representative of the 'globalist', establishment elite whose 'control [of] the levers of power' and protection of the financial interests of the wealthy have robbed ordinary working Americans of their incomes and deprived them of jobs.[3] Most blatant and sustained has been the use of images of Soros by Hungary's president, Viktor Orban. He blanketed the country during an election campaign with posters showing a picture of a smiling Soros and the words 'Don't let him get the last laugh', echoing, some historians said, the Nazi trope, used by Hitler in his speeches, of the 'laughing Jew'.[4] (Orban held Soros responsible for 'flooding' Hungary with Muslim migrants.) When the Hungarian government, under pressure, announced that it would remove the posters from the public sphere, it did not apologise for their antisemitic character, but declared that their aim had already been achieved.

Both Trump and Orban use these tropes, which are figurative or metaphorical rather than literal, in order to be able to claim that nothing they say is antisemitic, or at least to let others make such claims on their behalf. But tropes can also be more direct, leaving little to the imagination: fog-horn, rather than dog-whistle.

Many of the alleged incidents of antisemitism attributed to Jeremy Corbyn and other prominent members of the Labour Party were claims of verbal or written comments made about a Jewish person or a group of Jews that have, at their core, the repetition of an antisemitic trope. One of the most widely spread and publicised of such incidents occurred at the launch of the report and recommendations of the Chakrabarti inquiry into antisemitism and other forms of racism in the Labour Party on 30 June 2016.[5] While Corbyn and Chakrabarti were fielding questions, a Black Labour Party activist, Marc Wadsworth, was given the floor. While making a point about the under-representation of non-white racial groups at the launch, he said he saw the journalist from the *Telegraph* giving a copy of a press release, which he, Wadsworth, was handing out before the event began, to Labour MP Ruth Smeeth and thus claimed to have seen who was 'working hand-in-hand'. Ruth Smeeth is Jewish.

The Wikipedia account of what then happened states: 'At least one person in the audience heckled, angrily calling out: "How dare you". Journalist Kevin Schofield, the former senior correspondent at the *Sun* tabloid, muttered towards Smeeth that it is "antisemitism at an antisemitism inquiry". Smeeth walked out, followed by [*Telegraph* journalist Kate] McCann'. In the minutes immediately following the event, the media were reporting that Smeeth had left in tears. Later that day, she tweeted that Wadsworth had verbally attacked her by using a traditional antisemitic slur to accuse her of a media conspiracy, though did not specify the slur or the conspiracy. She wrote that:

> it is beyond belief that someone could come to the launch of a report on anti-semitism in the Labour Party and espouse such vile conspiracy theories about Jewish people, which were ironically highlighted as such in Ms Chakrabarti's report, while the leader of my own party stood by and did absolutely nothing. People like this have no place in our party or our movement and must be opposed.[6]

On 27 April 2018, the National Constitutional Committee (NCC) found that two charges of a breach of s.2.1.8 ('prejudicial and detrimental conduct') of the Labour Party Rule Book by Wadsworth were proven and decided to expel him from the party. The party had no specific formal rule about antisemitism or racism in general, but it was universally reported and understood that he was guilty of expressing antisemitism by accusing Smeeth of being 'hand-in-hand' with a journalist on a right-wing newspaper, thereby repeating the trope of Jews conspiring to control the media. And to make matters worse, Corbyn, who was fielding questions, was accused of deliberately allowing Wadsworth to say what he said out of sympathy for Wadsworth's alleged antisemitic views.

But detailed examination of what Wadsworth said and did before and during the incident provides no contextual evidence of antisemitism on his behalf. He states he did not know Smeeth was Jewish. McCann did hand a copy of Wadsworth's press release to Smeeth. Wadsworth's 'hand-in-hand' comment was, in effect, an aside—a common left-wing complaint about the mainstream media being collectively against the Labour Party—made prior to his main point about the inquiry having also been tasked with examining anti-Black racism, but that this was being ignored. So the charge against Wadsworth rested entirely on his 'hand-in-hand' comment.

The launch was broadcast live and recorded. There were many journalists present, including the BBC's political correspondent John Pinaar. And yet the mischaracterisation of what occurred as an antisemitic incident flowed through the media like a river that had burst its banks. That version of the Wadsworth story remains dominant, despite many online sources that reveal what really happened and what was really said. A report by the Media Reform Coalition, *Labour, Antisemitism and the News: A Disinformation Campaign*, which closely examined media coverage of the antisemitism issue in the party, reached this conclusion about the Wadsworth affair: 'Journalists covering the launch of Labour's antisemitism report in 2016 routinely misquoted an activist in ways that were entirely removed from his original comment, in spite of a video recording of the event that was readily and immediately accessible'.[7]

In Silow-Carroll's view, 'it is possible to partake of a trope without meaning to ... Sometimes bigotry is in the ear of the listener'. And this could very well be what happened in the Wadsworth case. After all, Smeeth appeared to delete her tweeted accusation that Wadsworth accused her of a 'media conspiracy'. (There is also no evidence of her walking out in tears.) Not that this has prevented the accusation from becoming and remaining received wisdom for so many others who 'found' antisemitism running rife in the Labour Party. An article in the *JC* subsequently accused Wadsworth of being involved in a group planning to target Jewish people in the Labour Party, but the High Court determined that Wadsworth had been defamed. The paper agreed to pay 'substantial compensation' and make a public apology.[8]

But there is something more fundamentally problematic about this trope accusation. It completely drains the term of anything to do with antisemitism: in effect making the mere mention of the word 'Jew' and 'journalist' in the same sentence, automatically 'partaking' of a trope—even if, as in this case, the word 'Jew' was not used, rather it was a Jewish MP, whom Wadsworth did not know was Jewish. And if a trope is to have any real antisemitic character, it must consist of more than just the close juxtaposition of two words.

If this were the only example of the misuse of the trope attribution, it would not be significant, but in reality we see a pattern of misuse, especially in relation to Corbyn and other figures in the Labour Party accused of expressions of antisemitism. It is a mindset that denies the possibility of any ambiguity in what might be alleged as antisemitism. And it treats tropes as fixed and eternal: Jew + media, Jew + power, Jew + lobby—whenever mentioned together, the spark of antisemitism is ignited. But as Bryan Cheyette explains, 'The Jew is a figure of ambivalence, not hatred or hostility. A protean figure which is good *and* bad (relating to context) rather than a fixed myth, image or trope'.[9]

Thus, the antisemitic trope or stereotype is both more subtle and plastic than you would realise from the way it is so often currently deployed. Jonathan Judaken argues that the nature of stereotypes about Jews is overdetermined: 'The concept of the Jew shapeshifts. These shifts help explain how myths about Jews have had different meanings at different moments or have signified differently to different people in the same era'.[10] Drawing on the work of Maurice Samuels and other scholars, Judaken writes:

> These myths cast light on particular cultural obsessions that nevertheless have meant different things at different historical junctures ... even when expressions of antisemitism are not expressed in a formal work of literature, they very often contain narrative elements. Antisemites tell stories. They concoct paranoid plots with devious characters to explain aspects of the world that escape their control. They blame Jews for imagined crimes: running the banks, controlling the media, plotting world domination. And they cast themselves as heroes who ride to the rescue of the hapless victim. The notorious antisemitic hoax *The Protocols of the Elders of Zion* (1903) is typical of this kind of text, which purports to be factual but contains all the elements of fiction.[11]

The understanding of tropes today represents a curious inversion of this process. The alleged antisemitism of Wadsworth and Corbyn, as expressed in the tropes that they are accused of using, is effectively devoid of any wider narrative. It is almost as if it were a barrister's killer fact in a case being prosecuted in court; whereas it is the accuser who 'invents' the trope, which is used to bolster a highly dubious narrative about the person accused. And the accuser styles themselves as the hero 'riding to the rescue of the hapless victim', the 'Jew'.

One such is the former Labour MP, now a Peer, John Mann (mentioned in Chapter 1), who gave up his seat after being appointed as the UK government's Antisemitism 'Tsar'. A self-styled champion of fighting antisemitism on behalf of the 'Jewish community', Lord Mann was one of Corbyn's fiercest critics from the moment he was elected leader of the party. Writing about the Wadsworth affair he opined: 'It was shameful that a Momentum activist [Wadsworth], took the opportunity to launch into one of the oldest antisemitic tropes as part of an attack on Ruth Smeeth. The unwelcoming environment for Jews remains and the press had the perfect example of just how it plays out'.[12] Mann treated a groundless accusation as unquestionable fact, and then proceeded to use it to prove that Jews are experiencing widespread antisemitism. Mann professes pro-Jewish sympathies, but such sentiments do not automatically confer on anyone innate expertise on antisemitism.

Another Labour MP, Joan Ryan, chair of Labour Friends of Israel (LFI) and strong critic of Corbyn, left the party in February 2019, saying it had become 'infected with the scourge of anti-Jewish racism' under Corbyn's leadership. In response, on 19 February, this tweet was sent from the Young Labour account: 'Joan Ryan Gone—Palestine Lives'. Among those immediately criticising the tweet as antisemitic was the outspoken Labour MP Jess Phillips, who told

Channel 4: 'My red line is the antisemitism … put[ting] "Palestine Lives" at the announcement of Joan Ryan leaving … that is antisemitic and it has to stop'. The tweet was soon deleted. Insensitive? Perhaps. But an antisemitic trope? Ryan is not Jewish. And while lack of sympathy for the Palestinians is by no means a requirement for chairing LFI, it would be true to say that LFI's understanding of the rights to which Palestinians are entitled and yet are denied, does not tally with how the issue is viewed by Labour Friends of Palestine.

Expressing pro-Jewish or pro-Israel sympathies, however, is no guarantee that the person expressing them is themself immune to using blatantly obvious antisemitic tropes. Mainstream Jewish organisations in the US and at least 75 per cent of political parties in the Israeli Knesset saw, and probably still see, Trump as Israel's, and the Jewish people's, best friend.

But in 2015 Trump employed an antisemitic trope more directly when he told the Republican Jewish Coalition (RJC): 'I'm a negotiator like you folks, we are negotiators. Is there anybody that doesn't renegotiate deals in this room? This room negotiates them—perhaps more than any other room I've ever spoken in'. Later he says, 'You're not gonna support me because I don't want your money. You want to control your politicians, that's fine'. After Trump made his 'negotiator' joke, the Jewish crowd roared with laughter.[13]

Jews sometimes base jokes about themselves on Jewish stereotypes, so does this make Trump's allusion to the haggling, money-grubbing Jew acceptable? There's no record of the RJC people receiving the second comment with laughter, however. Both comments play on antisemitic tropes, but deployed by Trump, with his proven ability to combine naivety and cunning, it is clear that a trope's character is contingent and not fixed for all time.

There is an element of the 'power/control' trope in the above; it is general and overarching. The 'Jews control-the-media' trope, as imagined to have been employed in the Marc Wadsworth/Ruth Smeeth incident, is a specific example of the alleged exercise of 'Jewish power'. However, there are features of the 'Jewish power' trope that require more extensive exploration (which can be found in Chapter 13).

Another example of trope misinterpretation is the dominant narrative about the mural created in September 2012 by the artist Kalen Ockerman, known as Mear One, on a wall of a private property in Tower Hamlets, previously used for public art. Although an emblematic instance of contradictory and confused judgements about and accusations of antisemitism, it is more complex than the Wadsworth case, but thereby further highlights the plasticity of stereotypes and the narratives we are predisposed to read into them.

Soon after the mural was completed, residents complained. Local Labour councillor and long-term resident Peter Golds urged the police to pursue the inflammatory artist under race hate laws. He said: 'When I saw the mural I was shocked. It's horribly similar to the propaganda used by the Third Reich in Nazi Germany. The money hoarding and hooked-nosed men is classic Nazi'.[14] The then mayor of Tower Hamlets, Lutfur Rahman, subsequently announced that he had instructed council officers to have the mural removed. 'Whether intentional or otherwise', Lutfur stated,[15] 'the images of the bankers perpetuate antisemitic propaganda about conspiratorial Jewish domination of financial and political institutions'.

The mural depicts six elderly men sitting passively around a table in the form of a Monopoly game board. One of them is counting a small wad of Monopoly banknotes. Propping up the table/board on their backs are figures representing the 'oppressed'. In the centre at the top of the mural is the symbol of the Illuminati, allegedly a secret, elite group associated with Jews. But on 2 October 2012, Jeremy Corbyn, having learnt of the intention to remove the mural, commented from his personal Facebook account: 'Why? You are in good company. Rockefeller destroyed Diego Viera's [sic] mural because it includes a picture of Lenin'. The reference was to a 1993 fresco, *Man at the Crossroads*, by left-wing artist Diego Rivera, seen as anti-capitalist, and removed in 1934 from the Rockefeller Center in Manhattan.[16]

The artist himself vehemently denied being antisemitic:

A group of conservatives do not like my mural and are playing a race card with me. My mural is about class and privilege. The banker group is made up of Jewish and white Anglos. For some reason they are saying I am antisemitic. This I am most definitely not ... What I am against is class.

He protested at the removal and posted: 'Tomorrow they want to buff my mural. Freedom of expression. London calling. Public art'. At the same time, the pseudonymous 'Lucy Lips' of the aggressively pro-Israel blog Harry's Place—generally believed to be David Toube, a lawyer and former lecturer[17]—questioned whether the mural was antisemitic and was initially prepared to give the artist the benefit of the doubt. 'I've seen more obvious stereotypes of Jews deployed in antisemitic art', he wrote.[18] Furthermore, unlike Corbyn, who arrived at his own initial judgement about the mural on the basis of a Facebook post probably viewed on his mobile phone, Lucy Lips had been to see the mural in situ, writes Bob Pitt. 'He decided he'd been wrong about it only after reading Ockerman's own comments[19] on his work, and even then stated that he would "oppose the whitewashing of the mural"'.[20]

Corbyn's Facebook comments only came to light in 2015. The *JC* referred to the mural then as having 'antisemitic undertones'.[21] But the issue was not picked up by other mainstream media.

Meanwhile, the artist made a number of subsequent remarks, the tenor of which suggested that antisemitic motives were indeed integral to his rationale for the mural, and revealed his close connection to David Icke and his antisemitic fantasies. In 2016 he produced a print version of the mural in which three of the seated figures are representations of living Jewish bankers and financiers, and two of four spectral figures in the background are also Jews.

The mural issue resurfaced in March 2018 when then Labour MP Luciana Berger publicly demanded an explanation of Corbyn's Facebook post. A spokesperson responded saying: 'In 2012 Jeremy was responding to concerns about the removal of public art on grounds of freedom of speech. However, the mural was offensive, used antisemitic imagery, which has no place in our society, and it is right that it was removed'. The Jewish Labour Movement said: 'Antisemitic art is antisemitism. It cannot be defended under any circumstances'. Berger declared the statement to be 'wholly inadequate … It fails to understand on any level the hurt and anguish felt about antisemitism. I shall be raising this further'.[22] The comedian and occasional columnist David Baddiel, writing in the *Sunday Times* on 1 April 2018, stated: 'The mural could be a cover of a reprint of *The Protocols of the Elders of Zion*'. After presumably approving of the cautious line taken by Marcus Dysch in 2015, that the mural had 'antisemitic undertones', by March 2018 the *JC* editor Stephen Pollard had apparently changed his mind, writing on his *JC* comment blog on 27 March 2018: 'the endorsement by Jeremy Corbyn of an unambiguously antisemitic mural was a step too far even for our naturally quiet community'. The 'Enough Is Enough' rally against antisemitism and Corbyn's handling of the matter, organised by Jewish communal organisations, took place on 26 March.

Bob Pitt's conclusion, from his lengthy and thorough analysis of the story, 'that the Brick Lane mural *was* essentially antisemitic', seems about right. But it should not obscure the fact that along the way, very divergent views were expressed of the existence, significance, nature and transparency of the trope or tropes that must be distillable to such a degree that one can speak of the mural as *having* an essence. Commentators regarded as the toughest and most uncompromising critics of Corbyn and the Labour Party, who tend to apply the antisemite label with some abandon, were initially circumspect about labelling the mural antisemitic. But when the issue resurfaced after Corbyn became leader of the party, and his Facebook post became a national story in 2018, these commentators changed their minds, even though the mural had been wiped in 2012 and they were not necessarily aware of Ockerman's subsequent comments.

Nevertheless, some of the characterisations of the mural demonstrated a woeful failure to differentiate between various levels of intensity of antisemitic imagery. So, when Baddiel says it could be a reprint of the cover of *The Protocols of the Elders of Zion*, a quick look at images of such covers on Google reveals nothing resembling the mural. Covers are either text, usually designed to indicate the 'seriousness' of the publication, or gross caricatures of Jews barely showing any resemblance to the men sitting around the Monopoly board. Similarly, commentators who have claimed that the mural and caricatures of Jews in the German Nazi Party's weekly tabloid format newspaper *Der Stürmer*, published from 1923 to 1945, are identical, are incorrect. The typical 'Jew' in *Der Stürmer* has an exaggerated hook nose, a bulging, protruding fleshy lower lip, an unshaven rather than always bearded face, eyes suggesting rapacious intent. The figures in the mural, irrespective of what Ockerman has said about them, look like cuddly teddy bears in comparison.

This does not mitigate the antisemitic nature of the mural, but it does illustrate again the confusion about what constitutes an antisemitic trope. It shows how people can be influenced in identifying an antisemitic trope by the pressure of the media, which collectively turned a six-year-old story that gained hardly any traction at the time into a *cause celebre*, an iconic example not only of antisemitism but of the kind of antisemitism of which Corbyn supposedly approved. Of course, the story would have remained something for the archives had there been no Corbyn connection. That connection was the spark, rediscovered at a time when the issue of antisemitism in the party had reached crisis levels, that ignited a furore.

And yet, the received wisdom about Corbyn's connection to the mural—that, in Pollard's words, he 'endorse[d] ... an unambiguously antisemitic mural'— is completely false. In the only piece of evidence on this—Corbyn's Facebook comment—he does not approve or endorse the mural; in response to someone else's previous post, in which the decision to remove the mural is mentioned, Corbyn merely asks 'Why?' His then reference to the removed mural of the left-wing artist Diego Rivera indicates that his sense of the mural was that it was a piece of anti-capitalist, public art. I write 'sense of what the mural was' because there is no evidence one way or the other as to whether he looked at the image of the mural at all, or whether, if he looked at it, he gave it enough attention to examine it carefully. As we know, Pollard's *JC* was originally cautious about the degree of antisemitism displayed by the mural, so one might as well indict the paper and its editor for downplaying antisemitism as accusing Corbyn of knowingly approving of an antisemitic mural. Once again, the media, through oversimplification and adherence to the 'Corbyn is an antisemite' narrative, played a major role in embedding in public belief that an unambiguously antisemitic incident had occurred and that Corbyn was responsible for it. In its report on Labour and antisemitism, the Media Reform Coalition concluded that: 'Several reports [that] focused on a controversial social media post by Jeremy Corbyn omitted any mention that it was made six years ago, with some emphasising a sense of currency and recency that failed to make clear the historical context of the post'.[23]

The Wadsworth and mural affairs are just two of many examples of how the concept of the antisemitic trope is both misunderstood and manipulated for political purposes. And in practically all the particularly significant cases, social media have played a crucial role. Judaken is right to point out that: 'Those who oppose Jews today continue to tell stories, and weave complicated plots, even if their favoured media are not the novel and the poem but the blog and the tweet'[24]—although as shorthand for the kind of social media, 'blog and tweet' are inadequate. Think Facebook, Instagram, YouTube, WhatsApp, TikTok and more. But it is equally important to note that those who claim to defend Jews are also instantly communicating their imagined, invented and confected notions of tropes through the same social media.

Among individuals targeted was the Jewish Labour councillor Jo Bird who made a joke about being personally investigated for antisemitism by speaking of the number of Jewish Labour Party members similarly treated as 'Jew process rather than due process'. Self-deprecating humour about your own ethnic group is not an antisemitic trope. The NEC member Peter Wilsman angrily questioned claims about antisemitism in the Labour Party by saying that some members of the Jewish community are 'Trump fanatics' and challenging the '70 rabbis' who wrote to the *Guardian* alleging that Labour had chosen to ignore the Jewish community[25] to 'show us the evidence'. This was labelled antisemitic.[26] Angrily or intemperately questioning claims about antisemitism in the Labour Party is not an antisemitic trope, nor is criticising rabbis for opinions they hold about matters which are essentially political.

A blanket allegation of antisemitism covering multiple internet sources was made in the Community Security Trust's report *Engines of Hate: The online networks behind the Labour Party's antisemitism crisis* (2019).[27] The report claimed that 36 accounts were conspiring to spread antisemitism. Some sites and tweets are antisemitic, but a definition of antisemitism it uses is based on the notion that if you criticise people who accuse Labour of antisemitism, that qualifies as antisemitism. This report lumps together 'different and entirely unrelated accounts' most of which contain no evidence of actual hate speech about Jews. Again, it is not an antisemitic trope to question the degree to which allegations of antisemitism are based on facts.

In January 2013, the Palestinian ambassador to the UK, Manuel Hassassian, addressed a meeting in parliament organised by the Palestine Solidarity Campaign (PSC). Among his remarks, he said: 'We, the Palestinians, the most highly educated and intellectual in the Middle East, are still struggling for the basic right of self-determination. What an irony. How long are we going to suffer and be patient with Israel?' In response, he reportedly said:

I'm reaching the conclusion that the Jews are the children of God, the only children of God and the Promised Land is being paid by God! I have started to believe this because nobody is stopping Israel building its messianic dream of Eretz Israel to the point I believe that maybe God is on their side.

Richard Millett, a Zionist activist, challenged Hassassian over what he had said.[28] Also speaking at the event were Labour Party Shadow Justice Minister Andy Slaughter MP, Liberal Democrat MP Sarah Teather and Corbyn.

At a subsequent conference later in 2013, recorded on video, Corbyn referred to Hassassian's speech and said:

We had a meeting in Parliament in which Manuel [Hassassian] made an incredibly powerful and passionate and effective speech about the history of Palestine ... This was dutifully recorded by the thankfully silent Zionists who were in the audience on that occasion; and then came up and berated him afterwards for what he had said. They clearly had two problems. One is they don't want to study history and, secondly, having lived in this country for a very long time, probably all their lives, they don't understand English irony either. Manuel does understand English irony and uses it very very effectively. So I think they needed two lessons, which we can perhaps help them with.

When a video of Corbyn making these remarks suddenly surfaced in 2018 he was accused of a triple trope antisemitic misdemeanour. First, using the word 'Zionist' as a derogatory term to denote 'Jew'; second, implying that Jews don't belong in Britain, that they aren't real 'Englishmen', because they don't understand irony; and third, expressing the kind of antisemitism that supposedly prevails among shires-born, privately educated, privileged individuals.

The problem with this indictment is that, in order to believe it you would have to hold a preconceived opinion of Corbyn as an antisemite, because the facts are more prosaic. First, the individuals Corbyn was referring to were prominent figures in a right-wing Zionist group, who are proud to call themselves Zionists, and who often attend such pro-Palestinian meetings where some of them sometimes behave in a very disruptive manner. It cannot be antisemitic to call a Zionist, who proudly self-identifies as a Zionist, a Zionist. Second, in his talk Hassassian had clearly flagged his use of irony in the segment of his speech quoted above, but it seems that, in their questioning of Hassassian, they had taken his 'Children of God', 'Promised Land', etc., references literally. To point out that the two critics did not understand the irony in Hasassian's remarks is not antisemitic. Third, you would have to assume nefarious motives on Corbyn's part to believe that the 'having lived in this country for a very long time, probably all their lives' comment was either a deliberate or subconscious antisemitic othering. First, it was not beyond the bounds of possibility that the activists had not been born in the UK. Jewish migration to the UK did not suddenly come to an end in the years immediately after the war. During the Aden and Suez crises (1947 and 1956), many Jews felt endangered or were forced out, and came to Britain. Another explanation would put it in the context of Corbyn's occasional clumsiness when speaking off the cuff, here looking for a way of saying 'they should have known better', or it could have been Corbyn's own attempt to make a little joke, itself mildly ironic. It was hardly proof of repeating an unambiguous antisemitic trope. Finally, as for labelling him a little Englander antisemite, I've no doubt that many who loosely have the same background are Tory antisemites, but there is nothing in Corbyn's record to indicate he ever related to Jews in that way. On the contrary, as I noted in the Introduction, throughout his parliamentary political career he has stood in solidarity with Jews when they have been under attack and also used his role and influence as an MP to assist the strictly orthodox Jewish communities living in his constituency.

Finally, to return to the Jewish power trope, nothing epitomises more clearly the way the notion of power that informs an antisemitic trope can become detached from its moorings than an interpretation of an off-the-cuff short speech Corbyn gave in 2017 at the opening of an exhibition about minority community media. A video recording shows him saying the following:[29]

> The Jewish community coming to London in the 18th and 19th centuries and in larger numbers in the 20th century fleeing from Nazism, the value of their newspapers was very very serious to them, kept them together, kept them powerful and kept them in a position to influence the politics of the environment.

The video clip is carried on a website under the title 'Jeremy Corbyn engages in antisemitic trope'—Jewish control of the media, of course.

Actually, Corbyn is praising minority community media, in particular that of the Jewish community. He is explaining how recent Jewish immigrants to the UK used newspapers they distributed amongst themselves to empower and bolster their struggle against antisemitism of the time, and against Mosley's antisemitic Blackshirts.

*   *   *

It is one thing to disagree over whether something said is antisemitic or not. But as I have shown in this and the previous chapter, we face something much more problematic. It is not merely widespread confusion that can be dispelled by patiently delivered information, education and explanation. The failure to understand or accept that antisemitic tropes cannot be wielded like sledgehammers as if they are eternal, unchanging and identifiable merely by the juxtaposition of something or someone possibly signifying a Jew, Jewishness, or a Jewish institution, with words like 'money', 'power', 'media', 'banks' and so on, is evidence that the politicisation of the subject has reached such a disruptive and compromising level, there is no longer a common language in which such matters can be discussed. That language has been displaced by a confrontational, adversarial discourse from which there seems to be no escape.

3
Motivated by Antisemitism?
Challenges to Zionism 1975–1989

On 10 November 1975, by a vote of 72 to 35 (with 32 abstentions), the United Nations General Assembly (UNGA) adopted Resolution 3379, which 'determine[d] that Zionism is a form of racism and racial discrimination'. Although it did not come as a complete surprise, there was shock and consternation among Israel's Western supporters. Daniel Patrick Moynihan,[1] the US Ambassador to the UN, spoke passionately against the move saying: '[The United States] does not acknowledge, it will not abide by, it will never acquiesce in this infamous act … A great evil has been loosed upon the world'. Israel's leaders condemned the decision in the strongest terms. Chaim Hertzog,[2] the country's ambassador to the UN, asserted that not only was Zionism not racism, it was in fact a liberating force for the country's Arab population. 'For us, the Jewish people', he said, holding the resolution in his hand, 'this resolution based on hatred, falsehood and arrogance, is devoid of any moral or legal value. For us, the Jewish people, this is no more than a piece of paper and we shall treat it as such'. At which point, he tore the document in two.

There were many states that formally declared themselves to be anti-Zionist, though this did not prevent some of them from doing business with Israel. It was common for them to repeat formulaic condemnations of 'the Zionist regime', though these were mostly rhetorical and also not surprising given that so many states in the Middle East and the Third World, as it was then called, looked to the Soviet Union for development support, the country at the centre of marshalling anti-Zionist sentiment at the UN.

There had been changes at the world body resulting from both Israel's victory in the Six-Day War of June 1967 and the destabilising vulnerability it displayed in the 1973 Yom Kippur War. Growing disquiet over the continuing occupation of Palestinian land, and the awareness that, although Israel prevailed in the 1973 war, it no longer looked invulnerable, contributed to making the Palestinian national movement a voice to be listened to. The Resolution 3379 vote took place approximately one year after UNGA 3237 granted the PLO Permanent Observer status, following PLO President Yasser Arafat's 'olive branch' speech to the General Assembly in November 1974. In addition, decolonisation was changing the power balance and the nature of concerns in the General Assembly, further focusing attention on what was increasingly perceived as the settler-colonial reality of Israel's policies in the West Bank and Gaza.

At the same time, there had been a surge of Jewish support for Israel and Zionism since the 1967 war, largely prompted by the apocalyptic warnings Jewish communal and Israeli leaders endorsed that the Jewish people once again faced the possibility of something like another Holocaust. The rapid victory brought some instant relief but also generated exaggerated assessments of Israel's military might, as was revealed during the 1973 war. The outcome was traumatic for the country and the reckoning was still going on when 3379 was adopted and seen in Israel and the Jewish world generally as adding insult to injury.

It was the Soviets who engineered the adoption of the resolution with the aim of achieving a major blow against the West, with which it was in competition to be the primary partner for the developing world. In fact, neither the West nor the East was able to fulfil their promises to these countries, leading the Soviets to resort to ideological gestures among which anti-Zionism was a special favourite as it was used by Soviet leaders as a cloak for their antisemitism. Leonid Brezhnev, who became general secretary of the Communist Party of the Soviet Union and the most powerful figure in the regime, was closely associated with this campaign.

There is no doubt that Abba Eban, Israel's foreign minister between 1966 and 1974, was *au fait* with the way the anti-Zionist winds were blowing during these years. Indeed, he was far ahead of his time in identifying anti-Zionism as 'the new antisemitism' in a 1973 article for *Congress Bi-Weekly*, a periodical of the American Jewish Congress (AJCongress):

[R]ecently we have witnessed the rise of the new left which identifies Israel with the establishment, with acquisition, with smug satisfaction, with, in fact, all the basic enemies ... Let there be no mistake: the new left is the author and the progenitor of the new antisemitism. One of the chief tasks of any dialogue with the Gentile world is to prove that the distinction between antisemitism and anti-Zionism is not a distinction at all. Anti-Zionism is merely the new antisemitism. The old classic antisemitism declared that equal rights belong to all individuals within the society, except the Jews. The new antisemitism says that the right to establish and maintain an independent national sovereign state is the prerogative of all nations, so long as they happen not to be Jewish. And when this right is exercised not by the Maldive Islands, not by the state of Gabon, not by Barbados ... but by the oldest and most authentic of all nationhoods, then this is said to be exclusivism, particularism, and a flight of the Jewish people from its universal mission.[3]

Eban's claim that Zionism and the establishment of the state of Israel represent the fulfilment of the purpose of the 'oldest and most authentic of all nation-hoods' is highly questionable. But even before Eban, according to French philosopher Pierre-André Taguieff, the first wave of what he describes as '*la nouvelle judéophobie*'[4] emerged in the Arab-Muslim world and the Soviet sphere following the 1967 War. In his book *Rising From the Muck: The New Antisemitism in Europe*, he cites papers by Jacques Givet from 1968 and historian Léon Poliakov from 1969 in which was discussed the idea of a 'new antisemitism' rooted in anti-Zionism.[5]

However, it would be fair to say that these early references to 'new antisemitism' did not lead directly to a consistent, coherent development of an idea or set of ideas. The word 'new' served multiple purposes. For example, in 1921 the Board of Deputies of British Jews published *The New Antisemitism: The Official Protests of the British and American Jewish Communities* 'in an attempt to describe the twin threat of Nazism in Germany and Mosley's fascism at home'.[6] In 1936, the British Jewish historian Cecil Roth used the phrase, in quotation marks, for the antisemitism based on racial theories[7] that emerged towards the end of the nineteenth century. Even the 1974 book sometimes referred to as the first to formally frame anti-Israel and anti-Zionist discourse as antisemitic, Forster and Epstein's *The New Antisemitism*, cannot carry such a weighty responsibility.[8] The authors were heads of the Anti-Defamation League (ADL) and their book essentially sums up their understanding of the state of antisemitism in the United States in the early 1970s, their title constituting more of a warning about trends they felt presented a new danger than an indication that the book focused on antisemitic anti-Zionism. In a 1975 review of the book, A. Roy Eckardt wrote:

> the adjective 'new' in the title is seen as insufficient. The antisemitism the authors describe is an essential and diabolic continuity with that most 'ancient and barbaric of European myths' (James Baldwin). Thus we have heard it all before. The Jews are 'canny, crafty, usurious, power-mad, conspiratorial, unassimilable, pushy, clannish, aggressive, weak, greedy' (p. 101). They are vengeful. Their god is the almighty dollar. Secretly, they control finance, industry, the media, entertainment. They are experts in dual loyalty. They dictate foreign policy. In Israel, Jews specialize in torture, genocide, racism, and imperialism. 'Jew-Zionism is the spearhead of the anti-Christ'.[9]

During the first two decades after Israel came into being, its urgent tasks—apart from absorbing hundreds and thousands of immigrants, some of whom were Holocaust survivors, but most were from Arab and Muslim countries—were neutralising the threat of destruction by the 'Arab foe' and realising the promise of Zionist ideology, in its Ben-Gurion iteration, which was to achieve sovereignty—negating the exile and eliminating the antisemitism associated with it. For the first two decades of the state, the Arab threat was not generally understood as antisemitism. Zionism rejected the '[t]raditional Jewish myth [which] regards antisemitism as an ever-present hatred regardless of Jewish conduct or political status. This tradition depends on the rewriting of biblical stories into foundational myths in descriptions of this hatred', write Asaf Turgeman and Gal Hadari in their article '"Arab antisemitism debate": the birth of new antisemitism in public and academic discourse in Israel'.[10] When Yehoshafat Harkabi, chief of Israeli military intelligence from 1955 until 1959 and afterwards a professor of International Relations and Middle East Studies at the Hebrew University of Jerusalem, challenged the Zionist narrative by concluding from his research that Arab attitudes towards Israel were suffused with antisemitic tropes and sentiment, he was roundly condemned and attacked. But his 1965 article set off a debate about traditional Jewish myths relating to antisemitism and whether the Zionist narrative still held its ground. In the debates on this during the 1960s and 1970s, the term 'new antisemitism' came to be applied by some to what was a merging of the Jewish mythical approach and the modern historical experience of Arab attitudes to the Jewish state. The leading figure articulating this idea was the expert on Zionist historiography and antisemitism Shmuel Ettinger. He wrote an introduction, titled 'Hatred of Israel as an historical continuum', for a collection of academic essays edited by Shmuel Almog, *Sinat Yisrael ledoroteiha* (*A History of Hatred of Israel*), published in 1980. Ettinger reached this stark conclusion:

> Today, more than ever, it is clear that anti-Zionism and antisemitism are one and the same. Or more accurately, anti-Zionism is the direct historical and psychological continuation of antisemitism. There is no evidence that the existence of a Jewish political centre, of Jewish political and social, directed and collective activity, will disrupt the continuum of stereotyping or the centrality of the Jews in people's consciousness.

Harkabi, who expressed considerable anger at the reception his 1965 article received, wrote an article for the collection entitled 'The new Arab antisemitism', in which he reflected recent debates during which Israelis had shown themselves to be more comfortable with his strictures about the subject. The debates, Turgeman and Hadari explain, reflected

> the tension between the historical and the mythical in Israeli discourse as well as the sea change in the Zionist view of antisemitism. Harkabi's essay points to antisemitism as a dominant motive in the Arab–Israeli conflict

thereby seeming to contradict the historical Zionist view of antisemitism as relevant only if there exists a helpless victim: the exilic Jew. The historical approach to antisemitism, based on classical Zionist beliefs and the political importance of sovereignty, was expressed in the extensive criticism to which Harkabi's articles were subjected when first published in *Ma'ariv*. In face of this criticism, Harkabi now presents a new approach to antisemitism which necessitates conducting an 'objective' examination 'without distortions rooted in ideology and faith'.[11]

A key factor in this change was the adoption of UNGA Resolution 3379 equating Zionism with racism in November 1975. The outburst of rage and indignation led to furious condemnations, an explosion of writing, replete with satire and loaded with nationalist slogans, reaching far beyond the event under discussion. It was described as 'new antisemitism', or 'UN antisemitism', which 'operated within the mythic cycle linking Israel with Jewish fate throughout the generations, thus restoring significance to Zionism'.[12]

The following extracts from Turgeman and Hadari's paper give the flavour of Israeli reaction: 'Calling for the abolition of Zionism is equivalent to a call to destroy the Jews'. 'Those who defined themselves as anti-Zionist' had the faces of Nazis 'thought to have disappeared beneath the ruins of the Third Reich'. This is '"the war of annihilation" against the people of Israel'. The UN is the 'carrier of Hitler's flag in our generation'. The resolution is 'the greatest danger befalling us since the establishment of the state'. The UN 'ought to be called "United Nazis"'. The UN is a 'racist antisemitic organization' whose location 'on 42nd St. in New York—a street of pornography and drugs—is no coincidence'. 'With the UN becoming the centre of antisemitism, it is perhaps the right time to pin the following notice on the door of every Jew, wherever he may be: "I am a Jew, I am a Zionist" ... We must wear our Zionist identity as a badge of pride ...'. The countries voting, 'hands raised in favour of the destruction of the State of Israel', are provocatively ignoring the only meaning of racism, since 'racism is not just a scientific theory' but a theory 'which has been ultimately refined and implemented in one concrete instance—the Final Solution to the Jewish problem'.

Turgeman and Hadari note 'these commentaries' particularist point of view: they endorsed the claim that the single most concrete implementation of racism was the Holocaust. This singular connection between racism and the Jews as the exclusive object of its theory and practice loosened the columnists' critical reins'. Various African countries, most of which supported the resolution, were the principal targets of this, which included naked racism. They had revealed not only their 'hatred' but also 'ingratitude' towards the Jewish state, which had tried to 'drag them into the civilized, developed world'. Another contribution from the same writer was headed: 'Climbing down from the trees and denigrating Zionism':

> The resolution passed by the General Assembly of the United Nations has put an end to the historical argument fiercely conducted between various sectors of the Jewish people. This resolution has undermined and utterly destroyed any wall or barrier dividing the Jew from the Zionist. Now a new—although actually ancient and rooted in Jewish sources—*halakha* [religious dictate] has been determined: that Judaism and Zionism are one, and that the Jew is in any case a Zionist.

Harkabi believed that the Arab antisemitism, of which 3379 was in part a product, 'was different from the antisemitism of the past, because of its main object, hatred of Israel, with Jew-hatred coming second, if it exists at all'.[13]

From my description in Chapters 1 and 2 of the present bitter, intra-Jewish arguments over the issues Harkabi was so certain about in 1980, it is obvious that his characterisation of the generation of a new Jewish unity, though perhaps momentarily apparent, has proved to be highly inaccurate. It could be argued that 3379 marked the beginning of the end of any Zionist consensus among world Jewry, such as it was. However, what is particularly striking about Harkabi's view was his prediction that antisemitic hatred of Israel could replace classic Jew-hatred altogether and that 'Judaism and Zionism are one', both of which, we will see, have become central to 'new antisemitism' thinking 40 years later.

Although the Ben-Gurion Zionist position on antisemitism survived 3379, a change did occur in academic and public perceptions of antisemitism. It was not so much the perceived antisemitism embedded in 3379 that engendered this, but rather a realisation that Harkabi's revelations about Arab antisemitism were valid and could no longer be denied, and that the enemies of the state were using antisemitism as a weapon to galvanise their populations in support of their manifestly unsuccessful efforts to prevail over the Jewish state. However, any temptation to use this in support of an eternalist, or cyclical eternalist view of antisemitism would be mistaken. As Turgeman and Hadari argue:

> we see a historical crisis leading to the adoption of an updated, mythistorical, Zionist perspective in which myth is intertwined with history in the way Zionism views antisemitism. *Thus, myth and history could no longer be thought of as mutually exclusive, or myth as extraneous to Zionist thought.* Instead, there was a pendular movement between the two, in keeping with current events.[14]

This 'pendular movement', which relies on being comfortable switching between fundamentally incompatible ways of thinking, is displayed in the quite

51

extraordinarily particularistic response to the 'Zionism is racism' resolution. It came at a time when Israel was quietly patting itself on the back for the under-the-radar relations it was developing with sub-Saharan Black African states, based to a great degree on the supply of agricultural aid and expertise. Although these relations cannot be seen exactly through the lens of developing Black–Jewish relations on the American Jewish model, there was an element of promoting racial equality about it and supporting decolonisation and Black African independence movements. In addition, 3379 did not single out Zionism alone for condemnation. It rested on the condemnation of other forms of racist nationalism, colonialism, imperialism; it references apartheid, and so on. And yet it seems that the tenor of the entire reaction took for granted that, on the one hand, it was inconceivable that Jews, especially Zionist Jews, could be racist; that having experienced the Holocaust, this further immunised Jews against behaving in this way towards others; that the very accusation was in effect calling for a new genocide against the Jews. As if antisemitism were the very quintessence of racism.[15] And Jewish leaders, Jewish Israeli politicians, Zionist intellectuals, writers, columnists saw 3379 as antisemitic, an affront to Judaism and demanded that people make it plain that being Zionist and Jewish were inseparable: 'If you attack me as a Zionist, you are attacking me as a Jew.' But as Brian Klug points out, 'the text reflects territorial, economic and political interests along with general principles of justice and human rights; not antisemitic prejudice'.[16] In the red mist that had descended on them, Israeli commentators could not countenance this fact, and deemed it to be perfectly acceptable to vilify Black African leaders who voted for 3379 using the worst racist language imaginable.

* * *

Outside of Israel, the major Jewish organisations in the US and Europe mobilised to campaign against the resolution and to have it revoked. Predictably, Jewish anti-UN sentiment increased. Most Jewish groups dismissed the idea that this was simply an anti-Israel argument, one based on the view that Israel was a 'colonial settler state illegally occupying Palestinian land', and therefore just a matter of the Palestinian case being stronger than the Israeli one. Accompanying arguments that no collective Jewish existence in *any* part of former mandatory Palestine could be recognised 'proved' that the aim of 3379 was antisemitic since there was nowhere else where Jews could enjoy collective emancipation as a people. In short, this anti-Zionism was regarded as devoid of any legitimacy. Behind every plausible anti-Zionist argument was an attempt to undermine the basis of Israel's existence even if not everyone making such arguments had this motivation.[17]

Where anti-Zionists and Zionists agreed was in seeing the liberal intelligent-sia in the West as pivotal both in providing legitimacy for the Zionist argument and in undermining it by supporting the Palestinian cause. For British Zionist Jews who had hitherto taken such liberal support more or less for granted, it was bewildering to see the liberal intelligentsia, from new left university students to prominent, seasoned intellectuals, increasingly looking at what they thought was a progressive socialist state with a moral claim on the conscience of the enlightened world to accept Jewish nationalism as legitimate, now revealed as the settler-colonial state ideologically driven to treat the indigenous Palestini-ans in Israel as second class citizens and those in the occupied territories as not entitled to any rights at all.

To explore how discussion of the relationship between antisemitism and anti-Zionism developed from this time and then how this was subsumed into or reframed as arguments for and against the notion of the 'new antisemitism', I take as my starting point the example of how the matter was broached in the UK in a political-academic context that was both locally specific and general, given the international status of the body involved.

*   *   *

In 1980, the London-based Institute of Jewish Affairs (IJA)[18] (where I was working at the time as a research officer), which was the research arm of the World Jewish Congress (WJC),[19] a body then headquartered in Geneva that represented the political interests of organised Jewish communities worldwide, began examining the issue.

Established in New York in 1942 and headed by two prominent international lawyers, Nehemiah and Jacob Robinson, the IJA's main tasks were documenting the effect of the Nazi onslaught against the Jews and developing the legal prin-ciples for obtaining post-war reparations from Germany for its crimes. Facing closure by the WJC in the mid-1960s, it was reprieved and moved to London in 1967 where an expert in international law, Dr Stephen Roth, a Hungarian Jew who came to London in 1947 after surviving incarceration by the Gestapo in Budapest in 1944, was appointed director. He already held the post of head of the WJC's European branch.

While Roth was a major figure in the Zionist movement in the UK, the IJA itself was not formally a Zionist organisation. Nonetheless, most of its 20-odd staff were, if not explicitly Zionist, at the very least strong supporters of Israel. (One such, the journalist Josef Fraenkel, a Revisionist Zionist, had written a biography of Theodor Herzl.) Nevertheless, a few were distinctly sceptical about Israel's policies and Zionist claims.

Roth developed a programme of research, publications and public activities dealing with a wide range of Jewish issues, including antisemitism, studied in

53

the context of racism in general, Israel's international position and changing perceptions of Zionism and the broader question of the defence and promotion of human rights. The high level of its work, and the absence of any other Jewish body like it in the UK, gave Roth a platform from which he successfully developed a network of prominent Jewish and non-Jewish academics, political figures, businessmen and financiers in the UK, continental Europe, Israel and the US. Lord Goodman (Harold Wilson's lawyer) was the IJA's president. Lord Lever, the Labour Peer and former government minister, was Chairman of its Research Board; Sir Keith Joseph, one of Margaret Thatcher's gurus, was a member. Before he was appointed Chairman of the Board of Governors of the BBC in 1981, Stuart Young was Chairman of the IJA's Policy Planning Group.

The IJA was not well known even within the organised UK Jewish community, and it would not be correct to consider it to have been influential in any concrete political or communal policy sense. Roth did have such ambitions for the institute, but trod a very cautious path since there were tensions between the IJA, which was funded almost entirely by the WJC and not answerable to any other body, and the Board of Deputies of British Jews, which was the British affiliate of the WJC. Nonetheless, its ability to tap into the thinking of leading Jewish academics, politicians, journalists, businessmen and cultural figures—also across Western Europe by dint of Roth's role as head of WJC's European branch—more than suggests that its reflection of current Jewish concerns is a good guide to how the anti-Zionism/antisemitism issue emerged.

So, when Roth in 1980 decided to initiate a series of discussions under the rubric of 'The Erosion of Liberal Support for the Jewish Position' he was clearly responding to increasing concern expressed among the institute's key academic and intellectual advisers about the changing status of Israel and Zionism among Britain's thinking classes. The phrase 'Jewish position' was more than just a reference to the specific issues of Israel and Zionism; it was an expression of a sense that support for the Jewish state among Jews had become integral to Jewishness. Roth saw it as the one political issue that practically all Jews agreed upon, and that there was no longer any ideological issue of any significance dividing Jews.

In a background paper I wrote for the discussion on 11 June 1980,[20] one year after I joined the IJA, I argued that '[The general Jewish perception was that] support for Israel was not only automatic in liberal circles and among social democrats, but Israel was also seen as an example of the strength of liberal pluralistic and social ideas'. But many felt that an attitude had developed that claimed that

Israel and Jews throughout the world cannot continuously rely on European feelings of guilt regarding the Holocaust to ensure support of positions which are politically and morally unacceptable to the rest of the world ... Rather, there is now a clear tendency for liberal opinion to swing towards groups who openly oppose Israel, Zionism, the notion of Jewish nation and statehood, on the grounds that such groups also have legitimate rights which must be satisfied.

If this were so, I suggested, Jews should look for an explanation both in what Israel and Jews are doing and in developments in the wider world. Jews themselves had been moving away from the liberal position and had become more conservative, and that the liberal position in general—that is, the liberalism which aligned itself with the idea that a benign state could be instrumental in solving the problems of justice, inequality and racism—had increasingly come under attack.

'The formulation [of the subject for discussion] actually reflects Jewish insecurities and uncertainties', and the way forward, I argued, was 'to confront ourselves ... to move away, as far away as possible, from any notion of a monolithic "Jewish position"'.

There is no surviving record of the discussion or who participated in it, but later that year the IJA participated in an initiative taken by the World Zionist Organisation (WZO) to establish high-level seminars in diaspora Jewish communities to re-evaluate and regenerate Zionist ideology. This was undoubtedly a reflection of the way that the international Zionist movement was responding to what Roth's IJA had termed 'erosion of liberal support for the Jewish position', meaning weakening support for and increasing criticism of Israel.

The WZO initiative arose out of a series called the Continuing Seminar on World Jewry, held in Israel under the auspices of the then president of the state, Ephraim Katzir. The proceedings of these seminars were published in 1980, in a volume titled *Zionism in Transition*, edited by Professor Moshe Davis, through the Institute of Contemporary Jewry (which he founded) at the Hebrew University of Jerusalem.[21] Political success for the hard right, with Ronald Reagan and Margaret Thatcher coming to power in 1980 and 1979, and the establishment of right-wing Likud hegemony in Israel at the same time, must have reinforced moves to lay the blame for mounting anti-Israel and anti-Zionist sentiment on the 'new left', already described by former foreign minister Eban in 1973 as 'identifying Israel with the establishment, with acquisition, with smug satisfaction'.[22]

In his foreword, Katzir described it as 'an invaluable source book on the growth and present state of Zionism in various countries' and acknowledged the primary role of the WZO in the enterprise by 'testifying to the validity of the categories proposed by the Chairman of the WZO, Arye Dulzin: distressed, tolerated, emancipated and (in Israel) auto-emancipated Jewish communities'.[23] The diversity of these communities was recognised, more as a challenge and a problem than a source of strength, and the essays all focused on how Zionism, seen as a living, multifaceted ideology, could, through a process of renewal and transformation, help these communities by, as Davis wrote, 'intensif[ying] the content of Jewish life everywhere'.[24]

Although there is very little reference to antisemitism or anti-Zionism in the close to 400-page book, it seems clear that the seminars were a response to the decline in support for Israel since the Six-Day War, the attack on Zionism from 3379, and the damage these developments were doing to Jewish identity in Jewish communities in the diaspora and Israel. The WZO would certainly have noted the reaction to 3379 in Israel and approved of the popular demand that 'We must wear our Zionist identity as a badge of pride'. The thinking was that only the renewal and transformation of Zionism could make this happen. There was nothing fundamentally wrong with the Zionist idea.

In Latin America, where Natan Lerner, an international law expert at Tel Aviv University, said 'antisemitism must be examined against the general picture of weakening democracy, suppression of individual rights and growth of political violence', he added that it 'has been a major factor in bringing many Jews to Zionism'.[25] Writing about the UK, Schneier Levenberg, London representative of the Jewish Agency, saw the universities and the new left political battles being fought there, as the only significant locus of anti-Zionism, but also as places where 'a growing number of academics choose Zionist themes as topics of research'. 'As in the case of antisemitism', Levenberg wrote, 'which has always made assimilated Jews conscious of their identity, so the anti-Zionist campaign today has its positive results: it leads some alienated Jews to an identification with Zionism'.[26]

One seminar in the WZO series focused specifically on the impact on Jewish communities and Israel of 3379. Avraham Schenker, head of the Jewish Agency's Executive Organization and Information Department, argued that diaspora Jewish involvement with Israel hid a growing sense of isolation and unease of Jewish communities regarding their 'vulnerability' within their home societies. Resolution 3379 'highlighted both the centrality of Israel and that sense of isolation of Jews and Jewish communities': 'anti-Zionism and antisemitism were increasingly identified in Jewish minds as having the same roots' and therefore 'reflect[ed] an inseparable link' between Israel and the diaspora.[27] However, Schenker showed no concern that the UN anti-Zionism resolution was a manifestation of antisemitism. Rather its significance lay in shifting the Arab–Israeli conflict 'from the political to the ideological arena. By equating Zionism with racism the issue was shifted from the search for a political solution (whether imposed by force or through negotiation) to questioning the very basis of Israel's existence'. In response, Jews throughout the world declared themselves to be Zionists, expressing 'Jewish support for the survival of Israel. It was a great demonstration', Schenker wrote, 'of the central position of the Zionist idea in modern Jewish history'. What this demonstrated, Schenker asserted, was that 'the State of Israel was in danger and had to be protected and strengthened. It was not the Jewish continuity in the diaspora, but the State of Israel which was put in question'.[28]

The only writer in *Zionism in Transition* to put antisemitism at the heart of the challenge to reformulate Zionism was Professor Yehuda Bauer, then head of the Institute of Contemporary Jewry. In stark contrast to Schenker, Bauer saw a bleak future for diaspora Jewish communities which faced 'demographic decline' and 'decimation, if not extinction' through assimilation. Without a 'Jewish people' outside of Israel, what future could there be for Zionism?

The second major challenge to Zionism was

the re-emergence of antisemitism. The Jew-hatred of the late 1970s is directed against Israel, the legitimate expression of the Jewish right to self-determination. One may be critical of Israel without necessarily being antisemitic. However, when one denies the right of Israel to be where it is, then one is denying the right of Jews to form a society of their own, and the right of that society to create a polity to its liking. It represents a denial of the Jews right to national existence, just as in the past their right to a separate religion was denied.[29]

Bauer admitted that Zionism had failed in one of its key objectives: eliminating antisemitism. However, he argued that 'While Zionism may ... have failed to fulfil its messianic promise as an end to antisemitism which would coincide with the establishment of a Jewish state, it did furnish the only possible tools with which to fight the enemies of the Jewish people'.[30] By this, Bauer meant 'self-defence', becoming a political force, something Zionism achieved in its struggle to create the Israeli state, and which American Jewry achieved 'dating from Abba Hillel Silver's leadership of American Zionism in 1943–44'.

There is little evidence that Bauer's view that modern Jew-hatred was directed at the state of Israel, found an echo in the contributions of other participants. But Annie Kriegel, a prominent French Jewish academic historian, made a point of objecting to the idea:

I would like to express here my negative attitude to a formula which has been frequently used. I object to the formula, 'Israel, the Jew of nations', first of all because it implicitly denies the Zionist achievement. In the light of this formula, Zionism has attained nothing else but to transfer Jewish oppression from the individual to the group level. That is not true.[31]

The political events that followed publication of the Davis volume prompted even more intense questions about the future of Zionism and the link between criticism of Zionism and the actions of the state of Israel and expressions of antisemitism. In 1982 Israel invaded Lebanon, ostensibly to remove the PLO, which was using that country as the base for continuing its struggle against the Jewish state, but in reality it was a move inspired by Ariel Sharon's grand plan to remodel the Middle East to serve Israel's future security interests.[32] International condemnation was ignored as the IDF moved rapidly to reach the outskirts of Beirut and, with Israel's Christian Falangist allies, consolidated its control of most of the south of the country. The entire enterprise had already turned poisonous when Sharon allowed his Falangist allies to enter the two Palestinian refugee camps of Sabra and Chatilla and massacre between 1,390 and 3,500 men, women and children. Not only was there widespread international outrage at what Israel had done, or at the very least allowed to happen, but opposition in Israel itself took public form in a huge demonstration in Tel Aviv, which gave birth to the Peace Now movement.

Criticism of Israel reached a crescendo. The newspapers, radio and television were awash with it, sparking a hurt and defensive reaction on Israel's part and pro-Israel Jewish communities and organisations around the world. Jewish commentators and non-Jewish commentators supporting Israel saw more than just criticism in what was being published and broadcast. Many said there was antisemitic animus in much of the coverage, and a furious Jewish backlash against the media emerged.[33]

In the light of these developments, Roth's plans to take up the WZO challenge to diaspora Jewish communities that they re-evaluate and revivify Zionism took a rather different course. The IJA was involved in organising some such seminars, but independent of that initiative, he decided to set up a small working party to plan a study of anti-Zionism, but with the principal aim of exploring the connection between anti-Zionism and antisemitism. The Chairman of the group was Professor Sammy Finer, the Gladstone Professor of Government and Public Administration at Oxford University. There were three others: Stephen Roth himself, Professor Julius Gould, a sociologist with Hayekian views and a founder of the Social Affairs Unit, and Lord Max Beloff, the prolific historian and former principal of the private University College of Buckingham, another prominent right-wing public intellectual. I was assigned to service the group and to prepare a paper outlining what such a study might look like. The group met twice in the first half of 1983.

All four were supporters of Zionism, but all were also deeply critical of the form of Zionism as represented and 'practised' by Menahem Begin. For any proposed study to meet their approval, it would have to find a way of bridging these two positions: accepting that there was a Zionism responsible for certain unacceptable acts and positions, and another Zionism that, for example, conformed to a universalist, 'semi'-definition Professor Shlomo Avineri used in his book, *The Making of Modern Zionism: The Intellectual Origins of the Jewish State*:[34] 'the supremacy of the public, communitarian, and social aspects at the expense of personal ease, bourgeois comfort, and good life of the individual'.[35] This universalist idea allowed for adaptation and change in Zionism, whereas Begin's Zionism could be labelled as particularist and clearly outside of this definition. This, at least, was Avineri's analysis. Even though Avineri, Professor of Political Science at the Hebrew University Jerusalem and former Director General of the Ministry of Foreign Affairs (1975–1977) during the Labour government headed by Yitzhak Rabin, was then one of Israel's most respected academics, the group did not want to be seen as endorsing any study that appeared to question the fundamentals of Zionism, which they understood Avineri was in some sense doing. And equally important, they did not want an exploration of the relationship between anti-Zionism and antisemitism in a high-level study to be making a distinction between the two that could be exploited by antisemites. The 'distorted' version of Zionism had nothing to do with the essence of Zionism and could therefore be put to one side. 'Anti-Zionism' could be safely studied as a phenomenon that fundamentally or deliberately misunderstood Zionism. I was asked to write a paper that would present a way of resolving the conflicting priorities, and I used this 'good' Zionism/'bad' Zionism distinction to achieve this.[36]

Perhaps understandably, given the tortuous reasoning I deployed, when the group discussed this proposal at its second meeting in May, they could not agree to endorse this basis for what was ultimately intended to be a book. No more meetings of the group took place. It may also be the case that being mostly right-wing, members of the group were not inclined to back a proposal based on the thinking of a left-wing figure like Avineri. (I confess that my own critique of Zionism had by then reached a point where I was not convinced of the validity of Avineri's distinction between a universalist and a particularist Zionism. Both were integral to Zionist ideology; versions of a nationalist project, the aims of which were the same.)

The group's discussion and its subsequent abandonment is perhaps only a minor footnote in the path I am charting, showing how the 'anti-Zionism is antisemitism' formulation gained increasing acceptance. And yet it is instructive because it shows how some significant Jewish academic figures, who clearly understood that Israel was coming under attack for actions taken in the name of the fulfilment of Zionism, were so sensitive about giving ammunition to antisemitic enemies that their natural disgust with what the Israeli government was doing could not be openly exposed.

The book proposal was shelved, and instead Roth and some academic colleagues in the USA and Israel decided to hold a conference on anti-Zionism and antisemitism, which took place in London in 1984. Out of that conference eventually emerged the book of essays, *Anti-Zionism and Antisemitism in the Contemporary World*, edited by one of the participants, Robert S. Wistrich, who, at the time of publication in 1990, was Professor of Modern European and Jewish History at the Hebrew University.[37] It contained papers from the event, together with other specially written or adapted material. (Since the volume only appeared six years after the conference took place, most of the conference papers published were updated to take into account interim developments. Other essays in the book were either written especially for it or were updated versions of pieces first published in various journals. I discuss its contents after focusing on some work published between 1983 and 1990.)

Meanwhile, we see a radical change in focus on the nature and extent of contemporary antisemitism. Writing about the state of antisemitism for *Survey of Jewish Affairs 1983*,[38] a yearbook sponsored by the WJC and edited in London, Bauer responded to the question of whether antisemitism was a 'real threat': 'Are we faced with a wave of antisemitism in the contemporary world? Are those who are saying such a wave exists guilty of exaggeration? Is anti-Zionism identical to antisemitism? Are we or are we not bringing together under the general term of antisemitism quite disparate phenomena?' Bauer's first sentence may come as a surprise to many, given that we naturally associate the notion of an alleged 'wave of antisemitism' with our own times, more than 20 years into the third millennium. No such phrase cropped up in the *Zionism in Transition* volume. But Bauer was referring to concerns widely expressed, if not openly acknowledged by all Jewish communal organisations. In *Turbulent Times: The British Jewish Community Today*, Keith Kahn-Harris and Ben Gidley record that in the late 1970s and early 1980s there were arguments between establishment leaders and anti-racist groups about how to respond 'to the rise in antisemitic violence from the late 1970s, a rise recorded by *Searchlight* but not publicised by the communal leadership'.[39] Note that this was not an argument about the *nature* of that antisemitism. The default position of communal leaders at that time was to play down the threat of antisemitism and work with the police and government behind the scenes to combat it.

Bauer gave no definitive answer to the question posed, but the thrust of his essay was to insist that current dangers worldwide needed to be taken very seriously. 'Many Jews will simply refuse to look where it is unpleasant to look', he wrote, and find all kinds of reasons to play down the significance of what is happening.[40] He was in no doubt, however, of the significance of the attacks on Israel and Zionism as expressions of antisemitism, especially emanating from the forum of the UN. 'Phraseologies and code-words develop into a liturgy that is used at international gatherings, exorcising the Zionist—i.e. the Jewish—devil. The Zionist is the cause of all the misfortunes'—an adaptation of the late nineteenth-century antisemitic German historian Heinrich von Treitschke's infamous statement from 1880: 'Die Juden sind unser Unglück'.[41]

> The Jew, through his collective political existence in Israel, again becomes a symbol. The position of the pariah Jewish state is beginning to approximate the pariah status of the individual Jew in pre-modern society. Put differently, the status of the Jew has changed form, not in basic content. Instead of being attacked as an individual, he is attacked as a community; the motives, and even much of the detailed irrational arguments, are similar.

By contrast, a parallel essay by the American academic and West Coast Jewish community leader Earl Raab in the same volume, confronting the same overall question, surveyed the world scene and warned that 'It is always a strategic mistake to confuse the active and the actual with the potential. To homogenise the dangers of antisemitism is to render us less capable of dealing with them. But, on a true variety of grounds', Raab concluded, 'there is no reason for complacency anywhere'. As for anti-Zionism, he stated that 'it is important to note that the currency of political anti-Zionism is a grave dimension of active antisemitism in today's world'.[42] But in his conclusion he was more specific about where it was most dangerous: 'Modern political antisemitism from the "left", that is, political anti-Zionism, will continue to flourish in the Soviet Union, to the peril of Soviet Jewry, and in Third World radical circles. Those radical circles will have more marginal influence in Western Europe than in the United States'.[43]

Concerns about rising antisemitism were taken up at an 18-month-long series of meetings, again under the auspices of the Israeli presidency, then occupied by Chaim Herzog. Now renamed the Jerusalem Study Circle on World Jewry and chaired by Bauer, whose idea it was to take up the issue, the meetings were held at the president's residence during 1984–1985. The discussions, under the heading 'Present-Day Antisemitism', culminated in an international conference in December 1985, attended by a large group of 'scholars, thinkers and public figures'. In the foreword to the volume of proceedings published in 1988, Herzog wrote: 'Antisemitism today is very far from being an abstract issue. Its recrudescence can be directly linked to Arab terrorism and is expressed in the increasing number of attacks on Jews and Jewish property throughout the world'.[44]

In his preface, Bauer summed up the question that the conference sought to address: '[Are we] facing a new wave of antisemitism and if so, whether this wave has novel characteristics that cannot be dealt with in the same way as were the old forms'. Participants were to focus on what might lead to pragmatic action, but premised on the idea that effective measures must be based on research, analysis and understanding. 'It is essential, I believe, to ascertain whether, in fact, there is a new type of antisemitism or whether it is the old disease in a new guise'.[45] He continued:

Most of the experts with whom we met and discussed this problem during the last year and a half believed that we were witnessing a different type of antisemitism, in which the novel element is the existence of the State of Israel, which is often perceived, particularly by antisemites, as the 'Collective Jew' and a convenient target for antisemitic attack.

In his summary Bauer concluded:

The topic most discussed at this seminar has been the relation between anti-Zionism and antisemitism. If we wish to enable policy and decision makers to translate their thoughts into action we must clearly define the terms. It seems to me that a general consensus was reached regarding this definition: when anti-Zionism takes the form of denying Jews the right to have their own national-political entity, then we would define this as anti-semitism. However, when anti-Zionism means opposition to policies of the State of Israel or an ideological disagreement about Zionism—the dream and the reality—this would not necessarily be antisemitic.[46]

Whether or not Bauer's formulation constituted 'clarity' is, at the very least, an open question. He, and presumably most of the other participants, do not seem to have allowed for the fact that 'an ideological disagreement about Zionism' could cover a critique of what 'their own national-political entity' precisely meant and entailed. But it is not my aim here to take issue with such arguments, but rather simply to reveal the way thinking about antisemitism and its rela-tionship to anti-Zionism emerged and developed, within 'mainstream' Jewish leadership organisations, the world Zionist movement and Israeli government circles.

Many of the participants echoed Bauer's views. Irwin Cotler, Professor of Human Rights at McGill University, Montreal, and later to become Canada's Justice Minister, wrote: 'The UN has stigmatized Israel as the poisoner of wells, as the Jew among the nations. The UN formula for the delegitimisation of Israel is the equation of Zionism with racism and sometimes, in its more demonological form—Zionism as nazism—the ultimate metaphor of evil in our time'.[47] Robert Wistrich wrote: 'It is precisely the equation of Zionism with Nazism which is in my opinion the most characteristic mode of the new antisemitic anti-Zionism in the early 1980s, one which inverts all our assumptions and therefore deserves special attention and consideration'.[48] 'Anti-Zionism continues the discriminatory theory and practice of classical antisemitism, transferring it to an international plane'.[49] In Shlomo Avineri's view: 'if anti-Zionism means the delegitimization of the Jewish National Movement—the denial of the Jewish People's right to political self-determination—then there is a persuasive analogy between anti-Zionism and traditional antisemitism and as such it is totally unacceptable'.[50] David Sidorsky, Professor of Philosophy at Columbia University New York, put it another way:

> [The] focus of Jewish energies on the security and development of the State of Israel made Israel the symbolic center of Jewish moral honor. There may be some recognition of that fact in the focus on Israel, as noted in the 'Zionism as Racism' resolution, as the symbolic target of contemporary antisemitism. It has been often noted, and perhaps most brilliantly described by Jacob Talmon, that several of the salient features of the historical antisemitic charge against the Jewish people have been transferred to Israel.[51]

Clearly, by the mid-1980s, much opinion among Jewish academics—historians, political scientists, philosophers, theologians and so on—as well as politicians, legal experts, Zionist officials and communal leaders, was moving firmly in the direction of equating anti-Zionism with antisemitism. This was often couched in terms of 'new forms of antisemitism', though the term 'the new antisemitism' was, as yet, rarely being used in any systematic manner. There were still significant voices urging caution in giving too much weight to the salience, rigidity or permanence of this relationship. In the *Present Day Antisemitism* volume, Herbert Strauss, founding director of the Zentrum für Antisemitismusforschung in Berlin, warned against mistaking the 'actual significance of antisemitism in its traditional and hitherto known antisemitic forms and the attention being paid to it by Jewish organization personnel in most countries of the West'.[52] Bernard Lewis, the controversial Princeton University Oriental Studies Professor who was accused of misrepresenting Islam, but nevertheless had a level-headed understanding of the extent and significance of antisemitism in the Arab and Muslim worlds, had no sympathy with equating anti-Zionism and antisemitism. 'The term antisemitism is often used to denote "normal" prejudice against Jews, and sometimes even to describe political opposition to Israel or ideological opposition to Zionism', he wrote, 'This practice, though perhaps inevitable, is misleading'.[53] He argued that

> It is easy to identify individual Arab rulers or writers whose hatred of the Jews is as deep and as consuming as that of any classical European or American antisemite. But for most it still seems true that despite its vehemence and its ubiquity, Arab or Muslim antisemitism is still something that comes from

above, from the leadership, rather than from below, from the society—a political and polemical weapon, to be discarded if and when it is no longer required.[54]

At approximately the same time, Lewis wrote an essay for the *New York Review of Books* entitled 'The new antisemitism' in which he dispatched two myths.[55] The first, 'that Arabs cannot be antisemites since they themselves are Semites' is meaningless. '[A]ntisemitism has never been concerned with anyone but Jews, and there is in any case no such thing as a Semite. Like the Aryan, he is a myth, and part of the same mythology'. Lewis continued:

> Among Israelis and pro-Israelis there is another common myth which equates enmity to Israel or to Zionism with antisemitism and depicts Arafat as a new and unsuccessful Hitler and the PLO as the present-day equivalent of the Nazi SS. This is a false equation. The Arab–Israeli conflict is, in its origins and its essence, a political one—a clash between peoples and states over real issues, not a matter of prejudice and persecution.

And possibly most interesting were the words of Haim Cohn, the former Justice of the Israeli Supreme Court, who, while acknowledging that anti-Zionism was a 'new ... form of expression ... of antisemitism',[56] was more concerned 'with our subjective moral deficiencies'.[57] 'How can we Jews', he asks,

> complain about the religious roots of antisemitism, of religious and cultural intolerance and restrictions, while we practice similar intolerance and restrictions in the Jewish State of Israel ... Are we really competent to criticize the actions or missions of Gentiles towards us, when we behave similarly towards them? ... For Jews in Israel there is only one way to combat antisemitism. That is not to imitate.[58]

But Cohn's was a lone voice.

4

'New Antisemitism': Competing Narratives and the Consequences of Politicisation

The collapse of communism and the end of the Cold War had very significant consequences for how antisemitism was perceived and who could be considered a reliable authority on the problem. On the one hand, Jewish populations in former communist states were suddenly free to practice their religion and organise cultural activities, and the new governments either restored, or opened anew, diplomatic relations with Israel. The dissemination of officially sanctioned anti-Zionist propaganda ceased. These changes contributed greatly to the improvement in Israel's international position and opened the door to what were then widely considered to be new opportunities for the pursuit of Middle East peace. A remarkable revival of Jewish life took place and a spirit of guarded but nevertheless palpable optimism prevailed. On the other hand, the new freedoms gave political parties with antisemitic tendencies the opportunity to organise and spread their views in the public space, thereby provoking considerable alarm among all Jewish defence organisations, especially in the US, and prompting a radical increase in the analysis and commentary they produced.

In Israel, a new agency had already been established in 1988, the Israeli Government Monitoring Forum on Antisemitism, with the aim of implementing a new policy putting Israel at the head of international Jewish efforts to combat antisemitism (a development covered in full in Chapter 5). By 1992, not only had international Jewish cooperation on monitoring antisemitism increased, so too had competition over assessing and determining the narrative about what was happening. And with competition came two kinds of increasing politicisation of the issue. First, a struggle among Jewish organisations as to who exerted the most influence over public understanding of the threat antisemitism posed. And second, an increasingly charged debate about the relationship between anti-Zionism and antisemitism, and whether, if they were synonymous, it necessitated being called 'new antisemitism'.

By the early 1990s we see further shifts, with increasing focus on discussion of the antisemitic nature of anti-Zionism and greater use of the phrase 'new antisemitism', which is used not only to characterise anti-Zionism, but equally to refer to what many perceived as a resurgence, or revival of political antisemitism in former communist countries, where any popular expressions of antisemitism were suppressed and only state-sponsored manifestations of anti-semitism, mostly in the guise of anti-Zionism, were allowed.

* * *

In his introduction to *Anti-Zionism and Antisemitism in the Contemporary World*, while Wistrich acknowledged that 'The relationship between anti-Zion-ism and antisemitism ... is in reality notoriously difficult to define in objective terms',[1] he believed '[a] future historian might be forced to conclude that since the Six-Day War, anti-Zionism has provided the ideological framework in which a new antisemitism could be incubated'.[2] Emmanuel Sivan, Professor of Middle East history at the Hebrew University, noted that in Egypt, in response to the stability of the Egyptian–Israeli peace treaty and the Israeli invasion of Lebanon in 1982, 'Anti-Zionism came to take pride of place, presented as the modern-day incarnation of the authentically Islamic hostility to the Jews' and that the 'combined impact of the Israeli-Arab conflict and the Iranian revolution propelled the anti-Zionist theme into greater prominence among the funda-mentalists in the early 1980s'.[3] In essays by Barry Rubin, Fellow at Johns Hopkins School of Advanced International Studies, on 'The non-Arab third world and antisemitism', and Natan Lerner on 'Anti-Zionism and antisemitism in Latin America', the anti-Zionism-antisemitism nexus was seen as less apparent and more contingent on the political character of emerging regimes in both con-tinents, given their status as regions in flux and facing uncertain futures. But writing about the UK, Julius Gould claimed

> the campaign against Zionism in recent years has been nothing other than a thinly-coded expression of the fight against Israel ... While Jews inside and outside Israel may have felt justified (even obliged) to dissent from declared policies of Israeli governments (or from motifs within these policies), they recognised attacks on Zionism as attacks on the right of Jews to enjoy a *collective* emancipation as a people. They regarded this as a form of collec-tive discrimination against the Jewish people that recalled past (or present) denials to *individual* Jews of equality of citizen-rights.[4]

Yehuda Bauer, who, in considering the relationship between anti-Zionism and antisemitism, concluded that there was a distinction without a difference, was not blind to the role 'Israeli behaviour' was playing in 'influenc[ing] antisemitic reaction'.[5] 'Antisemitic reaction', he wrote, was 'triggered rather than caused by' Israel's invasion of Lebanon and its 'behaviour on the West Bank'. It 'influenc[ed] antisemitic and anti-Zionist propaganda', solidifying 'anti-Zionist antisemitism'. But it seems he was less concerned about those affected by Israel's actions, than by what it did to Israel's 'self-image'.[6]

Jews and non-Jews contributed brief essays to a symposium, 'Antisemitism in the 1990s', published in the IJA journal *Patterns of Prejudice* in 1991.[7] Among a series of questions posed, two were key: in the light of commonplace talk of a revival or resurgence of antisemitism, is such talk justified? To what extent is antisemitism today taking the guise of anti-Zionism?

Most saw something of a revival or resurgence, but not all in the same areas. There was a degree of concentration on Arab and Muslim antisemitism, with some regarding it as very dangerous, but little reflection of the view that anti-Zionism and antisemitism were one and the same. Both were threatening for Jews and Israel, but a conceptual linkage was mostly avoided. The political scientist Daniel J. Elazar, president of the Jerusalem Center for Public Affairs asserted that 'The conflict between Israel and the Arab world offers the "safest" outlet for antisemitism among today's antisemites, both ideological and genteel'.[8] David Cesarani, Director of the Wiener Library, was more concerned about the impact of 'Israel and the Jewish-Arab conflict' in complicating relations with Muslims and Blacks, 'increas[ing] the numbers of those moved by a visceral hatred of Jews. Much of this antagonism could be diffused if pro-Israel activists refrained from conflating or confusing anti-Zionism with antisemitism'.[9] Helen Fein, a leading sociologist and genocide scholar, made a similar point:

> Although neither anti-Zionism nor criticism of Israel is necessarily antise-
> mitic, 'Zionists' is very often used as a code word for Jews. This depends on
> context and affect. Some Jewish organisations have interpreted all criticism of
> Israel as antisemitic. But branding all those who criticise Israel as antisemites
> blurs the issue; moreover, it could become a self-fulfilling prophecy.[10]

Isi Liebler, a prominent Australian Jewish community leader, trenchantly argued that 'Jews throughout the diaspora today have greater reason to fear for their future than at any time since the Second World War' and that 'In country after country, there has been a recrudescence of antisemitism on a scale not known since the Holocaust'.[11] He was particularly concerned about the growth in Holocaust denial, but wrote: 'Anti-Zionism is almost as dangerous, for it frequently gives legitimacy to antisemitic views that are couched in "political" rather than "racial" terms and are thus deemed to be more socially acceptable. This is the favoured mode adopted by antisemitic intellectuals, politicians and others on the left-wing of politics'.[12] While all the contributors recognised the existence of new challenges facing Jews—Black–Jewish relations in America, growing nationalism in Europe, far-right political parties like the Front National and the Austrian Freedom Party, the resurfacing of political antisemitism in former communist states, antisemitism emanating from Arab and Muslim sources—none were as pessimistic or alarmist as Liebler. Earl Raab, a University of California, Berkley academic extremism expert, averred that 'The world's most virulent and hard-core anti-Jewish prejudice flourishes [in the Middle East], amidst massive discontent of various kinds, and the antithesis of institutionalised constraint, either political or religious', yet

> the increased strength of political constraints in the significant sectors of the Western world suggest an important difference between the 1930s and the 1990s. There is even evidence to suggest that throughout the significant sectors of the Western world, the Jews have become less of a traditional target than they once were. That is always a reversible phenomenon, but it should remind the Jews that antisemitism is not a genetic condition.[13]

Robert Wistrich acknowledged that there had been an increase in antisemitism in Europe and to an extent in the United States, but thought it 'exaggerated' to call it a global phenomenon. His main concern was a reiteration of views we have already encountered from earlier writings:[14]

> The Arab-Israeli conflict and especially the Palestinian cause have in my opinion been a major factor in the past twenty years in fostering anti-Jewish sentiment, even among people who vehemently deny that they have any prejudice and claim to be unequivocally anti-racist or antifascist. Anti-Zionism—as I have argued many times—provided, since the late 1960s, a respectable intellectual framework for the expression of sentiments that were not 'respectable' in any other context. When talking about Israel, one can say things about Jews that would be unthinkable in other situations or would be instantly seen to be antisemitic.

It is interesting to note, however, that he believed 'Only the Palestinians did make a serious intellectual effort to distinguish between anti-Zionism and anti-semitism, though the meaningfulness of such distinctions for the Arab masses is much more doubtful'. Nevertheless, he remarked on what he believed was a significant change, presaging views that would become increasingly expressed:

> Though anti-Zionism in the late 1970s and the early 1980s seemed to me to be providing a kind of mask for antisemitism, more recently this disguise seems to have been less pertinent and unnecessary. When the radical right in Western Europe, Russia and America, vilified 'Zionists' or denounced the world Zionist conspiracy, it was always clear that they meant Jews. The distinction is usually drawn by the left, though the omnipotence, the diabolical qualities and the conspiratorial character attributed to Israel and Zionism often seem to mirror similar characteristics traditionally ascribed by anti-semites to Jews.[15]

Although the contributors were from many countries and disciplines, and one was the Chief Rabbi of the United Synagogue, Emmanuel Jakobovits, direct references to 'new antisemitism' were made by only three contributors: the first, cautiously, the other two, in sceptical terms. Herbert Strauss (see Chapter 3) saw dangers in 'social cultural and fiscal anxieties' in the West, but

> If the 'old' antisemitism has thus not been used in this complex social crisis—social tensions that had activated it in the past survive only among juvenile outsiders in marginal organizations—some observations point to the emergence of a potentially 'new' antisemitism. One [that] derives from Zionism, the Arab-Israeli conflict, and the hostility that was connected with it in Soviet policies since 1967 or 1948.[16]

Michael Marrus, then Professor of History at the University of Toronto, wrote:

> Diaspora Jews have become extraordinarily preoccupied with how the media present the confrontation between Israel and Palestinian nationalism, unable to understand the negative image of the Jewish state except as an expression of implacable hostility toward Jews. By the same token, disinclined to see the confrontation between Israel and her enemies as anything other than a struggle of right against wrong, many see any divergence from the position of the Israeli government or any critical judgement of Israeli policy as manifesting a 'new antisemitism'—essentially the old antisemitism, with an opportunistic focus on Israel.[17]

I was the other sceptic, writing:

> Those who see in opposition to Israel the source of a 'new' antisemitism—the notion that denial of Jewish collective rights is the modern equivalent of the classic antisemitic denial of individual rights to Jews—seem to be ignoring [the] decline in anti-Zionism [that has accompanied the collapse of communism], which takes place at a time when the policies of the Israeli government are not exactly popular internationally.[18]

There was a perceptible sharpening up of views among the prominent academics, intellectuals and Jewish communal and institutional officials during the early years of the 1990s. In 1994, the Hebrew University historian of Zionism, Professor Shmuel Almog, articulated an assessment of the relationship between anti-Zionism and antisemitism that presaged the far more specific formulation of the idea of Israel as the 'collective Jew', which would be developed by Irwin Cotler and others:

Moreover, the State of Israel—the result of Zionist efforts for more than a century as well as a haven for Jews escaping from antisemitism—seems to have drawn much of the fire that was once directed against individual Jews living in a non-Jewish society. It is now customary to attribute to Israel the role of the metaphorical collective Jew. An ironic twist of history if one remembers that the Jewish state was originally proposed as the definitive answer to the dangers of antisemitism.[19]

Yehuda Bauer saw in the treatment of Israel at the UN the continuation of antisemitism:

The Jews are a minority culture, except for Israel, hence their aggressions, while a very great danger to themselves and to their immediate surroundings, are no threat *to* the world at large. But antisemitism, the traditional expression of frustrations and aggressions, on a historical foundation, in the Western world, is such a danger. It now attacks Israel, as *a Jewish* state. The pariah position peculiar to the Jews in medieval Europe is still occupied by Israel in the United Nations, despite the resumption of diplomatic relations between Israel and most of the world's countries, under the Likud government, and an improvement of Israel's position under the new government, even as we speak.[20]

This reference to Israel's improved position is an important reminder of the context in which these views were being expressed. Continued concern about the post-1989 resurfacing of antisemitism in the former communist countries was accompanied by an intensified focus on the UN as a site of 'antisemitic anti-Zionism' and the growth of antisemitism coming from Islamic fundamentalist sources. However, the signing of the Oslo Accords in September 1993 and the Israeli–Palestinian talks that then took place in order to turn rapprochement into concrete agreements, undoubtedly resulted in a moderation of antisemitic propaganda from mainstream Arab sources. At the same time, a major source of anti-Zionist pressure and propaganda had largely dissipated as the vast majority of the states of the former Soviet bloc and sphere of influence rapidly transformed their relationships with Israel as part of the rejection of communist, anti-Western foreign policy.

Powerful evidence of the sense that a resurgence was underway came in the form of a conference sponsored and organised by the WJC titled 'My Brother's Keeper: World Conference on Antisemitism and Prejudice in a Changing World', held in Brussels from 6 to 8 July 1992. In the words of Elan Steinberg, WJC executive director, having successfully completed the campaign to free Soviet Jewry and unmask Austrian presidential candidate Kurt Waldheim as a serving

Nazi officer, the WJC was turning its attention to 'the eradication of antisemitism'. Several heads of state attended along with hundreds of representatives
from Jewish communities in more than 60 countries. An 'Appeal to Humanity'
authored by Elie Wiesel and signed by President Bush and three dozen other
heads of state was presented at the opening session by Edgar Bronfman, WJC
president. The highlight of the conference was a speech given by the Black
activist and politician Jesse Jackson in front of a capacity crowd of over 1,000.[21]
(Bronfman invited Jackson to speak as part of an attempt to improve his relations
with American Jews, which remained relatively fragile after he referred to Jews
as 'Hymies' and New York as 'Hymietown' in the 1980s—'Hymie' being a pejo-
rative word for 'Jew'. Black–Jewish relations, once seen as a successful alliance
working for civil rights during the Martin Luther King period, had deteriorated
over the previous decade or more, and it was also in the context of repairing that
relationship that Jackson came to Brussels.)

Among the many parallel sessions, one attracted special attention. This was
a panel discussing 'the role of the UN in shaping the human rights agenda and
fomenting antisemitism'. It was chaired by Professor Ruth Wisse, former Harvard
Jewish historian and Yiddish expert, and the speakers were Jean Kirkpatrick,
former US Ambassador to the UN, Morris B. Abram, then US Representative
to the European Office of the UN and US Permanent Representative to the UN
Commission on Human Rights in Geneva, and Professor Irwin Cotler from
McGill University, Montreal. Writing about the event, Abram's biographer said
it 'turned out to be the conference highlight'.[22]

A partial account of the session was given by Cotler in a chapter he contributed to a book on religious human rights and published in 1996.[23] He referred
to the conference as 'consider[ing] the explosive question of racial and religious
hatred which was stalking across Europe and other global stages'. And wrote
that the panel 'addressed the question of the development of a "new antisemitism", and the anchorage of that antisemitism in the United Nations itself'.

He then quotes from one of the 'participants'—actually, himself:

What Jewish NGOs are witnessing today—and which has been developing
incrementally, almost imperceptively [sic], for some 25 years now—is a new
antisemitism—grounded in classical antisemitism, but distinguishable from
it; anchored in the 'Zionism is Racism' Resolution but going beyond it; a
new antisemitism which almost requires a new vocabulary to define it—but
which can best be defined as the discrimination against, or denial of, national
particularity anywhere, whenever that national particularity happens to be
Jewish.

In a word, classical antisemitism is the discrimination against, or denial
of, the right of individual Jews to live as equal members of a free society;

the new antisemitism involves the discrimination against, or denial of, the right of the Jewish people to live as an equal member of the family of nations. What is indigenous to each form of antisemitism—and common to both—is discrimination. All that has happened is that it has moved from discrimination against Jews as individuals—a classical antisemitism for which there are indices of measurement—to discrimination against Jews as a people—the new antisemitism—for which one has yet to develop indices of measurement.[24]

The two principal 'indices or varieties of the new antisemitism' were, he claimed, *political antisemitism* in the form of 'the discrimination against or denial of the legitimacy, if not existence, of the state of Israel' and *ideological antisemitism*, 'the "demonising" of Israel, the attribution to Israel of all the evils of the world, the portrayal of Israel as the enemy of all that is good and the repository of all that is evil, not unlike the medieval indictment of the Jew as the "poisoner of Wells"'. To make Israel 'the metaphor for a human rights violator in our time exposes Israel as the "new anti-Christ", with all the "teaching of contempt" for this "Jew among the nations" that this new antisemitism implies'.[25]

The last of five other indices Cotler gives is what he curiously refers to as being 'the cutting edge of this antisemitism in the form of Holocaust Denial'— curious because by 1992 Holocaust denial was at least four decades old, hardly new—'which moves inexorably from denying the Holocaust, to accusing Jews of fabricating the "hoax" of the Holocaust, to indicting Jews for extorting false reparations from the innocent German people in order to build their "illegal" state of Israel on the backs of the real indigenous owners, the Palestinians'.[26]

We know from Cotler's contribution to the Israeli president's seminar in 1985 that he was already then fiercely critical of the UN as a primary initiator and purveyor of what he was referring to as 'Today's new antisemitism' or 'the new anti-Jewishness'.[27] Among differences in his 1992 remarks, apart from a more fully worked out rhetorical formulation of his thinking, was what followed practically from the panel discussion and was in fact already in the process of being set up and became a formal recommendation of the Brussels conference:

the establishment of a new NGO—to be called 'United Nations Watch'— whose mandate would be to 'monitor the United Nations and to measure that organization's performance by the yardstick of the UN Charter'. In particular, UN Watch would investigate the 'new antisemitism' ... as a case study of UN compliance with its own charter.[28]

UN Watch was duly set up in 1993 in Geneva by Morris Abram (now no longer a US ambassador) with the financial backing of the WJC. In 2001 it came under the control of the American Jewish Committee (AJC), of which Abram was once president. Although it officially became independent in 2013, UN Watch is chaired by Ambassador Alfred H. Moses, former US ambassador to Romania and Special Presidential Emissary for the Cyprus Conflict—and a former president of the AJC. Irwin Cotler has been associated with UN Watch since its inception and is a member of its international advisory board.

UN Watch was probably the first NGO established specifically to confront the 'new antisemitism' as conceptualised—or perhaps more accurately, *in the process of* being conceptualised—by Cotler.

While the now largely forgotten Brussels conference clearly reflects what was then a growing concern about the resurgence of antisemitism in both old and 'new' guises, it was by no means the only persuasive narrative commanding attention in the early 1990s. For example, a much-commented on essay in the *New York Review of Books* by a leading liberal figure in the American Jewish community, Rabbi Professor Arthur Hertzberg, a historian and expert on Zionism, was titled 'Is antisemitism dying out?'[29] Widely seen and remembered as a clear and unambiguous affirmative answer to the question, in reality the essay was a far more subtle and differentiated review of at least ten books and reports on current antisemitism and an engagement with other historians and public intellectuals. Herzberg compared antisemitism with the challenge then being mounted to 'the most ingrained of all stereotypes, that women are less intelligent than men', stating that 'Whatever may be the result of the feminist revolution, this stereotype will not persist in its inherited form'. He continued:

> Perhaps antisemitism is now at a comparable point in its long history. All the premises of the older forms of antisemitism have been undermined: it would be foolish to say it is dead, but it seems to be dying out and to have force only when it is redefined.
>
> In its history of twenty-five centuries, antisemitism has been redefined three times: by pagans, by Christians, and by modern ideologues on the right and left.[30]

Herzberg acknowledged heightened fears among Jewish leaders and populations in the United States, Europe and the former Soviet Union that antisemitism had increased but quoted opinion poll evidence from many countries that supported a more optimistic view. One poll in Poland, Hungary and Czechoslovakia found that there were fewer negative feelings towards Jews than towards other minority groups, including 'Gypsies, former Communist officials, international business representatives, Arabs, Asians, Blacks, etc.'. 'The people surveyed', Hertzberg wrote, 'were nearly unanimous in agreeing that the state of Israel has a right to exist, but over 75 per cent of the people in all three countries joined in agreeing that "Zionism is racism"'.[31] Antisemitic publications and articles in newspapers in Ukraine and Russia were on the increase, but the new governments were supporting the revival of Jewish communities and returning synagogues and other former Jewish communal properties to those communities.

Hertzberg argued that when societies turned towards xenophobia and the populist urge to discriminate against the 'other', Jews suffered too. But he insisted that 'the principal threat now is not to Jews as such but to people who are considered strangers'. Growing ambivalence about newcomers in New York and California, for example, were based on economic fears; 'this is the tinder for ethnic conflict', Hertzberg concluded.

His optimism was guarded:

> there is a mystery at the core of antisemitism ... It is clear that there is no specific cure for this endemic disease. We know only that it will flare up in troubled times. It is most likely to appear among those who resent their low and precarious place in society. Hate will lessen among the poor if they are helped to have better lives.

He tentatively raised the question of whether 'Jews have some responsibility for their own difficulties, as Hannah Arendt did thirty years ago in *Eichmann in Jerusalem* (or, for that matter, Theodor Herzl in *The Jewish State*)'.[32] Attributing excessive power to Jews is a classic antisemitic trope, but 'The Jewish establishment has been asserting for a generation that it wants political power beyond its numbers and it has been getting it. Why is it antisemitism', Hertzberg asks, 'if non-Jews are aware of this desire?'[33] Yet 'if anyone dares to suggest [such things], Jewish organizations and spokesmen tend to react with explosive anger. Such suggestions contradict the thesis that antisemitism is a disease spread by others'.[34]

Hertzberg concluded his essay again anchoring the future for Jews to the state of social and economic conditions:

> The ethnic and economic convulsions that are increasing in the world today dwarf the ancient issue of antisemitism. Hatred of Jews seems likely to diminish if ways can be found to quiet the ethnic angers that have become widespread with the end of the cold war, to relieve the condition of the resentful poor, and to help the less developed nations to support their own people. The Jews were long hated as outsiders. Today, for the most part, they are no longer weak or alien, but their destiny remains linked to the destiny of the displaced and of those who are seen as strangers.[35]

Hertzberg referred to the Brussels conference twice in his essay, but made absolutely no reference to 'new antisemitism' or to the claim that anti-Zionism was synonymous with antisemitism. There is barely a mention of antisemitism emanating from Arab or Muslim sources, or of Israel as a primary object of antisemitic sentiment. Since there was already much discussion, comment and writing on these matters, as already established above, it is highly unlikely that Hertzberg was unaware of such issues. He is therefore possibly open to criticism on this front. However, the absence of any consideration as to whether fears of a resurgence were linked to a 'new antisemitism', spread by the United Nations, for example, clearly indicates that it was perfectly possible to be a central player in the discussion of contemporary antisemitism without feeling it necessary to directly confront the views then being expressed by leading figures such as Yehuda Bauer, Robert Wistrich, Irwin Cotler, Shmuel Ettinger, Daniel Elazar and others, that Israel was now bearing the brunt of antisemitic vilification.

* * *

Although the vast majority of people participating in these debates and discussions were academics representing a variety of disciplines, there was quite obviously, and in no way hidden, a strong diaspora-Jewish and Israeli-Jewish organisational influence in the marshalling of the discussants and the framing of the formats in which the discussions took place. The influential seminars, held under the auspices and with the involvement of the Israeli president, with significant input from the WZO, quite naturally excluded any anti-Zionist voices. However, as we have seen, there were significant areas of disagreement among the participants. This was even more apparent in the contributions to the *Patterns of Prejudice* 1991 symposium, which drew on a wider range of opinion, not all Jewish, despite also at that time being the house journal of an arm of a major international Jewish organisation.

A parallel symposium of written contributions, far fewer in number, was published in an entirely independent periodical, the *Jewish Quarterly*, in spring 1991.[36] In the wake of a number of antisemitic incidents in 1990, the editors asked: 'How real is antisemitism today? Is it a latent ineradicable evil that continues to permeate British society? Are Jews in general justified in feeling that there is widespread discrimination against them?' Respondents included playwright Arnold Wesker, commissioner of the Commission for Racial Equality Aubrey Rose, novelist Rosemary Friedman, journalist Melanie Phillips, former chairman of British Steel Sir Monty Finniston, and historian Professor Geoffrey Alderman. While none of the writers dismissed concerns about current antisemitism, there was little evidence of any sense of great alarm about imminent dangers to British Jews. Only a couple of respondents featured Israel and anti-Zionism in any significant way in their remarks, with one in particular singling out what he regarded as the one 'additional element, previously totally missing' in expressions of antisemitism: 'virulent and well-funded and organized anti-Zionism ... [which calls] for the physical destruction of the Jewish state' and justifies 'physical attack and harassment' of 'Jewish and/or Israeli individuals, buildings and institutions'. In such an outlook 'the dividing line between legitimate comment and actual antisemitism disappears'.[37]

We have already seen that Wistrich, for example, was speaking of 'the new antisemitic anti-Zionism' at the end of the 1980s (see Chapter 3). In 1993 he was issuing this kind of stark warning:

> The virus of antisemitism is embedded, as it were, in the heart and very blood-stream of European society and culture, ready to be activated at the first major crisis—whether it be war, revolution, the fall of empire, economic depression, or the unleashing of ethnic conflict. With the end of the Communist era, many of these conditions are now in place—a not very encouraging prospect.[38]

Meanwhile, in early 1994, Cotler, pursuing the arguments he made at the 1992 Brussels conference, was speaking of 'classical antisemitism [which is] now finding its way into the popular culture and political discourse', 'the emergence of Holocaust denial as the cutting edge of the new antisemitism', 'a new antisemitism abroad in the land today, represented, in a word, in the on-going delegitimization of Israel as the Jewish people, reflected if you will, in the emergence of Israel as the Jew among the nations'.[39]

Daniel Pipes, then director of the Philadelphia-based Foreign Policy Research Institute, spoke on 'The new antisemitism' at the 1992 Brussels conference, though his remarks did not include any reference to the specific 'Israel as the "collective Jew" among the nations' discourse, or to the specific question of whether anti-Zionism was the same as antisemitism. However, he was, even then, singling out Islam and Muslims for their increasingly vitriolic antisemitism directed at Jews and Israel, and it was this that he was implying constituted the 'new antisemitism'. His remarks are more interesting for reinforcing the reality of the presence of two narratives:[40]

> There are some important positive and negative trends. On the positive side, some of the main sources of antisemitism are quiet. With the collapse of the Soviet Union, the vast propaganda machinery of hatred coming out of Moscow has been silenced. And more than that, there is no more pressure on the Muslim countries to adopt the Soviet line ...
>
> Desert Storm and the American pre-eminence of the last couple of years have also been important. Governments are cutting back on spreading antisemitism—and by the way, antisemitism very commonly includes anti-Americanism. The Kuwaitis and the Saudis in particular have refrained

from this propaganda. [The Madrid] Peace talks are currently underway with no fewer than eleven countries across the table from Israel. So at the state level, there are significant changes in a positive direction.

In the introduction to the collection of essays *Antisemitism and Jewish Security in America Today*, published in 1995, the editor Jerome Chanes, research fellow at the Center for Jewish Studies at the City University of New York, saw the term as fulfilling a rather different function: a category highlighting what we '*don't know about antisemitism*':[41]

> There are forms of antisemitism that are difficult to observe and measure, namely hidden and latent antisemitism. Additionally, traditional, cruder forms of antisemitism may not have been eliminated, but may have been revamped and repackaged for a new generation. This 'new' antisemitism, articulated in a different, perhaps less blatant manner, more subtle and nuanced, calls for study. The difficulty is that while new forms of antisemitism may be open and observable (as compared with the hidden and latent kinds), they are often encrypted.

Pipes returned to the subject in an article he wrote for the *Jewish Exponent* in 1997 titled 'The new antisemitism', but his subject was exclusively the issue of antisemitism among the Muslim population of the United States.[42]

> the main locus of anti-Jewish speech and deeds has moved from the Christian countries to the Muslim world ...
>
> [P]erhaps more ominously: even in the predominantly Christian countries of Europe and the Americas, Muslims today increasingly carry the banner of antisemitism and constitute a physical threat to Jews. That's not to say that antisemitism among Christians has evaporated, but that it has distinctly less punch than does the Muslim variety.

It is clear from these writers and others that there was no consensus about what was new in current antisemitism, but clearly a distinct desire to categorise it as such: for example, Holocaust denial, anti-Israel bias at the UN, militant new left sympathy for the oppressed Palestinians, the designation of Zionism as racism and the threat posed to Jews from Muslim populations in Western countries harbouring anti-Jewish hostility. And while the specific question of the relationship between anti-Zionism and antisemitism remained central to this disquiet, it was not sufficient in itself to encapsulate the range and variety of fears, threats and enemies Jews were said to be experiencing or confronting.

In the few years prior to the millennium, something of the flavour of those contradictory feelings characterised public comment. Writing in the *Observer* in February 1997, Michael Freedland, a freelance author and broadcaster who hosted a Jewish community radio programme for many years, referred to 'growing evidence of antisemitism'. In May 1998, Melanie Phillips wrote a piece in the same newspaper headed: 'Jews are society's pit canaries. Attacks on them warn of deeper prejudice. Be warned then, as the baiting has begun'. In August 1998 Helen Womack, Moscow correspondent for the *Independent*, wrote: 'Antisemitism is as strong in Russia today as it was in the rest of Europe before the Second World War'. In 1994, United Synagogue Chief Rabbi Jonathan Sacks, writing of 'Israel's continuing isolation', argued that it 'showed the sheer tenacity of antisemitism, now transmuted into anti-Zionism'.[43]

But there were voices rejecting these views. In a lecture to the Institute for Jewish Policy Research in London in 1998, Rabbi Professor Hertzberg, still faithful to the views he expressed in his 1993 *New York Review of Books* article, said: 'Despite the noises, antisemitism doesn't exist in any real sense'. In the same year, the Paris-based intellectual historian Diana Pinto wrote:

Never in Europe's millennial history have Jews on this continent lived in such individual and collective freedom and well-being as today ... The most important historical cornerstone of European antisemitism, Christianity, has not only turned its back on antisemitism, it has finally acknowledged the negative role played by the hierarchies of the Churches in the unfolding of the *Shoah*.[44]

In a *Washington Post* book review in 1996 Franklin Foer wrote:

For the first time in their three and a half centuries as a community in America—and perhaps for the first time since the dawn of the Jewish diaspora, two thousand years ago—the Jews had no greater enemy than themselves ... [T]he threats [of antisemitism] had not ended. Still, a detached, fair-minded observer of Jewish life might well have concluded that the Jewish people had achieved a historic reversal of fortune at the close of the twentieth century, in America and around the world.[45]

By the year 2000, whatever the term 'new antisemitism' actually referred to, a step change in its use became evident. In France, the sociologist Michel Wieviorka, while not a promoter of the 'new antisemitism' thesis, used the term in October 2000 after a wave of antisemitic incidents occurred.[46] The abstract of a critical 2012 article by Brian Klug, 'Interrogating "new antisemitism"', begins: 'Since the breakdown of the Middle East Peace Summit at Camp David in 2000 and the start of the second Palestinian Intifada there has been a voluminous literature that asserts that hostility to Israel and Zionism is a new form of antisemitism'.[47] The chapter 'New antisemitism, new insecurity' in *Turbulent Times* appears to locate the beginning of sustained debate on 'new antisemitism' in the wake of increased manifestations of antisemitism at the beginning of the 1990s, but practically all the books and documentary material it refers to are from the beginning of the 2000s.[48]

Was the increasingly prominent 'new antisemitism' discourse a result of the successful refutation of other understandings of contemporary antisemitism at this time? Could it be said that the argument over whether anti-Zionism and antisemitism were one and the same had been settled and the promoters of the proposition had won? Or did events—anti-Jewish manifestations, marked increased production and dissemination of the kind of anti-Jewish propaganda that was judged to be evidence of the 'new antisemitism'—prove that something unprecedented was occurring? Or were there other factors influencing the widely acknowledged turn?

That there was some kind of watershed moment is something on which both promoters of 'new antisemitism' theory and its critics tend to agree. But there had been no successful refutation of other understandings of antisemitism. While there was a strong element of absolute, unshakeable certainty in many accounts of 'new antisemitism', there was no diminution of work criticising the notion. The space devoted to those arguing that anti-Zionism was antisemitism most certainly increased, but there was no let-up in very forceful opposition to the idea. The matter was far from closed. And the same applies to claims that anti-Jewish hostility had reached unprecedented proportions. It remained perfectly possible to acknowledge that such manifestations had increased, but given that so much of that hostility was linked to actions of the Jewish state, there was ample opportunity to dispute the degree to which criticism levelled at vocal Jewish supporters of whatever Israel did was antisemitic.

While the urge to adjudicate between these narratives is strong, it does not help in understanding what was happening to antisemitism at this time. They obviously appear contradictory and reflect a sharpening of the differences emerging in the 1990s. On the other hand, the possibility that both narratives could reflect some aspects of reality should not be ruled out. To untangle this further, other crucial factors impacting on the understanding of antisemitism must be taken into account.

To consider them we next explore the role of major national and international Jewish and Zionist organisations in identifying and prioritising for attention the sources of antisemitism that posed the greatest danger to Jewish communities. Israeli governmental and state institutions were involved in this too, but in a fragmentary fashion given that the country was preoccupied with the crumbling Oslo process and then, towards the end of the decade, with intensified violent Palestinian protest, of which it was the suicide bombings that caused the greatest havoc.

This brings us face to face with intra-Jewish communal and Israel–diaspora political rivalries and struggles for power over who would set the antisemitism agenda, although it soon became clear that the direction of travel was increasingly towards making 'new antisemitism' the primary focus of attention for all players. But the journey to this end was not straightforward. The next chapter examines how this came about and what then emerged by way of institutional preparedness for the anticipated dangers ahead.

5
The Development of Institutions
Combatting Antisemitism 1970s–2000

Justified or not, in the first few years after the turn of the century, the alarmist atmosphere framing reports about antisemitism was palpable. The key events were the beginning of the al-Aqsa Intifada in September 2000, which was followed by a wave of attacks on Jewish property, especially in European countries with large Muslim and Arab minorities.[1] The following summer, Jewish organisations attending the NGO forum before the UN conference on racism in Durban, South Africa, were disturbed by what they saw as antisemitic attacks on Israel and the adoption of vicious anti-Israel resolutions. 'The NGO declaration at the Durban conference, written in highly politicized language, reflected a concerted effort to undermine Israel', NGO Monitor wrote at the time.[2] Durban was followed by 9/11, which gave rise to the circulation of various antisemitic stories on the internet, the most common of which claimed that Jews working in the World Trade Center were forewarned and stayed away. After 11 September, the Sharon government intensified its crackdown on Palestinian resistance leading to a further upsurge in anti-Jewish incidents in some European countries. Some synagogues were torched and vandalised, and a small, prefabricated synagogue in Marseille burned down. In April 2002, the *Independent* published a front-page picture of a desecrated synagogue in north London; with it ran the headline 'A picture that tells a shocking story: the rise of antisemitism in Britain'.

Headlines are one thing. Far more significantly, by this time there was a wide and growing variety of formal and informal organisations and groups,[3] especially in North America, across Europe and in Israel, engaged in studying, monitoring, documenting, analysing, reporting on, educating about and seeking policies to deal with the problem of contemporary antisemitism. To a greater or lesser degree, all were involved in fighting antisemitism. Included among the range of forces engaged in this effort were university-based research institutes, think tanks both independent and associated with universities or other institutions, antisemitism units or departments in national, regional or global representative Jewish organisations, independent national and international NGOs, parliamentary groups (like the All Party Parliamentary Group Against Antisemitism in the UK) and anti-antisemitism groups set up as private charities. In addition, certain international governmental bodies, such as the Organization for Security and Cooperation in Europe (OSCE) and the Task Force for International Cooperation on Holocaust Education, Remembrance and Research (ITF, which was renamed and institutionalised permanently as the International Holocaust Remembrance Alliance (IHRA) in 2012), while not solely dedicated to combatting antisemitism, developed significant roles as leading participants in the fight.[4] Finally, Israel as a state was also part of this panoply of entities engaged in the battle through the Israel Government Monitoring Forum on Antisemitism and the Mossad, the national intelligence agency, responsible for intelligence collection, covert operations, and counter-terrorism. And because of the increasingly pervasive argument that anti-Zionism and strong criticism of Israel was antisemitism, Zionist organisations, Israel advocacy groups and other pro-Israel bodies—parliamentary, civil society, Christian evangelical, etc.—also entered the fray as actors in this drama. In the UK, prominent among them was BICOM—Britain Israel Communications and Research Centre—founded in 2001, essentially as an Israel lobby organisation, but with a strong interest in promoting the supposedly academic study of 'antisemitic anti-Zionism'. (BICOM replaced a not entirely dissimilar body called BIPAC—Britain Israel Public Affairs Committee—which ceased to exist in 1999 after its backers withdrew funding, having concluded that it was no longer what was required in the Oslo era, and that it had anyway not proved very effective.[5])

* * *

Nothing like this existed when the discussions about the relationship between anti-Zionism and antisemitism were gathering momentum from the late 1970s. When problems of antisemitism did arise, they were largely dealt with on a national basis by the particular Jewish community affected, even if some American national Jewish organisations and the WJC, through its regional groupings, did issue statements condemning antisemitic incidents. When the issue of the status of Jews beyond the Iron Curtain became a matter of international Jewish concern, local activist groups in some Western countries mobilised to raise awareness of their plight, with major engagement by the WJC. But while Soviet antisemitism played its part in generating a basis of concern, the campaign to pressure the Soviet Union to allow its Jews to emigrate was based on appeals to fulfil human rights obligations under the Helsinki Agreements. It wasn't until the Brussels conference of 1992 that the WJC itself decided to prioritise combatting antisemitism directly. Its major policy concerns had been Soviet Jewry, the Waldheim affair and, post-1989, the restitution of Jewish property and assets in the former European communist states.

The London-run European branch of the WJC, renamed the European Jewish Congress (EJC) in 1986 and moved to Paris, and from then formally the

European affiliate of the WJC, had a commission on antisemitism comprising representatives of national communities responsible for dealing with antisemitism. It was serviced by the IJA during the early 1980s, but it ceased to function for a number of years. The IJA then attempted to revive it in the early 1990s, holding a meeting of Europe-wide Jewish community representatives in 1993.

There was no other European-wide forum that could discuss the actual problems of antisemitism facing Jewish communities, which could then, in principle, lead to political action by the EJC leadership.

At the meeting of the commission that I chaired in London on 29 March, I spoke of the existence of a general consensus that there had been a significant revival of antisemitism in Europe, and that it was clear that there were significant connections between antisemitic events and movements throughout Europe, giving the meeting added significance. I added that the meeting was 'potentially significant in another way too: it seemed that many groups and organizations regarded it as their right, even duty, to initiate some kind of activity against antisemitism in Europe—whether it's the Simon Wiesenthal Center or other groups like the ADL and the AJC'. There was nothing to prevent any private group from seeking to combat antisemitism, and it may well have been that what such organisations were doing was of some help. But 'antisemitism seems to be an area in which there is great duplication of effort and this cannot be good. A commission like this could play a significant part in preventing duplication'.[6]

There is no single reason why, by the early 1990s, the growing differences in identifying, assessing and making judgements about the state of antisemitism were accompanied by the proliferation of institutional actors whose various approaches and priorities with regard to combatting antisemitism reflected these differences. Jews virtually everywhere were feeling a greater sense of security in their daily lives and were more prepared to be publicly assertive about the positive benefits of their Jewishness. But that same assertiveness was applied to social and political developments perceived to have negative impacts—anti-Zionism equated with antisemitism, criticism that allegedly demonised Israel, the resurfacing of antisemitism in the former communist states, the claim that antisemitism in Muslim communities in Europe was posing an increasing threat to Jews. It became increasingly common to bring such issues to public attention, and more significantly to the attention of the powers that be: at the national level—government, political parties, the churches, the police—and at the international level—the UN and its individual agencies, regional multilateral structures like the EU and the Papal authority of the Catholic Church. The New York-based leadership of the WJC, which effectively seized control of the then Geneva-based body in 1981, with the election of Edgar Bronfman to the presidency, and the subsequent appointment of Dr Israel Singer as secretary general, led the way in this with a confrontational style, and skilful, blunt public relations, driven to a great degree by a fierce intention to hold the world to account for the Holocaust, public awareness of which had dramatically increased in the 1970s and 1980s. Promises of financial support, public spectacle and cajolery brought most national Jewish leaderships, previously very cautious, into line behind the WJC's assertive campaigns on Soviet Jewry,[7] the Waldheim affair,[8] the return of or compensation for Jewish assets seized by Axis states and their communist successors, and on raising awareness of resurfacing antisemitism in the former communist states. The WJC, though in 1980 an international body with offices in Geneva, Jerusalem, Paris, Buenos Aires and London, transferred its centre of gravity to New York and was increasingly seen as an American Jewish organisation, competing for attention in the United States with the other major American Jewish organisations. The AJC, ADL and the SWC, all of which had ambitions to extend their influence beyond North America, and had footholds in Europe and elsewhere, substantially extended their international reach in the wake of the impact being made by the WJC. And the fundamental political struggle which each body claimed it could wage more effectively than its rivals was the fight against antisemitism. At the same time, all of these organisations were increasingly placing the defence of Israel, perceived as an object of demonisation and delegitimisation on the international stage, at the heart of their political campaigns. In the new Europe, a public reckoning with responsibility for the Holocaust, coupled with a perceived resurgence of the very political movements and parties espousing the racist ideology that led to the genocide, were taking place, at the same time as a Jewish cultural and religious revival was clearly evident in the newly free states of Eastern Europe as well as in the countries of Western Europe. The region became the battleground that provided all of these organisations with a seemingly endless supply of material that was used to give legitimacy and appeal to their organisational goals.

An increasingly complex array of political players on the anti-antisemitism field had developed by the first years of the twenty-first century. But while one participant of great importance in this 'movement' (if it can be described as such), Israel, has been mentioned a great deal, it appears to have the character of a passive recipient of the attention of attackers and defenders. However, its role has never really been entirely passive, though the posture it adopted during the first 40 years of the existence of the state can be construed as a form of passivity, certainly when measured against the activism of many of the other players already mentioned. Most people who observe and take an interest in antisemitism, or who are actively engaged in combatting it, would probably assume that Israel, in its self-styled role as the Jewish state, has always, since its founding, been at the forefront of tackling antisemitism. In fact, nothing could be further from the truth. Writing in the *Jerusalem Post* in 1997, commentator David Weinberg, who became deeply involved in subsequent government engagement with the issue, asked and answered this question: 'Is the struggle against antisemitism around the world Israel's fight? For close to thirty years the official answer to this question was a resounding no. Now that's changed, and there are policy implications'.[9]

In the early years of the state, Israel wanted to have nothing to do with antisemitism for two basic reasons. First, if Jews faced problems of antisemitism where they lived, they could escape them by emigrating to Israel. Second, a central tenet of Zionism was that its realisation would bring an end to antisemitism, since the state would normalise the position of Jews throughout the world. To engage in openly fighting antisemitism in diaspora communities would be tantamount to admitting that Zionism had failed.

This is not to say that Israel was declining to act as protector of the Jewish people. On the contrary, the state was declared to be just that. It 'took upon itself the role of protector of the kin communities, the Jewish faith and the demographic viability of the nation, absorbing the ancient idea that Jews are mutually responsible, that they are their brothers' keepers', write Yossi Shain and Barry Bristman.[10] And the state exemplified this by its 'foreign policy [which] placed a high priority on saving Jews individually and as groups, expending great resources to free Jews in Syria, the USSR, Argentina, Romania, Ethiopia and elsewhere'. But there was always a significant caveat. Such 'rescue' efforts were 'always done in the context of the Zionist vision of the ingathering of the exiles, of ultimately uniting the nation inside the state, and not of perpetuating Jewish communities in their foreign domiciles'. In the 1950s and 1960s, Israeli leaders downplayed diaspora involvement in supporting Israel, which consisted, among other things, in providing considerable funds to bring Jews clandestinely to the developing Jewish state. It wanted to convey an image of Israel as 'taking care of its own defence and reaching out to extend this security to the Jews of the diaspora. The deeply rooted perception of diaspora-born weakness was essential to Zionist ideology, which considered diasporic existence nationally degenerating'. Prime Minister David Ben-Gurion's 'Israelocentrism' meant that the diaspora was always a secondary concern. Israeli security was synonymous with Jewish security. Ben-Gurion himself said:

It was always my view that we have to consider the interests of diaspora Jewry—any Jewish community that was concerned. But there is one crucial distinction—not what they think are their interests, but what we regard as their interests. If it was a case vital for Israel, and the interests of Jews concerned were different, the vital interests of Israel came first—because Israel is vital for world Jewry.[11]

It was this principle that lay behind Israel's policy of supplying arms to Argentina during the years 1976 to 1983 when that country was ruled by a military junta, a brutal regime which, as part of its 'dirty war', persecuted, detained and 'disappeared' an estimated total of 30,000 left-wing activists, of whom 2,000 were Jews.[12] Appeals to Israel by left-wing Argentinian Jews fell on deaf ears.[13]

So too with the case of South Africa under apartheid. While initially sympathetic to the struggle against apartheid, Israel switched sides in the early 1970s. From 1976, not only did it develop very close military cooperation with South Africa, selling the country arms, helping it build its own arms manufacturing capability and even going so far as to give South Africa its nuclear weapons capability,[14] but the two countries found ideological affinity in their determination to maintain Jewish and Afrikaner majority rule in perpetuity. In fact John Vorster's National Party had a long history of antisemitism. When apartheid was introduced there was genuine concern that formal discrimination against Jews might also be introduced. It is not surprising, therefore, that 'the Jewish establishment shied away from confrontation with the government', wrote *Guardian* journalist Chris Greal.[15] 'The declared policy of the [South African] Board of Deputies was "neutrality" so as not to "endanger" the Jewish population. Those Jews who saw silence as collaboration with racial oppression, and did something about it outside of the mainstream political system, were shunned'. 'By and large', Helen Suzman told Greal, 'Jews were part of the privileged white community and that led many Jews to say, "We will not rock the boat"'. At no time did Israel act in any other way than in line with what it regarded as its own interests. The fate of South Africa's 120,000 Jews was secondary.

Writing in 2001, Shain and Bristman concluded that

> Israel still privileges the health of its bilateral relations with other countries over the interests of Jewish communities resident there, though it certainly does not ignore them. In the same way, while Israel denounces antisemitism worldwide as a dangerous phenomenon in general, it is selective in its particular condemnations, hesitant when interests it perceives as more important are at stake.[16]

More recently, in 2013, Dov Waxman and Scott Lasensky wrote: 'Above all else, Israeli policy-makers have sought to defend and advance the interests of the State of Israel. If there is a conflict between the interests of a particular Jewish community and those of the State of Israel, the interests of the latter will generally prevail in determining policy'.[17]

Meanwhile, I return to the change in Israeli policy on fighting antisemitism that David Weinberg identified in 1997. Though this is when his article was written, he is not suggesting that the change took place then. He argues that Israeli attitudes began to change in the 1970s. He first singles out the growing attack on Israel's legitimacy by 'the Arabs after the [1973] Yom Kippur war', which he says Israelis saw as an anti-Zionism 'indistinguishable' from antisemitism. The rue Copernic bombing in Paris in June 1980, in which four were killed and 46 wounded, led Prime Minister Begin to decide that Israeli officials should advise Jewish communities abroad on security measures. 'Those in Israel who always had believed that "the whole world is against us", like Begin, made potent political use of this theme, and [a] response to antisemitism rapidly found its place on the national agenda'.[18]

And yet the first time that antisemitism was mentioned in an Israeli government resolution was in 1970, and it dealt with the question of Soviet Jewry. Israel still saw its main efforts in tackling antisemitism as rooted in Zionist ideology, 'in *aliya*, Jewish immigration to Israel. This is the essence of the Zionist hope' wrote Elyakim Rubinstein, the former government secretary.[19] And the right to emigrate is what the government stressed, though it also vowed to continue the struggle against antisemitism. However, when the government denounced the passing of UNGA Resolution 3379 in November 1975, which declared that 'Zionism is a form of racism and racial discrimination', it made no mention of the term 'antisemitism'.[20] When the peace talks with Egypt began after President Sadat's visit to Israel, Egyptian newspapers were still featuring reports with antisemitic connotations, prompting a relatively mild government resolution expressing 'the hope that insults to the Jewish people would be avoided'.[21] Even after the rue Copernic bombing in Paris in 1980,[22] an event that prompted the government to declare that 'there is no distinction between anti-Israel and anti-Zionist phenomena, and antisemitism, which has brought catastrophe and disgrace on all mankind',[23] there is no mention of antisemitism in government resolutions until 1987.

It was then, Rubinstein writes, that 'some of us felt that it was time to be more precise, and more focused on the subject, since ugly incidents were taking place. We proposed to Prime Minister Yitzhak Shamir to establish a forum monitoring these phenomena'. The Israel Government Monitoring Forum on Antisemitism began operating in early 1988, under the direction of Rubinstein:[24]

consisting of representatives of all relevant government authorities, Foreign Ministry and others, and the [World] Zionist Organization, also accompanied by a wider forum, meeting once or twice a year, of academic people and representatives of Jewish organizations—to monitor the subject. We have been reporting to the Prime Minister and to the Foreign Minister every month, and to the full government about once a year.

Rubinstein stressed that 'we do not panic and we do not cry wolf'. Nevertheless, while a few years earlier Israeli embassies were sending few cables reporting on antisemitism, 'Now, you find them quite often almost on a daily basis or a few times a week. And the reasons are', Rubinstein argues, 'on the one hand, more awareness—but on the other hand, many problems in the world at large. Therefore, Israeli embassies, as part of their normal job, report home and contribute to the struggle against antisemitism.'[25]

From these accounts, we begin to get a clearer picture of a significant change in Israeli government policy on antisemitism, with the machinery of the state being deployed in what looks to be a transparent fashion, guided by Zionist principles. However, Shain and Bristman already referred to *clandestine* government efforts 'saving Jews individually and as groups', which were being undertaken from the earliest days of the state and in fact continued a process that the security forces of the Yishuv were engaged in before 1948.[26] Though sources I have quoted so far do not refer to it, post-1948 'clandestine' means Mossad, Israel's national intelligence agency, formally founded in 1949.

The historic name of the department in the Mossad that has been responsible, among other things, for the struggle against antisemitism, is 'Bitsur' (which means 'fortification'), writes Israeli journalist and security expert Yossi Melman.[27] After the pre-state organisation responsible for illegal immigration, Mossad for Aliya Bet, was dismantled in 1951, immigration from 'problematic' countries was divided between Nativ (also known as Lishkat Hakesher)—dealing with contact with the Jews of the Soviet Union—and Bitsur—covering immigration from Muslim and Arab countries. As this required undercover secret operations, the task was given to Mossad, which set up Bitsur for the purpose.

One mission was organising secret immigration from North Africa, Syria, Lebanon, Iraq, Iran, Ethiopia and Yemen. The other, providing protection to Jewish communities throughout the world and helping them organise means of self-defence against antisemitic forces.

> Trainers and security experts were sent to the Jewish communities and young Jews came to Israel for training. The authorities in those countries that maintained good relations with Israel, did not raise objections to their young Jewish citizens training in Israel. Here they were taught by experts who lectured on intelligence and trained them in security methodologies. Back home, they took part in protecting Jewish community institutions.

Whether or not the UK came under the remit of Bitsur specifically, it was an open secret in the late 1980s and early 1990s that the defence department of the Board of Deputies was cooperating with the Mossad in the training of young Jewish volunteers for the purposes Melman describes. The organised community had developed a structure for defending Jewish institutions, monitoring manifestations of antisemitism, tracking antisemitic groups and liaising with the security authorities when necessary. A separate charity, Group Relations Education Trust (GRET), provided funds for the defence work until a new body was set up in 1994, the Community Security Trust (CST), which was a registered charity and independent of the Board of Deputies, a deliberative body the Jewish security experts and officials felt hindered their ability to respond in a timely fashion to manifestations of antisemitism and develop independent relations with the security organs of government and the state.

Meanwhile, the still relatively new Israel Government Monitoring Forum on Antisemitism, which, as a multi-agency body, included representation from the Mossad, was in the process of engineering a new relationship with Jewish defence bodies worldwide—a logical step, given that one of the motives for establishing the Forum was to fulfil the Zionist ideological imperative to act as 'protector of the kin communities', without losing sight of the ultimate solution to Jewish diaspora insecurity: *aliya* to Israel. A unit in the Mossad had, for a number of years before the Forum was set up, collated raw data on what it deemed to be expressions of antisemitism around the world, re-packaged it and sent it to Jewish defence bodies. The Forum took over the task of disseminating this material.

There were other reasons for the forum's efforts. The outbreak of the first Palestinian Intifada in 1987 and Israel's harsh response—symbolised by the then Defence Minister Yitzhak Rabin's order in January 1988 to break the bones of Palestinian 'inciters' as punishment—only deepened international hostility to the country, which was still suffering from the consequences of the 1982 Lebanon invasion and the massacre of Palestinians by Phalangists—supposedly Israel's allies in Lebanon—in the Sabra and Chatilla refugee camps. Strengthening ties with diaspora communities on the back of heightened concerns about antisemitism following the collapse of communism was a way of mobilising and exploiting pro-Israel sentiment in support of shoring up the country's image. Achieving this aim was easier said than done. European Jews supportive of Israel found themselves at increasing variance with their national governments, which had become more critical of Israel; with Western Europe becoming a 'surrogate battlefield' of the Middle East conflict in the 1970s and 1980s, they 'quickly realised that they were now implicated in Israeli affairs in general, and could not choose to be shielded from the negative consequences of Israel's conflicts'. So the forum's efforts to reach out to diaspora communities can be seen as a reflection of the Israeli government's concern about the implications of this vulnerability.[28] In addition, the decline in post-1967 identification with Israel and the increasing numbers of diaspora Jewish critics, especially among the younger generation, who were aligning with progressive forces in Israel, such as Peace Now, founded in 1978, was a cause of growing concern,[29] and another reason for encouraging young Jews to become engaged in another 'progressive' cause: combatting antisemitism. Nonetheless, as Gabriel Sheffer wrote at the time: 'At best it is highly questionable whether Israel has been able to contribute to Jewish well-being, except for national pride ... [Perhaps] Israel is a Jewish liability rather than an asset'.[30]

What was the practical outcome of the Forum's attempts at diaspora outreach? Although they do not refer to the Forum by name, Shain and Bristman are almost certainly judging its efforts when they comment: 'Israel's government ... tried to engage its west European counterparts in closer security cooperation, often without much success'.[31] It is perhaps not surprising, given the involvement of the Mossad, that accounts of this effort by those working for Jewish defence bodies, or other institutions engaged in fighting antisemitism, are, to say the least, hard to come by. But we know that the joint government-Mossad initiative faced two problems.[32]

First, the data being disseminated to Jewish community defence groups was crude and undifferentiated, to say the least. Ostensibly, these were lists of antisemitic incidents, but invariably they contained mentions of incidents that clearly had, at most, marginal antisemitic characteristics; incidents of crude daubings of swastikas or Stars of David in random locations that could easily have been mindless hooliganism, and incidents described in such a confused, contradictory and incomplete fashion as to be of very little value.

Second, Rubinstein had chosen to give government and Mossad involvement in the issue of antisemitism a public profile of a kind they never previously had, which 'involve[d] diaspora Jewish representatives and academics too'.[33] This raised the question of the academic credibility of any such enterprise. With the data being disseminated already regarded with great scepticism and judged to be produced by people who had little understanding of the phenomenon—bear in mind that country data was being sent back to experienced antisemitism watchers in those countries, who were invariably better informed about local developments and conditions than were Israeli officials working out of Israeli embassies—gaining the trust of genuine experts was difficult. So, a decision was taken to establish an academic monitoring and research centre in Israel to act as the public face of the Forum/Mossad effort. This was the Tel Aviv University Project on Antisemitism, headed by Professor Dina Porat, a historian, who was already directing the Weiner Library Documentation Centre at the university. The ADL, which had been seeking a base outside of the US to pursue its anti-antisemitism work on a global level for some time, was a joint founder.

Towards the end of 1990 the IJA began work on a booklet which examined the state of antisemitism in Eastern and Central Europe country-by-country, under common headings. Partly written in-house and partly using outside experts in the countries concerned, the booklet was published towards the end of 1991, shortly after I was appointed director. It was well received. Journalists, Jewish leaders and members of the institute seemed to find our research-based, balanced approach to antisemitism very useful.

This came at the end of a two-year period during which the WJC ceded oversight of the IJA to the ADL in exchange for a major injection of funds. During those two years, the IJA's freedom to publish on current political issues, especially antisemitism, was limited. We were subject to ADL management's political priorities. Had we tried to publish the Central and East European booklet while still under ADL control, it is highly unlikely that permission would have been given.

Nevertheless, while the WJC—once again sole major funder and ultimate arbiter—did not exert control in a heavy-handed fashion, the New York leadership expected the IJA to reinforce the political objectives of the organisation. IJA's long-term future had been in doubt since WJC agreed the management and financial deal with the ADL in 1989, and uncertainty then returned in 1991.

The IJA therefore had to play a significant role in the Brussels conference, although without any prior consultation about its format or programme. Its main aim was to send out a warning to the world of the danger represented by the upsurge of antisemitism in the post-communist states and to establish the WJC as being at the forefront of the campaign to combat it. Many of the sessions had serious titles and a number of prominent academics and experts in antisemitism were invited, but the WJC was far more interested in achieving a public relations success than in seriously analysing the problem. In the light of all of this, and in an attempt to combine seriousness of purpose with something that would capture the attention of the media, and therefore make the WJC sit up and take notice, I came up with the idea of building on the Central and East European booklet and producing an annual, worldwide, country-by-country survey of antisemitism, modelled on the annual human rights reports of bodies like Amnesty International. Each country entry would be organised according to set categories to enable comparisons to be made between countries and then over time. This would be the first document of its kind and fill a much-needed purpose. Indeed, it always surprised me that nothing like this had been done before. For the countries in which we had expertise, IJA research staff would write the entries. For other countries, we would commission experts we regarded as reliable to write the reports for us. But to maintain a high standard and quality control, each country entry was to be vetted by at least one other expert, and in the overall editing process, which would be done by IJA staff, we would draw on the institute's own data to augment or supplement entries where we saw fit.

We were already aware of a general problem with the quality of the data available. For some countries, there was excellent information, and this was largely because of the expertise of the individuals or agencies monitoring and analysing antisemitism in those countries. But the overall picture was muddied by a stream of raw data distributed throughout the world by Israeli government sources, as mentioned above. Most antisemitism researchers knew full well that this material was of very poor quality. It comprised lists of so-called 'antisemitic incidents', but in very many cases there was no evidence at all that the incidents were antisemitic. Even known antisemitic incidents were often distorted, exaggerated or wrongly described. The IJA had begun to cooperate quite closely with the Defence Department of the Board of Deputies of British Jews at the time and they were equally dismayed by the unsophisticated nature of this Israeli material. It was an irritant and a nuisance, as we had to examine the data, but it did not impede our work. The WJC knew to expect delivery of what we had decided to call the *Antisemitism World Report* in time for the July conference and staff worked furiously to complete it on time.

The institute's work on antisemitism raised its international profile, but it also meant that it was entering a rather complicated world in which the quality of research on antisemitism was secondary to political and ideological imperatives and rigid ideas as to how antisemitism should be combatted. I knew something about this world, since I had written about the politicisation of antisemitism back in 1985 in an editorial as editor of the *Jewish Quarterly* magazine, which was critical both of Jewish progressive groups and Jewish establishment organisations for instrumentalising antisemitism for political ends.[34] To my surprise, I was severely attacked by the Board of Deputies and the leading Zionist organisations for dissenting from what was portrayed as the 'communal consensus' on antisemitism, especially since I was employed by a research institute considered to be a major communal institution. The furore was reflected, among other ways, in the letters page of the *JC* where publication of correspondence on the affair continued for seven weeks.

At the time, I was still a novice as far as Jewish communal politics were concerned and the views I expressed then were largely based on my experience in the UK and stemmed from close observation of a field to which I was still something of a newcomer. But by 1992, I had worked closely with the ADL, the world's largest and most influential Jewish organisation fighting antisemitism, and had much more direct contact with the leadership of the WJC following their change of policy direction, making antisemitism their main concern. At the same time, as the IJA searched for experts worldwide, we increasingly came across a variety of individuals and agencies, some of which approached the issue from an ideological and political, rather than a research-based, perspective. Despite, by then, being far more experienced in the ways of this world, the degree of competition between many of these bodies still took me by surprise.

But the most troublesome of these actors were located in Israel, as we soon discovered.

Not long after it became known that the IJA was producing a world report on antisemitism for the WJC conference in Brussels in 1992, we learnt that the Mossad-linked Tel Aviv University Project on Antisemitism, and still something of a newcomer on the scene, was planning to produce something similar. This information was conveyed to us by a man who worked out of the Israeli embassy in London. Known to us as 'Mike', he had first been introduced to me by Michael Whine, then Government and International Affairs Director of the Defence Department of the Board of Deputies, with whom I developed a close working relationship. 'Mike' was a Mossad operative, and while he ostensibly had a formal embassy role as a counsellor of some kind, whatever else he was doing, one of his main responsibilities was antisemitism and Jewish security.

Although 'Mike' kept a low profile in his relations with the organised Jewish community—for example, he did not make himself available to speak about his work at public meetings—the full-time and honorary officials responsible for security matters understood that he was the representative of Israel's new approach of institutionalising the fight against antisemitism as part of the state's foreign policy when it founded the Israel Government Monitoring Forum. As 'Mike' put it to us at the time, he wanted to facilitate cooperation between the various Jewish institutions now working on antisemitism. To this end, the Forum, of which 'Mike' was effectively an unofficial representative, organised a meeting at the Brussels conference between IJA, SICSA, the Tel Aviv University Project, the ADL, the WJC and others. The first IJA *Antisemitism World Report* was successfully completed just in time for the conference, where it was distributed to all participants. Although widely welcomed and praised by individual participants, its reception by the Jewish anti-antisemitism institutions was less than fulsome. Past soured relations, new, increasingly adversarial competition, the WJC's repositioning to be the world Jewish leader in combatting antisemitism and its increasingly transparent intention to radically reduce its support for the IJA all contributed to this state of affairs.

Ostensibly called to discuss cooperation, it soon became apparent that the principal purpose of the meeting was to persuade the IJA to cease producing its world report on antisemitism, and rather to pool resources and produce one together with the other two academic institutes. SICSA's head, Yehuda Bauer, was lukewarm, but the Tel Aviv Project claimed that it had already made plans to produce its own world report and that it would proceed to do so unless we cooperated.

IJA declined, for two reasons. We strongly believed such a report would gain greater authority from being produced outside of Israel, since a report produced with Israeli institutions might attract the charge that it was distorted because of Zionist ideological objectives. And we did not think it wise to work so closely with the Forum given the distortions and inaccuracies in the data it produced. During the coming months, further efforts were made to persuade us to change our minds and we began to learn more about the way the Forum operated. This then furnished us with two additional reasons for maintaining our independence.

First, by then we knew that the Tel Aviv Project was the public, 'academic' face of the Forum and Mossad effort to implement government policy seeking a more interventionist coordinating role in the fight against antisemitism. To the IJA, such close links with a specific Israeli government policy and the Mossad, as well as state funding, further compromised the objectivity and credibility of the Tel Aviv Project. In addition, the ADL was a co-partner, making cooperation an even less attractive idea.

Second, by working with central Jewish monitoring bodies, the Forum followed a deliberate policy of attempting to act as a central coordinator of all monitoring being organised by Jewish communities. There were at least two very disturbing features of this activity. 'Mike' freely admitted that the main purpose of establishing the networks of people supplying the Forum with national information and then sending back the data collated from around the world, and supplemented by the Mossad operatives in embassies, in return was to sensitise and galvanise young Jews to the present dangers of antisemitism and thereby encourage *aliya*. Their attempts at persuading existing country monitoring organisations to cede some of their sovereignty to the Forum was resented by some of those bodies and, given the quality of the Data the Forum produced, regarded as risible.

So, in short, the Forum, the Israeli government's civil arm devoted to the problem of antisemitism, working hand-in-hand with the Mossad, was being used as a Zionist recruiting tool. This should not come as a surprise. On one level, the government's new policy on antisemitism, and its intention to lead the worldwide Jewish effort to fight antisemitism, was a significant departure from previous practice, it remained within the ideological and political parameters set by Ben-Gurion when he said that Israel would always act with the interests of the Jewish diaspora in mind, but according to Israel's determination of what those interests were.

IJA's stance was, to say the least, not to the Forum's liking, and as time went by they made this increasingly clear. We had agreed to organise a conference in London for researchers dealing with antisemitism and this took place in December 1993. The Forum took exception to some of the people we invited to attend—people who were part of the international network of researchers we had set up to help produce our world report; not operating within formal Jewish communal structures, they did not have the confidence of the Forum. But our sole criteria for engaging with researchers were the quality of their research and the measured nature of their conclusions. Being Jewish and receiving the stamp of approval of the official leadership body of a Jewish community was no guarantee of the value of an individual researcher's work. And we noted that, overall, the assessments of our diverse team of researchers were more objective, differentiated and balanced than reports in the media and from Israeli-based sources. Good media coverage, following a press launch of the yearly *Antisemitism World Report*, was encouraging. But the Forum made it clear that they did not like our conclusions. To counter our efforts, they pressed the Tel Aviv Project to proceed with producing its own report and we found ourselves in a race each year to be the first to publish.

In an attempt to handicap us even further, the Forum stopped sending us the raw data they produced on antisemitic incidents. At first they said it was an oversight. Then, when the incident reports continued to be denied to us, they justified it on the basis that they did not want the material to get into the hands of researchers they did not trust. From time to time, they would again raise the idea of producing a joint report, but we continued to resist. Unsurprisingly, as the Forum and the Mossad to an extent withdrew from the role of being a part of the public face of Israel's engagement with the issue of antisemitism, and ceded this task to the Tel Aviv Project, our relations with Tel Aviv, already strained, got worse. Eventually, when it was the turn of Tel Aviv to organise another in the series of conferences for Jewish researchers on antisemitism in 1994, we were deliberately excluded from attending.

I decided to alert the IJA Board of Directors to this problem and seek their advice on the policy we should follow. In a discussion paper written for the Board meeting on 15 March 1994, I expanded on the ideological and philosophical differences between the Tel Aviv Project and the IJA:

> The ethos behind the antisemitism work of Tel Aviv, which was set up at the urging of the Israel Government Monitoring Forum, is that only Zionism provides the answer to the problem of antisemitism. Thus, the tone of much of their work is highly alarmist and exaggerated and is directed at vulnerable communities and young people. Their network of contacts is based almost solely on central communal bodies, because they assume that those bodies will tacitly accept their assumptions.
>
> Our view is that the opinions and assessments of Jewish communities must be taken into account in reporting antisemitism, but that what is most important is a rigorous and objective approach. Only such an approach will command the respect of governments, international organizations and so on. Furthermore, although Israel has a very important role to play in the monitoring and researching of contemporary antisemitism, it is entirely wrong

for the government to be attempting to dominate this work, since they will always be seen to have questionable motives and because Israel's interests as a state are bound to diverge at times from the interests of Jewish communities.

Relations with the Forum reached a new low when a bizarre attempt was made by 'Mike' to justify their behaviour towards us. Not long after the bombing of the Israeli embassy in London on 26 July 1994,[35] 'Mike' asked me to meet with him at his office there. In fact, the room we met in was his temporary office. His original office had been damaged by the effects of the bomb, which injured 14 people. In no uncertain terms, 'Mike' tried to shame me and IJA by pointedly drawing my attention to the circumstances in which he and his colleagues now had to work. While his tone was ostensibly more one of sorrow than anger, there was an unmistakable implication that I was somehow complicit in what had happened, or at least that there was something in my 'uncooperative' attitude which helped create a climate in which such incidents could occur. I decided not to rise to the bait and waited for him to move on to what I presume he really wanted to say. Continuing in the same tone as before, he began to accuse me of discourtesy for not replying to letters he and the Forum had sent me urging the IJA to cease publishing its *Antisemitism World Report* and cooperate with the Tel Aviv Project. No such letters ever reached me and it soon became clear that this was a crude attempt to frame me and discredit the IJA. 'Mike' threatened to make it even more difficult for us to work in the field of antisemitism if we did not change our attitude.

With relations having deteriorated to such an extent that our ability to produce the *Antisemitism World Report* was affected—some significant communal monitoring bodies that had continued to work with us succumbed to pressure to end that cooperation—I thought the best way to resolve the situation was to meet face to face with the Israeli ambassador in London, Moshe Raviv, together with the chairman of the IJA, Peter Levy, and ask him to intervene with the Forum and to seek assurances that we would no longer be subject to its harassment. I had met the ambassador before on a number of occasions and had found him to be sympathetic, intelligent, softly spoken and thoughtful. To my surprise, we were given short shrift. Instead of being listened to sympathetically, he told us in no uncertain terms that we should cease producing our report, that we were novices in the matter of antisemitism and that this was something best left to the Israeli government to deal with and organise.

The meeting with Raviv only confirmed for me the conclusions I had already reached: on the basis of my experience, the Israeli government was not interested in objective assessments. It was determined to exert centralised control of the monitoring of antisemitism worldwide and was using antisemitism as a crude mobilising tool for Zionism and *aliya*.

I had not sought this confrontation. All we had done at the IJA was to try to develop the most comprehensive, objective and thorough research-based analysis and assessment of contemporary antisemitism, using the most carefully scrutinised monitoring material. We never had any intention to publicly criticise Israel over its handling of this issue. Even as I became increasingly aware of the systemic political and ideological manipulation of antisemitism through the 1990s, I merely wanted to let the quality of our work speak for itself. Surely this was the best way to underpin the fight against antisemitism. Not to identify closely with any political organisation. Not to do anything that would compromise the accuracy of what we were producing. We simply wanted to tell it like it was.

And we were not alone in thinking that this was the best way of approaching the issue. Many of the people we worked with approved of our system and our methodology. Many also sympathised with our criticisms of the Zionist-centric assumptions of the Israeli Government Monitoring Forum and Israeli institutions like the Tel Aviv Project. First and foremost were Michael Whine and Morton Creeger, the head of GRET, the charity funding communal defence work. They were very critical of the Israeli authorities, felt that the attempt to impose Israeli hegemony over the fight against antisemitism was entirely wrong and continued to deplore the quality of the material the Forum produced. (When the Forum sought to 'punish' us by ceasing to send us their lists of so-called anti-semitic incidents, Whine regularly sent on to us their copies of the material.) But since the Board of Deputies Defence Department and GRET maintained a relationship with the Israelis, especially with the Mossad, for the purposes of providing training in security expertise for the Jewish community security volunteers, Whine and Creeger were not in a position to take the kind of independent stand in relation to the Forum that the IJA needed to take.

In 1994, pre-empting a plan being hatched by the New York leadership of the WJC, to close the IJA in London and transfer it to New York, of which I had learnt from the WJC's representative in Brussels, Maram Stern, the IJA Board agreed confidentially to formally sever relations with the WJC. Funding by WJC was likely to end rather quickly, so efforts to replace it were made. The result was that the IJA entered into a five-year partnership with the AJC, a body whose more serious, research-based approach to understanding contemporary anti-semitism seemed to be more compatible with our principles and methodology. In addition, another new funding stream was secured from Yad Hanadiv, the British Rothschild family foundation based in Geneva and operating mostly in Israel. In 1992, Lord Jacob Rothschild had agreed to become President of the IJA.

The AJC and the WJC were bitter rivals, so one of the immediate consequences of the split was a change in the patronage arrangements for the

Antisemitism World Report. Until 1994, the *Report* was published in association with the WJC, whose logo was on the cover. From then on, we published with the AJC and displayed their logo. Meanwhile, as we anticipated, the WJC threw in its lot with the report now being produced by the Tel Aviv University Project, and already appearing under the patronage of the ADL. So, for the next three years, we were in intense competition with Tel Aviv to be the first to produce an annual report on antisemitism worldwide.

Already handicapped by having to live with the enmity of the Mossad, the Israel Government Monitoring Forum on Antisemitism and the Tel Aviv University Antisemitism Project (renamed the Stephen Roth Institute for the Study of Contemporary Antisemitism and Racism in 1996), we now had the WJC and the ADL working against us too. At first, we responded by devoting even more resources to the production of the annual volume, but this proved financially unsustainable. More of the Jewish community bodies around the world, which had been supplying us with data and reports, ceased to do so after pressure was put on them by the Mossad and the Forum. We had hoped that our relationship with the AJC would be of great benefit to the *Report* because we were relying on them to produce the entry for the United States, always one of the longest given the sheer size of the country and its Jewish community. But they were incredibly tardy in supplying their report, causing us no end of difficulty in sticking to our publication deadline.

We were also soon at odds with them over the interpretation of the data. During the first few years of producing the *Report*, we more or less went along with the consensus that there had been a resurgence of antisemitism since 1989 and that this mostly resulted from the collapse of the restraints on freedom of expression and political organisation that accompanied the fall of the communist regimes in Central and Eastern Europe and the Soviet Union. But especially from 1993 onwards, when, despite the rise of Islamic fundamentalism and the strain of antisemitism which came with it, which we were the first to identify, antisemitism in the Arab and Muslim worlds was moderating because of the 1993 Oslo Accords and the rapprochement between Israel and the Palestinians, we began to argue that there was an overall lessening in antisemitic pressures around the world. At the same time, the antisemitism in post-communist societies was not proving to be as significant as at first feared. The democratic structures developing in those countries, the political parties committed to fighting prejudice and the emerging civil society all seemed able to cope with and mitigate the dangers of antisemitic propaganda and activity. We were not alone in holding this view, but the AJC resisted when we wanted to introduce these assessments into the overall conclusions of the *Report*. Certainly, we were rather more sanguine about the current state of antisemitism at that time than were the Tel Aviv Project and its partners, the ADL, WJC and the Monitoring Forum. In general, we found that the message that antisemitism was declining was not one that many people wanted to hear. And since we were trying to raise funds, especially for our work on the *Report*, taking such a view did us no favours. As we already knew only too well: to attract donors to support work on antisemitism, you were under strong pressure to exaggerate the problem. But I was determined that we should not do this.

Two years into the partnership with the AJC, we tried to make a further, and final, effort to reach a better understanding with the Mossad and the Israel Government Monitoring Forum. Dr Joseph (Yossi) Alpher, the former head of the Jaffee Centre for Strategic Studies at Tel Aviv University and a Mossad intelligence officer for twelve years, leaving the agency in the late 1970s, had become the head of the AJC's office in Jerusalem. I had developed a good working relationship with him, and he fully understood the value of the independent antisemitism work we were undertaking. A man with very fine judgement and an open mind, Alpher seemed to me to be someone who could perhaps mediate a meeting between me and the Mossad official driving their activity in the field of antisemitism. He was more than willing to do this, and in the summer of 1995, I sat with Alpher and the Mossad official at Café Landwer in Tel Aviv to discuss our differences.

The encounter was polite but fruitless. Hard-faced and unforgiving, he told me that they were continuing to back the Tel Aviv Institute, but that now it was up and running they would be withdrawing into the background. He maintained that Jewish communities, under Israel's leadership, had to keep tight control of the monitoring of antisemitism. For him, this was non-negotiable and Jewish groups which set themselves outside of this arrangement were disqualifying themselves from having anything legitimate to say.

Nevertheless, with some reluctance he told me that the Mossad and the Monitoring Forum were no longer pursuing the same hegemonic role for Israel they had been in the late 1980s and the early 1990s. This was a significant admission. It meant that the Israeli government would no longer be giving the same priority to antisemitism as in the recent past. It was clear that he had accepted this policy change, but only grudgingly.

Withdrawal from Israel's efforts to lead and coordinate all organised Jewish efforts to combat antisemitism was a direct result of the conclusion of the 1993 Oslo Accords.[36] Prime Minister Rabin wanted a free hand to negotiate with the Palestinians, and this meant scaling back on involvement with the Jewish diaspora, which might result in him being subject to Jewish pressure that would hinder the achievement of his objectives. In essence, this was a return to the status quo ante. As Shain and Bristman wrote: 'The deeply rooted perception of diaspora-born weakness was essential to Zionist ideology, which considered diasporic existence nationally degenerating'.[37] This was not a rationale for doing nothing to help diaspora Jews. It translated into what Aharon Klieman identified: 'while the lot of Jewish communities outside Israel is not the number one determinant in Israel's foreign policy calculus, neither does it mean Israel is free to formulate its policy like other countries strictly on the basis of its own raison d'état'.[38] And although Israel's security services were ready to 'rescue' Jews anywhere—in theory at least—it was not fighting antisemitism in order to make Jewish lives permanently safer in diaspora communities. There was no question of Israel making public reliance on diaspora support a central feature of government policy, but it was taken for granted that this would be forthcoming.

While this was never made public, the wider policy of which it was a part had already become clear in the months after the signing of the Oslo Accords in 1993 and the taking of a new independent path by the government to pursue peace on its terms. Yossi Beilin, Israel's deputy foreign minister, was dispatched to address major Jewish communities, conveying Rabin's clear message that there had to be some alteration in the nature of the Israel–diaspora relationship. I was present at a meeting in New York when Rabin told an audience of mostly American Jewish leaders that the Israeli government would lead in discussions with the US administration on issues to do with Middle East peace and would no longer rely on the increasingly powerful AIPAC to speak on Israel's behalf. Beilin not only emphasised this policy change, which was not well received by some of Israel's right-wing Zionist supporters, he also told Jewish audiences around the world that Israel no longer needed diaspora Jewry's charitable funds, and that Jewish communities should spend that money on themselves.[39] This new policy direction not only reflected the assertion of Jewish and Zionist sovereignty, it also came about as a result of the fierce opposition in some quarters of the diaspora, particularly in America, to the path Rabin had taken. He did not want powerful Jewish organisations hindering his room for manoeuvre, his freedom to go his and Israel's own way. Nonetheless, neither Rabin nor Beilin expected there to be any fundamental change in diaspora Jewry's support for Israel. However, change was coming.

Evidence was beginning to emerge of a growing distancing of younger Jews from Israel, something that had been identified in the UK from the results of the first-ever survey of social and political attitudes of British Jews conducted in 1995, the results of which were presented at the launch of the Institute for Jewish Policy Research (JPR), the think tank into which the IJA had transformed itself, in 1996.[40] Based on the survey results, Barry Kosmin, Jacqueline Goldberg and I authored a study of the *Attachment of British Jews to Israel*,[41] which fleshed out the details and implications of these developments. The analysis of the data was mostly the work of my social scientist colleagues. The conclusions were mostly my work, but Kosmin and Goldberg endorsed them.

We argued that 'the attachment of British Jews to Israel can no longer be taken for granted'.[42]

Israel is part of Jewish ethnicity, but by no means as important to it as is generally assumed. Certainly, to call Israel the 'central focus of Anglo-Jewish identity' [as journalist Joseph Finklestone did in *The Jewish Year Book* 1997] is not justified by the JPR data. Some talk of Zionism Mark II, or of the renewal of Zionism, and it is not mere coincidence that they do so in this anniversary year. But this flies in the face of reality. The trend for Zionism is towards ideological irrelevance; and for Israel to be very present in, but diffused throughout, the increasingly complex mosaic that makes up contemporary Jewish identity.[43]

The survey data related to the situation in late 1995, after the assassination of Rabin on 4 November and the election of the first Benjamin Netanyahu government, which suggested that 'far from being a source of cohesion and consensus, in some respects Israel is becoming a source of communal division'. Giving the reasons for the increasing distancing of British Jews from Israel and Zionism, the paper asked:

In this light—and if Israel is integrated more into the Middle East—can Israel's centrality hold for all Jews? If these trends prevail, and if nothing happens or is done in the interim to change them, we could be seeing a turning of the circle in British Jewry's attachment to Zionism, and to the idea and the reality of the Jewish state; it began as the concern of a mostly secular minority, grew to embrace the entire community, and could be in the process of returning to be the concern of a minority, although now a minority with a mostly traditional or Orthodox religious outlook.

This situation can be viewed as a natural process and a product of the success of the Zionist project. Israel has grown up; it does not require the support of diaspora Jews as it once did since it is no longer under immediate threat. If there is to be a relationship with British Jews, why shouldn't it be based on practical and personal connections—visits, friends and so on— or on some kind of religious imperative? And meanwhile, British Jews turn increasingly to the problems of their own community or the world. This may be the normal position and those whose primary concern is Israel may simply have to adjust to this new reality.[44]

At that time, suggesting the demise of Israel's centrality for the Jewish people, even if it was a possibility supported by survey data, was almost certainly a lot more than many in the mainstream community were ready to contemplate. Nonetheless, the evidence in the report could be used to support the conclusion that, from a normative perspective, centrality was no longer appropriate and that there was a fundamental incompatibility between Israel and Jewish communities elsewhere arising out of the fact that Israel was becoming a state like any other state, and that its interests would no longer coincide with those of Jews owing loyalty as citizens to the countries where they lived. The survey data and the report provided an opportunity to raise questions about this key element of Zionist ideology in public forums; to challenge the officials of pro-Israel organisations, of groups which aimed to perpetuate the Israel–diaspora bond in the form of an unacknowledged subservience to what they claimed was the only place where one could live a full and free life as a Jew; and to call into question the view that, even though Zionist leaders and supporters may not choose to go to live there, it is the better place. These groups could respond in two ways: either acknowledge the new reality and adjust accordingly, or reject it and take determined action to shore up the relationship between Israel and the diaspora by making Israel an even more important factor in Jewish identity through concentrating on Zionist education and the development of strong attachment to Israel among young people—the very group that the survey revealed had looser ties with the country. The 'Israel first' elements chose the latter, but partly acknowledged the new reality by devoting more resources to improving Jewish education in the UK on the understanding that a more committed Jew, a Jew with greater Jewish literacy, was more likely to feel close to Israel. There was certainly no public recognition of the need for the kind of fundamental rethinking of the Israel–diaspora relationship hinted at in the report.

By 1998, with the rapidly growing use of the internet to convey the kind of data and analysis JPR published in the *Antisemitism World Report*, a decision was taken to turn it into an internet-based publication, as a way of making it as up-to-date as possible on a limited budget. It was, quite frankly, an admission of defeat: JPR could not sustain the labour intensive, independent, objective, non-partisan approach to producing an authoritative yearly report on antisemitism that IJA had chosen as the 1990s began, and which it developed and refined over the decade. And it was out of the question that JPR would abandon its principles and finally succumb to pressure that it had resisted for almost a decade. Indeed, reasons to continue keeping its distance from Israeli influence and Israeli government policy were getting stronger as the decade came to an end. The Stephen Roth Institute at Tel Aviv University had the backing of the Israeli government, after receiving financial support from the Mossad in its first years of operation, and the yearly report it was producing was endorsed by the government, but also by the ADL, the WJC and, in effect, by Jewish antisemitism monitoring bodies around the world, which were constrained not to cooperate with JPR.

* * *

Against a background of mounting concern, in some quarters, of rising antisemitism, the cumulative effect of this international intra-communal competition and realignment was heightened by the entry into the picture of other institutional players such as the almost century-old AJC, the relatively new Interparliamentary Council Against Antisemitism and the very new European Union Monitoring Centre on Racism and Xenophobia (EUMC)—initially described as an 'observatory'—set up in 1997. Also entering the fray, though already with a remit for engagement with the problem of antisemitism, was the Organization for Security and Cooperation in Europe (OSCE). According to Whine:

> It was the dramatic rise in antisemitism worldwide during the late 1990s that forced the Organization for Security and Cooperation in Europe (OSCE) and the EU to confront the problem, each in its own way, and eventually to encourage monitoring by national criminal justice agencies. The rationale behind this was that the problem is increasingly trans-national and therefore requires a 'joined up', Europe-wide approach to understand and defeat it.[45]

'The idea that the OSCE could be an effective vehicle for combating antisemitism came initially from the Jacob Blaustein Institute for the Advancement of Human Rights', Whine explains. But the body to which it was affiliated, the AJC, 'provided the focal point for the Jewish groups' campaign'.[46] The OSCE's Office for Democratic Institutions and Human Rights (ODIHR)[47] became an important agency for data collection on hate crime and antisemitism.

The growing significance of the AJC's role in the fight against antisemitism was also evident in its decision to assume full control of UN Watch (see Chapter 3) in 2001, which had been affiliated with its founding body, the WJC, until then. One of the main reasons for the establishment of UN Watch was to combat the 'new antisemitism', which its founders believed was being generated and promoted principally by the UN and its agencies.

While US-based Jewish bodies saw ever closer involvement in fighting antisemitism in Europe as fulfilment of an uncomplicated, altruistic duty—which is not how all Jewish representative bodies in Europe saw it—they were confronted with a far more complicated picture in the US itself. An assessment of the situation at the end of the 1990s by antisemitism expert Jerome Chanes began with this information: 'When questioned in surveys, Jews overwhelmingly and consistently say they feel "comfortable" in America. Yet eight out of ten American Jews believe that antisemitism is a "serious" problem in the United States'. The 'perception gap', he writes, 'among American Jews may be explained by wariness rooted in Jewish history, especially the recent history of the Holocaust', yet 'the reality of the Jewish condition in post-World War II America is that of a steady and dramatic decline in antisemitism.[48] In a similar but more forthright vein, the high profile American Jewish lawyer Alan Dershowitz, who believed that assimilation was a greater problem than antisemitism for American Jews, wrote:

> We continue to see antisemitism where it has ceased to exist, or we exaggerate it where it continues to exist in marginalised form. Indeed, some Jewish newspapers refuse to print, and some Jewish organizations refuse to acknowledge, the good news, lest they risk alienating their readerships or losing their membership. For example, in November of 1996 I saw a fundraising letter from a Jewish organisation which claimed that 'antisemitism ... appears to be growing more robust, more strident, more vicious—and more "respectable".' Well intentioned as this organization is, it seeks support by exaggerating the threats we currently face and by comparing them to those we faced during the Holocaust.[49]

But voices describing a more complex and far from alarmist situation were clearly proving less persuasive than those with more pessimistic accounts. In June 1999 in Berlin, Itzhak Nener, a founder of the international Association of Jewish Lawyers and Jurists and a member of the Israeli Liberal Party leadership and vice-president of the Liberal International, warned that 'there are some very disturbing signs' of rising antisemitism in Germany and across Europe, but that 'Germany is one of the few countries in Europe which has adopted legislation' to fight these trends.[50] Is there a chance that we are approaching a new era, free of antisemitism, hatred and racial prejudice he asked: 'Under the cover of democracy, freedom of speech and freedom of organization, the antisemites are again growing in strength', Nener said. The period between 1991 and 1996 was marked by a rise in expressions of antisemitism, resulting mainly from the collapse of the communist bloc in Europe and the reunification of Germany:

> In the past few months there has been another wave of antisemitism in some countries, because Jewish survivors asked for restitution of their property and assets robbed during the World War. Militant antisemitism has become a growing threat to Jews and antisemitism from Islamic sources has increased ...
>
> While in recent years, antisemitism in various countries has taken a less violent form, neo-Nazi and antisemitic parties and organizations have spread, or, where already in existence—have increased their strength and impact on the political life of their respective countries, including countries where no Jews live.

In contrast, an assessment of antisemitism in the UK made in a report on the future of multi-ethnic Britain, commissioned by the country's main race-relations think tank, the Runnymede Trust, and published in 2000, presented a more optimistic picture: 'Jews see themselves historically as an oppressed group. However, Jews in Britain today face relatively little discrimination; the number of antisemitic incidents is small; the impact of antisemitic propaganda is marginal; and antisemitism has ceased to be socially acceptable.'[51]

The *Report* was the work of a commission of 23 people, drawn from a wide range of ethnic, religious and cultural communities, race-relations experts, the police, the civil service, broadcasting and so on. It drew on advice sought from a very wide range of institutions, including the Board of Deputies of British Jews and other Jewish bodies.[52] Its conclusions were therefore not simply the judgements of a single individual. Giving reasons for its positive comments it stated that 'countervailing forces have strengthened. These include the adoption of legislation making race hatred unlawful, growing awareness of the Holocaust, greater acceptance of pluralism and many decades of successful assimilation— the wisdom of which, however, many in the Jewish community now question.'[53] Nevertheless, the *Report* cautioned that

> not all Jews recognise the improvements. In 1995, 40 per cent of Jews believed that antisemitism was worse than it had been five years earlier, despite the fact that the evidence of declining antisemitism came from data collected by the body that formally monitors such issues on behalf of the community, the Community Security Trust. In view of antisemitism's murderous conse-quences in the past, Jewish sensitivity is entirely understandable.[54]

In a 1998 paper, 'Nationalist challenges in the new Europe', Wistrich was pointing to an antisemitism continuously poised to unleash mass mayhem and havoc when he wrote: 'Neither Western nor Eastern Europe is immune from the spectre of economic disintegration, chronic political instability, moral nihilism and despair in which both fascism and antisemitism have tradition-ally flourished'.[55] And yet, less than two months before the beginning of the new millennium Wistrich acknowledged 'the current, relative immunity of Jews' to antisemitism.[56] He accepted that 'Jews in the West have never had it so good, that state-sponsored antisemitism has effectively disappeared in post-Commu-nist Russia and Eastern Europe, and that even militant anti-Zionism (of the "Zionism is racism" variety) is on the wane'. Nevertheless, he had serious res-ervations and spelt out where he thought dangers lay, asking 'why should we assume' that this situation 'will persist indefinitely?' He concluded:

To be sure, such irritants [in relatively tolerant Britain … as antisemitism] continu[e] to fester quietly beneath the surface as part of the more widespread antagonism to all those minorities who deviate from mainstream definitions of 'Englishness' … seem mild enough against the background of general prosperity and political stability in contemporary Western societies. Jews today quite understandably regard themselves as fully integrated participants in this beckoning new order.

But in the longer sweep of history, it would be a rash prophet who would predict the end of antisemitism in the 21st century. Past experience suggests that the anti-Jewish virus is never so dangerously unpredictable as when its obituary is being written.

As the twentieth century came to an end, institutional engagement—Jewish and general—with the problem of antisemitism was clearly increasing, albeit in a somewhat ad hoc fashion, driven in part by some coalescence around the view that manifestations of antisemitism were on the rise. But there was no settled narrative about how serious the problem was, and as we have seen, certain individuals—such as Wistrich and Dershowitz—who, only a few years later, were convinced that 'global antisemitism' was rising exponentially, were far more cautious about endorsing such claims, and in some cases argued strongly against that view.

Meanwhile, Israel continued to maintain its stance of having formally withdrawn from seeking to centralise the fight against antisemitism under its leadership, preoccupied as it was with the collapse of the Oslo process, the fallout from the second intifada, and the spate of suicide bombings that were having a very damaging effect on the population's sense of security. Nevertheless, ten years of a new policy of government and state involvement in the fight against antisemitism left its mark. Withdrawal from that activity was never fully realised and proved to be temporary. And the very fact that there now existed another institutional partner, and one of huge symbolic significance, for Jewish diaspora groups fighting antisemitism, meant that the landscape was transformed. Major Jewish organisations, both national and international, were increasingly receptive to the understanding that Israel, as both target and combatant, was central to future Jewish mobilisation aimed at fighting antisemitism. And the Benjamin Netanyahu, Ehud Barak and Ariel Sharon-led governments in power between 1996 and 2003 did not discourage the entrenchment of this view.

Although the increase in institutional engagement with the problem of antisemitism was, to a degree, ad hoc, by the turn of the century it was beginning to look like a coalition was coming into being almost by default. Anti-Zionism was the enemy, but it had no concrete form. And since it was Israel on the receiving end of alleged antisemitic anti-Zionism, whatever strategy might be devised to deal with it had to be done in concert with the Israeli government.

The 'new antisemitism' provided the common agenda around which the Jewish organisations and the Israeli institutions coalesced. Dissenters continued to argue strongly against the idea that there was such a thing as 'new antisemitism'. But events after the turn of the century resulted in a decisive shift towards the 'new antisemitism' becoming the 'new orthodoxy'.

6
The Turning Point: 'New Antisemitism' and the New Millennium

It is tempting to think that what many identified as an explosion of global anti-semitism beginning in the year 2000 was somehow linked to the apprehensions, fateful predictions, apocalyptic fears and exaggerated expectations generated by the coming of the end of the second millennium. There is no doubt, at least, that the numerous accounts of post-2000 antisemitism saw the moment as a turning point, even if they eschewed the notion that it had anything to do with millennial angst. And for many analysts, commentators, academics and so on there is a high degree of coalescence around the idea that it was from 2000 that the 'new antisemitism' increasingly came to function as the new orthodoxy, the principal form of Jew-hatred threatening Jews, Jewish communities and the Jewish state. As Dina Porat put it: 'Since October 2000 with the outbreak of the Second Intifada and the events which followed, a new term began to be used—"New Antisemitism"'.[1]

But as we have seen, Porat's contention was not correct. Not only was the term being used, albeit sporadically, more than 20 years and more before 2000, systematic efforts were being made by some academics, Jewish public figures in Israel and the diaspora and some commentators to shape discussion about current antisemitism around the notion of the 'new antisemitism' in the 1990s. While at first there was no consensus as to what 'new antisemitism' referred to, by 2000 that uncertainty had more or less faded away. In short, it comprises two complementary notions: 'anti-Zionism is antisemitism' and 'Israel is the "collective Jew" among the nations'.

As the preceding account of developing debate about the relationship between anti-Zionism and antisemitism demonstrated, some of the discussion had a rigorous, open-ended, inquiring and objective character, as we have seen from the disagreements there were about the matter. And these disagreements remained powerful and stark right up until the end of the century and beyond.

Broadly speaking, two narratives were dominant: one that characterised the 1990s as a time of significant and steady 'global' antisemitic resurgence, and the other that emphasised the countervailing forces that reduced the salience of manifestations of antisemitism and stressed the differentiation of antisemitism's impact from country to country. While the rhetoric around these contending narratives became sharper through the decade, reviewing the debates with some historical distance suggests that the positions being adopted were not mutually exclusive; that there was some validity in drawing attention to new forms of antisemitic expression, as well as validity in the view that diaspora Jewish security, vitality, sense of belonging, and sense of identity had never been stronger. Moreover, there were significant differences from country to country, which makes it necessary to be wary of generalising judgements made about 'European antisemitism' or references to the existence of something called 'global antisemitism'.

All the same, it would be naive and incorrect to imagine that what was going on was an academic debate about a very serious political issue, untainted by any influence from interested political elements, whether these were of a Jewish organisational character or stemmed from the institutions of the Israeli state. The high-level discussions at the residence of the Israeli president, organised and sponsored with the close involvement of the WZO, reflected Israeli-Jewish national and governmental concerns as well as concerns about the prospects of Zionism remaining an ideology not only supported by most Jews worldwide but also one that was still capable of generating significant *aliya*, fulfilling the Zionist aim of securing a Jewish majority in perpetuity. The participants were no stooges, handpicked because they could be relied upon to toe an ideological line. The enthusiastic Zionists were true believers. The proceedings reveal very significant and sharp differences of view. And yet, they *were* handpicked as being, at the very least, supportive of Zionism. There were certainly no Jewish anti-Zionists, non-Zionists or proto-post-Zionists among them.

Moreover, as I have demonstrated, through the Mossad and the Israel Government Monitoring Forum, considerable pressure was being exerted on Jewish communal defence and antisemitism monitoring bodies to cooperate with each other and avoid working with non-Jewish groups or individuals unless they were approved by the Israeli officials. And individuals from such Jewish bodies were among those participating in the Israeli president's seminars. With the creation of what became the Stephen Roth Institute for the Study of Antisemitism and Racism (the former Tel Aviv University Project on Antisemitism), the initiative of the WJC in organising the 1992 Brussels conference and reorienting its political agenda to tackle antisemitism worldwide, the establishment of UN Watch with the task of calling out antisemitism in UN structures, the deepening involvement of the major US Jewish organisations, the ADL, AJC and SWC, in focusing on antisemitism in Europe and at the same time stepping up their roles as pro-Israel advocacy bodies, and the increasing willingness of national and regional Jewish representative bodies like the Board of Deputies of British Jews and the European Jewish Congress (EJC) to take on the role of defending Israel at the public and political levels (a task previously undertaken by Zionist organisations that were now far less influential communally)—transnational racial governance institutions were playing a role in the policing and influencing of antisemitism narratives in a radically enhanced manner.[2] The particular role of the Israeli state waxed, waned and then became more diffuse during the 1990s, but it acted as a significant catalyst in driving Jewish organisations to work along the same lines, if not necessarily through formal cooperation. The American-based organisations went along with this approach to some degree, but the rivalry among them remained intense.

It is therefore necessary to look at the growth of the notion of the 'new antisemitism' not only as 'discourse',[3] or as 'theory',[4] but also as political projects, movements or institutions that were 'participants in wider power dynamics',[5] and to do this in tandem. The interplay, the mutual dependency between, roughly speaking, 'thought' and 'action' is crucial to understanding the role played by 'new antisemitism' in the redefinition of antisemitism.

I briefly focused on some of the institutions in the previous chapter. At the same time, I summarised the key incidents and manifestations that gave rise to the notion that the opening of the third millennium had triggered a radical explosion of global antisemitism. In this chapter, I take that summary as my starting point for examining how the alarmist narrative came to be framed so comprehensively by the discourse of 'new antisemitism'.

*　*　*

Even before the Durban conference took place, what was anticipated to occur there was being categorised as an expression of the 'new antisemitism'. On 9 August 2001, Israel's deputy foreign minister, Michael Melchior, having just returned from Geneva where the agenda of proposals was still being thrashed out by officials, briefed the foreign press on the draft text, which he said is currently 'using all the worst vocabulary which the world society knows to condemn Israel, its birth, its existence, and so on. It's "ethnic cleansing", it's "genocide", it's "neo-apartheid"'.[6]

> But there is a red line, and the red line is where you go over from condemning or a disagreement on a political level, to what I call an existential level of condemning, making Israel the Jew of the nations, making the condemnations and on an existential level delegitimizing Israel's existence. That is already going over the red line and becoming the new antisemitism. We are the new anti-Christ of the international community, or the devil of the international community.

On 23 September, in his speech at a Jewish community rally in Trafalgar Square organised by the United Jewish Israel Appeal after 9/11, Rabbi Jonathan Sacks focused on the hate directed at Israel, 'as if all the evils of the world have one source: us, we who have striven for peace, for blessing and for life',[7] making no distinction whatsoever between diaspora Jewry and the Israeli state. 'When the history of the twentieth century comes to be written, it will tell a simple story', Sacks said, 'of how fascism came and went; how Soviet communism came and went; and how antisemitism came and stayed'. Using more or less the same words a few months later he added:

> Its success is due to the fact that, like a virus, it mutates. At times it has been directed against Jews as individuals. Today it is directed against Jews as a sovereign people. The common factor is that Jews, uniquely, are denied the right to exist in whatever form their collective existence currently takes.[8]

Melchior was speaking before 9/11; Sacks was speaking twelve days after. What Melchior included in his list of 'libels' against Israel demonstrates the heightened level of anxiety that was already gripping the Jewish diaspora defence community and the Israeli officials tasked with monitoring and responding to antisemitism, but especially that which targeted Israel. Making Israel 'the Jew of the nations' was Melchior's 'red line'. Many reports of the NGO phase of the conference would have confirmed for Melchior that the 'red line' had indeed been crossed. Writing about Durban in the *Jerusalem Report*, Stuart Schoffman insisted: 'It's here, for real: antisemitism, the oldest social disease of the Western world, pernicious as ever ... It didn't die when Hitler shot himself in his bunker'.[9]

Sacks's remarks not only endorsed Melchior's, they also, and more significantly, reflect the way 9/11 almost immediately constituted a watershed moment validating all the dire warnings about a worldwide explosion of antisemitism and making Israel and Jews—with no distinction made between the two—the first victims of the Twin Towers tragedy. 9/11 was therefore crucial in generating global receptivity to the 'new antisemitism' argument, especially when linked, as it mostly was, to the string of events leading up to it: the second intifada, the suicide bombings, the collapse of the Oslo process, the electoral defeat of Prime Minister Ehud Barak and the Durban anti-racism conference.

The subsequent world events beginning with George W. Bush's proclamation of the 'war on terror' and then followed by the invasion of Afghanistan and the war against Iraq, were all factors that led to the strengthening of Israel's geopolitical situation (explored in Chapter 11), a development that made much of the world increasingly receptive to Israel's 'new antisemitism' complaint that the country was 'the persecuted "collective Jew" among the nations'.

* * *

Peter Beaumont, writing in the *Observer* in February 2002, acknowledged the rise in antisemitic attacks across Europe, said to be evidence of 'new antisemitism', which he defined:

> The new antisemitism—say those who argue most strongly for its existence—is not simply limited to attacks on individuals like Rabbi Gigi [Chief Rabbi of Brussels who was assaulted by a group of Arab-speaking youths] and to a spate of attacks on synagogues and Jewish schools and cemeteries. Instead, they say, it is a pernicious and widespread cancer infecting the media and political classes across Europe.[10]

But Beaumont argued that 'the problem with all this talk of a "new antisemitism" is that those who argue hardest for it are dangerously conflating two connected but critically separate phenomena': verifiable attacks on Jews and Jewish properties largely the responsibility of 'disaffected Islamic youths, a group itself that is victim of some of the worst race hate and discrimination in Europe', and 'criticism in the media and political classes of Europe of the policies of [Israeli prime minister] Sharon'.

In Murray Gordon's account, 'the "new antisemitism" first broke out in Western European countries in tandem with the "Al-Aqsa intifada" that began in September 2000'.[11] Nevertheless, at no point in his 17-page pamphlet does he provide a clear definition of what it is. A survey of expressions of antisemitism in a dozen Western European countries largely lays responsibility at the door of Arab or Muslim youth, 'lurid' and unbridled anti-Israel and anti-Zionist incitement involving the blaming of Palestinian deaths on Jews in general. Yet he concludes by admitting that 'What is referred to as the "new antisemitism", which resonates so powerfully in Western Europe today, is not exactly new'.[12] Attacks on Jews spiked before when Israel was in violent confrontation with its neighbours or the Palestinians. What was new was 'European governments and much of the media ... taking a one-sided position on the Israel–Palestine conflict'.

Claims about the 'new antisemitism' were accompanied by highly alarmist judgements about the severity of the intensified antisemitism of the new millennium. 'These are the worst antisemitic days in Europe since the end of the Second World War', wrote Dr Avi Beker, secretary general of the WJC, in April 2002. 'This is really reminiscent of the worst times of Europe', he told CBS News,[13] which also reported that 'the World Jewish Congress reiterated its controversial view that anybody who is against Israel must automatically be antisemitic'. In the same month, *Washington Post* columnist Charles Krauthammer wrote: 'In Europe, it is not very safe to be a Jew ... What is odd is not the antisemitism of today but its relative absence during the past half-century. That was the historical anomaly. Holocaust shame kept the demon corked ... But now the atonement is passed'.[14] Writing in March in the *Daily Mail*, columnist Melanie Phillips, looking on in 'horror' at the escalating violence in the Middle East and the fallout from it in the UK, admitted:

> I have never felt as gripped by such terrible foreboding as I do now ... The terrible thought that Israel may not survive is now forming itself ... And beyond even that, another dreadful anxiety is seeping into the minds of British Jews. The Jewish state, which was supposed by its founders to purge once and for all the poison of antisemitism, has not done so.[15]

She argued that the settlements in occupied territory 'are wrong and should be dismantled; and undoubtedly, human rights abuses are occurring for which there is no excuse', but this did not justify Arab terrorism or antisemitic attacks in the UK.

Among those prepared to call for a 'sense of proportion' when the headlines of so many reports and comment articles painted such a bleak and dangerous picture, was the prominent Liberal Rabbi David Goldberg, who wrote:

> when it comes to the alleged recrudescence of antisemitism in the wake of the intifada ... the notion strikes me as paranoid and exaggerated ... By any objective criteria, the modern, acculturated, broadly accepted, successful Jew in the Western world has never had it so good. We should never be complacent or cease to be vigilant about antisemitism. But at the present time, it is far easier and safer to be a Jew than a Muslim, a black person or an east European asylum seeker.[16]

The Israeli columnist Eliahu Salpeter averred that

> we could say we are again witness to a worldwide outbreak of hatred of the Jews. If, however, the differentiation between the 'old' [antisemitism which has its roots in Christianity] and the 'new' [now flourishing under the influence of Islamic extremism] is correct, then talk of a 'plague' is less realistic.[17]

Israel will only make matters worse, Salpeter argued if it fails to 'make every effort to separate antisemitism from anti-Zionism in the consciousness of the non-Jewish world'.

Brian Klug suggested that if there is an equivalence between the individual Jew in the old classical version of antisemitism and the state of Israel there can be no Herzlian Zionist solution to antisemitism since Israel 'cannot "take itself off" to another corner of the globe'.[18] If Israel really is 'the collective Jew among the nations', all it can do is 'fight for survival, defying the world and keeping it at bay'. It would mean that Zionism had failed. In an essay that does not confront directly the question of 'new antisemitism', Leon Wieseltier nonetheless contextualised contemporary antisemitism in such a way as to make clear that whatever Israel was facing by way of terror or the anti-Zionism and antisemitism in the Arab world, and despite the 'rise in anti-Jewish words and deeds in Europe', American Jewish imagination of disaster, of a 'second Holocaust', a 'new Kristallnacht', is completely groundless.[19] 'The Jewish genius for worry has served the Jews well, but Hitler is dead', irrespective of the fact that a few weeks earlier on 15 April 2002 in Washington, only a few blocks from the Holocaust Museum, Benjamin Netanyahu compared Yasser Arafat to Hitler.

'The problem with typological thinking about history', Wieseltier writes, 'is that it is not historical thinking at all. It is ahistorical thinking. It obscures and obliterates all the differences between historical circumstances in favour of a gross, immutable, edifying similarity'.

Anthony Julius noted that there was 'a developing sense that antisemitism itself is on the increase. But what is the evidence to support this intuition? It is, in the main, quite paltry, uncertain stuff'.[20] Though he accepted the existence of some of the features of the 'new antisemitism' discourse, seeing in anti-Zionism the message of a desire to dismantle the state of Israel—'a kind of antisemitism', he said, 'indistinguishable in its compass and consequences from any that has yet been inflicted on Jews'—he followed Wieseltier in seeing a lack of perspective on the past: 'the exercise of comparing relative levels of antisemitism in England over (say) the past 30 years is rather like debating the precedence of a flea over a gnat'. He concluded:

> While antisemitism cannot be eradicated, it can be kept at bay. It is too integral to western culture to be destroyed, but its menace can in large measure be neutralised. The threat of antisemitism, though it has always existed, exists at different times in varying degrees of intensity. While the threat today is real, and in many parts of the world, especially serious, this is not so here, in England, today.

Julius's *Guardian* article was included in slightly modified form in a collection, published in 2003, devoted to addressing whether there was such a thing as a 'new antisemitism': *A New Antisemitism? Debating Judeophobia in 21st Century Britain*.[21] By then, with continuing bloodshed in the Israel–Palestine conflict and more headline-making incidents of antisemitic violence and vandalism, discussion and argument about the meaning of what was happening intensified. The collection, jointly published by Profile Books and JPR, was not an evenly balanced set of essays, but to a degree did reflect the diversity of views on whether such a thing as 'new antisemitism' existed. Though not new, use of the word 'Judeophobia' in the subtitle to refer to hostility to Jews had become more common, indicating that the editors agreed with those who no longer considered the word 'antisemitism' as adequate to encapsulate the new form or forms of hatred to which Jews and Israel were being subjected.[22] In their conclusion, tellingly titled 'Globalized Judeophobia and its ramifications for British society', they wrote:[23]

> Therefore, is the question of the 'new antisemitism' just a question of collective psychosis—a hypersensitive minority traumatised by the events of 1933–45 and haunted by fears of genocidal victimization? The contributions to this volume appear rational enough to refute this allegation. Most argue that there is indeed cause producing an effect.

They said that 'the "new antisemitism" is not primarily to be found yet on the streets in Britain', rather 'it is to be found among certain elites: left-liberal elites in the media, churches, universities and trade unions. The phenomenon in evidence is more accurately described as "Judeophobia", as it involves a manifest hostility towards Jews, rather than the propagation of the racial ideologies of the old antisemitism'.[24]

As we will see, in the following years proponents of 'new antisemitism' theory largely rejected this distinction. But in the editors' final pages they used the 'Judeophobia' formulation as the foundation on which to build the case that hatred of the state of Israel constitutes the most extreme and vicious hostility to Jews at the beginning of the twenty-first century. 'Judeophobia provides a coalition of interest in Britain for the new left, the far-right, radical Islamists, and human rights campaigners and activists', they wrote, 'who may be more well-meaning, but in their singular obsession with Israel contribute to its demonization'.[25] They claimed that enemies of the West—marginalised geopolitically as the USA, its allies and the newly democratic pro-Western former communist states declared the triumph of liberal democracy and free-market values—regrouped, using the outbreak of the Al-Aqsa intifada and the Durban anti-racism conference to revive the 'Zionism is racism' campaign. Triumphalist Islamist groups, and elements of the old Marxist hard left, both openly and passively encouraged by developing countries and Western Europeans, constituted a 'new anti-Zionist coalition', boosted by elements who judged that American imperialism was getting what it deserved with the destruction on 9/11. Anti-Zionism appealed to the 'world's angry and frustrated losers on both the personal and state levels [and resonated beyond] these narrow circles because it has strong ideological roots in both traditional Christian theology and radical Islamist thought but more relevantly here in Marxist-Leninist ideology'. Wrapping up this trenchant argument, Iganski and Kosmin wrote:

> Moreover anti-Zionism seems to have a particular resonance among western-ers burdened by post colonial guilt who picture Israelis as European colonial interlopers in the Middle East. As liberal secularists they cannot abide the Zionist narrative that they are actually witnessing an exiled remnant returning to its ancient homeland as foretold in biblical prophecy.[26]

Although Jews in the UK were well placed to repel the 'continuing campaign of vilification' against them, 'Judeophobia could rapidly undermine aspirations for Britain to be a truly plural and tolerant society'. It is therefore 'incumbent upon the government, criminal justice system and the good people in every city and county in the land to stand up and proclaim that they will not allow Judeopho-bia to become an established fact in British society'.[27]

Whether or not you agree with this presentation of the nature and conse-quences of 'new antisemitism', it is a powerful statement of one interpretation of the phenomenon. As the selection of interpretations I quote above show, however, a variety of different approaches continued to circulate. However, there were significant developments taking place during 2000 to 2004, which began to have a major impact on the landscape.

*　　*　　*

Before the al-Aqsa intifada, the Durban UN anti-racism conference and 9/11, the Israeli government's policy to exert hegemony over the monitor-ing and combatting of antisemitism by Jewish groups worldwide was formally in abeyance, as I explained above (see Chapter 4). On the ground, however, it was still in place. The Israel Government Monitoring Forum on Antisemi-tism was still the state's vehicle for implementing policy on antisemitism, but given wider developments in the Israel–Palestine conflict, it is not surprising that antisemitism was not seen as a priority. The fallout from the assassination of Prime Minister Yitzhak Rabin, the increasingly tortuous efforts to turn the Oslo Accords into a permanent resolution of the Israel–Palestine conflict, the launching of Operation Grapes of Wrath by Prime Minister Shimon Peres, the intensive suicide bombing campaign, the collapse of talks in July 2000 between Prime Minister Ehud Barak and Yasser Arafat to reach a final status agreement, Ariel Sharon's controversial visit to the Temple Mount, the beginning of the al-Aqsa intifada in September—this was a period characterised by thousands of deaths, ongoing bloodshed and political turmoil with six prime ministers in office between 1995 and 2006, and it cast an increasingly dark shadow over the

Oslo process, which many expected, erroneously, would lead to the establishment of a Palestinian state alongside the state of Israel.

Nonetheless, behind the scenes, changes were afoot. In 1997, Cabinet
Secretary Danny Naveh replaced Elyakim Rubinstein and assumed Israeli
government responsibility for combatting antisemitism. Perhaps indicating a
more assertive role, Naveh advocated global legislation that would limit access
to sources of hate literature such as neo-Nazi websites on the internet. Many
American Jewish groups opposed this approach, however, because it suggested
limits on free speech. But it was also the case that, as David Weinberg wrote:
'back then some American Jewish leaders felt that global antisemitism wasn't
Israel's fight, that the struggle to educate and legislate against antisemitism
should be left to them. They resisted Israeli attempts to lead or coordinate
anti-antisemitism activity.'[28]

In 2000, the Israel Government Monitoring Forum on Antisemitism was
replaced by the Coordination Forum for Countering Antisemitism (CFCA).
The new name itself suggests that the government had decided on a more
proactive role in antisemitism matters. This seems even more likely given that
Rabbi Michael Melchior, deputy foreign minister in the Barak government, as
well as minister for diaspora and social affairs, was given the brief to chair the
beefed-up body. This was a clear upgrade since the previous body was chaired
by a government official not a minister. The CFCA described itself in these
words:[29]

> The Coordination Forum for Countering Antisemitism is a National Forum
> that monitors antisemitic activities throughout the world. It coordinates
> the struggle against this phenomenon with various government bodies and
> Jewish organisations around the world. The Forum receives information on
> antisemitic activity from a variety of sources, checks this information and
> publishes it in regular reports.
>
> Israel, as the Jewish State, gives the highest priority to the security of Jewish
> communities around the world and has undertaken to do everything in its
> power to eradicate anti-Jewish activity. The struggle against antisemitism
> must unfortunately persist and requires our constant attention. This entails
> learning and understanding the extent of the phenomenon and recruiting all
> the relevant resources to fight it wherever and whenever it appears.

Fine rhetoric, but as I have shown above, not an accurate reflection of what the
Israeli government was actually doing. Around the same time as the creation
of the CFCA, the Mossad began to increase its 'involvement in tracking down
and monitoring outbreaks of antisemitism and violence against Jews in different
parts of the world, in view of the threat to Jewish communities and institutions

abroad', wrote the security expert Yossi Melman in May 2002.[30] 'To this end, it has beefed up cooperation and exchanges of information with the relevant authorities in the various countries where there have been widespread incidents of antisemitism'. This is almost certainly a reference to, among others, Jewish community defence groups given that the news about 'beefed-up' Mossad involvement emerged 'from a public lecture given by the head of the Mossad's research department on antisemitism, called "Yossi", in the framework of the Jewish Agency's Forum for Zionist Thinking', wrote Melman. 'The lecture was due to have been delivered by the deputy head of the Mossad but he was unable to attend'.

By the beginning of 2002, Israeli government thinking on antisemitism had evolved further. Melchior chaired a press conference, accompanied by Professor Irwin Cotler, the Canadian MP, and Per Ahlmark, former Swedish deputy prime minister, and announced the establishment of a new body, the International Commission to Combat Antisemitism (ICCA). 'We are trying to create an overall body which is not specifically Jewish ... in which the various Jewish bodies, of course, as experts and as parts of the NGO community will be a part, but it will be concentrated on non-Jews'.

A clear indication of the main focus of the new commission was the presence of Cotler. Speaking immediately after Melchior, Cotler opened his statement by defining 'new antisemitism':[31]

> We are today witnessing a new anti-Jewishness—an anti-Jewishness, which is a dramatic transformation in the sense that it is grounded in classical antisemitism, but distinguishable from it—anchored in the 'Zionism is racism' resolution, but which goes beyond it. If we needed one line to summarise it, it would be: the discrimination against, or denial of Jewish particularity or peoplehood anywhere, whenever that particularity or peoplehood is Jewish. In other words, the singling out of Israel and the Jewish people for differential and discriminatory treatment in the international arena; traditional antisemitism was the denial of the right of individual Jews to live as equal members in a society.
>
> The new anti-Jewishness is the denial of the right of the Jewish people to live as equal members of the family of nations ... All that has happened is that there was a move from discrimination against the Jews as individuals to discrimination against the Jews as a people ...
>
> But it is the Jewish people in its collective sense, where Israel has become a word—the Jew among the nations—in which this new anti-Jewishness finds expression.

This definition is, to all intents and purposes, identical to the one he gave at the 1992 Brussels WJC conference, My Brother's Keeper (see above Chapter 3). What then is the significance of this deployment by the Israeli government of Cotler's definition and of the new Forum?

In fact, what was being called the ICCA did not immediately materialise as a functioning entity, probably as a result of the definitive collapse of the Clinton sponsored 'peace process' and of the 2001 general election, which resulted in a change of government from Barak's Labour-led coalition to the coalition led by Ariel Sharon and his Likud Party. By March 2003, Natan Sharansky had been appointed minister for diaspora, social and Jerusalem affairs, and he was also Chairman of the CFCA. A press release dated 23 March 2003 shows that the Israel cabinet was now regularly receiving reports from the CFCA on anti-semitism developments worldwide. The press release stated that 'Sharansky informed the ministers that the report of the Coordination Forum for Counter-ing Antisemitism for the year 2002 had been published several days earlier. The report shows a constant increase in acts of antisemitism, especially in Western Europe'.[32]

The new body, now called the Global Forum for Combatting Antisemitism (GFCA), which finally came into being in late 2003, was launched formally by Sharansky in February 2004 at a gathering in Jerusalem of 90 Jewish leaders from around the world. A CFCA press release described the body as 'Under the auspices of the Minister for Jerusalem and Diaspora Affairs, the Prime Minister's Office, Jerusalem', and stated that the task of the GFCA was to 'plan diplomatic initiatives against antisemitism, including the roll-back of Arab and Islamic antisemitism by enlisting the courts and regulatory agencies'.[33]

It seems that a highlight of the gathering was the forum's agreement on a 'defi-nition of "new" antisemitism':

This meeting of Sharansky's Forum may best be remembered for a unique intellectual achievement: a first-of-its-kind agreement among Jewish leaders worldwide on a definition of 'new antisemitism'. After lengthy discussion and debate, Global Forum participants agreed, unanimously, that 'when criticism of Israeli policies involves the application of gross political and diplomatic double standards against the State of Israel, or invokes demonizing termi-nology against Israel or Zionism, or denies Israel the fundamental right to exist—that criticism cannot be regarded as legitimate; rather it clearly consti-tutes antisemitism and should be labelled as such.

The range of organisations represented indicates the extent to which the fight against antisemitism was becoming increasingly institutionalised on a global level, with Israel now endeavouring to insert itself again into the forefront as principal coordinator.[34] Shortly before the GFCA meeting, Sharansky inaugurated Israel's National Day to Combat Antisemitism, the 'first national day of solidarity with Jewish communities around the world suffering from the rising tide of antisemitism'.[35] The day designated, 27 January, was chosen to coincide with the annual European commemoration of the Holocaust. 'Antisemitism threatens the Jewish people, the very existence of the state of Israel, and in fact the entire world', said Sharansky. 'We must raise awareness in Israel, strengthen the solidarity between Israel and world Jewry, and increase Israeli citizens' sense of responsibility regarding events in the Diaspora'. David Weinberg was then working for Sharansky and was the GFCA coordinator. Recalling events at the time, he later wrote, quoting Sharansky:

'The State of Israel has decided to take the gloves off and implement a coordinated counteroffensive against antisemitism', Sharansky said. 'The State of Israel will play, as it always should, a central role in defending the Jewish people'. Sharansky's intellectual leadership brought discipline and focus to global Jewish community activity against antisemitism.[36]

This was indeed a significant symbolic moment since, as established above, Sharansky was formalising a major departure from Israeli policy and Zionist ideology on antisemitism. Nonetheless, it is inconceivable that he would have loosened his deep commitment to Zionism to such a degree as to agree with the view of Israel's *Haaretz* newspaper at the time that 'The anxiety of some one million Jews [in Europe], members of proud and Zionist communities, should trouble their brethren in Israel, if only because Israeli policies and actions are a reason—or at least an excuse—for much of the local expressions of hostility to Jews'.[37] The paper continued: 'While the Israeli government cannot be expected to shape diplomatic or military policies according to their ramifications on Diaspora Jewry, those ramifications cannot be ignored. The strength and well-being of those Jews, particularly those living in the West, contribute significantly to the Jewish state's overall strategic strength'.

Yet other reasons were being advanced, beyond the confines of government institutions, for showing more than just verbal concern. The Jewish People Policy Planning Institute (JPPPI), set up by the Jewish Agency in 2002 ('Planning' was later dropped from the title), was another new body with antisemitism high on its agenda. It held a discussion on 11 March 2004 on the subject of 'Global strategic developments—the impact on the Middle East and the Jewish people'. The high-level list of participants included six representatives of the Foreign Ministry, the Finance Ministry and the Prime Minister's Office; one from each of the ADL, Israel Democracy Institute, AJC, Centre for European Studies Ben-Gurion University, Rothschild Foundation, the Begin-Sadat Centre; and eight from JPPPI itself. Antisemitism was the fifth of ten topics discussed, with Ambassador Dennis Ross from the US, Chairman of JPPI's Board of Directors, chairing. It was agreed that antisemitism would rise. Islamic antisemitism threatened the continent and greater efforts from European governments to fight its spread can be expected. As for implications for Jews, 'A comprehensive strategy to combat antisemitism and minimize the damage caused by it (for example, through improving crisis management systems) should be developed. *In addition, momentum can be exploited to encourage immigration to Israel'* (emphasis added).

The new level of engagement and the drive to assume leadership were unprecedented. And while the larger and well-established diaspora Jewish organisations that were investing very heavily in the fight against antisemitism retained independence of action, their reluctance to submit to Israel's earlier attempts at hegemonic leadership were now being put aside.

At the same time, a major effort to enlist the support of international organisations in Europe in combatting antisemitism was bearing fruit. Michael Whine reported on these efforts in 2004:

Jewish organizations led by the major American groups, have tried to alert international organizations to the threat that antisemitism and antisemitic violence in Europe again poses to Jewish communities and to democracy itself. At a series of conferences of the OSCE and the European institutions, these Jewish groups have overcome governments' reluctance to address the issue and have focused attention particularly on the threats posed by the spill-over of Middle East tensions and the antisemitic messages promoted by Arab states, their media and Islamist bodies.[38]

Notwithstanding the extent of institutional mobilisation against antisemitism—which was increasingly predicated on the belief that it was largely emanating from Islamic sources, particularly in Europe, was focused ever-more sharply on Israel and Zionism, clearly showed that there was little or no difference between anti-Zionism and antisemitism and assumed Jews worldwide were implicated in the ongoing 'ethnic cleansing' of Palestinians—there remained much debate in the public space about whether what was happening was a 'new antisemitism', an exaggeration based on alarmist responses to very serious, but still rare anti-Jewish incidents, a direct result of the bloody conflict on the ground in Israel–Palestine and so on.

In July 2004, at a gathering of Catholic and Jewish intellectuals in Buenos Aires, the Catholic Church formally agreed to a joint statement that equated anti-Zionism and antisemitism, the first time the church had taken such a step.[39] Abe Foxman, director of the ADL, was adamant that the 'Palestine–Israel conflict has been hijacked, resulting in an explosion of global antisemitism'. (Note that he does not say here a 'global explosion of antisemitism', but emphasises that there is some form of antisemitism that is global in nature.) He continues: 'Anti-Zionism has long been a code word for antisemitism. We have to define for ourselves when anti-Israel and anti-Zionism is antisemitism'. And Foxman was clear: 'anti-Zionism is antisemitism. There should be no doubt about that'.[40]

Acknowledging that 'genuine antisemitism—racial antipathy towards Jews— is resurgent in Europe', Max Hastings, former editor of the *Daily Telegraph* and the London *Evening Standard*, argued that Israel's repression of the Palestinian people is fuelling the resurgence of antisemitism. 'Attempts to equate anti-Zionism, or even criticism of Israeli policy, with antisemitism reflect a pitiful intellectual sloth', he wrote in March 2004. 'The most important service the world's Jews can render to Israel today is to persuade its people that the only plausible result of their government's behaviour is a terrible loneliness in the world'.[41] In February 2004, BBC News Online asked '12 experts on Jewish affairs from Europe and Israel to reflect on two questions: Is antisemitism really increasing? Is hostility towards Israeli policy in the Middle East becoming anti-Jewish?'[42] Opinions ranged from such comments as: 'People here [in Israel] have a sense of systematic stigmatisation and even a demonization of Israel' (Robert Wistrich); 'The line between valid criticism and antisemitism is being crossed' (Peter Sichrovsky, Austrian MEP); 'Jews are attacked because of their alleged unconditional support for the policies of the state of Israel' (Jean-Yves Camus, French political scientist); to 'Some people in the US have the idea that this continent is somehow a hotbed of antisemitism. This is absurd' (David Aaronovitch, UK columnist); 'It is wrong to talk of a new wave of antisemitism gripping Europe ... [This] idea is ... in part stirred up those Jewish communities in Europe who ally themselves closely with Israel, but also the Sharon government ... [which is] exploiting fears of antisemitism to persuade Europe's Jews to emigrate' (Henry Wajnblum, Union of Progressive Jews in Belgium); 'I don't think we can talk about antisemitism creeping back into Europe. This is a notion Israel has come up with in order to dismiss any criticism of its policies. It is nothing but propaganda' (Anneke Mouthaan, Another Jewish Voice, The Netherlands).

In a tightly and sensitively argued article in *Salmagundi*, the historian Martin Jay, professor of history emeritus at the University of California, Berkeley, attributed partial responsibility for the 'upsurge of global antisemitism'—the 'new antisemitism'—to the actions of the Sharon government on the grounds that: 'An account of antisemitism that assumes that the victims are in no way involved in unleashing the animosities they suffer cannot be historically persuasive'.[43] Jay, who is Jewish, attracted criticism for 'blaming the Jews'. One critic, Edward

Alexander, Professor of English Literature emeritus at the University of Washington, wrote:

> Jews who assign responsibility for anti-Jewish aggression to Jewish misbehaviour not only save themselves from the unpleasant and often dangerous task of coming to the defence of the Jews under attack but also retain the delightful charms of good conscience. Hitler's professors (to borrow the title of Max Weinreich's famous book of 1946) were the first to make antisemitism academically respectable and complicit in murder. They have now been succeeded by Arafat's professors: not only the boycotters, not only the advocates of suicide bombings, but also the fellow travellers like Martin Jay.[44]

Closing your mind to uncomfortable truths and relying on turning Palestinians into Nazis, is standard fare when the objective is protecting Israel at any cost.

Although there is a degree of consensus among these examples that there had been a worsening of expressions of antisemitism over the previous four years at least, there was little agreement about what that antisemitism consisted of, who or what in the countries affected was responsible for it, exactly what kind of threat it posed to individual Jews and Jewish communities, and whether Israel was in part responsible for it because of its alleged brutality towards the Palestinians—except among the growing number of voices endorsing the 'new antisemitism' argument.

Affirming that anti-Zionism was antisemitism, that criticism of Israel or of Zionism was antisemitic, greatly simplified matters. As did constant repetition of Cotler's definition of it: 'Israel is the "collective Jew" among the nations'.

The fallout from 9/11—including the spread of conspiracy theories about Jewish/Israeli responsibility for the event—not only boosted receptivity to the 'new antisemitism' discourse, it also greatly facilitated the codification of 'new antisemitism', which is discussed in the next chapter.

7

The Codification of 'New Antisemitism': The EUMC 'Working Definition'

By the early years of the twenty-first century the 'new antisemitism' narrative may have become the new orthodoxy, but there was no clamour for a formal, new definition of antisemitism. Among some scholars, antisemitism research-ers and Jewish monitoring groups there were a few people actively considering drafting one. This begs the question of what they considered to be the old one, and what was wrong with it. The very fact that the notion of 'new antisemitism' appeared to satisfy so many as a description of post-2000 Jew-hatred, seems to suggest that there was a consensus in many circles as to what antisemitism was, thereby obviating the need for a formal new definition.

Certainly, those few who were pressing for something new did not see things that way. For them, the central issue was indeed that existing definitions did not account for the 'new antisemitism'. And it is true that while the phrase 'new antisemitism' was popping up everywhere and in Jewish and Israeli circles was widely accepted as a correct appellation for the antisemitism *du jour*, we know that it was still a contested notion. In any event, given that it was quite clear that alleged antisemitism directed at Israel and Zionism were central to conceptions of 'new antisemitism', any new definition would naturally focus on those targets.

The view taken by one of the key voices in the demand for a new definition, and in the growing Israeli academic antisemitism industry, confirms this. In a 2002 paper written by Porat, where she incorrectly stated that discussion of 'new antisemitism' only began in 2000, she also wrote that 'the term still does not have a definition agreed upon by everyone, certainly not by the encyclope-dias. The situation is still at the boil: waves of violence are carried against the background of constant and increasing antisemitic and anti-Zionist expressions reaching world public opinion through the various communications media'.[1]

But at the time—or possibly even before—she wrote the above, Cotler himself was reprising his definition at the January 2002 press conference chaired by then deputy foreign minister, Melchior. Once Sharansky took over, and the new body, the GFCA got off the ground, the pace of activity on antisemitism at the Israeli government level quickened. As we have seen in Chapter 6, at its first interna-tional gathering in early 2004 the new GFCA agreed on a definition. Soon after,

Sharansky himself coined a definition which was contained in a short article published as a Foreword in *Jewish Political Studies Review*, the journal of the right-wing Jerusalem Center for Public Affairs, in autumn 2004.[2] Following the Cotler understanding that 'whereas classical antisemitism is aimed at the Jewish people or Jewish religion, the "new antisemitism" is aimed at the Jewish state', and since the key problem was how 'to distinguish legitimate criticism of Israel from antisemitism', his definition took the form of three tests, which he called the '3 Ds':

Demonisation: when the Jewish state is being demonised; Israel's actions are being blown out of all sensible proportion; Israelis are compared to Nazis, Palestinian refugee camps to Auschwitz. This is antisemitism.

Double-standards: criticism of Israel is applied selectively; singled out by the UN for human rights abuses while major abusers are ignored. This is antisemitism.

Delegitimisation: when Israel's fundamental right to exist is denied, alone among all peoples of the world. This is antisemitism.

Sharansky made a special point of emphasising that the borders between 'antisemitism, anti-Americanism, and anti-Westernism have become almost completely blurred', thereby making Israel and the US partners in a 'clash of civilisations' war of which the fight against antisemitism was an integral part. He argued that the level of naked, state-sponsored antisemitic propaganda in Arab and Muslim countries was so egregious, antisemitism should become a much more prominent issue in the bilateral relations between the US and the Arab and Muslim worlds.

Revisiting the definition agreed at the GFCA gathering in February, it is obvious that that text already reflected Sharansky's thinking. Two of the '3 Ds' are in the text: 'double-standards' and 'demonising terminology', and the third, 'delegitimisation' is present, but not used, in the words 'denying Israel the fundamental right to exist'.[3]

Sharansky's '3 Ds' have certainly had an impact on understandings of 'new antisemitism', and as we will see, in some major jurisdictions, the '3 Ds' formula was adopted as a standard test for when criticism of Israel becomes antisemitism. But far more significant in the longer term has been a document rather inconspicuously posted on a website in Vienna in 2005.

* * *

In March that year, the European Union Monitoring Centre on Racism and Xenophobia (EUMC), located in the Austrian capital, published a 'working definition' of antisemitism on its website, although it was dated 28 January. It emphasised that it was 'part of an ongoing process having no legal basis', and that it was one of several articles on its website that appeared under the disclaimer that they 'do not necessarily reflect the official position of the EUMC'.[4] Five years later, the then head of research at the CST, Dave Rich, would write: '[the 'working definition] has become a metaphor for all debates about contemporary antisemitism over the past decade'.[5]

The creation of the EUMC in 1997 was a political act: to provide the data to formulate policies to fight racism. For its drafters, the 'working definition' was officially supposed to deal with a specific political problem and contribute to the taking of more effective action against antisemitism by governments and law-enforcement agencies. And the framing of the 'working definition' was taking place in a period when the politicisation of the monitoring, analysis and discussion of contemporary antisemitism had markedly intensified. From the very beginning the EUMC was subject to political lobbying and pressure from all kinds of European and non-European political organisations.

The 'working definition' was not conceived or drafted exclusively by academics, and those involved have explicitly stated that 'it is not a theoretical academic definition'.[6] So, how did it come about?

The AJC's veteran antisemitism specialist, Kenneth Stern, actually credits Porat, then head of the Tel Aviv University Stephen Roth Institute for the Study of Racism and Antisemitism (the former Mossad funded Project for the Study of Antisemitism), for first articulating the idea of a 'common definition' in discussion with him at a conference in Berlin in April 2004. But it was Stern himself, dissatisfied with the definition of antisemitism used in the EUMC's report on antisemitism in 2002–2003 released by the EUMC in March or April 2004, who personally took the initiative to draft a new definition.[7] That draft was published on the Roth Institute website in a paper by Stern called 'Proposal for a redefinition of antisemitism' in July 2004.[8] He shared the draft with some unspecified others. Then, at a conference in Israel in October that year,[9] in his own words:

I recall bus rides … discussing and tweaking the definition. In particular Mike Whine [CST], Jeremy Jones [Australia/Israel and Jewish Affairs Council], Roni Stauber [TAU Roth Institute], Felice Gaer [AJC Blaustein Institute], [Professor] Yehuda Bauer, Michael Berenbaum [former head of the USHMM Holocaust Research Center] and [Rabbi] Andy Baker [AJC International Affairs director] were very much part of that process.

He continues: 'What we produced was changed somewhat by EUMC, after a very exhausting meeting between Beate Winkler [director, EUMC], Mike [Michael] Whine, Andy Baker and my AJC colleague Deidre Berger [AJC Berlin]. But the key components remained'.

Indeed, they did. Stern's first draft and the final 'working definition' are remarkably similar. From both of Stern's papers it is quite clear that the primary motivation behind what became the 'working definition' was creating a definition that provided a basis for determining when criticism of Israel is antisemitic. His main criticism of the definition used in the EUMC's *Manifestations of Antisemitism in the EU 2002–03* report is that it failed to provide this. But even the most cursory reading of the EUMC report proves this to be incorrect.[10]

However, Stern was opaque about how his personal initiative morphed into a process adopted by the EUMC and then a document officially released by them. To establish this, we need to backtrack. The available evidence seems to confirm that the link came about through the relationship between AJC's Andy Baker and Beate Winkler.[11] As Stern wrote in 2010: 'my colleague Andy Baker, probably alone in the organized Jewish community, had not blasted EUMC and its then director, Beate Winkler, over the earlier suppressed report, and had smartly developed a working relationship with her instead'.[12]

The report he is referring to was prepared by the Zentrum für Antisemitismusforschung at the Technische Universitat Berlin (ZfA) in 2002, but was shelved by the EUMC Board in rather murky circumstances, after it questioned the researchers' findings that young Muslims were responsible for many attacks on Jews. A representative of the European Jewish Congress (EJC) on the Board leaked the report to the press in December 2003, just a week after the bombing of a Jewish school near Paris and suicide attacks on two Istanbul synagogues, complaining that appeasement of Europe's large Muslim population was behind the decision not to publish, and plunged the EUMC into a major public controversy. The EUMC's official line was that the report was of 'poor quality', that its methodology was flawed and its findings deemed to be biased.[13] But it was widely believed that the real reasons for the suppression of the report were different. Some members of the Board were unhappy that hostility to Israel was included and that the report laid the blame on young Muslims and pro-Palestinian perpetrators for much of the post-2000 upsurge in antisemitic incidents in Europe. 'Flawed methodology' meant an inappropriate definition of antisemitism. The authors vehemently rejected these charges.

Winkler was particularly embarrassed by the affair. Baker, seeing that Winkler felt damaged by the criticism and had no plan for restoring the EUMC's reputation, suggested that she could extricate herself and the EUMC from the crisis by getting the EUMC to develop a definition that would clarify where criticism of Israel became antisemitism, and to do that by first consulting with Jewish antisemitism experts and groups.[14] She agreed. It seems reasonable to assume that Baker at the very least informed Stern about this at some point, thereby triggering the drafting process that Stern undertook, which then came under the auspices of the EUMC.

The 2004 EUMC report, *Manifestations of Antisemitism in the EU 2002–03*, lamented the fact that no common definition of antisemitism is used by the sources providing data for the report, but the authors state quite categorically: 'Future data collection and assessment should be commonly based on the definition of antisemitism *provided in this report*'). And there is an extensive and comprehensive section that ends with the formulation of their definition. It therefore seems reasonable to conclude that the EUMC's official position is expressed in their report on antisemitism, which was adopted by their Management Board.[15] In that definition there is a full exposition of the basis on which the report distinguishes between anti-Zionism and antisemitism, between criticism of Israel and antisemitism. It is this rationale that Stern objected to and which he sought to supersede in his draft, which eventually became the 'working definition'.

In the initial stage of discussions about Stern's draft, and in the subsequent 'wider' consultation on the draft, only people favourably inclined towards the idea of the 'new antisemitism' were invited to comment on the text.[16] According to the EUMC these were the EJC, the CST (UK), the Consistoire of Paris, the Stephen Roth Institute, the Berlin Antisemitism Task Force, AJC, the Blaustein Institute for the Advancement of Human Rights (part of AJC), ADL, B'nai B'rith International, the Tolerance Unit of ODIHR-OSCE and Professor Yehuda Bauer, adviser to the International Task Force on the Holocaust (eventually to become the International Holocaust Remembrance Alliance, IHRA), and others. Porat characterises this by saying: 'Quite a number of scholars and institutions took part in this attempt to meet the challenge':[17] Whine sees this somewhat differently. In his account of the process, the EUMC was not satisfied with the definition in the 2002–2003 antisemitism report and was also troubled that no two experts could agree on one. '[T]herefore', he writes, '[The EUMC] asked *selected* [emphasis added] Jewish NGOs and academics to provide a simple working definition that would encompass antisemitic demonization of Israel, and which could also be used by their own RAXEN network of national focal points[18] and by law enforcement agencies',[19] referring to 'final draft negotiations' involving 'representatives of the American Jewish Committee and European Jewish Congress'. But while the EUMC list above gives the impression of being substantial and broad-based, almost all are Jewish organisations, some with very close institutional links to each other. There were no independent academic experts. Porat's claim that 'The one-page "Working Definition of Antisemitism" (WDA) ... evolved as a result of the concerted efforts of a large number of institutes and individual experts [whose] efforts lasted for two years (2003–2004), during which time many questions were elaborated regarding both the principles and parameters of the definition',[20] simply does not accord with the facts. Moreover, the fact that the final version of the 'working definition' released in

2005 was so very close to Stern's original draft also casts very serious doubt on the claims made that it was the result of wide consultation with a range of experts.[21]

In brief, the content of the 'working definition' comprises a short opening definition, followed by two lists. Each list, made up of five points, is prefaced by this statement: 'Contemporary examples of antisemitism … could, taking into account the overall context, include'—and the five examples follow. The first list focuses on what are, for want of a better word, classical manifestations of antisemitism, the antisemitism which is not new. The second list contains examples all focusing on Israel and Zionism. The 'working definition' does *not* state that the examples *are* manifestations of antisemitism, but that they *could be*. The second list could be regarded as a breakdown of the essential components of 'new antisemitism'.

The crucial difference between Stern's original draft and the final text is this element of conditionality. The sentence prefacing Stern's list of classical manifestations of antisemitism reads: 'Contemporary examples of antisemitism in public life, the media, schools, the workplace and in the religious sphere include, but are not limited to', etc.

The sentence prefacing his list of examples focusing on Israel and Zionism reads: 'Examples of the ways in which antisemitism manifests itself with regard to the State of Israel include'.[22]

Quite clearly, Stern was convinced that the examples were always, in every instance, antisemitic. He could not have been pleased when the review process instigated by Winkler resulted in the inclusion of this significant, though ultimately widely ignored, element of conditionality.

Whine bracketed the April 2004 Berlin Declaration on antisemitism of the Organization for Security and Cooperation in Europe (OSCE) and the EUMC 'working definition' as significant: 'Of the initiatives undertaken by European organizations in recent years to combat antisemitism, [these] two appear likely to be more effective than others'.[23] However, referring specifically to the 'working definition', he also wrote: 'Will it lower the number of future antisemitic activities or mute antisemitic expressions? The year 2004 was better than 2005 in terms of antisemitic violence'.

The initiators of the 'working definition' were encouraged by the international response. It was 'Unofficially adopted by the participants of the OSCE's Conference on antisemitism and on Other Forms of Intolerance in Cordoba in June 2005'.[24] Six years later Porat wrote:

Barely half a year [after publication], reference to the working definition was made by the participants of the next OSCE conference (Cordoba) as a matter of fact. Since that time, numerous national and international bodies used the definition, cited it, or recommended using it.[25] These included the UK National Union of Students (2007); the US State Department (2008); and the London Declaration of the Interparliamentary Coalition for Combating Antisemitism (2009). Courts of justice (in Lithuania and Germany) also found it useful, as did law-enforcement agencies in a number of countries preparing police officers to investigate general hate crimes, not necessarily directed against Jews. To facilitate its use, the Working Definition has been translated into thirty-three languages used by the fifty-six OSCE member states.[26]

Support also came from the US Commission on Civil Rights, and in 2006 the All-Party Parliamentary Inquiry into Antisemitism urged the British government to adopt it formally. It was also said that the 'working definition' had been 'recommended internationally for adoption by universities and law enforcement agencies'.

In August 2012 a bill passed in the California state legislature, which 'calls upon [educational institutions in the state] to increase their efforts to swiftly and unequivocally condemn acts of antisemitism on their campuses', cited the EUMC

> working definition in support of its decision. The text concludes that colleges and universities should 'utilize existing resources, such as the European Union Agency for Fundamental Rights' [FRA, which succeeded the EUMC in 2007] working definition of antisemitism, to help guide campus discussion about, and promote, as appropriate, educational programmes for combatting antisemitism on their campuses.

The bill passed without discussion.

In 2010, Whine surveyed the growth of institutional means and methods of combatting antisemitism throughout the decade, singling out the EUMC 'working definition' as '[having] been of real lasting benefit'.[27] An interlinked series of gatherings took place under the auspices of the OSCE, the Council of Europe, ECRI, and the EU, with the UN (seen at the beginning of the decade as a primary source of the 'new antisemitism', particularly after the 2001 Durban anti-racism conference, by many Jewish groups and activists) making its own contribution by denouncing antisemitism in 2002 and 2005, and establishing 27 January as the International Day of Commemoration for Holocaust Victims, as well as issuing an unequivocal condemnation of Holocaust denial signed by all states except Iran. The organisational 'map' was extended further by increasing numbers of parliamentarians coming together to condemn and seek ways of combatting antisemitism. Whine concluded:[28]

It might be argued that ten years of diplomatic effort to counter antisemitism have been of little avail, given the dramatic increase in incidents and the deterioration in discourse, particularly following Israel's 2009 Operation Cast Lead.[29]

This would, however, miss the point. At the turn of the millennium, governments were reluctant to even recognise that antisemitism was once again growing. They could see antisemitism only through the prism of the far right, which was in retreat politically, and not through that of Islamism and the left, which were ascendant. They also underestimated the phenomenal power of information and communication technologies and the viral nature of internet social networking sites. Since then, states have recognised the dangers to societies' health by not combatting the phenomenon, have agreed upon a common yardstick by which antisemitism can be defined and measured, and have recognised that it now also comes from new and different directions. Many states have also legislated against incitement of antisemitism in its various forms, including Holocaust denial. Those that have not yet done so, in Europe, at least, will have to do so by the end of 2010.

...

The progress made in confronting and combating antisemitism since the 1990s has been neither continuous nor consistent, but without the determination of some governments, international agencies, and a handful of Jewish NGOs, the progress made thus far would not have been possible.

Given the manner in which the diplomatic initiatives have evolved, the onus remains on the Jewish (and other leading human rights) NGOs to ensure that progress continues to be made. In this task, they must work ever closer with governments, parliamentarians and international agencies.

I quote Whine at length here because it summarises the result of the central strategy that the main Jewish bodies were pursuing, especially in relation to diplomatic actors which they were relying on to take action against the sources of antisemitism Whine and his colleagues identified, And it is very striking that even though his opening words were about the increase in antisemitism 'particularly following Israel's 2009 [sic] Operation Cast Lead', he makes no attempt to explore any of the implications about Israel's actions fuelling the antisemitism he is so concerned about.

Why it 'misses the point' to suggest 'that ten years of diplomatic effort to counter antisemitism have been of little avail', given the continuous rise in antisemitic manifestations, is unclear and not supported by Whine's claim that, 'At the turn of the millennium, governments were reluctant to even recognize that antisemitism was once again growing', an assertion of doubtful validity in the light of media reports and the very strong statements quoted above about what was happening at that time.

After 2005, efforts were made by the promoters of the EUMC 'working definition' to introduce it in all the forums in which combatting antisemitism was a central objective.

But precisely what was being promoted was far from consistent. We find many instances in which the fact that it remained a '*working* definition' of an EU agency, not of the EU Commission or the Council of Ministers, is ignored. It was variously referred to as '*the* EU definition',[30] 'the European Union's own definition of antisemitism',[31] 'the common European definition of antisemitism',[32] 'the most widely accepted definition'.[33] In 2007 Porat wrote that 'the definition presents a list of acts and statements *that are antisemitic*' (emphasis added), ignoring the explicit conditionality in the text.[34]

Then there are many examples of inappropriate attempts to apply the 'working definition' in specific circumstances. The SWC demanded cancellation of the 'Israel Apartheid' conference at the University of Paris VIII, claiming it was 'a clear violation of the European Union Fundamental Rights Agency's Working Definition of Antisemitism'. The One State Conference at Harvard in March 2012 was described in an article on the website of CAMERA, a pro-Israel media-monitoring operation, as 'an exercise in antisemitism' according to 'the working definition of antisemitism developed by the [FRA]'.[35] NGO Monitor said: 'BDS campaigns that single out Israel explicitly violate the European Union Working Definition of antisemitism'.[36]

Some of the principal promoters of the 'working definition' were unhappy about aspects of its use: both inappropriate and insufficient application. In 2010, Stern, the original dafter of the text, said: 'most Jewish organizations have not sufficiently used the definition' and 'some Jewish organizations ... are using it in an inappropriate way'—undermining free speech. Then in 2011, Stern again expressed his concerns about the 'working definition' being used to stifle freedom of speech. Some reactions to incidents on university campuses leading to allegations of antisemitism, he wrote, 'are making the situation worse by distorting the provisions of Title VI of the Civil Rights Act of 1964, and what has been called the "working definition of antisemitism"'.[37] In 2010 Whine wrote:

> The current reality is that ... US State Department and OSCE ODIHR use the Working Definition but not FRA itself. Indeed, FRA currently does not even notify its RAXEN Network of NFPs [National Focal Points] that it even exists, let alone ask them to use it. It is true that FRA's mandate has widened enormously ... but monitoring antisemitism still remains a core activity.[38]

The General Union of Palestinian Students was expelled from the UK National Union of Students (NUS) conference in 2008 for distributing a leaflet that bore the headline (in capital letters): '*WHY "JEWISH STATE" NOT A SECULAR*

STATE?' and carried two cartoons by the Brazilian anti-Israel illustrator, Latuff. The NUS conference agreed with concerns raised by the Union of Jewish Students (UJS) that the leaflet was antisemitic. In doing so, both NUS and UJS invoked the EUMC *'working definition of antisemitism'*, previously adopted by the NUS in 2007.[39] Dave Rich wrote: 'This is the only example I am aware of in which an organisation in the UK has adopted the Working Definition as official policy, and then successfully enforced it in this way'. And while the 2006 Report of the All-Party Parliamentary Inquiry into Antisemitism endorsed the 'working definition' and urged the UK government to adopt it, the government declined, citing 'EUMC's evidence to the Committee that the definition is in fact a work in progress and has not been recommended to states for adoption. We undertake to re-examine this if and when the EUMC's successor body the Fundamental Rights Agency do so'.[40]

If this suggests a certain caution in the EUMC's ambitions for the 'working definition', this is even more clearly seen from other evidence. From the outset the EUMC said the 'working definition' had 'no legal basis' and 'did not necessarily reflect the official position of the EUMC'. The EUMC itself did *not* adopt it. In reply to a letter from European Jews for a Just Peace, dated 13 October 2005, strongly criticising the 'working definition', on 28 November Winkler replied: 'Currently the draft guidelines and working definition, which should be viewed as "work in progress", are under review in the light of feedback received, *with a view to redrafting them* in 2006' (emphasis added).[41] While the EUMC website still existed, the URL of the document included the word 'draft' in the title.[42]

Even as the 'working definition' was making further inroads institutionally and giving further legitimacy to notions of the 'new antisemitism', the Fundamental Rights Agency, successor to the EUMC, was—as indicated by Whine above—proving itself rather reluctant to fully embrace the 'working definition'. In 2008, the FRA informed the UK government that 'initial feedback and comments drew attention to several issues that impacted on the effectiveness of the definition as a data collection support tool'.[43] In other words, it wasn't useful. 'Since its development we are not aware of any public authority in the EU that applies it', an FRA official added. Moreover, 'The FRA has no plans for any further development of the "working definition"'.[44] That was in August 2010. In February 2011, Ioannis N. Dimitrakopoulos, Head of the Department of Equality and Citizen's Rights at the FRA, said:

The paper that was produced had no legal basis or value. It was published in the interests of transparency. The publication of documents was under the responsibility of the Director ... the FRA applies the terms racism, xenophobia, antisemitism and intolerance as developed and used by the

Council of Europe, namely the European Commission against Racism and Intolerance (ECRI).[45]

He said that he was not aware of any public authority within the EU that applies the document in any way, e.g. as a tool for data collection. Asked why he thought this was so he replied: 'one reason might be that public authorities need to rely on a legal definition to develop any relevant guidelines, and to my knowledge no such legal definition exists as regards EU Member States'.

In 2010, Whine said that the FRA 'does not even notify' partner organisations in EU countries that the definition exists, 'let alone ask them to use it',[46] according to the Kantor Center's conference programme for the 2010 conference reviewing the progress of the 'working definition'. Speaking in Washington in December 2011, Baker told a congressional hearing that

> the EUMC adopted[47] a working definition of antisemitism. It provided an overall framework, but it went, as well, to provide specific examples of how antisemitism can manifest itself with regard to the state of Israel. It was endorsed by parliamentary conferences in London and Ottawa. The State Department special envoy sitting next to me here [Hannah Rosenthal, special envoy to monitor and combat antisemitism, Department of State] has adopted it for her own work and analysis. And I share it and recommend its use when I travel in my OSCE capacity. *But it still meets with some opposition, including from the EUMC's successor organization, and thus it bears repeating whenever possible* [emphasis added].[48]

David Feldman said that 'the EUMC working definition was never, so far as I understand it, an official EUMC line'. The FRA, he pointed out, 'appears to be taking a different approach and has commissioned a survey that focuses on Jews' perceptions and experiences of antisemitism'.[49]

But there is no doubt that the FRA had become a stumbling block on the path to further dissemination and adoption of the 'working definition' by state parties and other international bodies. The FRA did not actively seek to play this role. The fact that it had disowned the EUMC's position and eventually withdrew the 'working definition' from its website only emerged and was then confirmed when researchers inquired with the FRA as to the status of the document. It was obvious that the controversy surrounding the shelved and leaked antisemitism report of 2002 and the mixed reception given to the 'working definition' convinced the FRA that, if it were to be effective, it had to make a clean break with its predecessor's involvement in this area. Nevertheless, this by no means stopped the drive towards international acceptance. On the contrary, to a great degree the 'working definition' had taken on a life of its own. If individuals and organisations could misread it, misquote it, make false claims about it being 'the EU definition' of antisemitism, read the examples on Israel and Zionism as incontrovertible manifestations of antisemitism, ignoring the conditionality clause that prefaces them, why would they stop acting as if nothing had changed regarding its status? It now belonged to the expanding field of transnational anti-antisemitism governance and was proving to be a very useful and influential form of codification of the 'new antisemitism'.

*   *   *

Further evidence of this came from the renewed engagement in combatting antisemitism on the part of the Israeli government and state structures. This effort began gathering pace before the EUMC 'working definition' saw the light of day in January 2005. But the Israeli offensive already had its own two complementary definitions to work with, one of which was already in well-worked out form more than a decade before: Cotler's 'Israel as the "collective Jew" among the nations' formulation. This was given further public exposure when, in November 2002, the Jewish People Policy Planning Institute published a pamphlet by him titled *The New Anti-Jewishness* with this text on the front cover: 'The new anti-Jewishness consists of the discrimination against, or denial of, the right of the Jewish people to live as an equal member of the family of nations'.[50] A fuller title is given on the first page: 'Human Rights and the New Anti-Jewishness: Sounding the Alarm'. The pamphlet was reprinted in September 2004. In 2012, interviewed by David Sheen for *Haaretz*, Cotler, who co-founded the International Parliamentary Coalition to Combat Antisemitism, was as consistent as ever:

> Since the start of the 21st century, the world has been witnessing a new and escalating, globalizing, virulent, and even lethal antisemitism ... one which substitutes hate for the Jewish person with hate for the Jewish state. We had moved from the discrimination against Jews as individuals, to the discrimination against Jews as a people, to Israel as the targeted collective 'Jew among the nations'.[51]

The second definition was Natan Sharansky's '3Ds' (see above), which he was ideally placed to disseminate as a government minister responsible for Jerusalem, Social and Diaspora affairs between 2003 and 2005, and having implemented a proposal of his predecessor in 2003 to establish the Global Forum for Combatting Antisemitism (GFCA), involving Jewish leaders and intellectuals. Sharansky's test was adopted by the US Department of State in 2010. In special antisemitism envoy Hannah Rosenthal's words: 'Our State Department uses Natan Sharansky's "Three Ds" test for identifying when someone or a government crosses the line from criticising Israeli policies into antisemitism: when Israel is demonized, when Israel is held to different standards than the rest of the countries, and when Israel is delegitimized'.[52] (Note that Kenneth L. Marcus wrote that: 'While Sharansky's 3D test is helpful in part for its mnemonic cleverness, I have argued in Jewish Identity and Civil Rights in America[53] that it lacks sufficient rigor to be used without modification for scholarly or governmental purposes'.)

However, to confuse matters further as to the status of competing, or rather complementary definitions, at a meeting of the US Commission on Security and Cooperation in Europe in 2011, the Chairman, Hon. Christopher H. Smith, said in his opening remarks: 'The Interparliamentary Coalition for Combatting Antisemitism, which held its most recent major conference in Ottawa last fall, has been a crucial forum for parliamentarians to work across national boundaries to address common problems of antisemitism'. At the body's meeting there in November 2010, a Protocol was agreed which stated: 'We reaffirm the EUMC—now Fundamental Rights Agency (FRA)—working definition of antisemitism'. It looked as if the FRA's attempt to quietly shelve the EUMC 'working definition' was not going to succeed.

8

Responding to 'New Antisemitism': A Transnational Field of Racial Governance

As 'new antisemitism' theory achieved the status of orthodoxy—never without its critics of course—a number of academic bodies, research institutes and Jewish communal defence organisations adopted its premises. And by formally broadening antisemitism to embrace hostility to Israel, space was created for new institutions, websites and anti-antisemitism campaigning and pressure groups to come into being with the express purpose of researching, analysing and raising public awareness of it, but especially confronting and defeating it.

Under Yehuda Bauer and his successor, Professor Dalia Ofer, SICSA certainly acknowledged and promoted the study of the worsening antisemitic climate, but never, as an institution, formally accepted that there was such a discrete phenomenon as 'new antisemitism'. When asked, in 2007, is there a 'new antisemitism' and how do you define it, Bauer replied:

> You see Western antisemitism is not new. This concept of 'New Antisemitism' is, I think, quite false. It is the old pre-Hitler antisemitism that utilises occasions to come to the fore when something triggers [it]. Now it is the Israeli situation. If tomorrow there was suddenly a change in the situation in the Middle East and serious negotiations started between Israel and the Palestinians ending with even a temporary compromise for a number of years, that would mean, I am quite sure there would be a decline in antisemitism in the West because the trigger is gone. But the antisemitism would not disappear, it would still be there and there would then be another trigger. It's a very slow process to deal with, latent antisemitism.[1]

When Wistrich was appointed director of SICSA in 2002, the body became a *de facto* promoter of 'new antisemitism' theory. Wistrich himself, however, was somewhat more circumspect about declaring the existence of 'the new antisemitism'. In response to the question posed to Bauer, Wistrich gave a far more discursive answer of which this extract is indicative:

Governments are reluctant or afraid to address the newer forms of anti-semitism, anti-Israel and anti-Zionism, especially those adopted by radical Islamic, anti-Western currents in the Muslim community. The infiltration of Islamism into the western Muslim diaspora is alarming and brings with it a serious problem for Jewish communities, which is aggravated by the general mood of appeasement. Only in the US and Australia is there a more robust posture in defending Western core values.

Much of this touches on elements of 'new antisemitism' theory, and during the rest of the interview he added more of its components. This was therefore 'new antisemitism' in all but name. In 2008 he was equally trenchant about antisemitism's contemporary manifestations but more direct in giving it a name:[2]

[Israel] must reconnect with the roots of its existence in Zion and with the meaning of Jewishness and Judaism in the world as a whole. It is this value-vacuum which facilitates endless and pernicious clichés about Israel as a narrowly nationalist 'anachronism' or as the last European colonial project. Israeli leaders often seem helpless when confronted with malicious propaganda branding them as flouters of international law, serial violators of human rights, lackeys of American imperialism, colonialist occupiers, 'ethnic cleansers', founders of an apartheid state or heirs of the Third Reich. Silence in the face of such grotesque demonisation in Europe and the Middle East is not an option. This rhetoric has been aggravated by the prevalence of so-called 'progressive' Jews in the front line of the Israel-bashing chorus.

None of this poison is going to disappear on its own. The struggle against the 'new' antisemitism will have to face this challenge, while accepting the right to Jewish dissent, to engage with alternative voices.

There is no doubt that the programme of seminars, conferences and publications of SICSA under Wistrich fully reflected an approach to antisemitism grounded in an assumption that new antisemitism, as defined in the EUMC 'working definition', Cotler's 'Israel as the collective Jew among the nations', or Sharansky's '3Ds', was the central focus of attention.

Wistrich steered SICSA in this direction until his retirement in 2014. In 2015 he died suddenly of a heart attack in Rome. In a letter published posthumously in the *Jerusalem Post*, he wrote, 'The Islamists are the spearhead of current antisemitism, aided and abetted by the moral relativism of all too many naïve Western liberals'.[3]

Porat's project was established in 1991, 14 years before the EUMC 'working definition' was published. In 1996 it was renamed the Stephen Roth Institute for the Study of Contemporary Antisemitism and Racism. She headed it until

2010. Effectively backed by the Israeli state from its earliest days, it became a principal incubator for 'new antisemitism' thinking. From 1994, Porat's outfit was holding a biennial international seminar for antisemitism researchers, backed by the ADL, WJC and Israeli state and government agencies. The only researchers invited to attend were those formally linked to Jewish communal bodies, most often a country level Jewish representative body. The fact that it was her institute that staged a conference in Paris reviewing the 'working definition' five years after it was posted on the EUMC website, is an indication that she played a major role in its emergence and dissemination.

But she was never entirely consistent in her writing and commentary on 'new antisemitism' (see Chapter 7), at times appearing to be more detached in her judgements, but this seems to have been formulaic rather than substantive. Interviewed in 2007, and asked whether there is a 'new antisemitism', she began by concurring 'in principle' with Professor Wolfgang Benz, head of the antisemitism research centre at the Berlin Technical University, that 'there is really no new antisemitism', 'it's just that it has a new envelope'.[4] She then seemed to contradict herself, saying:

> Today, a new and violent form of antisemitism exists in the countries of Western Europe from Scandinavia in the north to Spain and, less so, to Italy in the south.
>
> For the present, one may say that the image of the Jew and his [sic] supposed intentions are no different from those in the past, only the arena is now the world of radical Islam.

Moving ever closer to describing the main characteristics of 'new antisemitism', she says: 'the differentiation between antisemitism and anti-Zionism which had existed in the past ... is becoming increasingly less clear. And at this stage, attacks that were once directed against the individual Jew are now directed against his state'.

Eight years later, at a hearing of the Knesset's Immigration and Absorption Committee in December 2015, Porat stated: 'It's obvious that anti-Israelism and anti-Zionism are acquiring an increasingly antisemitic tone'.[5] She lamented the fact that the FRA had taken down from its website the 'working definition' and argued strongly for its restoration: 'it needs to be everywhere'. And she emphasised the importance of the five examples that 'define when anti-Israelism and anti-Zionism, the singling-us out, and comparing us to Nazis and calling us racists ... is antisemitism'—as before, ignoring the conditionality in the examples).

Scott Ury of Tel Aviv University's Department of Jewish History, a noted critic of the notion of 'new antisemitism', took over as director of the Stephen Roth

Institute in 2010 and took it in a different direction. However, Porat remained a key figure in the field.

The Kantor Center for the Study of Contemporary European Jewry was inaugurated in May 2010 at Tel Aviv University,[6] with Porat installed as its head. The Center provides 'an academic framework for the interdisciplinary research of European Jewry from the end of World War II until the present day'. One of its four subject areas is: 'Worldwide legislation and enforcement in the promotion of minority rights, non-discrimination, and against racism, hate crimes, hate speech, antisemitism, and Holocaust denial'. Much of its output seems to concentrate on antisemitism. In its opening year it hosted the 10th biennial seminar on antisemitism, the subject of which was 'The [EUMC] Working Definition of Antisemitism—Six Years After'.

Meanwhile, in the United States, the Yale Initiative for the Interdisciplinary Study of Antisemitism (YIISA) was founded at Yale University within the Institution for Social and Policy Studies in 2005 by Charles Small, who became its director. (It started life as the Institute for the Study of Global Antisemitism and Policy, ISGAP, but changed its name in 2006.) From its inception, Small made it clear that YIISA would promote the notion of the 'new antisemitism', focus heavily on criticism of Israel and prioritise the issue of 'Muslim antisemitism'. Very well-funded, it rapidly became the leading body hosting academics and Jewish defence researchers who were writing, from a 'new antisemitism' perspective, about these topics. YIISA was the standout example of the academic or quasi-academic bodies being set up in this period—the Roth Institute and the Kantor Center included—which operated more as Israel advocacy organisations than as independent, objective, scholarly research centres, and was attracting much criticism for this from some prominent academics.

These reservations were also being expressed within Yale's governance bodies. In a shock move on 7 June 2011, Yale University notified YIISA that it would be closed at the end of July. A Yale spokesman stated that the initiative did not meet 'its academic expectations and has been cancelled'. Donald Green, director of the Institution for Social and Policy Studies where YIISA was housed, said in a statement that it had 'generated little scholarly work that earned publication in highly regarded journals, and its courses attracted few students'.

There were immediate protests from the two most prominent American Jewish organisations. The ADL's national director, Abe Foxman, complained: 'Yale's decision is particularly unfortunate and dismaying ... it leaves the impression that the anti-Jewish forces in the world achieved a significant victory'. David Harris, AJC executive director warned: 'If Yale now leaves the field, it will create a very regrettable void'. Less measured was a report in the *New York Post* headed 'Yale's latest gift to antisemitism'.[7] The writer claimed Yale ordered closure 'because YIISA refused to ignore the most virulent, genocidal and common form of Jew-hatred today: Muslim antisemitism', but offered no evidence for this charge. The *Jewish Chronicle* reported[8] that 'Some American Jews, who had felt safe from antisemitism, will now be hurting'.

But many academics welcomed the decision, among them the Holocaust historian Professor Deborah Lipstadt, who, after at first calling the decision 'strange, if not weird', consulted people at Yale and then concluded that YIISA's efforts had 'migrated from the world of scholarship to that of advocacy'. I argued that the organisation was politicised and that its demise should be welcomed by those who 'genuinely support the principle of the objective, dispassionate study of contemporary antisemitism'.[9] In a damning judgement, Jerry Haber, a Jewish Studies professor with posts in the US and Israel, who blogs under the name 'The Magnes Zionist', wrote the following:

> The moral of this story? Take an important phenomenon which is worthy of study and have it hijacked by people with an ideological agenda, who organise conferences that revel in Islamophobia and right-wing Zionism, mixing mediocre academics and non-academics with serious scholars, all of whom have axes to grind—in short, trivialize antisemitism in order to silence critics of Israel—and sooner or later, God willing, real academics will write it off as an embarrassment.[10]

Yale moved quite quickly to scotch accusations of abandoning the fight against antisemitism by announcing on 20 June the establishment of the Programme for the Study of Antisemitism (YPSA) as a replacement for YIISA, to be convened by existing faculty and sponsored by the Whitney Humanities Center.[11] A tenured professor of French Jewish history, Maurice Samuels, who contributed to the *AHR* roundtable on 'Antisemitism in historical perspective', was appointed to convene the new body, of which the Provost of Yale, Peter Salovey, said: 'I am hopeful that this programme will produce major scholarship on the vitally important subject of antisemitism'. This development was a significant, though small, distancing by Yale from a 'new antisemitism'-based research programme.

YIISA supporters soon had good news, however. The body, still headed by Small, reverted to its first name, the Institute for the Study of Global Antisemitism and Policy (ISGAP), and relocated to Manhattan, from where it still operates, not affiliated to any university or other academic institution, and still functions as a leading promoter of 'new antisemitism' theory and the 'working definition' of antisemitism.[12] Not that you will find the term 'new antisemitism' in its mission statement or in the general description of what it does. But a look at the subject matter of its conferences, seminars and publications shows the emphasis on, for example, Israel, anti-Zionism, Islamic antisemitism, Palestinian political activism on American campuses and the Boycott, Divestment and Sanctions (BDS) movement. To take but one specific example, highlighted on its website as I write,[13] under the headline 'Officially sanctioned hate at the University of Michigan', is

> The 2020 Youth for Palestine Conference ... taking place from January 25–26 at the University of Michigan Ann Arbor. The conference will be hosted by Midwest Students for Justice in Palestine (Midwest SJP), Palestinian Youth Movement (PYM) and Students Allied for Freedom and Equality (SAFE). The conference is also being sponsored by the American Muslims for Palestine (AMP), an organisation described by the Anti-Defamation League as "the leading organization providing anti-Zionist training and education to students and Muslim community organizations in the country ... AMP seeks to delegitimize and demonize the Jewish state. Its materials are prominently featured at its events and conferences, in its publications and through materials available on its website". As Natan Sharansky has famously demonstrated, the delegitimisation and demonisation of the Jewish State is a clear and common manifestation of antisemitism.

The item fleshes out what ISGAP regards as the antisemitic nature of this enterprise and concludes: 'How much longer will antisemitism be tolerated on our campuses? What is the damage of inaction as more students across the nation are being exposed to this oldest of hatreds?'

In its 2015 publication, *The Yale Papers: Antisemitism in Comparative Perspective*, a 542-page collection of 28 seminar and workshop papers, lectures, and conference presentations from its Yale period dedicated to the memory of Robert Wistrich, it lists the heads of ISGAP centres in Asia, Israel, Italy, France, Canada and Chile.

More modest in size and scope, but styled ISGAP's counterpart in Europe, is the Berlin International Center for the Study of Antisemitism (BICSA), Germany, directed by Dr Clemens Heni, a Yale University post-doctoral associate. Founded in January 2011 and described as 'a think tank in Europe dedicated to the analysis of all forms of antisemitism [whose] purpose ... is to conduct high-profile scholarly research without being stuck in the ivory towers of academia'. 'Anti-Zionist, anti-Israel, antisemitism is the new form of well-respected, mainstream hatred of Jews',[14] Heni wrote on 11 April 2012. The centre holds an annual lecture in memory of Robert Wistrich on the anniversary of his death, 19 May. He was at one time a member of the editorial board of the *Journal for the Study of Antisemitism*, founded in 2009. The current board constitutes a list of scholars, politicians, activists, journalists and public figures, almost all of whom are associated with 'new antisemitism' theory.[15] Heni was also the first editor of the *Journal of Contemporary Antisemitism*, the first edition of which was published in January 2018,[16] which is one of a number of publications focusing on perceived antisemitism in discourse on Israel and Zionism, in the BDS movement and Palestinian activism more generally, and among anti-Zionists.[17] The current editor is Lesley Klaff, senior lecturer in law at Sheffield Hallam University. On its editorial board are many of the main figures—both academic and non-academic—associated with promoting the notion of the 'new antisemitism'.[18]

Also in the UK, the Israel lobby organisation BICOM (Britain Israel Communication and Research Centre) publishes an online journal, *Fathom*, which devotes much of its space to what its editors call 'antisemitic anti-Zionism' and gives a platform to many academics who write in this key.[19]

This is just the tip of an iceberg, though it should be emphasised that there are differences in emphasis among these institutions, websites and periodicals. Moreover, there are academics who can be found contributing their work in both camps. But one additional thing they have in common is a dedication to exposing left-wing Jewish critics of Israel and Jewish anti-Zionists as antisemitic.

It should be understood that there is no clear distinction between, on the one hand, the bodies and periodicals I have mentioned so far, which all purport to adhere to high academic standards, and, on the other hand, the more overtly politically motivated organisations dedicated to combatting antisemitic hate, defending Israel, etc. National Jewish representative organisations, activist groups like the ADL, AJC, CAA, CST have their own 'research departments', loosely defined, and often operate in alignment with think tanks and university departments. However, a major difference between the two kinds of organisations is that the latter focus intently on securing media coverage for their work, and they do that very successfully.

In 2009 Professor Alvin Rosenfeld founded the Institute for the Study of Contemporary Antisemitism at Indiana University (ISCA).[20] Conferences ISCA organised in 2014 and 2016—Deciphering the 'New' Antisemitism, 5–9 April, and Anti-Zionism, Antisemitism, and the Dynamics of Delegitimization, 2–6 April—are representative of Rosenfeld's focus on 'new antisemitism'. In December 2006 he wrote a highly controversial pamphlet for the AJC titled *Progressive Jewish Thought and the New Antisemitism* (see Chapter 1), which accuses various left-wing Jewish non-Zionist and anti-Zionist academics and writers of 'typif[ying] one of the most distressing features of the new antisemitism—namely, the participation of Jews alongside it, especially in its anti-Zionist expression'[21]—barely a hair's breadth away from saying such people are Jewish antisemites.

The Louis D. Brandeis Center for Human Rights Under Law[22] was established in 2012 as 'an organization uniquely devoted to utilizing the law to combat antisemitism'. The Center's mission is 'to advance the civil and human rights of the Jewish people and to promote justice for all'. Kenneth L. Marcus was its founding head. He stepped down in 2018 to become the Trump administration's Assistant Secretary for Civil Rights at the United States Department of Education, but returned as chairman of the Board in mid-2020. Prominent on the institute's website are various references to 'new antisemitism' demonstrating a clear pre-occupation with the topic. A volume on *Deciphering the New Antisemitism* (Indiana University Press 2016), edited by Rosenfeld of the Indiana University antisemitism institute, who is an academic adviser to the Brandeis institute. Marcus contributed a chapter on 'The ideology of the new antisemitism' to the volume.

The Canadian Institute for the Study of Antisemitism (CISA), founded in 2010 and based in Winnipeg, 'produces scholarship and education on the subject of antisemitism in its classic and contemporary forms', its website declares.[23] CISA's director, Dr Catherine Chatterly, is editor of the journal *Antisemitism Studies*, which is published by Indiana University Press and closely associated with the Rosenfeld antisemitism institute. Like the other academic bodies focusing on 'new antisemitism', appointees to its governance structures are drawn from a familiar list of people promoting 'new antisemitism' theory: Cotler, Porat, Bauer, Lipstadt, Rosenfeld, Wisse and Wistrich.

There are two internationally known antisemitism research institutes that have never been engaged in promoting 'new antisemitism' theory, but do not ignore it and indeed make it an aspect of their overall field of scholarly enquiry. First, the Birkbeck Institute for the Study of Antisemitism at Birkbeck University of London, founded in 2010 and headed by David Feldman, and first referred to in Chapter 1. (Formerly named the Pears Institute, after the Pears Foundation that established it and provided most of its funds, in 2021 the foundation, unhappy about public interventions by the director on contemporary political controversies relating to antisemitism, announced that it was withdrawing the use of its name and cutting back its funding. This was undoubtedly a serious blow to a first-rate institution. The university announced that it would maintain its support and gave the institute the university's name.) It sums up its objective approach to 'new antisemitism' like this:

> 'The new antisemitism' is a term used by some to refer to criticism of Israel and/or criticism of the policies of its government. This is an important area of public and scholarly debate in which there is no consensus. There is a pressing need to engage with these issues in ways that are intellectually and politically inclusive.[24]

Second, the Zentrum für Antisemitismusforschung (Centre for Research on Antisemitism, ZfA) at the Berlin Technical University, established in 1982 and now headed by Stefanie Schüler-Springorum.[25] Since 2012, the ZfA has been part of the international research network International Consortium for Research on Antisemitism and Racism (ICRAR), which coordinates joint research initiatives of the participating institutes. Birkbeck is one of the bodies in the consortium. 'ICRAR involves leading scholars from universities and institutes across Europe, Israel and the US who share the common goal of revitalising and reshaping the study of antisemitism. It was launched in November 2011'. Scott Ury's appointment as head of the Roth institute led to that body also associating itself with the consortium.

According to the consortium, one reason why the understanding of antisemitism remains underdeveloped 'relates to the politicisation of antisemitism. Too often its study has been shaped and corralled by immediate political concerns. This has not only foreshortened our understanding of antisemitism in the past and present, but it has also undermined the specific contribution academics can make to overcome it'. This suggests it is reasonable to see ICRAR as a group of individual scholars and institutions fundamentally sceptical about 'new antisemitism' and its inextricable links to the most distorting aspects of the politicisation of antisemitism. The work of some of the scholars involved is clear evidence of this sceptical approach.

Nevertheless, there is no comparison between the outreach of the consortium members and that of those associated with promoting 'new antisemitism' studies. Although it would be accurate to say that virtually all scholars of contemporary antisemitism see themselves as engaged in work that could contribute to combatting the phenomenon, those following 'new antisemitism' theory are far more politically engaged and networked than those who are not convinced by, or openly oppose, 'new antisemitism' theory. Robert Wistrich, Dina Porat, Irwin Cotler, Kenneth Marcus, Alvin Rosenfeld and others, made or make frequent appearances on the international stage, whether that is at events organised by such organisations as the OSCE or the EU, or by the Israel-based, mostly government-sponsored anti-antisemitism forums.

There is also a hinterland of less formal entities, largely internet-based, which comprise academics or purport to be driven by academic standards, pursuing a 'new antisemitism' approach. One such, based in the UK, is Engageonline,[26] founded and still headed by David Hirsh, a sociologist at Goldsmiths University of London, who has spoken at YIISA, ISGAP, the Stephen Roth Institute, the Kantor Center, and at international NGOs and American Jewish organisations. Initially founded in 2005 to fight the campaign to boycott Israeli universities, it describes its mission as to 'challenge left and liberal antisemitism in the labour movement, in our universities and in public life'. It emphasises that it is a single-issue group, left-wing and not exclusively Jewish. The prominent *Observer* columnist Nick Cohen, a supporter, described Engage's position as pointing out that 'the act of singling out Israel as the only illegitimate state—in the absence of any coherent reason for doing so—is in itself antisemitic, irrespective of the motivation or opinions of those who make that claim'[27]—a classic tenet of the argument for the existence of a 'new antisemitism'. Described by Hirsh as a left-wing project, Engage is a home for a range of academics supportive of and comfortable with the site's focus on left-wing antisemitism as manifested in, for example, BDS anti-Zionism.[28]

NGO Monitor, based in Israel and founded and run by Professor Gerald M. Steinberg, is a more formal operation with an international profile, but also purporting to focus on a single issue. It does not appear to have the fight against 'new antisemitism' in its aims, but it is obvious from its activity that it looks at alleged anti-Israel bias through a 'new antisemitism' lens. It claims to be 'independent' and 'non-partisan', 'dedicated to promoting transparency and accountability of NGOs claiming human rights agendas, primarily in the context of the Arab–Israeli conflict'.[29] Its establishment in 2002 followed the 2001 Durban UN anti-racism conference, described by some as an 'antisemitic hate-fest', where 'NGOs adopted a strategy of using the instruments and language of "human rights" and "international law" to isolate Israel and undermine its right to sovereign equality'. These assertions very strongly echo the long-held views of the UN by Cotler, Wistrich and others, and NGO Monitor's campaigning approach is similar to that of UN Watch (see Chapter 5), which describes itself as 'a leader at the UN in the struggle against antisemitism'[30]—*at* the UN.

Steinberg and Anne Hertzberg contributed a chapter on 'The role of international legal and justice discourse in promoting the new antisemitism' to Rosenfeld's *Anti-Zionism and Antisemitism: The Dynamics of Delegitimization* (2019).[31] Such claims are not new. Michael Galchinsky writes:[32]

> Beginning in the 1970s Jewish NGOs began to identify such behaviour [ostracising Israel from the community of nations] as a 'New Antisemitism', designed to turn Israel into a pariah and deny the Jewish people their right to self-determination. In some cases, the tension produced by commitments to international human rights and Jewish nationalism caused activists to withdraw their support from the human rights system. More often, NGOs continued their work with various human rights bodies while expending a greater and greater proportion of their resources defending Israel from its critics and pushing for reforms in the UN system.

*　*　*

Such NGOs and the research institutes discussed earlier needed no prompting from Israeli governments to attack the UN and its agencies for demonising Israel. Indeed, it could be argued that at the turn of the century it was the other way round. Ambivalence about relations with the diaspora, preoccupation with dealing with the internal security threat and political instability all impacted on the nature of Israel's response to the concerns about 'new antisemitism'. But as we have seen, by 2005, with the establishment of the Global Forum, publicity given to the EUMC 'working definition' of antisemitism and Sharansky's '3Ds' and the apparent deterioration of Israel's international position as the Oslo process collapsed, a new understanding of the importance for the state of the widespread heightened alarm about 'global antisemitism' had emerged. This view catches some of Israel's response:[33]

> Meanwhile, rather than fixing the main cause of its unpopularity—the military occupation of territory assigned to the Palestinians under international law—Israeli policy makers blamed 'viral antisemitism' together with an ineffectual communications strategy.[34] All Israel required, or so they thought, was a radical overhauling of its hasbara (giving highly selective public relations information about Israel) and a more proactive approach to communicating with the international community.

But this was only one aspect of the government's response. After the first meeting of the new Global Forum Against Antisemitism in Jerusalem in February 2004, which marked a significant upscaling of government engagement in the issue, the advantages of giving priority to antisemitism on the international stage became evident at the 28–29 April 2004 OSCE Berlin conference on antisemitism. The final declaration included the following: 'Declare unambiguously that international developments or political issues, including those in Israel or elsewhere in the Middle East, never justify antisemitism.'[35] This apparently reflected the fact that, for the first time, the conference 'confirmed the Israeli government's claim that criticism of its policies was sometimes used as a camouflage for the expression of antisemitic attitudes'.[36] In the following year, the UNGA, long seen by Israel as congenitally hostile, passed by an overwhelming majority an Israeli proposal to declare 27 January as International Holocaust Remembrance Day. And in January 2005, following the Tehran Holocaust denial conference held on 11 and 12 December, the UNGA voted to condemn the phenomenon.

Despite these successes, and the higher profile Sharansky had given to an Israeli engagement with antisemitism, there was no evidence of a consistent policy being followed. Falling back on Israel's traditional stance on antisemitism, that it would put its national interests above getting involved in publicly attacking antisemitism in any particular country, seemed so often to be the default position. This was also reflected in developments within the Mossad, which was the one state agency that had often played a role in supporting the security of diaspora Jews, when it suited the government of the day to do so. We

147

saw the results of their engagement on antisemitism in the early 1990s and the subsequent stepping back after the Oslo Accords.

Mossad units Bitzur and especially Nativ have found it difficult in recent years to define their mission. Apart from France in recent years, there has been little immigration to Israel from Jewish communities, and even the very alarmist publicity given to French Jews allegedly leaving in their thousands is questionable, given that many already had second homes in Israel and there is much movement back and forth for business and family reasons (which is known as 'Boeing *aliya*'). Even for those Jews who do intend to emigrate permanently, they can do so freely and do not need the help of Mossad departments like Bitzur and Nativ. And where there are pockets of Jews who require welfare support in countries where neither Jewish communal organisations nor state institutions can properly service these needs—Holocaust survivors in Ukraine and Russia, for example—the Jewish Joint Distribution Committee (JDC), based in America, continues to fulfil its traditional role in helping such individuals. (At one time it needed Mossad help to do this, but this is no longer required.)

Nevertheless, it is in the DNA of the Israeli intelligence services to see themselves as responsible 'not only for Israeli citizens' security, but also for that of Jewish communities abroad', writes security expert Yossi Melman. 'This doctrine—of "the Jewish people's intelligence services"—can be traced back to the Mossad Le'Aliyah Bet, a branch of the Haganah underground that brought in illegal Jewish immigrants under the nose of the British Mandate, and remained in operation after the establishment of the state'.[37]

But during the 2000s, personnel at the Foreign Ministry, the Jewish Agency, the Immigrant Absorption Ministry, the Prime Minister's Office and within the Mossad itself, were 'pushing to shut the [Bitzur and Nativ] units down. But someone always comes to their defence'. While the former Soviet Union is not entirely free of states where restrictions exist on citizens' freedoms, emigration is largely open to all, so the logic of shutting down Nativ was strong. But Bitzur was another matter. Though moves were made to cut its personnel and downgrade its administrative status, in the light of terrorist threats to Jewish communities, Bitzur's demotion was reversed, and in Melman's words, it 'experience[ed] a renewal' and 'was given the status of a division'.

Despite sensitivities about interfering in other countries' affairs—Israel would hardly countenance other countries acting in that way—the Mossad has taken action to defend Jews abroad. For example, in Morocco, Tunisia and Algiers in the 1950s, and in South America (Argentina and Uruguay) in the 1960s.

Based on such precedents, one can only assume that the governments of Israel continue to find ways to implement the doctrine of 'Jewish intelligence'. This is done mainly through close cooperation with intelligence communities and police forces abroad. [Much information has been uncovered about world jihad activists gathering intelligence on Jewish institutions … in Europe, North America and Asia.] To counter these threats, the security chief of Jewish communities in cooperation with the respective local security services and police forces, as well as the 'Jewish intelligence', have in recent years stepped up their preparedness to tackle any terrorist threat.

At the same time as the Mossad was brought back firmly to the front line of fighting antisemitism, Israel's wider offensive expanded. In 2006 a government decision was taken 'to coordinate activities dealing with the problem of anti-semitism'.[38] From 2003 to 2005 Sharansky, as minister without portfolio with responsibility for diaspora affairs, dealt with the issue and endeavoured to give the new Global Forum Against Antisemitism—the international face, if you like, of the government body, the Coordination Forum for Countering Anti-semitism (CFCA)—a place at the table where bodies like the OSCE and the EU were making decisions intended to commit states to taking concrete actions to fight antisemitism, forums where Jewish groups such as the AJC, SWC, WJC and CST had become increasingly active over the previous ten years.[39] Coordi-nating the fight against antisemitism and defending the Jewish people were key government aims according to Sharansky',[40] but he was probably overstating the government's intentions at that point. And 'defending the Jewish people' inside the countries with diaspora Jewish communities when it came to antisemitism, rather than just urging Jews 'under threat' to emigrate to Israel, was still not regarded as a Zionist objective across the range of right-wing Zionist parties in the Knesset. But Sharansky left the government in 2005; the portfolio was left vacant for over a year and at some point between late 2006 and early 2007 a decision was taken to close the unit for diaspora affairs that operated within the prime minister's office.

Against this background, the then foreign minister, Tzipi Livni, decided 'to take the Global Forum under her wing',[41] no doubt recognising the political value of the fight against antisemitism in the conduct of the government's foreign policy.

The foreign ministry wants to retain control of the Forum, even if a new minister for diaspora affairs is appointed. It is true, as the Israeli diplomats claim, that the foreign ministry is the only governmental body that has the organizational ability and the global reach to pull together a conference on antisemitism at an international level. That ability was proven by the unprec-edented number of participants the ministry was able to attract, with less than three months to organize the event, and no budget to begin with. Credit for the achievement goes largely to the new Department for Combating Antisemitism, headed by Aviva Raz-Shechter, and the Department for Jewish Communities, headed by Akiva Tor.

Barkat claims that had Livni not taken 'the Global Forum under her wing ... it is doubtful whether the struggle against antisemitism would have attracted any attention at all from the present Israeli government'. This may or may not be the case. In any event, the Global Forum has been a fixture of Israel's attempts to showcase, in an international setting, its leadership of the 'war' against antisemitism. Between 2007 and 2018, the Forum has held an international gathering six times, with varying gaps between meetings: 2007, 2008, 2009, 2013, 2015, 2018. But during these years, Israeli governments, especially since Netanyahu became prime minister in 2010, expanded the way in which they instrumentalised the politicisation of antisemitism to help further their strategic goals.

As the emphasis on the central features of modern antisemitism shifted from traditional forms associated with the far-right, neo-fascists, neo-Nazis, white supremacists and so on, to demonisation of the Jewish state, questioning its legitimacy, arguing that Zionism is a racist ideology, advocating boycott, divestment and sanctions, aided by the increasing ubiquity of references to the EUMC 'working definition' of antisemitism and Sharansky's '3Ds' test, so new vehicles were put in place to ram home the significance of this new emphasis. This brought most solace to Israel advocacy groups, Israel lobbying organisations and an Israeli government that was increasingly convinced of the usefulness of antisemitism accusations as a shield against external criticism of its actions. In Professor Neve Gordon's words: 'The Israeli government needs the "new antisemitism" to justify its actions and to protect it from international and domestic condemnation. Antisemitism is effectively weaponized, not only to stifle free speech ... but also to suppress a politics of liberation'.[42]

At the same time, the decision by the FRA to distance itself from its predecessor's association with the 'working definition', was not taken lightly by the international Jewish organisations, the dedicated anti-antisemitism organisations and the institutes promoting 'new antisemitism' theory. Although the EUMC text had taken on a life of its own, those who promoted it and those who subsequently joined in championing it, felt that the European international imprimatur had been very useful in extending the reach of the 'working definition', and set about finding another international framework through which its influence could be spread even more widely and be less subject to challenge.

Two crucial institutional developments at the turn of the first decade brought into alignment the Israeli government's antisemitism policy designed to serve, first and foremost, national interests, and the anti-antisemitism offensive of the major international and national Jewish organisations.

Israel's Ministry of Strategic Affairs (MSA) had an uncertain start. Founded in 2006 for Avigdor Lieberman, whose party joined the coalition government, it was abolished in 2008 after he left, only to be resurrected in 2009. Until then, the task of combatting the '3Ds', Sharansky's definition of the nature of the 'new antisemitism', at the government/state level resided with the Ministry of Foreign Affairs (MFA), and with the various incarnations of a minister or Ministry of Diaspora Affairs—also called the Hasbara Ministry—sometimes within the Prime Minister's Office and sometimes within the MFA. After Sharansky ceased to be Minister of Social and Diaspora Affairs in 2006, when Ehud Olmert became prime minister heading a centre-left-religious coalition, the Labour Party's Isaac Herzog became Minister of Diaspora, Society and the Fight Against Antisemitism. A further change was implemented when the Likud came to power in 2009 and Yuli Edelstein became Minister of Public Diplomacy and Diaspora Affairs, in a stand-alone ministry of the same name, from 2009 to 2013. The ministry itself was abolished in 2013 and then re-established as part of the Ministry of Strategic Affairs in 2015, when 'finally it was determined that it would lead the public diplomacy effort from within Israel'.[43] In 2009, with the reestablishment of the MSA, Prime Minister Netanyahu said it would play 'a central role in coordinating the government efforts to fight the attempt to damage Israel's legitimacy'.[44] Yossi Kuperwasser, who headed the research division of military intelligence during the second intifada, was appointed director-general of the MSA in that year, and served until 2014. He and the prime minister identified 'delegitimisation' as one of three central threats to Israel—BDS was defined as an 'existential' or 'strategic' threat. The core issue for the prime minister and the MSA was whether 'the BDS movement was going to be successful in implanting in international discourse that Israel is illegitimate as a Jewish state'.[45]

Although this tortuous journey looks like a 'Yes Minister!'-style parody, it actually reflects a very significant double truth: first, that Israeli political leaders knew that, as the target of the 'new antisemitism', the Jewish state had to develop a serious response both out of fear of what they believed to be the real impact of 'delegitimisation, dehumanisation, and double standards' and as a way of strengthening ties with the Jewish diaspora to mobilise it as a strategic asset; and that they were at sixes and sevens regarding how to achieve these tasks. So, by 2015, the MSA was being presented as the central state agency leading Israel's offensive against 'new antisemitism'. As the State Comptroller's annual report put it:

the political-security cabinet ... determined that the Ministry of Strategic Affairs would be responsible 'for guiding, coordinating, and integrating the activity of all the government ministries and civil bodies in Israel and abroad on the issue of fighting the efforts to delegitimize Israel and the boycott movements'.[46]

The MFA retained a major role in this effort, with its 106 representative offices around the world and the fact that 'its emissaries had unmediated access to, among others, people in sympathetic organizations and their counterparts'.[47] And there is evidence that the Mossad was also involved in the offensive against 'new antisemitism'.[48]

The MFA determined that efforts to delegitimise Israel were being strengthened significantly by the BDS movement from 2005 and the government saw this as a 'severe threat'. It therefore began tailoring hasbara activity at BDS specifically in a struggle over public opinion. Hasbara agencies began using social media—Facebook, YouTube, Twitter, etc.—for this purpose, and the MFA established a Division of Digital Diplomacy to develop the media tools to disseminate hasbara in dozens of languages.[49] It also founded the Spokesperson's Division for Arabic. In 2009, it began using 'ordinary' Israeli citizens and diaspora Jews to spread Israel's message, not just establishment figures. A first project, 'Presenting Israel', 'succeeded beyond expectation': between February 2010 and July 2012 more than 100,000 'instruction' pamphlets were distributed to Israelis at Ben-Gurion Airport. Another project was then started, Faces of Israel, which involved sending delegations to North American campuses. Given special training in how to 'show Israel's real and diverse face', these delegations were exposed to more than 2,000 students across the United States. Also judged a success by the MFA—though there seems to have been no formal evaluation of these projects—officials decided it was worthwhile to invest further in similar schemes, targeted at young American Jews, such as Taglit—free, organised ten-day trips to Israel for 18–32 year-olds—and Masa—internship, study and volunteer opportunities all over Israel lasting between five and twelve months, as well as Eye2Israel, a collaborative effort with the ORT educational network. The national airline El Al sent crew members to tell personal stories to Jewish groups. Another hasbara project, the Situation Room—based on the White House brainstorming method, but for young people at summer camps to produce Israel-friendly activity programmes—established at the Interdisciplinary Centre in Herzlia during the Gaza wars of 2012 and 2014 became a permanent part of the Act. IL app programme, created by the MSA. Young people with this app received messages to comment on Facebook defending Israel or attacking its enemies. But to make messages more effective among liberal groups—Democratic Party supporters who believe in pluralism and criticism, for example—a directive was given to allow a limited amount of criticism of Israel's policy after it was agreed that Israel had the right to exist. This replaced the classic Israeli hasbara tactic of posing a dichotomous choice: either for or against Israel.

A parallel choice was to avoid foreign, defence and Palestinian issues, and stress instead Israel's hi-tech achievements, the humanitarian aid it provides to disaster areas, contributions to science and the humanities and the pluralism that prevails in Israel—all of which were at the heart of the 'Brand Israel' project.[50]

But the hard core work of the MSA, under its ministerial head Gilad Erdan, who was also Public Security Minister and held both posts from 2015–2020, given its task of coordinating all anti-delegitimisation efforts, was far more uncompromising. As Joshua Leifer, an editor at *Dissent* magazine put it in 2019:

> The Israeli government long ago adjusted its public relations strategy for the post-two-state reality … so that today, the Israeli hasbara apparatus's most active front is the attempted redefinition of anti-Zionism as antisemitism, with the goal of rendering any opposition to the occupation [or] Zionism— or even simply Israeli policies themselves—beyond the pale of mainstream acceptability.[51]

'In recent years, Israeli officials have enthusiastically embraced the "new antisemitism" framework in their attacks on Palestine solidarity activism'. This emerges clearly in Ayelet Shaked's 2016 interview with the *Washington Post*: 'In the past, we saw European leaders speaking against the Jews. Now, we see them speaking against Israel. It is the same antisemitism of blood libels, spreading lies, distorting reality and brainwashing people into hating Israel and the Jews'.[52] For Shaked, BDS supporters are 'using the same kind of antisemitism but instead of saying they are against the Jews, they say they are against Israel'.

From 2015, mobilising against BDS was stepped up.[53] What was identified by the government as a 'severe threat' in 2005, ten years on was generating even more concern. In response, Friends of Israel groups in various countries were encouraged to fight BDS with legal instruments 'advancing legislation in many countries making boycott illegal'. Between 2014 and 2016, more than 100 measures targeting boycotts and Palestinian rights advocacy had been introduced in state legislatures and congress. Sima Vaknin-Gil, director-general of MSA, reported 'making progress' with an $11m budget in 2015, but refused to disclose details: 'A lot of what we do is under the radar' she told a Knesset Committee.[54] Nevertheless, as legal materials submitted to the Supreme Court on 7 August 2018 reveal, the Israeli government declared that 'the Knesset [is permitted] to legislate laws everywhere in the world' and that it is authorised 'to violate the sovereignty of foreign countries via legislation that would be applied to events in their territories'.[55] In December 2018, Erdan announced that the MSA would invest $800,000 over the following two years to create an international legal network to fight BDS. By April 2019, 27 US states had adopted such anti-boycott laws and five executive orders against BDS had been issued by state governors.

Allegations made of close links between BDS groups and Palestinian armed factions never amounted to more than 'vague accusations', but they helped bolster the claim that BDS was antisemitic. And the government's efforts met with some success as 'dozens of fundraising accounts associated with Palestine solidarity and BDS groups were closed "on grounds of alleged connections to terrorism'".[56]

There was never much reluctance on the part of the MSA, the MFA and all of the other Israel-associated bodies fighting delegitimisation to acknowledge their belief that BDS was innately antisemitic. And the propensity to say this ever-more openly, and also attack its supporters, increased. In August 2018, the Act.IL app 'issued a "mission" for social media users to make comments against Labour Party leader Jeremy Corbyn, accusing him of antisemitism'.[57] In 2015 Corbyn had backed a boycott of Israeli universities involved in arms research.[58] (Although, as party leader, he did not support the full BDS agenda.)

On 25 September 2019, Erdan was at the European Parliament in Brussels telling politicians that the Palestinian-led BDS movement was 'an antisemitic campaign'. He was there to launch an Israeli government report *Behind the Mask: The Antisemitic Nature of BDS Exposed*. With him at the subsequent press conference was Elan S. Carr, the US State Department's special envoy to monitor and combat antisemitism, who attacked BDS as 'classical old antisemitism, repackaged and rebranded, cloaked poorly as anti-Israel rhetoric'. The report was the work of the MSA and demonstrated 'how the BDS leadership hides behind a mask of liberal values and human rights, while disseminating content relating to Israel which is blatantly antisemitic', according to an MFA press release.[59] At the same press conference European Jewish Association director Rabbi Menachem Margolin declared the BDS movement 'responsible for the vast majority of physical attacks and social media hatred against Jews in Europe'.[60]

In May 2019, the German parliament voted to condemn BDS as antisemitic.[61] The motion said a BDS campaign calling for Israeli products to be labelled with 'Don't Buy' stickers was reminiscent of the Nazi-era boycott of Jewish businesses, known in German as 'Judenboykott', which used slogans such as: 'Don't buy from Jews'. Israel's ambassador to Germany, Jeremy Issacharoff, welcomed the Bundestag decision. He said the motion had broader European significance given that 'BDS makes no attempt to build coexistence and peace between Israel and all of its neighbors', he tweeted.

On 22 October 2019 the lower house of the Czech parliament passed a non-binding resolution, with an overwhelming majority, strongly condemning 'all manifestations of antisemitism directed against individuals, religious institutions, organisations as well as the state of Israel, including the denial of the Holocaust'. It condemned 'all activities and statements by groups calling for a boycott of the state of Israel, its goods, services or citizens'. 'We regard Israel as our true ally in the fight against Islamic terrorism', far-right MP Tomio Okamura said, adding that the Jewish state 'should be a role model' for his country.[62] Afterwards, Israel's ambassador to Prague expressed appreciation for the chamber's 'unequivocal condemnation of antisemitism and steadfast support of Israel', while Israeli Foreign Minister Israel Katz tweeted his own thanks, calling 'on more Parliaments to follow suit'. Jan Bartošek, the head of the Christian Democrats faction who introduced the resolution (that was also partially formulated by the Czech Foreign Ministry) hailed Israel as the Czech Republic's 'strategic partner and ally in the Middle East'.

Clearly buoyed by its conclusion that investing resources in attacking BDS, pro-Palestinian activism, anti-Zionist groups (including Jewish ones), campus debates which entertain the idea of a single democratic secular state for Israel–Palestine and so on were paying dividends, and doing so by basing its actions firmly on the increasingly ubiquitous features of 'new antisemitism', the Israeli government had even more reason for satisfaction with the other main institutional development over the decade to 2020: the adoption by the International Holocaust Remembrance Alliance (IHRA) of a 'working definition' of antisemitism and the text's subsequent worldwide dissemination.

*   *   *

In this chapter and to an extent the previous chapter I have only been able to give a flavour of the 'cast of actors'—from international governmental and non-governmental organisations to websites, university think tanks to MSA app programmes, parliamentary committees to uncompromising civil society groups, Israeli intelligence agencies to NGO watch bodies, European racism monitoring agencies to Jewish community-based defence groups and so on—which make up the transnational field of governance that operates on the basis of anti-'new antisemitism' thought and practice and on the Jewish particularism that underpins it.

We should bear in mind, however, that this field of governance is by no means static, and the effectiveness of the way it operates is to be assessed on the basis of its identifiable impacts. Such impacts may or may not reflect claims made by institutions that are active in the field. And their influence may fluctuate, especially if they are political creations, like the MSA for example. While its centrality to the 'war' on antisemitism has been strongly emphasised by the Israeli government in recent years, since its original establishment it has had a chequered history. Despite being handed many millions of NIS, the government decided to abolish the ministry in July 2021, on the grounds that its tasks— fighting delegitimisation and BDS, for example—were best undertaken by the MFA, which has been involved in this kind of activity itself over many years. Some were convinced that it wasted money and had always been used as a perch for a particular politician who needed a special favour.[63] Others judged that it had done important work in pushing back on BDS.[64] What is certain is that the anti-antisemitism activity in which it engaged will still be a key feature of Israel's foreign policy.

There are many reasons why the governance works on such a broad front and with multiple sources of direction, and a great deal of self-direction. The delegitimising of the ideology of multiculturalism, an audience attentive to the blaming of 'new antisemitism' on the human rights agenda and the organisations that support it (see Chapter 10), the sympathy of right-wing groups who see Jewish complaints about antisemitism not being taken seriously as an assertion of a Jewish particularist identitarianism opposed to the universalising framework of Christian humanism and the Enlightenment—all these are political and ideological positions that those who hold to them would find compatible with anti-'new antisemitism'.

9

The Redefinition Project and the Myth of the 'Collective Jew' Exposed

In the *New Shorter Oxford English Dictionary*, a 'definition' is defined as: 'A precise statement of the nature, properties, scope, or essential qualities of a thing'. Neither the EUMC nor the IHRA 'working definition' of antisemitism follows this explicit form. Their creators insist that it is the entire text—in both cases comprising a short opening definition in a box, followed by examples— that constitutes the 'working definition'. Their length alone, from the opening sentence in the box—507 words for the EUMC version; 506 words for the IHRA version—makes dubious their claims to qualify as definitions. But more tellingly, all of the examples, which are ostensibly given to help identify when something is antisemitic, are conditional: they could or could not be antisemitic, depending on context—thereby rendering the 'working definitions' not definitive. They fail to tell us what constitutes the 'essential qualities of a thing'.

There is no guarantee that a shorter definition would be any better. For example, Roni Stauber of the Tel Aviv University Kantor Center, an institution that has done more than most to promote the term, writes: '"new antisemitism" can be defined as: a clear conflation of Jewish communities and Israel, which are perceived as a single evil entity'.[1] While this may unintentionally capture— or perhaps rather express—something of the confusion which characterises our understanding of antisemitism today, it is utterly inadequate as a definition: it may be a manifestation of antisemitism but is not a definition of it.

Moreover, it flatly contradicts the often-stated position of former Prime Minister Benjamin Netanyahu, self-styled 'leader of the Jewish people', and other far-right Israeli political leaders such as Naftali Bennet (Israel's prime minister at the time of writing), who see the conflation of 'Jewish communities and Israel' as a core tenet of Zionism, the fulfilment of Jewish destiny.

Since the IHRA's 2016 adoption of its 'working definition'—a marginally revised version of the EUMC 'working definition' of 2005—the very opposite of clarity has been introduced into the matter of defining antisemitism. For *any* definition of antisemitism to be given the publicity that the IHRA 'working definition' has received would have been extraordinary. For the prolix IHRA 'working definition'—leaving aside any questions about its intelligibility, coherence or status as a definition—to have become so ubiquitous seems scarcely credible.

Its promoters would argue that there was an urgent need for a new definition of antisemitism. In 2019 Mark Weitzman, then director of Government Affairs for the Simon Wiesenthal Center, presented his rationale for using the IHRA as the vehicle for reinserting the EUMC working definition into the public domain internationally, following a period when the FRA had in effect disowned the EUMC 'working definition' and withdrawn it from its website: 'It was our feeling that in order to begin to address the problem of antisemitism, there must be clarity as to what antisemitism actually is'.[2] In his paper 'Two steps forward and one step back: diplomatic progress in combating antisemitism', originally delivered in the YIISA 2009–2010 seminar series, Michael Whine claimed that 'what has been of real lasting benefit is the EUMC Working Definition of antisemitism. Until its creation and dissemination, no two experts could define antisemitism in the same way'.[3]

Irwin Cotler had argued in 1992 that there were as yet no indices of measurement of the 'new antisemitism'—'discrimination against Jews as a people'. And he made the same claim almost 20 years later in his 'Global antisemitism: assault on human rights', a working paper published in the *Yale Papers* collection edited by Charles Small.[4]

In a *Times of Israel* blog on 1 December 2016, Rabbi Baker gave his response to the need for a new definition, and his and the AJC's role in creating it, reinforcing the accounts of Weitzman and Whine. Under the title 'To fight antisemitism, first define it', Baker wrote: 'The search for a definition began some fifteen years ago, when governments were slow in responding to the resurgence of antisemitism in Western Europe'.[5]

Giving testimony before the Knesset's Aliya, Absorption and Diaspora Committee on 29 December 2015, Porat said: 'I think it's necessary to renew recognition of this definition [EUMC "working definition"], international recognition ... because from all you have said and from every situation it's clear that anti-Israelism and anti-Zionism [are] more and more acquiring antisemitic tones'.[6]

In this jumble of justifications for the claim that a new definition was needed there is much to unpack. A strong *ex post facto* rationale has been imposed on the formal redefinition process, which reached its climax in 2016.

Starting with the IHRA itself, the organisation felt a new definition was needed in order, the text states, 'To guide IHRA in its work'. Yet IHRA exists to 'strengthen and promote Holocaust education, remembrance and research worldwide', and 'recognises that international political coordination is imperative to strengthen the moral commitment of societies and to combat growing Holocaust denial and antisemitism'.[7] It therefore seems odd, at the very least, that a body initially founded in 1998 as the Task Force for International Cooperation on Holocaust Education, Remembrance and Research (ITF), could undertake any Holocaust education, presumably to ensure that genocide could never happen again, without a clear understanding of what antisemitism is. And in a 'Statement by Experts of the UK Delegation to the IHRA on the Working Definition of Antisemitism', issued formally on their behalf by the IHRA office in Berlin on 7 August 2018, the seven-person group insisted that: '[the IHRA's] network of experts was compelled in 2016 to address the global rise in antisemitic incidents by putting forth a clear "gold standard" definition of what antisemitism consists of'.[8] But how could they know there was a global rise in incidents if no adequate definition of antisemitism existed? This is no mere logical quibble since later in their statement, when insisting that altering anything at all in the document before adopting it—at that time the Labour Party was considering adoption but with some amendments—would automatically mean that it 'is no longer the IHRA definition', they justify this injunction by making the following bizarre assertion: 'We would once again revert to a world where antisemitism goes unaddressed because different entities cannot agree on what it is'. Dismissing all anti-antisemitism work prior to the IHRA adopting its 'working definition' as effectively worthless is not only wrong, but appallingly arrogant and a rewriting of history, placing so-called 'expert status' at the service of politicised institutional rigidity and conformity.

Where does this notion of an absence of an agreed definition, leading to unaddressed antisemitism, come from?

Some say that governments and security services failed to acknowledge that a rise in antisemitic incidents post-2000, largely perpetrated by Muslims, were linked to vicious anti-Israel and anti-Zionist sentiment that they did not recognise as antisemitic; that, hypothetically, a visibly orthodox Jew attacked in anger at Jewish support for Israeli attacks on Gaza would be treated as political and not as a hate crime. This would then be put down to police not having a definition of antisemitism that explained that attacking a Jew as a Jew, irrespective of the reason for the attack, is experienced as antisemitic. Some put down such recording errors not just to confusion or ignorance, but to deliberate playing down of Muslim-based antisemitism or to police sympathy for pro-Palestinian sentiment.

The scenarios may well happen, and security personnel may be confused or biased, but the cause is not the absence of a definition. As I have already shown (see Chapter 4), once antisemitism from Islamist sources became a significant factor in certain countries in the 1990s, antisemitism monitoring data collated for *Antisemitism World Report* clearly reflected this. There seemed to be no need to produce a new definition of antisemitism in order to identify the problem. The Introduction to the 1994 report included this paragraph:[9]

In regard to the question of defining antisemitism, a strictly common-sense approach has been adopted. It was found that when those who concern themselves with the phenomenon in a serious manner were asked to report on it, there was a remarkable degree of unanimity about what was being described. The only significant area where differences emerge is on the question of the relationship between anti-Zionism and antisemitism. Here we have erred on the side of caution, including only those elements of anti-Zionism which are patently antisemitic or had antisemitic effects.

The final sentence offered a practical way of dealing with the dilemma.

But if it is argued that this is not exactly a definition and it would be better to have one, there are perfectly good ones already in existence. One such definition was drafted by the Oxford philosopher Brian Klug, a leading expert on modern uses and abuses of the term 'antisemitism'. Klug emphasises that to the antisemite, 'the Jew is not a *real* Jew at all' and therefore, as in his following short definition, should always appear enclosed in quote marks: 'At the heart of antisemitism is the negative stereotype of "the Jew": sinister, cunning, parasitic, money-grubbing, mysteriously powerful, and so on. Antisemitism consists in projecting this figure onto individual Jews, Jewish groups and Jewish institutions'.[10] He fleshes out this imagined 'Jew' as the antisemite would see him:

The Jew belongs to a sinister people set apart from all others, not merely by its customs but by a collective character: arrogant yet obsequious; legalistic yet corrupt; flamboyant yet secretive. Always looking to turn a profit, Jews are as ruthless as they are tricky. Loyal only to their own, wherever they go they form a state within a state, preying upon the societies in whose midst they dwell. Their hidden hand controls the banks, the markets and the media. And when revolutions occur or nations go to war, it's the Jews—cohesive, powerful, clever and stubborn—who invariably pull the strings and reap the rewards.

Klug then extends the definition to cover discourse about Israel and Zionism by stating that

if [a] text projects the figure of 'the Jew' directly or indirectly (a) onto Israel for the reason that Israel is a Jewish state, or (b) onto Zionism for the reason that Zionism is a Jewish movement, or (c) onto Jews, individually or collectively, in association with either (a) or (b), then that text is antisemitic.[11]

Klug acknowledges that applying these definitions to real phenomena is by no means always straightforward. But that does not justify the abandonment of what would have been seen as a reasonable consensus definition of antisemitism 30–40 years ago. And make no mistake, this is not an argument about semantics, but rather about coming to terms with changing political realities. On the one hand, as Klug does by building on accumulated academic knowledge; on the other hand, as proponents of the concept of the 'new antisemitism' do by abandoning almost all of that knowledge for reasons of Jewish particularism: national, ethnic or religious identification and loyalty, as well as political ideology.

Whine's assertion that 'Until [the EUMC working definition's] creation and dissemination, no two experts could define antisemitism in the same way' sounds so matter-of-fact that the uninitiated are likely to accept the statement without question. But if such a statement were true, there could be no genuine discussion and dialogue, even in a field of study in which there may be differences. My own experience of marshalling the work of scores of antisemitism researchers around the globe to produce a world survey addressing a phenomenon that they all recognise as the same multifaceted thing, proves the absurdity of Whine's statement.

Cotler's insistence that decades have gone by since he first gifted the public his definition of 'new antisemitism', and yet there are still no indices for measuring it, is another shock-into-silence statement. If true, it follows that the consensus that had formed around the 'new antisemitism' by 2005 was not based on any systematic or reliable evidence.

When Baker claims that 'The search for a definition began some fifteen years ago, when governments were slow in responding to the resurgence of antisemitism in Western Europe', what search is he referring to? He gives the impression of an endeavour in which many people were involved, when in reality it was a politically motivated effort initiated by Baker and his colleagues in the AJC themselves, with the backing of a few others, including Porat and Whine. There was a perfectly good, if rather long, discussion of definitions of antisemitism in the EUMC report on antisemitism in the EU 2002–2003, published in 2004[12] which contained the building blocks of a definition that could easily have been the basis of a consensus understanding of contemporary antisemitism, had the EUMC's director's authority and confidence not been undermined by the furore generated by the leak of the controversial report. (The board member who leaked the report was Jean Kahn, a leader of French Jewry, former president of the European Jewish Congress and founding figure of the EUMC.)

Porat's drive to entrench the EUMC 'working definition' not only as the sole, legitimate definition of antisemitism—by implication the one all dictionaries should adopt—but also as mostly focused on critical discourse about Israel and Zionism, made a mockery of the EUMC's own continued insistence that the 'working definition' was for discussion only and was never formally adopted by the EUMC.

There is no reason whatsoever why anyone should shy away from discussing definitions of, or what constitutes, antisemitism. The academic discussion of such definitions is quite common, and why it takes place is understandable. The word 'antisemitism'—without a hyphen—only came into common usage when the German journalist Wilhelm Marr popularised it in 1879 with the setting up of the Antisemites League and the publication of his book *Victory of Jewry Over Germandom*. The word then eventually came to be used to describe all forms of hostility to Jews going back more than two millennia. But that hostility has taken different forms over this period. Christianity saw Jews as blind unbelievers and Christ killers; economic antisemitism was based on the supposed stranglehold of 'the Jews' over finance and capitalism; cultural antisemitism, which saw Jewish rationalism as responsible for Marxism and other 'modernist' developments; conspiracy theory antisemitism, whereby Jews were said to be involved in a supposed secret plot to control and take over the world, a plan 'revealed' in the 1903 Tsarist forgery *The Protocols of the Elders of Zion*; and then, with Marr and others, the emergence of racial antisemitism which saw 'the Jew'—the imaginary Jew—as having evil and corrupting racial characteristics that polluted the indigenous nation, and thus justified not just expulsion of Jews from human society, which is what the Nazis wanted at first, but then also their elimination—mass murder, 'extermination'—as the only way to rid the world of this malign influence. Whether the same word can be used to describe all of these and other forms of Jew-hatred is a subject of ongoing robust and often undignified academic debate.

Defining *current* antisemitism also involves rigorous academic study and discussion, up to a point. However, with incomplete data and little historical perspective, definitive accounts of antisemitism are hard to come by, their judgements proving to be very ephemeral. As we have seen, the main purpose of exploring definitions is in relation to combatting antisemitism, to clarify the targets of the struggle against it.

And there is a strong link between scholarly, historical discussion of antisemitism and arguments over what antisemitism is today. Broadly speaking, and at the risk of oversimplification, there are two approaches: one that sees a linear pattern of development of a singular phenomenon; a transnational continuity between anti-Jewish hostility's first emergence and its present manifestations; sometimes called 'eternalism'. The other finds even the word 'antisemitism' problematic because it implies a continuity that does not reflect reality; in this view a historicist approach is required because antisemitism has meant different things to different people at different times, and is made up of different components interacting dynamically with each other.[13] There is another approach that purports to get beyond this dichotomy and that is to see antisemitism as 'cyclical': each form of manifestation of antisemitism is 'nothing but the latest repetition of an eternal cycle that has perpetually plagued Jews, triggered by the same set of causes'.[14]

Those who have insisted on the need for a new definition generally see a clear shift from what is often called, arguably very inappropriately, 'classic' antisemitism, generally referring to the essentially racially-based Jew-hatred of European provenance that originated towards the end of the nineteenth century, to the 'new antisemitism' that targets the Jewish state and the ideology of Zionism upon which it is based. At the same time, both phenomena are located within the wider frame of seeing antisemitism as 'the longest hatred',[15] a 'very light sleeper',[16] a phenomenon sufficiently singular to warrant, for Robert Wistrich, the writing of a comprehensive history titled *A Lethal Obsession: Antisemitism from Antiquity to the Global Jihad*.[17]

But the fact that there is nothing unusual or inherently political in discussing definitions only raises further questions about why the definitional issue seemed to have become so controversial. Some observers felt that the understanding of what antisemitism was at the turn of the century was inadequate for encompassing the alleged antisemitic hostility to the Jewish state emanating from Muslim sources and, it was argued, increasingly from the left. However, there is no hard evidence that such inadequacy actually existed.

For those working in the field of monitoring and studying antisemitism for the purpose of combatting it in the late 1970s/early 1980s there *was* a common understanding of what antisemitism was. When in 1982 the IJA's international journal *Patterns of Prejudice* invited an international cross-section of leading academics, intellectuals, politicians and Jewish leaders to assess the state of antisemitism in short essays, no contributors asked for a definition and the editors felt no need to offer one.[18] It was rightly taken for granted that the diverse range of 21 respondents would have no doubts as to whether they were all writing about the same thing. The second question posed to contributors covered the issue of anti-Zionism's relationship with antisemitism: 'Are we now experiencing entirely new forms of antisemitism, which come from the extreme left as well as from the right, and are expressed in the form of "anti-Zionism"? How far would you regard such anti-Zionism as synonymous with antisemitism?' None of the respondents felt that a new definition of antisemitism was required for the purposes of discussing these questions.

Ten years later, when the IJA began preparations to publish an annual, country-by-country, human rights-style world report on antisemitism, cooperating with dozens of researchers, monitoring organisations and academics around the world, no one involved asked the editors or compilers to define antisemitism for them. And when the IJA and its successor JPR presented their findings each year to journalists at well-attended press conferences, no one asked 'what do you mean by antisemitism?'

In 1991 *Patterns of Prejudice* repeated its 1982 symposium on 'Antisemitism Today', this time under the title 'Antisemitism in the 1990s'. There were 27 responses to the invitations to contribute essays. Some were contributors to the 1982 symposium, but most were new names and included up-and-coming younger academics. Four questions were posed. The third covered the issue of anti-Zionism/antisemitism: 'What role, if any, do you think the conflict between Israel and the Arab world is playing in fostering anti-Jewish sentiment? How important is the emergence of Islamic fundamentalism in this context? To what extent is antisemitism today taking the guise of anti-Zionism?'[19] Once again, no definition of antisemitism was given and none requested.

Throughout the 1990s it was concern about how to interpret evidence of rising antisemitism in the former Soviet Union and the former communist states of Eastern and Central Europe that preoccupied observers. As the decade ended attention shifted to the 'is anti-Zionism antisemitism?' question and to whether 'new antisemitism' theory helped or hindered reaching an answer. There was a new definition of antisemitism in circulation, and it had been for more than a decade—Irwin Cotler's 'Israel is the "collective Jew" among the nations'—but there was no mounting clamour promoting Cotler's project or for any other new definition as the century drew to a close.

The 9/11 watershed moment, coming on top of the Al-Aqsa intifada in October 2000, and the NGO Forum Against Racism at the Durban UN World Conference Against Racism in August and September 2001 (already discussed in Chapter 6), radically altered the balance of opinion about the salience of anti-Jewish and anti-Israel hostility. There was a spike in high-profile antisemitic incidents during those years and beyond, and it was Israel that came to be seen as the modern antisemite's principal victim. At the risk of oversimplification, it can be said that there are two ways of looking at what happened next.

To those who wanted a new definition, or more accurately, a redefinition, it was a perfect storm. The antisemitic incidents constituted a global resurgence. Islamist and left-wing sources were responsible. A plethora of articles placed 'new antisemitism' at the heart of the discourse about what was going on, but they claimed that the world did not want to know. In short order the first 'new antisemitism' books were published: Phyllis Chesler's *The New Antisemitism: The Current Crisis and What We Must Do About It*,[20] and Pierre-André Taguieff's *La nouvelle judéophobie*.[21] Then in February 2004, Sharansky's new Global Forum agreed to his proposal of a new definition of antisemitism, which was given formal status in an article he wrote for *Jewish Political Studies Review* in autumn 2004, in the form of the '3 Ds': demonisation of the Jewish state; double standards applied to Israel; delegitimisation, or denying Israel's right to exist.

I have covered in greater detail in Chapter 7 how, only a few months later, in January 2005, the EUMC posted on its website its 'working definition' of antisemitism, based on AJC antisemitism expert Kenneth Stern's proposal for a redefinition of antisemitism. And so, 'new antisemitism' was formally codified.

The other story belongs to those who, while fully aware of the spike in incidents, were very wary of putting it down to Islamist and left-wing Jew-hatred. The turmoil in Israel–Palestine, the genuine and justified resentment at continued occupation, the sense of hopes betrayed when the mid-January 2001 Taba peace talks collapsed,[22] the indecent rush to lay the blame on Muslims and the patent illogicality and historical distortion of equating anti-Zionism with antisemitism—these critical factors were being ignored. It followed from their rejection of the notion of the 'new antisemitism' that they believed the demand for a redefinition was precisely in order to define anti-Israel speech by Muslims and the left as antisemitic. Its relevance for other forms of antisemitic expression was merely incidental.

The staying power of the EUMC 'working definition' has proved to be extraordinary; and its influence expanded greatly after a slightly amended version of it was adopted by the IHRA in 2016.

There is no doubt that this process has been crucial to the crystallisation of the struggle against antisemitism. Anti-'new antisemitism' activists, researchers, monitors, academics, Jewish defence and representative organisations now had a codified version of the misdemeanours of the alleged antisemitic Israel-haters in an unamendable form—despite it still being called a 'working definition'.[23] It rapidly acquired the aura of a holy text as its key promoters and the IHRA secretariat policed the adoption process and slapped down anyone who suggested anything other than that the entire 506 words constituted the definition: the opening short, bland statement about antisemitism, plus the eleven examples of what could be antisemitic depending on the context, eight of which refer directly or indirectly to Israel. There is no memorable or quotable phrase or sentence in the text summing up the pithy essence of the definition, not even in the opening paragraph, which is printed in bold type and enclosed in a box. In fact, taken as a whole, there is no pithy essence. (This gives it malleability, meaning that any part of it can be taken and used to justify virtually any allegation of antisemitism, because there is nothing else in the text that prevents you from doing so: a key factor in why it has proved so useful.) Cotler's 'Israel is the "collective Jew" among the nations' has been, as part of a discourse, far more influential. Nevertheless, the 'working definition' has strong symbolic value derived from its association with Holocaust remembrance and the high-level institutional approval it rapidly acquired.

I first criticised Cotler's definition in *Prospect* magazine in August 2002 as part of a wider attempt to contextualise the alleged rise of antisemitism in Europe, arguing that it was exaggerated—largely a mix of paranoia and a means of deflecting criticism from Israel.[24] Although I did not quote Cotler directly—

partly because many others had by then incorporated versions of his formulation into their own arguments about the nature of current antisemitism—I summed up his definition in this way:

> Most supporters of the 'new antisemitism' argument [argue that we are witnessing a] form of criticism of Israel which is so hostile that it can only be explained as hatred of Jews [and] lump all criticism [of Israel] together and label it anti-Zionism. And given that Zionism is the ideology of Jewish national liberation, opposition to it is deemed to be antisemitic. Just as traditional antisemitism was the denial of the right of the individual Jew to live in society as an equal citizen, so the new antisemitism is the denial of the right of the Jewish people to live as equal members of the family of nations.[25]

Later, I gave as an example of the argument that 'anti-Zionism = antisemitism' the then Chief Rabbi of the United Synagogue Jonathan Sacks's statement to the Parliamentary Committee Against Antisemitism that 'accusing Israel of "racism, ethnic cleansing, attempted genocide, crimes against humanity" is itself antisemitic'.[26] I continued: 'Yet to exempt Israel from such allegations is to set the threshold of where legitimate criticism tips over into antisemitism impossibly low. If we say a British institution is racist, does this imply an ideological anti-Britishness? If Milosevic is accused of crimes against humanity, does that imply racist anti-Serbianism?'[27]

I then sought to show the illogicality and counterproductive nature of Cotler's definition:

> The anti-Zionism equals antisemitism argument drains the word antisemitism of any useful meaning. For it means that to count as an antisemite, it is sufficient to hold any view ranging from criticism of the policies of the current Israeli government to denial that Israel has the right to exist as a state, without having to subscribe to any of those things which historians have traditionally regarded as making up an antisemitic world view: hatred of Jews *per se*, belief in a worldwide Jewish conspiracy, belief that Jews generated communism and control capitalism, belief that Jews are racially inferior and so on. Moreover, while theoretically allowing that criticism of Israeli governments is legitimate, in practice it virtually proscribes any such thing. Following Sacks's reasoning, an Israeli soldier who sees elements of racism and the denial of human rights in policies towards the Palestinians must be antisemitic.[28]

One of the elements of Cotler's definition of 'new antisemitism' that is common also to Sharansky's '3Ds' and both the EUMC and IHRA versions of the 'working definition' is the centrality of the state of Israel itself as the object of antisemitic hate. While criticism of Israeli governments' policies may or may not be antisemitic, in all three definitions the potential for any and all criticism of the state—the *only* 'Jewish state' we are always reminded, as if this acts as some blanket refutation of any allegations against it of human rights abuses or racial discrimination—to be deemed antisemitic is built into the text, notwithstanding any caveat such as the statement in the IHRA 'working definition' that 'criticism of Israel similar to that levelled at any other country cannot be regarded as antisemitic'. Cotler's rationale for this *sine qua non* is explicitly stated. In the 9 November 2010 version of his definition, which appeared in an article he wrote for the Canadian *National Post*, he stated: 'The new antisemitism involves the discrimination against, denial of, or assault upon the right of the Jewish people to live as an equal member of the family of nations, with Israel as the targeted "collective Jew among the nations"'. This is a simple, persuasive and appealing formulation—the Jewish state is the individual Jew writ large—and I suppose that if you accept the principle that Jewish people's attachment to Israel is, in UK legal terms, for example, 'a protected characteristic', the same as your ethnic or religious identity, then you would find the equivalence to your liking. However, the last time a legal claim was made of anti-Jewish discrimination on the grounds of attachment to Israel being a protected characteristic, it was summarily dismissed.[29]

Cotler's formulation works as poor poetry or mere rhetorical flourish, but nothing more. It is fundamentally flawed on four interrelated levels.

First, asserting a fundamental equivalence between a human being—living, breathing, feeling, making moral and ethical choices and (in Judaism) with free will to do good or evil, on the one hand, and on the other hand a state—a form of human organisation that can have neither will nor agency of its own, is a *category mistake*, the ascription of a property to a thing that could not possibly have that property.[30]

There are various definitions of a state, and no single definition that commands consensus. Possibly the most often quoted is the sociologist Max Weber's means-related definition that the state is 'a human community that (successfully) claims the monopoly of the legitimate use of physical force within a given territory'.[31] A Marxist definition is ends-related: the state exists to perpetuate class domination in favour of the ruling class. Also ends-related is John Locke's definition:[32] the goal of the state is 'the preservation of property', referring not only to personal possessions but also to one's life and liberty. The state is not synonymous with government.

All of these definitions of a state depend for their existence on human agency. Human beings can construct a state to be, or transform one into, an instrument, for example, for doing good or evil, for intrusive intervention in the lives of its citizens, for maintaining a *laissez-faire* approach to the way its population live their lives, for coercing groups into second class status, and so on. But a state could not possibly have the attributes of a human being. The notion of the state being like a 'Jew' is a nonsense.

Second, of course, the parallel is not with a living Jew but with the 'collective Jew'. Now while at least an individual Jew—or Christian, Muslim, Hindu or Jain for that matter—exists, is real flesh and blood, the 'collective Jew' does not exist. It is a mythical construct. As myth, it only works if it explains the world and human experience. In this instance, it stands for the state of Israel. By being made analogous with the individual Jew experiencing antisemitism, we are supposed to believe that antisemitism is something a state can experience too. But since we have already established that the state cannot have the properties of an individual, the claim that the state can experience antisemitism cannot be sustained. Let us be generous and call the 'collective Jew' a mythical construct in search of a meaning.

A third fundamental fault in speaking of Israel as 'the collective Jew' is that it reduces 'Jews' to a singularity—it stands for all Jews. It implies that all Jews are the same (See Chapter 1 for the first reference to this issue.) On the one hand, this takes us to the idea that the 'hate' or 'vicious criticism' directed at the state of Israel is the *eternal* hate experienced by all Jews over millennia. Quite apart from the weakness of the eternalist theory itself, and its ahistorical nature/assumptions, the very notion of Jews as a singularity is made nonsensical by Jewish history. There was always diversity: of identity, experience, religious practice and so on. As David Biale's *Cultures of the Jews* so majestically shows, there has never been a single Jewish culture.[33] Moreover, the Jewish world, post-Holocaust and post-the establishment of Israel is deeply divided as to what it means to be Jewish. The strict, narrow definition of 'who is a Jew', which applies in Israel by diktat of the religious authorities, whose writ is recognised by the state, clashes starkly with the pluralist Judaism common to the vast majority of American Jews. As Shlomo Fischer puts it: 'American and Israeli Jews no longer agree on what it means to be "Jewish"'.[34]

On the other hand, singularity takes us in the opposite direction, so to speak. 'Jews are all the same' is a classic antisemitic trope. To the antisemite, Jews are a certain type: devious, cunning, secretive, conspiratorial, greedy—all of them, without exception. That a redefinition of antisemitism is based on a logic that can itself be understood as antisemitic is quite absurd.

Fourth, the Cotler formulation also implies that the Jewish state is beyond criticism.

No one would seriously suggest that a person, even one who suffers persecution because of their colour, ethnicity, faith, etc., is beyond doing anything that might be morally wrong, or illegal, or gratuitously cruel. But the experience of the Holocaust has led us to see murder of a Jew in the gas chamber of a

Nazi death camp as the ultimate antisemitic act. And the naked human being facing that death is, at that moment, innocence personified. It is this quality of innocence that is conferred on the Jewish state in the formulation of 'Israel, the "collective Jew" among the nations'. And if the Jewish state has this quality of innocence and purity, the only thing it can be compared to is the deity. And like the deity, Jews should hold it in reverence. It has been our deliverance, our redemption. Jews should worship it. And it seems that many do. Therefore, the state is now deified.

Reverence also leads in another direction, *away* from the state as the innocent and *to* the state as the fulfilment of Judaism. In such a claim, Zionism is not the nineteenth-century political movement for Jewish self-determination that histories of Zionism say it was. Rather the state it wanted to bring into being would be sacrosanct, therefore implying that it would be the climax of Jewish history: in itself the pinnacle of Jewishness, the symbol of a pure Jewish identity, central to Judaism, such that every form of defence of it, every form of counter-attack or pre-emptive strike against its critics, is justified. Yet there is nothing in Judaism, or in biblical Jewish history of the united kingdom of Israel or its subsequent fragmented formations that suggests that a state of the Jews is in itself a fulfilment of God's decree.

By granting it this degree of reverence, critical speech calling for action to achieve change in Israel—advocating BDS, proposing the transformation of Israel into a state belonging to all its citizens, granting Palestinian refugees the right of return, replacing the current legal constitutional framework with a secular, democratic constitution, granting Palestinians full equal rights, including national rights—is easily characterised as a dire, existential threat, endangering the very essence of what Jews have created and the very existence of the state's Jewish population: the foundational belief that Israel's survival as a Jewish majority state equals Jewish survival.[35]

Some Zionists were well aware of the dangers inherent in this kind of thinking, understanding that the lure of nationalism and seeing its necessary realisation in the form of a unitary state could lead to disaster. In 1921, the philosopher and theologian Martin Buber, who was a key figure in Brit Shalom, a Zionist group in Palestine that was active in arguing for ways in which the Yishuv could fulfil the aims of national regeneration without establishing an exclusive Jewish state and by sharing the land with the Arab population, wrote presciently:[36]

A nationalist development can have two possible consequences. Either a healthy reaction will set in that will overcome the danger heralded by nationalism, and also nationalism itself, which has now fulfilled its purpose; or nationalism will establish itself as a permanent principle; in other words, it will exceed its function, pass beyond its proper bounds, and—with overemphasized consciousness—displace the spontaneous life of the nation. Unless some force arises to oppose this process, it may well be the beginning of the downfall of the people, a downfall dyed in the colours of nationalism.

Abraham Joshua Heschel, one of the leading Jewish theologians and philosophers of the twentieth century, wrote: 'Judaism is not a religion of space and does not worship the soil. So, too, the state of Israel is not the climax of Jewish history, but a test of the integrity of the Jewish people and the competence of Judaism'.[37] 'New antisemitism' is effectively predicated on the notion that the state can do no wrong.

As a people, Jews have been encouraged to see themselves as 'a light unto the nations'. But this image has been tarnished in recent years. The callous killing of children in Gaza. The evidence of apartheid. The schisms within the religion. Our flaws are more visible than ever. Never mind. The miracle of the state is above the messy reality of the Jew as a human being like any other human being. And so, the state can do no wrong. It is the state that is now 'a light unto the nations', no longer the people. But the state is an entity that has no innate value, whether or not we wish to invest our faith in it. And thus the reverence in which it is held is tantamount to idolatry. This fetishising of the Jewish state is a heresy.

The Sharansky definition and the EUMC/IHRA 'working definition' do not explicitly conflate the individual Jew with the Jewish state. But in reality, in both cases, when what they say is (or could be) antisemitic when said about the state, about the ideology that underpins it, and about the basic laws that are in effect the state's constitution, the result is much the same: to throw around Israel the mantle of protection from accusations of antisemitism as one would around an individual Jew being victimised by expressions of antisemitism.

The primary purpose of the state is to be the vehicle that realises the national goals of the Jewish people, and those goals are the quest for ethno-nationalist supremacy in perpetuity. And the purpose of the state's engagement in the fight against antisemitism is to defend that goal at all costs. Can it not do that in some other way? The answer is no, because the process of achieving that, and the achieving itself, violates human rights. The best way to justify that violation is to trump it by claiming the existence of a greater violation against yourself, a violation for which those whose human rights you are violating are deemed responsible: 'The Palestinians hate us. They want to drive us into the sea. They incite hatred against us. They are terrorists. We can only secure our future by fighting their antisemitism—which is bolstered by left and Muslim forces worldwide—and going full steam ahead to reclaim all the land'. On these grounds, Israel justifies its position that Palestinians do not deserve rights. Quite the opposite: not only is the military occupation 'a force for good', writes

Natasha Roth-Rowland, 'not only for the safety of Israel and the Jewish diaspora, but also as the "West's" last line of defence against "the forces of radical Islam"'.[38]

In an article for *Forward*, the American online news periodical, Jonathan Judaken offered 'Ten Commandments for thinking about modern antisemitism', which he calls 'post-Holocaust Judeophobia'. His sixth commandment was: 'Thou cannot define the problem away'. The specific 'problem' he was referring to is the use of Nazi analogies in the bitter arguments in America over contemporary antisemitism—analogies used by both sides in debate about it that is 'a dialogue of the deaf waged as a battle to the death'. He reasons that 'free speech protections will uphold people's right to make these analogies and arguments'. But his useful corrective—which also affirms the value of analogies and metaphors in seeking explanations—has wider applications. The very idea that a formal, universally agreed definition of antisemitism is a fundamental necessity for conducting the struggle against antisemitism is fanciful. There is no evidence that definitions of antisemitism have ever been put to effective use in combatting the phenomenon, or that they offer Jews any credible refuge from Jew-hatred. Deep disagreements among Jews about the IHRA 'working definition' have only intensified intra-Jewish conflict over the questions of the relationship between anti-Zionism and antisemitism, and attitudes towards the Palestinian-Israeli conflict.

The definitional obsession has also had the effect of making Jews *more* vulnerable to antisemitism, not *less*. The IHRA 'working definition' has widened the scope of what can be considered antisemitic by insisting that its conditional examples are part of the definition. Why stop at eleven possible expressions? There could be many more. On what grounds would others be excluded? The consequence is that, if almost anything is antisemitic, then nothing is. The word is rendered useless. Or as Brian Klug put it: 'when antisemitism is everywhere, it is nowhere. And when every anti-Zionist is an antisemite, we no longer know how to recognize the real thing—the concept of antisemitism loses its significance'.[39] (And indeed, the thrust of the Sharansky and Cotler definitions have contributed significantly to this devaluation of the word.)

It is not a criticism to state categorically that, while the obsession with defining the 'new antisemitism' has not been an entirely centralised project, it has always been fundamentally political. And since combatting antisemitism has always been a political task, this was to be expected. As the task of scaling up the fight was undertaken and it was increasingly conceived of as a 'war', whether this was necessary, appropriate, helpful, efficacious, or sensible, academic and discursive justifications for the redefinition of antisemitism were readily available and grew rapidly, directly encouraged by Jewish institutional involvement, various branches of the Israeli government and national and international governmental and non-governmental bodies. As Israel has been increasingly identified, and has identified itself, as the central target of the anti-Jewish hate network, it is hardly surprising that Judaken concludes that 'too much of what passes for thinking about antisemitism amounts to reductive apologetics or polemics'.[40] Not that states and their changing relationships with Jews have been overlooked in the intellectual and cultural history of the term antisemitism, David Feldman points out,[41] adding: 'This symbiosis [between Jews and states] continues anew with the state of Israel—the Jewish state—now transforming the meaning of antisemitism once more', though, as I would argue and have tried to demonstrate, in a more deliberate, organised and politically focused manner than I think Feldman means. Definitions of the 'new antisemitism', especially Cotler's category mistake formulation of 'Israel as the "collective Jew" among the nations', or just 'the Jew', not only transform the meaning of the term, they also legitimise taking the short step to replacing all previous definitions, and then further to argue that no other kind of antisemitism exists. This may seem bizarre, but Bernard-Henri Lévy, France's most prominent and possibly most influential public intellectual, could, with his trademark portentousness, confidently make such a claim in his 2008 book, *Left in Dark Times*,[42] writing that the 'new antisemitism' of the twenty-first century would be 'progressive—or nothing at all'—meaning essentially left-wing and radical groups representing the interests of the underclass and oppressed, including Islamist organisations like Hamas and the Muslim Brotherhood. And we need to look no further than the brazenly transparent policy of Netanyahu and all his far-right and orthodox allies in the Knesset for a concrete example of this transformation, as they were perfectly happy to accept the support of right-wing populists and former neo-Nazis, neo-fascists and Christian evangelicals who express their admiration and love of Israel, and turn a blind eye to the classic antisemitism these forces still promote and encourage, directed at liberal elements in their countries, including liberal and left-wing Jews. When the prime minister of the Jewish state does not criticise the antisemitic campaign waged by Hungary's President Orban against George Soros, the Hungarian-born Jewish philanthropist, and encourages others to openly condone it, the damage that the redefinition of antisemitism has caused is plain.[43] Surely, any moral legitimacy Israel arrogates to itself as the self-proclaimed centre of the Jewish world and leader of the Jewish people in the fight against antisemitism crumbles when it pursues narrow, national interest that endangers Jews who do not live in Israel.

There is plenty of critical, scholarly and intellectually persuasive literature which should have been sufficient to undermine fatally the credibility of the IHRA 'working definition' and the entire redefinition process. But this has not happened. A key reason is that so much of that critique has accepted the assumption that a new definition was needed, or that the IHRA text could be acceptable with appropriate amendments. As a result, a number of alternative definitions have been devised, the most comprehensive and best known to date being the Jerusalem Declaration on Antisemitism (JDA), into which a great deal of thought and strategic planning was invested.[44] Nevertheless, neither the JDA nor any other new definition has been a decisive challenge to IHRA, in great part because such efforts fight this battle on IHRA's ground— matching one prolix definition with another—and also assume that intellectual argument can win the day. IHRA has penetrated so deeply at international and national governmental levels, in academic institutions, state or local govern- ments, civil society groups of certain kinds, that the idea it could be pushed from its perch by circulating another visually similar definition was, although well-intentioned, misjudged. IHRA has effectively refused to engage with those promoting other definitions. However, some supporters of the 'working defini- tion' have done so on the crudest, dismissive level. The redefinition has always been a fundamentally political project, not an opening gambit in an intellectual or scholarly exchange. Fighting one long definition with another was a strategic error first and foremost, but also an academic and intellectual mistake. The only good definition is a short one.

Some of the key promoters of the IHRA 'working definition' know only too well the advantages of concision, or rather the combination of language slippage and concision. The Experts of the UK delegation to the IHRA issued a statement on 7 August 2018 calling the 'working definition' 'the "gold standard" definition' of antisemitism.[45] The CAA now brazenly refer to it simply as 'The International Definition of Antisemitism'.[46]

10

Human Rights: the 'Mask Under Which the Teaching of Antisemitic Contempt for Israel is Carried Out'

The role of villain played by human rights law, culture and activism—Cotler's *bête noire*—in the 'new antisemitism' has already figured in various places in this book. It is a key driver of UN delegitimisation of Israel and the basis on which left-wing groups and parties unfairly criticise Israel's treatment of the Palestinians, according to successive Israeli governments since the late 1960s, as well as to Israel advocacy groups and Zionist organisations. They view human rights as nothing more than a cloak to hide the antisemitic anti-Zionism of its network of affiliated forces. But from the landmark events relating to antisemitism at the turn of the century and the subsequent EUMC and IHRA redefinitions of antisemitism in 2005 and 2016, there has been a sharp increase in the significance of Jewish disillusionment with and growing attacks on the human rights movement broadly defined. This chapter traces how this unfolded. In doing so, in order to grasp its full importance, some of the pre-2000 developments relating to human rights and the 'new antisemitism' are briefly reprised.

* * *

We have seen how one of the key promoters of 'new antisemitism', Irwin Cotler, has made an integral part of his often-repeated narrative the antisemitic manipulation of human rights culture, norms and institutions, fleshing out his view that Israel is 'the "collective Jew" among the nations', which was given a full exposition in 1992 at the Brussels My Brother's Keeper conference (see Chapter 3). But as Michael Galchinsky points out: 'Although Diaspora activists embraced international human rights during the 1950s and 1960s, their enthusiasm began to cool in the mid-1960s'.[1] He explains this as resulting from the

> many members of the new UN majority—including the Communist bloc, Arab states, and newly independent African and Asian states—[which] began to use the human rights system not just to criticize Israel for particular violations but to ostracize it from the community of nations. The General Assembly's resolution of 10 Nov. 1975 (A/RES/3379) equated Zionism with

174

racism and initiated decades of condemnations of Israeli rights practices by various UN bodies.

The attempt to ostracise Israel from the UN system may have continued long after the Zionism = racism resolution was revoked on 16 November 1991, but it had lost any serious practical, negative consequences in the wake of the post-1989 geopolitical changes. Moreover, Israel made its revocation a condition of its participation in the Madrid Middle East peace talks, which took place from 30 October to 1 November 1991. The signing of the Oslo Accords took place two years later and generated optimism that a formal reconciliation would soon be concluded by the Palestinians and the Israelis. Although the Oslo process looked to be in serious difficulty by the turn of the century, the impact of any singling out of Israel for attack was progressively weakened as geopolitical realities led to Israel's relatively steady integration into the global political system.

Galchinsky argues: 'Beginning in the 1970s Jewish NGOs began to identify such behaviour [condemnation of Israel] as a "New Antisemitism", designed to turn Israel into a pariah and deny the Jewish people their right to self-determination'. There then began a steady retreat from seeing the codification of human rights as a major achievement in creating an international order in which something like the Holocaust could never happen again. Even during the period of the 'Oslo process', optimism did not prevent the critique of human rights culture from transmogrifying into the establishment of organisations, such as UN Watch (see Chapter 4), dedicated to exposing the alleged antisemitic ends driving the singling out of Israel and Zionism for condemnation in human rights forums. (Some of those behind the setting up of such bodies were never convinced that Oslo was a good deal for Israel in the first place.)

It was at the 1992 Brussels international conference on antisemitism that the rationale for UN Watch was set out by Irwin Cotler, speaking on a panel together with Morris Abram (see Chapter 4). His remarks were written-up as a chapter of the book *Religious Human Rights in Global Perspective: Religious Perspectives* published in 1996. '[I]n a world in which human rights has emerged as the new secular religion', he wrote with uncompromising vehemence,

> the portrayal of Israel as the metaphor for a human rights violator in our time exposes Israel as the 'new anti-Christ', with all the 'teaching of contempt' for this 'Jew among the nations' that this new antisemitism implies ... human rights becomes the mask under which this 'teaching of contempt' is carried out.[2]

No less emphatically, the indictment continues:

> the problem, as UN Watch has put it, is not that Israel as the 'Jew among the nations' seeks to be above the law, but that it has been systematically denied

175

equality before the law; not that Israel must respect human rights—which she should—but that the human rights of Israel have not been respected; or that human rights standards should be applied to Israel—which they must—but that these standards have not been applied equally to anyone else.[3]

Despite Cotler's unrestrained attack on those who seek to hold Israel to account for its treatment of the Palestinians, in comparison to NGO Monitor, established by Gerald M. Steinberg in 2001 in Jerusalem, with a focus on NGOs in general but with the UN very often in its sights, UN Watch's early reports critical of the UN's treatment of Israel were milder than the message conveyed by Cotler. By then, most of the major national and international Jewish organisations were adopting stances highly critical of the UN and other NGOs, especially Christian bodies such as War on Want and the World Council of Churches.

Nevertheless, among Jewish human rights activists there were those who refused to join the anti-human rights culture bandwagon. Especially interesting is the internal debate in the AJC as recounted by Galchinsky. In the late 1970s, activists in the AJC 'responded to the Zionism = Racism resolution in seemingly contradictory ways. In public, they mounted a substantial public defence of Israel's rights record'. Privately, however, the director of AJC's human rights arm, Sidney Liskofsky, discussed with his staff "'the Jewish ambivalence re: the Israel-human rights question". The staffers wrung their hands over whether there was any substance to the charges of abuse, and worried that such abuses might cause a negative backlash against Diaspora Jews'. On 18 October 1977, Abraham Karlikow, AJC's European director in Paris, sent a letter 'marked "Confidential" to Liskofsky and other staffers frankly discussing this ambivalence.[4] Recognizing "the special difficulties Israel faces," he nonetheless called for AJC to help build "a human rights-impartial body inside Israel"'. Intervening in Israeli human rights politics for the first time, AJC worked confidentially with Israeli Supreme Court Justice Haim Cohn and a group of non-governmental Israelis to establish the Association for Civil Rights in Israel (ACRI), a body now under regular attack from the political and religious right, and no longer one that finds favour in AJC circles.[5] As Galchinsky delicately but pertinently concludes: 'The split between AJC's public and private responses illustrates in stark terms the difficulties of balancing commitments to international human rights and Jewish nationalism'. A blatant example of this came in 2002 when, despite helping draft the 1998 Rome statute of the International Criminal Court, Israel nonetheless declined to ratify the treaty. 'The sticking point', Galchinsky explains, 'was a clause criminalizing a state's resettlement of its own civilians in territory it occupies. Israel interpreted this clause as the world community's attempt to restrain the West Bank settlement enterprise. Hence it decided not to join a court designed, among other things, to punish the perpetrators of genocide'.

In a speech in 1997, Diana Pinto, the influential intellectual historian based in Paris—who had been arguing for some years that in post-1989 Europe conditions had never been so favourable to foster a Jewish renaissance: 'a new religious and cultural creativity within a democratically pluralist Europe'—issued a warning: 'The risk today is that Europeans will become potentially anti-Israeli because Israel itself is not measuring up to the democratic, human rights and pluralist standards which Jews have come to expect of their European countries'.[6] While Pinto's critical view would have been sympathetically received even late in the decade of 'new Europe' optimism, by the mid-2000s, the Israeli mindset that determined the state should not ratify the ICC treaty was increasingly influential among organisations and leaders prosecuting the 'war' on antisemitism. In a Memorandum submitted by the Parliamentary Committee Against Antisemitism (PCAA) to the UK parliament's Select Committee on Home Affairs, and published in March 2005, the PCAA asserted:[7]

> The sin of the Jews is no longer deicide, nor are they are accused of possessing sinister racial traits. In the modern world, the methods of the antisemite are far subtler. It is antisemitism with a 'social conscience', often based on human rights and the demand of a homeland for the Palestinian people. Today's Jewish 'collective crime' is Israel. The Jews stand accused of supporting a racist state, and as such, they are collectively deserving of reproach. These people are using the veil of criticism of the state of Israel to mask their antisemitic sentiment.

To turn the human rights-based 'demand of a homeland for the Palestinian people' into nothing more than one of the 'methods' of the antisemite, especially since it had been their homeland for centuries and was guaranteed to them when the UN voted for partition in 1947, the resolution that the Zionist leaders and leaders of the Yishuv took as the international seal of approval for the declaration of a Jewish state, makes a zero-sum game out of what are supposed to be universal rights. It is significant to note, however, that those framing this argument feel it necessary, without any empirical justification, to dismiss the contemporary relevance of classic expressions of antisemitism in order to 'make way', as it were, for 'new antisemitism' as manifested in the application of human rights standards to Israeli political and military actions, yet this was featuring increasingly in the rhetoric of the 'war' on antisemitism. One writer suggests that Elie Wiesel, in his 1978 book *A Jew Today*,[8] and the Canadian academic Anne Bayevsky, whose website eyeontheun.org fulfilled a similar function as UN Watch, were early exponents of this, framing their criticisms of the UN as *the* modern antisemitism.[9] Also helping foster this anti-human rights climate was the then recently released text of the EUMC 'working definition' of antisemitism. Since its 2005 publication 'to the present', writes Rebecca Ruth Gould, 'no proponent of the working definition has been able to reconcile its exclusionary claims with fundamental human rights, to integrate it into a programmatic anti-racist agenda, or to use it to facilitate Jewish and Palestinian coexistence in the occupied territories'.[10]

More recently, as pressure mounted on governments, intergovernmental organisations, international NGOs, political parties, local authorities, universities and colleges to adopt the IHRA 'working definition', attacks on human rights groups resisting occupation have increased. David Weinberg, vice-president of the Jerusalem Institute for Strategic Studies and former coordinator of the GFCA, complained that

> much of the self-styled human rights community has studiously ignored the IHRA framework. Groups such as Amnesty International, Human Rights Watch and the World Council of Churches reject the [definition] ... and frequently stray into antisemitic territory in their incessant and fierce criticism of Israel. They also have studiously ignored the vast amounts of antisemitic materials emanating from the Arab world.[11]

Weinberg clearly feels that the case against human rights groups and human rights culture is strengthened by erroneously associating them with antisemitic propaganda emanating from Israel's 'enemies', as if the unsubstantiated accusation of turning a blind eye to it makes them actually responsible for it in some way.

With the success of this kind of guilt by associative contamination, other things that would ordinarily be protected on the grounds of free speech, such as advocacy of BDS, get caught in the antisemitic net. So, in 2019, Israel's Minister of Strategic Affairs Gilad Erdan could go to the European Parliament in Brussels, after more than a decade of targeting human rights culture as antisemitic, to launch, and be sure of a sympathetic hearing for, an Israeli government report, *Behind the Mask: The Antisemitic Nature of BDS Exposed*, which he said demonstrated 'how the BDS leadership hides behind a mask of liberal values and human rights, while disseminating content relating to Israel which is blatantly antisemitic'. Sitting alongside the minister at the subsequent press conference was Elan S. Carr, the US State Department's special envoy to monitor and combat antisemitism, who slammed BDS as 'classical old antisemitism, repackaged and rebranded, cloaked poorly as anti-Israel rhetoric'.[12]

Critics of this aspect of antisemitism's redefinition claim that its primary purpose is to shut down debate on Israel's human rights violations or, for example, provide a smokescreen for the illegal expansion of settlement activity in the West Bank. In response, the Israeli government and its supporters in the

Jewish diaspora say this is antisemitism denial, explicitly or implicitly dismissing antisemitism as a 'non-problem'. And having already successfully branded the UN and human rights organisations as antisemitic, this can 'bolster Israel's justificatory arsenal for its refusal to abide by UN positions on human rights matters'.[13] In addition, the extension of antisemitism to human rights culture is used by Israel to shore up its legitimacy as the Jewish state. That isn't to say all claims of antisemitism are intended to justify Israel's existence but, Josh Kaplan argues, 'that this is an omnipresent possible interpretation shapes the politics of anti-antisemitism claims-making and the way it is evaluated'.[14]

Excoriating censure is not the only form of critical engagement with the behaviour of human rights organisations and culture with regard to Israel and Zionism. Some anti-antisemitism campaigners are working to persuade international intergovernmental bodies to de-couple Israel's actions from antisemitic manifestations, with some success. The model, in some respects, is the so-called Berlin Declaration, agreed at the OSCE meeting there in 2004: '[We participants] [d]eclare unambiguously that international developments or political issues, including those in Israel or elsewhere in the Middle East, never justify antisemitism'. Ethically, this is fair enough. Nothing *does* justify antisemitism. But there is a clear correlation between military and security operations carried out by Israel and spikes in expressions of antisemitism. Israel is not necessarily setting out to *cause* antisemitism, which is not to say that it is necessarily bothered if it does, but that may be the *effect* of its actions. And the media reflect this sequence of events. Meanwhile, because of the relentless drive to embed in the public space the redefinition of antisemitism as almost always being about Israel, it is very difficult and frankly rather dubious about insisting that there is no cause and effect involved.

The reaching out to intergovernmental organisations and extensive use of the media is in great part intended to convey the message that antisemitism is not a Jewish problem, but society's problem, the world's problem. Constant references to lines like 'first they come for the Jews ...', or 'the Jews are the canary in the mine', are seemingly intended to prick consciences and persuade others to act. But, as Kaplan writes: 'The fact that several Jewish advocacy organizations have portrayed prominent human rights organisations as antisemitic and biased against Israel only further reinforces the impression that antisemitism is a Jewish problem and not a human rights problem'.[15] It comes back to Anijar's assertion that the 'war' on antisemitism 'hardly knows its allies'. In his paper, Kaplan does not dispute that Israel is 'disproportionately' singled out for criticism; but he suggests that reasons other than anti-Jewish animus are arguably responsible. 'There is, of course, another way of looking at Israel's human rights record at the UN and among NGOs—that the content of the criticism is generally deserved'.[16]

* * *

The erosion of Jewish and pro-Israel affinity with human rights culture[17] is one of the key factors that has led to the burgeoning of ever-closer ties between some Jewish groups, Israel advocacy organisations and the state of Israel itself on the one hand, and right-wing, predominantly American, Christian Zionist evangelical groups, far-right populist leaders, some white supremacists, political parties with pro-Nazi and pro-fascist roots, etc. on the other.

For the Christian Zionists, Jerusalem will be the setting for the Second Coming of Christ and the Battle of Armageddon. The lands of Israel need to be united and ready for the day of the 'Rapture', when all believers will be transported to meet the Lord, while everybody else perishes. Millions of Americans believe therefore that God requires them to offer unconditional financial, political and military support to Israel, even if all Jews will perish too. This may sound like a very strange kind of philosemitism: unequivocal support for Zionist Jews because they are indispensably dispensable, if not sacrificial. But the Israeli extreme right, which is the country's dominant political force, and the Christian Zionists have the same political aim based on totally opposing religious convictions. After all, antisemitism is deeply engrained in this ideology; some evangelicals even dismiss the Holocaust as God's punishment of 'the wrong kind of Jew'. Naturally, they have no time for left-liberal Jews who oppose the occupation and the anti-Palestinian policies of Israeli governments on human rights grounds.[18] If Christian Zionism were purely a religious movement, it could be ignored. But, especially after 9/11, its influence on Washington's foreign policy strategies was very strong during the presidency of George W. Bush. Fast forward to 2016 and the election of Donald Trump as president, and ensconced in the White House was a new ally of both the Christian Zionists—and even more open to their ideology—and the governing Israeli settlement-supporting, Zionist coalition of right-wing, far-right and strictly orthodox parties. Trump put Christian Zionists in a number of key administration positions, notably Secretary of State Mike Pompeo, who brazenly inserted his evangelical beliefs into discussions of foreign policy.[19] Vice-President Mike Pence openly acknowledged that his support for Israel was rooted in his evangelical Christian faith.[20]

For the motley collection of far-right forces, what they broadly have in common is the 'apologies' they have made for past antisemitism, which gives legitimacy to their enthusiastic support for Israel as an ally in the struggle against Islam. Not only do they welcome Israel's central role in this struggle, which is largely focused on the alleged 'Islamisation of Europe', they expect most Jews to support their Islamophobic agenda given that Islamist and jihadi tendencies are seen as Jews' principal antisemitic enemies.[21] Again, left-liberal Jews, as personified in the demonised figure of the billionaire philanthropist George Soros in Hungary, are excluded from this philosemitism.

By making Israel ever-more central to what is defined as hatred of Jews, and legitimising the corollary, that support for or 'love' of Israel has become the test of what being pro-Jewish means, it could be said that the definition of an anti-semite has been transformed from being someone who hates Jews to someone whom Jews hate. Or another way of characterising this is that (some) Jews are saying: 'my enemy's enemy is my friend'—where the principal enemy is not just anyone who is judged to have criticised Israel unfairly, but also anyone who advocates for the national and human rights of the Palestinians, for redress and justice for the ethnic cleansing they suffered, for the end to the occupation of Palestinian land, for full equality for all who live in the Palestine–Israel area. So, what has become central to the 'war' on antisemitism is not a set of anti-rac-ist principles, a fundamental belief in the inherent ethical and moral wrong of racism, of which antisemitism is an integral part—in short, the full panoply of human rights— but rather the defence of a powerful state on the grounds that it confers special protected status on itself by virtue of self-defining as 'the Jewish state'.[22]

The historian and memory studies scholar Professor Michael Rothberg and his colleague, English scholar Neil Levi argue that we have moved into a new, unsettled political context in which Jews and Jewishness occupy very ambiva-lent positions. Because of their absolute commitment to Israel

conservative Jews can be networked into ethno-nationalist alliances, but Jews as a group also remain targets of the far-right. Meanwhile, many Jews have aligned themselves with the multiracial social movements of the left, yet Jew-ishness and the status of antisemitism remain sources of unease and tension in such coalitions, not least because of the vexed Israel/Palestine question.[23]

Rothberg further points out that while charges of antisemitism are actively being promoted by Israel and its allies around the world in the context of the anti-BDS campaign, there has been a 'shocking rise of violent antisemitism in recent years', including armed attacks and murders, not without connection to Donald Trump becoming president of the USA, but these are coming from the far right, not from critics of Israel.[24]

Rothberg does not deny that there is antisemitism on the left or among critics of Israel:

But the attention to them at the expense of focus on the far right has made Jews (and racialized minorities) more vulnerable, and it has allowed actively anti-semitic regimes, like those in Hungary and Poland—not to mention Trump's White House—to legitimate themselves through alliance with Netanyahu's government. The world has been turned upside down when antisemites like

Orban and Trump consort with Jewish leaders, while Jews who are critical of the occupation of Palestine are targeted as 'antisemites'.[25]

The successful elevation of concern about antisemitism to the international level, whether that derives from the cooperative, ally-seeking approach of some of the international Jewish organisations and one 'face' of Israeli policy on antisemitism, or from the critical, condemnatory camp, which includes UN Watch groups and another 'face' of Israeli policy in the form of the activities of the Israeli Ministry of Strategic Affairs, can be presented as the 'war' on antisemitism seeking to universalise the underlying nature of the problem. In other words, portraying antisemitism as 'society's' problem or as a 'global' problem, an undermining of democracy, to presage the intensification of racism among other groups. But in reality, what the 'war' is achieving is precisely the opposite: namely, to reinforce antisemitism as a special case, and therefore legitimise Jewish exceptionalism, which governments are ready to go along with because it is an easy, tick-box way of displaying moral rectitude. It therefore validates Israel's role and place in the Islamophobic coalition that brings together democracies and authoritarian regimes alike.

We see this exceptionalism in the international drive to designate 'Zionist identity', the 'pro-Israel sentiment of Jews' and 'identification' with 'the Jewish state' as protected characteristics in law, either directly through legal challenges,[26] or by engineering the outlawing of BDS advocacy, banning Israel Apartheid weeks on campuses organised by pro-Palestinian groups. And also in the entirely false claim that the so-called Macpherson principle or definition of racism—an insupportable reading of comments in the 1999 Macpherson Report of the inquiry into the murder of the Black teenager Stephen Lawrence in 1993, which does not contain any such definition—gives Jews the exclusive right to determine for themselves what antisemitism is.[27]

This rejection of human rights values as antisemitic and of the authority and legitimacy of the institutions set up in the post-Second World War period, in order to codify and promote measures that combat abuses of human rights and pre-empt such abuses by enforcing the introduction and practice of human rights laws, is baked into the agendas and mindset of the vast majority of pro-Israel and pro-Zionist advocacy groups. Much of their activism and advocacy work involves pushing back against campaigns like BDS, which base their legitimacy on well-established evidence that Israel has been in the past and is now a major instigator of human rights abuses—from the ethnic cleansing of Palestinians in the 1948 war to the treatment of Palestinians in the occupied Palestinian territories today. This includes attacking human rights organisations in Israel that monitor and document such abuses, organisations widely regarded by right-wing and religious Zionist forces in Israel as effectively a 'fifth column'.

When the International Criminal Court (ICC) announced that it would be opening an investigation into alleged Israeli war crimes in Palestine since June 2014, Prime Minister Netanyahu accused it of hypocrisy and antisemitism. (When the ICC ruled on 6 February 2021 that it had jurisdiction to open such an investigation against Israel, Netanyahu immediately called such a probe 'pure antisemitism' and 'vowed to fight it'.[28]) In a videotaped statement on 3 March 2021, he said:

> Israel is under attack this evening ... the ICC, which was established to prevent a repeat of the horrors the Nazis instigated against the Jewish people, now turns against the state of the Jewish people. Of course, it doesn't say a word against Iran and Syria, and other tyrannical regimes, frequently committing real war crimes ... I promise you we will fight for the truth until we will annul this scandalous decision.

The court also indicated that it would investigate alleged crimes committed by Palestinian militants.[29]

But all this moralising, holier-than-thou indignation, and shameless invocation of the Holocaust, cannot hide the fact that Israel refused to join the ICC, alongside, among others, the United States, China, India, Iraq, Libya, Yemen and Qatar. A state fully committed to upholding universal human rights is hardly likely to want to be seen in the company of most of these countries.

The political ideology of Zionism, in the only form of it that currently has any agency in Palestine-Israel—expansionist, colonising, influenced by strictly orthodox religious messianism and far-right political thinking and activism: a continuous project to purify the tribe that also draws support from so-called liberal Zionists and some Reform Jews—is bullish in its exceptionalism on the question of rights, especially national rights for Jews, in Israel–Palestine. 'Why should the Jewish state not do what it can legally do to maintain a Jewish majority?' asks Eric Yoffie.[30] But for him this is a purely rhetorical question. That 'so many of the champions of the Zionist left ... find it difficult to affirm what is so clearly sensible and right' is practically inexplicable. After all, the fulfilment of Zionism is about 'creating a democratic state with a Jewish majority ... the loss of a Jewish majority means the end of Zionism and the disappearance of the State of Israel'. Never mind the fact that where 'loss' is concerned, it is the indigenous population of Palestinians who experience this 'Jewish democracy' in the form of ethnic cleansing, rejection of their national rights, dispossession, apartheid—and not simply as 'the past', but as something ongoing. Redress for this abuse of human rights cannot be forthcoming since there is no admission of guilt. However, Yoffie airily states his support for a Palestinian-majority state alongside Israel, as if any credible enthusiasm for a two-state solution really existed, beyond formulaic utterances of politicians around the world who want to avoid being dragged into the Palestinian-Israeli minefield.

Yoffie avoids using the words 'human rights' altogether, as if the mantra of a 'democratic state with a Jewish majority' is a secure basis for achieving justice for Israeli Jews and Palestinians; as if there were some equality of suffering since the Jewish state came into being, rather than an inbuilt structural bias towards the realisation of Jewish rights in what is a bi-national reality across the entire area controlled by Israel, but one that Israeli governments and the constitutional shape of the Jewish state refuses to recognise. So, when Yoffie rails, however sincerely, against the forces which have allowed 250 illegal settlements to exist and balances this criticism with an excoriation of the 'left' for allowing itself to be seduced by talk of a single, secular democratic state or a 'Jewish–Arab confederation',[31] he is in denial about the nature of the theory and practice of Zionism today and dismisses any solution grounded in the principle of equal rights for all, which would give primacy to the culture and pursuit of universal human rights. When he says 'If the outpost [of Evyatar] remains, and it probably will, it will be yet another victory for the creeping annexationism that is eating Zionism alive', he is oblivious to the reality that 'creeping annexation' is precisely what *is keeping* Zionism alive.

Yoffie is the former president of the Union for Reform Judaism, American Judaism's largest denomination, which he headed from 1996 to 2012. While this puts him at the centre of American Jewish life, it would be wrong to claim that his views are representative of American Jewish opinion. Rather it would be fair to say that the contradictions and tensions among American Jews on the key issues of Israel, Zionism, antisemitism and anti-Zionism are reflected in what he writes, and that therefore the absence of any reference to human rights signifies the extent to which it has become problematic in the context of modern Jewish experience and the existence of Israel.

Deplorably, there is no doubt that the individuals and organisations that have spearheaded the transformation of human rights into a central source of anti-semitism, using the myth of Israel as 'the Jew among the nations', have scored a considerable success. It is enough to note how this strain of thinking consti-tutes the backbone of the IHRA 'working definition' of antisemitism, with its principal focus on the characterisation of human rights-based criticism of Israel as potentially antisemitic. Yet, at the same time as human rights advocacy is branded as integral to the 'new antisemitism', those engaged in this aggressive critique lay claim to a Jewish religious, educational and political tradition of pro-tecting rights, especially of the stranger, which is promoted as being a precursor of the modern human rights movement and superior to it. In other words, we Jews should be recognised as the true guardians and carriers of the flame of human rights, and our authority in this area is made even more definitive given our experience of 'the most horrible event in the history of the nations', to use the words of Yair Lapid, Israel's foreign minister.[32] In a confused and rambling critique of the way Israel and Jewish anti-antisemitism organisations have handled the problem of antisemitism—and in his view failed to combat anti-semitism effectively—he places the issue of antisemitism at the centre of Israel's international concerns:

> I see part of my job as Israel's foreign minister—if not my main role—as addressing the need to find ways to deal with the crisis of modern antisemitism. We need to conduct a thorough discussion about the state of antisemitism and how to address it. Without that, there is no Israeli public diplomacy, there is no coherent Israeli story and there is no way to enlist the world's support.

The conclusion Israel must draw from the Holocaust is that

> we must survive at any price. No one will come to save us. No one will fight our wars. We must live because life is the decisive response to hate. We must live by virtue of our own power in an independent country with a strong army that is not afraid of using force to defend itself and that does not apologize for its power. We are determined never again to be the victim.

But a second conclusion is that 'we must be a moral people', especially during wartime. 'Antisemitism is not just racism, but it is also racism'. Therefore 'Israel needs to be at the forefront of the fight against racism. We need opposition to racism to be part of our policy in every field—military, diplomatic and civil'. While indicating that in practice this means a more judicious and measured approach—'We also need to lower the level of hysteria in the face of criticism. Maybe every antisemite would oppose Israeli policy in the Gaza Strip, but not everyone who opposes Israeli policy in Gaza is an antisemite'—'If we want the world to continue to deal actively with hatred of the Jews—and more than that, hatred of the Jews who live in Israel'—we must 'actually' put the Holocaust 'at the top of ... a discussion of the tragedies that racism has caused'. According to Lapid, 'we must emerge from our isolation'—though he presents no evidence of such isolation, and all the evidence presented so far belies this notion—and 'enlist the Western world to stand at our side, to give the battle against anti-semitism a contemporary context'. However, included in this 'battle' is targeting those who accuse Israel of the 'ethnic cleansing' of Palestinians, of advocat-ing BDS, of being 'against Israel'—views held by significant numbers of people who rely on data and history impeccably researched by Israeli and Palestinian human rights organisations, as well as by the leading international human rights organisations, Human Rights Watch and Amnesty, and who also believe in the human right of free speech.

Whatever Lapid has attempted to do for domestic political reasons by attempting to stake out a new position on antisemitism for the Bennet–Lapid coalition, it is quite clear that any link with those Jewish Israelis like Justice Haim Cohn who, in earlier decades, were sensitive enough to the troublesome aspects of Israel's human rights record to find it necessary to establish a human rights watchdog, has now been severed. It takes quite a degree of chutzpah for Lapid to state baldly that 'The new antisemites are not focusing on the state of Israel as a result of something we have done, but only because Israel constitutes the biggest concentration of Jews in the world'. Especially when, by 'new antisemites', he is referring to, among others, 'the hatred of Jews that led to a demonstration by young supporters of the boycott, divestment and sanctions movement on the streets of Madrid'. But this is precisely how the IHRA 'working definition' is used, whether or not the original authors intended this to be so. Licence to deflect criticism of Israel's human rights record is built into it, and Lapid is just as prepared as Netanyahu was to exploit this.

At heart, Lapid is an eternalist, demonstrating in his support for the IHRA 'working definition' that there is a continuous link between 'the hatred of Jews that led to pogroms in Alexandria in 38 CE' and the young BDS supporters in Madrid. But this connection is, first, tenuous. Sandra Gambetti states that '[s]cholars have frequently labeled the Alexandrian events of 38 CE as the first *pogrom* in history, and have often explained them in terms of an *ante litteram* explosion of antisemitism'. In her book *The Alexandrian Riots of 38 CE and the Persecution of the Jews* (2009), however, Gambetti 'deliberately avoids any words or expressions that in any way connect, explicitly or implicitly, the Alexandrian events of 38 CE to later events in modern ... Jewish experience' as this would 'require ... a comparative re-discussion of two historical frames'.[33] Similar analytical, historicist-based differentiation can be applied to the Jewish experience of hostility over the centuries, disproving the sloppy assumption that all hostility towards Jews has been the same, and Jewish/non-Jewish relations have followed a rigid pattern. This misreading of history has gone hand-in-hand with an equally facile narrative of a universalist Jewish tradition of social justice, respect for rights, often bundled together under the heading of *Tikkun Olam* (repair of the world), and as such, Jews and the promotion of human rights have always gone together. As Galchinsky explains, the picture is far more complicated: 'Jews have played every role in the human rights drama. They have been victims, advocates, violators. and judges'.[34] But protecting themselves from abuse of rights has not been a permanent feature of diaspora Jewish history. Galchinsky continues:

Yet while it is useful to look for precursors to human rights concepts in ancient and medieval Jewish sources, one should not assume that Jews or any other group in Europe had begun thinking about human rights much prior to the French Republic's Declaration of the Rights of Man and Citizen in 1789. For most of human history, Jews—like everyone else—did not articulate an explicit concept of human rights because they did not conceive of their humanity as having a political dimension.

For orthodox Jewish theologians, this makes perfect sense. When Justice Haim Cohn set out to explore the relationship between human rights and Jewish law he wrung out of Jewish texts as much support for human rights principles as possible,[35] but could not overcome the fundamental truth that, in Judaism, since all moral authority derives from the word of God—*torah min hashamayim*—Jews do not have access to a conception of human rights that derives from any other source. The late, former Chief Rabbi of the United Synagogue, Lord Sacks, seen as progressive on matters to do with difference, equality, justice, refugees, rights and so on, and a prominent public figure, made this clear when he wrote about the subject, mostly from a critical standpoint. In his 2002 book *The Dignity of Difference*, he claimed that the universal code of human rights 'understates the difficulty and necessity of making space for strangers—the very thing that has been the source of racism and exclusion in almost every society known to history'.[36] In October 2016, Sacks told the European Council on Foreign Relations:

> Throughout history, when people have sought to justify antisemitism, they have done so by recourse to the highest source of authority available within the culture. In the Middle Ages, it was religion. So we had religious anti-Judaism. In post-Enlightenment Europe, it was science. So we had the twin foundations of Nazi ideology, Social Darwinism and the so-called Scientific Study of Race. Today the highest source of authority worldwide is human rights. That is why Israel—the only fully functioning democracy in the Middle East with a free press and independent judiciary—is regularly accused of the five cardinal sins against human rights: racism, apartheid, crimes against humanity, ethnic cleansing and attempted genocide.[37]

An authoritative-sounding, quotable, grand sweep across the centuries, perhaps. But one that does not stand up to scrutiny. Once again the myth of Israel as the 'collective Jew' is used to neutralise and discredit charges of the Jewish state's human rights abuses. And while the culture of human rights as it developed in the post-Second-World-War era has become a very important yardstick for judging how humans treat each other, and was specifically targeted at preventing the recurrence of the attempted genocide of European Jewry (which Sacks conveniently omits to mention), many of its most prominent advocates are only too well aware of the fragility of its authority, the flaws in its practice and the political games states play in deflecting accusations of human rights abuses by declaring their accusers unfit to stand in judgement given their own human rights records. What gives human rights the degree of influence it may have is the moral and ethical codes of human beings, which do not always align, and therefore do not constitute a single 'highest source of authority available within the culture'. 'Authority', after all, has no automatic connection with morality. This is why the nation-state and the reassertion of state sovereignty is arguably *the* highest authority of our time, having briefly and erroneously been seen as in long-term decline.

Returning to Lapid's eternalist framing of antisemitism and its second weakness, its clear connection to the description of antisemitism as the 'longest hatred', popularised by Wistrich, allows Lapid to exceptionalise the Jewish experience of racism and avoid the significance of the post-war human rights movement's role in establishing an international standard for combatting anti-semitism and all forms of racism. He sets Israel up as the supreme moral actor with the unimpeachable credentials for heading the world's fight against racism, with antisemitism as racism's foremost evil. Once again, in Lapid's narrative, we see the Holocaust pressed into service to provide the moral legitimacy for Israel's right to pick and choose what does and does not constitute the abuse of human rights, effectively ring-fencing Israeli actions from free and open scrutiny. While Galchinsky may be right in arguing that 'While acknowledging the flaws in the current [human rights] system, some Jews will keep working to improve its fairness and efficacy ... because they believe it is better to struggle for human rights than to revert to the old system of unquestionable state sover-eignty',[38] the essence of Lapid's message is that the Jewish state has firmly opted for the latter.

The turn of events making human rights a principal antisemitic enemy of Jews is perhaps unsurprising. Galchnsky reminds us that

As a matter of fact, human rights were embodied in an international legal and institutional framework only after World War II. Philosophies and theol-ogies of Judaism and human rights tend to confuse the rights of monarchical subjects, in biblical times, or of members of a *kehillah* in the medieval period, with international human rights in the contemporary era. While the rights found in ancient and medieval texts were certainly human rights precursors in their concern for justice and the individual's dignity, they did not conceive of themselves as global in scope and reach. The term 'state' ought not to be used interchangeably for an ancient monarchy and a modern nation-state.[39]

Understanding this makes it harder to locate Jewish human rights activity within a centuries-old context of Judaism's social justice tradition, which is more mythical than actual.

Apart from the fact that rights in Judaism are God-given and not inalienably attached to human beings, the Jewish social justice movement has never seriously penetrated Jewish orthodoxy, in great part because—as the orthodox would see it—of its secular origins and connections, which make it the invention of the sceptical, non-observant Jew, the *apikoros*, the one who does not have a share in the world to come. Moreover, the revival of orthodoxy in the last 50 years and its radically increased role in determining the nature of modern Zionism and the policies of the Jewish state have diminished the Jewish appetite for participation in Jewish human rights activity. As did the way the UN structure allowed evidence of Israeli abuses of Palestinian human rights to be given so much attention. Meanwhile, Israeli-Jewish human rights activity increased considerably, only to be subjected to vicious and vindictive attacks by right-wing and orthodox religious Zionist political groups and civil society organisations.

The attack on human rights as a principal source of antisemitism is central to the notion of the 'new antisemitism'. The IHRA 'working definition', as the codification of the 'new antisemitism', has a mutually reinforcing, symbiotic relationship with the Jewish anti-human rights drive. And providing the conceptual underpinning, without which this tangled web might not remain intact, is the myth of Israel as the 'collective persecuted Jew' among the nations.

Meanwhile, it looks likely that the demolition of a Jewish connection to human rights still has further to run. A book by Jonathan Neumann, *To Heal the World? How the Jewish Left Corrupts Judaism and Endangers Israel*,[40] attacks the concept of *tikkun olam* (repair of the world), which has been, for many left-liberal Jews, the inspiration for their commitment to the human rights cause. Neumann's argument, as summarised by Adam Sutcliffe, is that *tikkun olam* has 'no authentic roots in the Jewish tradition, and has been promoted through highly selective and wilful interpretations of biblical and other religious texts to advance a leftist political agenda that is not only alien to Judaism but injurious to it'. Preaching this liberal agenda to others has led Jews 'to a hypocritical rejection of their own particularity, while celebrating diversity in others; a special hostility to Israel; and the abandonment of the true duty and purpose of Jews, which is to support or live in Israel, and to prioritise the security and welfare of Jews in the diaspora'.[41]

Neumann, and supporters of his views like the columnist Melanie Phillips, who notoriously called Jews critical of Israel 'Jews for genocide', gives a further dimension to Cotler's accusation of 'human rights as a teaching of antisemitic contempt for Israel' by apportioning a major share of blame for it to left-wing Jews.

Geopolitics, Israel and the Authentication of 'New Antisemitism'

The Israeli government, many of the country's civil society organisations and political think tanks, as well as the vast majority of its university departments and research institutes dealing with the issue of current antisemitism, have all accepted the fundamental tenets of 'new antisemitism', and in large part follow the government's lead in exploiting its value as a key weapon in the state's foreign policy arsenal. Jewish community antisemitism defence and monitoring groups around the world, who were once unhappy with the mixing of serious work combatting antisemitism with Israel's Zionist objectives, abandoned such reservations after a series of influential events that occurred at the turn of the century, including, most prominently, the beginning of the second intifada, the Durban UN anti-racism conference and 9/11.

Both the promotion of, and opposition to, or acceptance of, or at least acquiescence in, the notion of the 'new antisemitism'—the process of redefinition—were, until the early 2000s, largely an internal Jewish matter. But from then on, use of the term to characterise what many commentators judged to be a growing wave of antisemitic manifestations increased internationally at governmental levels. While it was being vigorously promoted by some academics, research institutes and pro-Israel advocacy groups, their efforts alone, often undertaken in a concerted fashion, could not have been the decisive factor in securing that support. A necessary precondition, yes, but one that might have remained, ultimately, of real significance only within the Jewish world. So why did it happen?

* * *

For Israel and its supporters, from the mid-1970s to the early 1990s, the UN General Assembly 1975 Resolution 3379, engineered by the Soviets, which declared that 'Zionism is a form of racism and racial discrimination', stood as the most prominent and shameful marker of much of the world's hostile attitude to the Jewish state. In Yehuda Bauer's words, written in 1990:

It has been pointed out by many observers that the UN resolution, by ostracising Israel, seeks to place the Jewish state in a position analogous to that of the Jew in pre-modern society. The attack now is on the collective rather than the individual Jew, and that is a special feature of this antisemitism.[1]

For 16 years, the UNGA resolution publicly linked Zionism with what came to be regarded, in the years following the end of the Second World War, as the ultimate form of evil: the Nazi racist ideology that justified the attempted mass murder principally of the Jews, on the grounds that they were parasitic vermin worthy only of eradication. Resolution 3379 therefore gave anti-Zionism a form of international legitimacy and status which it had hitherto lacked.[2] At the time, the anger and disgust with the UN expressed in Israel was palpable.[3] While Jewish groups and pro-Israel organisations made efforts to reverse 3379, there was little hope of achieving success. But when the political climate did change after 1989, with the collapse of the Soviet Union, the fall of communist regimes in East-Central and Eastern Europe and the tearing down of the Berlin Wall, the preconditions were in place that led to the revoking of 3379 in December 1991. Jewish and pro-Israel groups had little to do with this process though they were of course among its beneficiaries since the suppression of Jewish life under communism ended and Jews were free to revive their communities, emigrate or simply enjoy the new freedoms. The changes came as a surprise for most— Western experts on communism included—so much so that the WJC were endeavouring to help prop up the GDR regime in order to complete a Holocaust reparations agreement they had been secretly negotiating with the Honecker government. Meanwhile, the Israeli government had made revoking 3379 a pre-condition for its participation in the October–November 1991 Madrid Peace Conference. By then, no one could have been in any doubt that the geopolitical tectonic plates had shifted.

The image of Israel as grossly and unfairly isolated by the international community was still deeply entrenched in assessments of the country's geopo-litical position, even as its relations with the United States strengthened and the influence of AIPAC, the pro-Israel lobby, was openly seen across the main-stream political spectrum as increasingly significant.

Fast-forward to the present and there is widespread acknowledgement of a new reality. A report from the Brookings Institute concluded that 'Israel enters the 2020s looking toward its region from a position of confidence'.[4] The authors referenced normalised relations with the United Arab Emirates (UAE) and Bahrain, the beginning of a normalisation process with Sudan—developments 'deepening and making public dramatic shifts in Israel's regional position. Relative to its neighbours, Israel enjoys military prowess and economic strength'. In a piece titled 'Israel and the geopolitics of the Middle East', a Spanish analyst argued that 'Israel is also beginning to be a point of reference for its Middle Eastern neighbours, who foresee that economic development and what is known as Economic Intelligence could be the key to the necessary change of paradigm in this troubled region.[5] Further normalisation came in December 2020 when Morocco established diplomatic relations with Israel. Commenting on this and the other normalisation developments, Elie Podeh noted that Israel now 'had relations, public or secret, with thirteen out of twenty-two members of the Arab League'.[6] In January 2021, the new partnerships

> prompted Trump to transfer Israel from the responsibility of the US European Command to the US Central Command (CENTCOM), which oversees the territory of the Middle East. CENTCOM has twenty members, including Egypt, Jordan and the Gulf states. This administrative decision was the culmination of a long process of Israel becoming a recognised—and desired—partner in the Middle East by major Arab players and the West in the war against mutual enemies such as Iran.[7]

Despite this geopolitical reality, the Israeli government continues to present itself as isolated and under threat. At the fifth gathering of the Global Forum for Combatting Antisemitism in 2015, Netanyahu spoke of the current 'treatment' of Israel as no different from that 'of our forebears. The Jewish state is being treated among the nations the way the Jewish people were treated for genera-tions'[8]—a repetition of the eternalist, 'new antisemitism' mantra. Even though Netanyahu was successfully ousted from the premiership with the formation of the Bennett-Lapid government in June 2021, and Lapid, in his role as foreign minister, seemed to distance himself from Netanyahu's policy on antisemitism in what many regarded as a controversial speech to the GFCA, in an op-ed clar-ifying that speech, the rhetoric of mounting, worldwide threat to Jews echoed that of the departed prime minister:

> Reports gauging hatred of the Jews in the world are unprecedented and hor-rifying. The year 2019 set a record for the number of hate crimes directed at Jews, and 2020 did not witness a drop in the figures, despite the coronavi-rus pandemic (which even generated a new blood libel, to the effect that the pandemic was being deliberately spread by the Jews). And it's already clear that the data for 2021 will surpass those of the two previous years.[9]

In the 'war' on antisemitism, Israel's geopolitical position is of great impor-tance. How then to understand the way these two contradictory narratives work and coalesce? On the one hand, Israel is the dominant military and economic power in the region, steadily turning its behind-the-scenes relations with Arab states into formal, diplomatic partnerships, and enjoying the benefits of being a strategic asset for the West, yet close to Russia and positively engaged with

China and India. On the other hand, a sense of fragility prevails, 'even if the state does not appear to be in any danger, and no regional army can match the IDF in the "dangerous neighbourhood" so frequently invoked by Israeli politicians'.[10] We are told that 'global' antisemitism poses an existential threat to the Jewish state, which has become—and has been for many years now—antisemitism's principal target, subject to 'viral delegitimisation', such that there is no longer a 'Jewish Question', but an 'Israel Question', resulting in the 'Israelisation of antisemitism', the objective of which is genocide (according to an influential line of thinking among some Israeli and diaspora Jewish academics, which will be discussed in Chapter 15).

*   *   *

It is important to recognise the significance of Israel's direction of travel over the last 30 years, especially because its leaders on both the left and the right wish to convey a sense of continuity in relation to its self-characterisation as a liberal democracy and an egalitarian society. For the state's first 30 years, this was framed by the country's socialist image and the ruling Mapai Party's membership of the Socialist International. But it is now 'those on the right wing of the political spectrum who lavish admiration and support upon Israel, and view it as a bulwark against the alleged "Muslim onslaught"'.[11] Israel did not simply slide unwittingly into this ideological camp.

Momentous change in the geopolitical environment in 1989 was highly conducive to the path modern Israel took and to the country's self-image. When the European communist regimes began to collapse in that year, speculation about what it all portended ranged from unbounded hopefulness about the positive results the new-found freedoms could bring, to dire warnings about the revival of destabilising, militant nationalism. What gave the former a clear edge over the latter was the broad consensus that the Cold War, bi-polar political configuration was at an end, and the possibility of military conflict between East and West had all but disappeared. This opened the space for the spreading of fanciful notions about the 'end of history' and the triumph of liberal democracy, which shaped a decade when expectations were initially high for social, political and economic transformation, especially in the countries and regions most affected by the changes. Central to developments was the fracturing and collapse of the influence of Soviet Russia over its satellite states in East-Central and Eastern Europe, and states in the Caucasus that were part of the USSR itself. The reunification of Germany set the scene for the expansion of the EEC, with many of the former European communist states lining up to join the body, which changed its name to the European Union after the creation of the single market in 1993. Europe—now increasingly referred to as 'the new Europe'—rapidly became a continent in which almost all its states could, in theory at least, exercise economic and political freedom. Countries forced to follow foreign policies dictated by Moscow could now determine such matters for themselves. And one fundamental change they almost all made was to normalise their relations with Israel. While this was something expected of states now positioning themselves as part of the 'West', it also reflected the positive view of Israel, held by many of the new political leaders in these countries, as a fledgling state, 'pluckily' struggling to maintain its sovereignty and independence in a difficult environment. They saw parallels with their own struggles as suppressed oppositional movements seeking to overcome forces that prevented genuine national self-determination and fundamental democratic reform. And during the 1990s most of these states embraced neoliberal economics, as did Israel.

Other non-European states that invariably supported UN, non-aligned and 'third-world' (as it was then called) condemnation of Israeli policies towards the Palestinians, often strongly influenced by their relations with the Soviet Union, also used the new, more fluid geopolitical situation to switch to a more pragmatic relationship with Israel.

From the 1990s, neoconservative writers and thinkers in the US, many of them Jewish, found sympathetic partners in Israel who rejected the socialist model and strongly advocated a neoliberal economic and political agenda.[12] And it was Netanyahu who willingly adopted and, from the time he came to power, implemented the neoconservatives' neoliberal dream. This was not presented as a rejection of egalitarianism, but rather as a rejection of state-enforced uniformity and the freeing-up of private initiative and provision of equality of opportunity.

These changes contributed to producing the positive geopolitical atmosphere that secured international support for the Oslo Accords, which in turn contributed to Israel becoming a more significant player in maintaining the so-called 'liberal world order'. Yet for all that the Oslo Accords were hailed by some as a major advance in Israel's integration into the Middle East, as Podeh argued: 'In contrast to conventional wisdom, Israel was never completely isolated and ostracised in the region. In the post-1948 period, most Arab states were formally at war with Israel and boycotted it economically. But Israeli decision-makers still managed to find allies willing to cooperate secretly against common enemies'.[13] For example, an intelligence apparatus called Trident enabled sharing of information between Israel, Turkey and Iran, which operated until the Islamic revolution in 1979.

Israeli leaders and policymakers never saw their particular understanding of 'comprehensive peace' in these terms. In the immediate aftermath of Oslo, legend has it that President Mubarak of Egypt said to Israeli Foreign Minister Shimon Peres: 'Now Israel can surely become part of the Middle East'. But Peres demurred, responding: 'Israel will always look first and foremost towards

Europe, from which it emerged and whose values it embraces'. To which Mubarak replied: 'Then Israel will never truly find peace with its neighbours'. We now know that the discourse of cooperation that was fashionable in the 1990s, and even had its moment in the Middle East after Oslo when Peres was being feted for advocating an EU-style arrangement of economic cooperation as a way of consolidating the peace agreements that would flow from Palestinian–Israeli reconciliation, was hollow. Rabin never wanted an independent Palestine,[14] rather just enough autonomy for the Palestinians to give the impression that Arafat's surrender could look to the world like a negotiated settlement among equals.

Multilateral cooperation, the spread of liberal democracy, the embrace of neoliberalism—while these developments were initially seen as auguries of a positive future, a more accurate reflection of things to come were the years of the break-up of Yugoslavia, which led to the Balkan or Yugoslav wars, and the widespread resurgence of extreme nationalist sentiment, especially where it had been either suppressed or rigidly controlled by the communist authorities. At the same time, far-right and populist Eurosceptic reactions to an overreaching, top-down, intergovernmental management and leadership of the EU were manifesting themselves in many of the original member states of the EU. As the 1990s ended, it was the reassertion of state sovereignty, the acquisition of it by nationalist movements driven by exclusivist ethno-nationalism and a whitewashing of pre-Second World War pro-Nazi and fascist nationalist leaders and organisations that had become the norm.

For its part, whether by choice or necessity, Israel always sought to build a strong, centralised state structure, a path equally ideologically compatible with Mapai's dirigiste socialism on the left and Likud state-led economic liberalisation on the right. At the same time there was little doubt that Israel would see itself as part of the triumphant liberal democratic West versus the rest. So, as the third millennium opened and the 'End of History' narrative[15] was crumbling, political and ideological fragmentation had set in and jihadi terrorism began to wreak havoc, Israel was perfectly comfortable signing up to a new, simplistic, good-versus-evil story based on those who lined up to fight the 'war on terror' and those who condoned, promoted and perpetrated it. The suicide bombings, Hamas rocket attacks from Gaza and the simmering confrontation with Hezbollah were more than just the 'scars' Israel could display to show how it was a veteran when it came to combatting terrorism; they were presented as evidence that Israel was in the front line experiencing and confronting jihadi terror.

It was therefore perfectly natural for Israel to want to be part of the post 9/11 'coalition of the willing', initially couched as coming together in the cause of the 'war on terror' announced by President Bush, which would oust Al Qaeda from Afghanistan and protect and project liberal values internationally. When it rapidly became clear that this 'coalition' embraced illiberal, dictatorial, authoritarian and anti-democratic regimes, and not just the so-called democratic West as personified by North America and the states of the European Union, Israel still had no reservations in judging that it was in the country's national interest to be part of it.

This coalition, which would later be significantly bolstered by the failure of the Arab Spring, was a strange-looking creature from the start, since it had a fundamentally anti-Islam basis, even if this was undeclared and couched only in terms of the dangers of Islamism. And yet some Arab regimes, like Saudi Arabia, Egypt and the Emirates, which had more to fear from jihadism than the UK, France and America had, were integral to it. Even before 9/11, the Western media narrative—shaped by major columnists and academics who were supporting and promoting this coalition—on Middle Eastern developments, especially the tensions between Iran and Saudi Arabia, the instability of Lebanon, the alleged 'weapons of mass destruction capability' being advanced by Iraq, 'have always reduced matters of extraordinary depth and complexity to a mere snapshot, which more often than not has catered to an orientalist audience that regards Arab or Muslim cultures as backward and to security-focused policymakers', wrote Kim Ghattas in her study of Saudi-Iran rivalry from 1979 to the present.[16] 'Over time', Ghattas continued, 'those two groups have worked to reinforce each other, merging to such an extent that everything was viewed through the prism of the security of the West, especially after 9/11'.

This suited Israel well, because successfully presenting itself as a key component of the security of the West, in the front line against militant Islam, increasingly characterising any violent Palestinian resistance to Israel's tightening control of Gaza and the West Bank as all of a piece with jihadi terrorism became easier and more convincing.

* * *

A factor in Israel's global standing has been the

> dynamism of its high-tech—and particularly military—industries. Israeli exports as well as cooperation agreements for the production of military materiel help consolidate relations with the elites of several countries, even those where public opinion views Israel negatively. Arms sales not only ensure the viability of the Israeli military industry, but also facilitate the country's international relations.[17]

Israeli security know-how is exported across the globe; the IDF is involved in the training of armed forces in several countries; and there are various police collaboration agreements, some of which have attracted unwelcome public controversy.

Israel also maintains multifaceted relations with the post-Soviet countries. Mass immigration of highly educated Soviet Jews—that many intensively engaged Jewish groups had been working to achieve for three decades or more, in collaboration with a branch of the Mossad known internally as Nativ and to the activist groups such as Lishkat Hakesher (the Contact Agency)—which began during the perestroika period and for whom socialism was a dirty word, intensified for some years after that, and strengthened the country's right and radical right political tendencies and its defence industries. While immigration from Putin's Russia is no longer significant, relations between the two countries have become very close.[18]

The strength of Israel's geopolitical situation has been further bolstered by the way it has greatly benefited from economic and financial globalisation, in common with countries like China, India, Indonesia, Brazil, Germany, Japan and Finland (at various stages of their economic development). But at the same time, it has participated in the widespread backlash against what many countries have seen as the negative social, political and cultural effects of globalisation: increased and unwanted migration, the fragmenting of borders, the dilution of national identity, a weakening of 'indigenous' culture, conflict between religious groups and so on. Populist parties—largely right- or far-right—have exploited the fears generated by these changes, offering social and political governance based on nativism, ethno-nationalism, opposition to migration and support for illiberalism.

Although Israel's government leaders and its apologists in academia and the media continue to characterise the country as the only true democracy in the region, an open and tolerant society, yet comfortable in its Jewish skin, from a geopolitical perspective it occupies a place closely aligned with the states driven by perpetual striving to realise an ethno-nationalist, illiberal agenda. The logic of its far-right, religious messianism-inflected Zionism simply cannot accommodate any challenge to the sovereignty, which influential, right-wing political thinkers believe to be fundamental to the stability, security and Jewishness of the Jewish state. This is a zero-sum game in which the Palestinians are the perpetual losers.

In the region, there is no doubt that critical public and governmental opinion about Israel's treatment of the Palestinians remains a limiting factor in the state-to-state normalisation process. And there is no serious, viable plan or process in play to bring the Palestinian–Israeli confrontation to an end. On the one hand, it serves Israel's interests to emphasise the ongoing, destabilising dangers of this situation, thereby justifying extreme, repressive measures against anti-settlement activity in the occupied territories and the application of severe military retaliation in response to rocket attacks from Gaza. But on the other hand, the Israeli government is well aware that neither states like Egypt, Saudi Arabia or Jordan, nor the European Union, and certainly not the Biden administration, are making it a priority to pressurise Israel to engage in any kind of internationally sanctioned peace process. On the contrary: increasing insistence by Israel and its Western allies on recognition of Israel as a 'Jewish state' as a precondition to any negotiations with the Palestinians; the adoption of the Nation State Law which declares that Israel is 'the national home of the Jewish people' and that the right to realise self-determination in the state is unique to them,[19] thereby formally classifying Palestinians as second class citizens; and the insistent drumbeat of annexation talk, sometimes toned down when allies express disapproval (invariably rather mild), amplified when the internal political situation demands it and the world is looking elsewhere, all prove that Israel knows it has an effective way of managing the Palestinian issue, and minimising risks. Four years of Trump—during which he moved the American embassy to Jerusalem, initiated a 'peace plan' which had no provision in it for an independent Palestinian state, installed a new ambassador who unashamedly supported illegal settlement in the occupied territories—only bolstered Israel's policy of marginalising and paying little more than lip service to a 'peace process'. Even the April 2021 violence, Hamas rockets and intercommunal conflict across pre-1967 Israel, which followed expressions of Palestinian anger at provocative Israeli security actions on the Temple Mount and took many by surprise, prompting talk of a new reassertion of Palestinian national identity and a shock to 'ordinary' Israelis for whom the occupation either no longer existed or at best was out of view and easily ignored—now that the dust has settled, Israel confidently continues with its consolidation of administrative, legal and military control over the Palestinians in the occupied territories.

There is precious little sympathy in Jewish-Israeli society with the plight of the Palestinians. Zionism saw Arabs as ambiguous figures: at best, capable of being 'civilised' by the 'new Jew' bringing modernity to Palestine; at worst, a backward, racialised enemy whose Palestinian identity had to be denied because accepting its reality—many centuries of Palestine as their home—undermined Jews' exclusive, biblically based claim to the land. If at first Palestinian resistance was seen as fundamentally political, anti-Palestinian discrimination was justified on the grounds of security, controlling the enemy within. But as Palestinians increasingly developed their ability to tell their own national story, both through historical and cultural narrative and armed resistance, and therefore demonstrated that they would not accept their dispossession, Jewish Israelis came to explain Palestinian stubbornness by branding it a form of antisemitism. With the development of 'new antisemitism' theory it was easy to slot Palestinian 'hatred' of Jews into the eternalist understanding of antisemitism—their total opposition to Zionism and a Jewish state was simply a form of delegitimisation and demonisation; denial of the right of the 'collective Jew' to self-determination and national self-expression—just as the individual Jew was demonised and persecuted throughout Jewish history.

The seeds of this process began long before the state embraced neoliberalism. In Ronit Lentin's account of race and surveillance in Israel–Palestine,[20] 'once racially configured, the other [the Palestinian] becomes a threat that the state must contain and control'. The state has done this, and continues to do it in various ways by, *inter alia*, 'citizenship regimes, border controls and census categorisations, but also invented histories and traditions that construct state memory, ceremonies and cultural imaginings, and the evocation of ancient (in Israel's instance biblical) origins'. Central and East European Jews, mostly socialist atheists, conceived of Zionism as a movement to create a state in Europe's image, but 'nonetheless mobilized biblical promises and the Jewish religion to their cause'. This led to the creation of 'a racial state par excellence', in which

> exception [became] the rule and the constant state of emergency enable[d] one rule (life) for the state's Jewish citizens (as well as Jewish people from around the world who are entitled to citizenship upon immigration to Israel), and another (death, threat of death, threat of expulsion) for the state's Palestinian and other non-Jewish subjects, not entitled to citizenship and whose lives are rendered 'bare'.

Lentin summarises this with a quote from David Theo Goldberg: 'Palestinians are treated not *as if* a racial group, not simply *in the manner* of a racial group, but *as* a despised and demonic racial group'. To maintain Israel as a 'haven' for the Jewish people—with a Jewish majority in perpetuity—the state 'regards the control of 1948 Palestinians, 1967 Palestinians and diasporic Palestinians as an imperative born of necessity and emergency'.

While this 'emergency' justification for control remains, it was given two other dimensions with, first, the establishment of the Palestinian Authority (PA) in 1994 pursuant to the Oslo Accords; and second, the influence of the state's embrace of neoliberalism.

Although public perception was that the PA would be the embryonic structure for the establishment of a Palestinian state, in reality it became an enforcer of the racialised control structure of the Israeli state. Leaders of 'the despised and demonic group' derived their legitimacy from the Israelis and were therefore obliged to police and suppress manifestations of dissent in areas under the PA's control, thereby becoming complicit in their own racial subjugation.

Coterminous with the establishment of the PA was the consolidation of Israel's adoption of neoliberal social and economic policies. And this is one area in which the 'exception state' did not apply, as the PA adopted neoliberal policies too. Efraim Davidi writes:

> As of now, the Palestinian Authority is not taking any significant steps towards ending its reliance on Israel and achieving economic independence. The Palestinian Authority's economic policies have been, for many years, monitored closely by representatives from the World Bank and the International Monetary Fund (IMF), the tentacles of capitalist globalisations. The representatives of these international (i.e. American) bodies, together with their Palestinian colleagues, whose worldview was formulated based on neo-liberal economic theory, contribute their part to implementation of the Israeli neo-colonial formula. As it turns out, there are also Palestinians who make profit of—and therefore have interest in—continuing Palestinian reliance on the Israeli economy.[21]

Neoliberal is most often defined in economic and political terms, as the entry in Global Social Theory demonstrates:[22]

> The term neoliberalism is generally used to mark the shift away from the socio-economic and political-cultural values, relations and processes of the post-Keynesian era ... and a turn to forms of economic and political thought and governance which place emphasis on free markets, free trade, strong property rights, privatization and individual responsibility.

In practice, this means that 'the state withdraws from certain areas of social provision (e.g. healthcare, welfare and social services), yet continues to play a critical role in establishing and guaranteeing the institutional, socio-economic and socio-political conditions' in which such provision can be made. There is an assumption that an underclass will always exist and some social security provision is required, but it is intentionally kept as low as possible. The principles behind the welfare state, as articulated towards the end of the Second World War by the economist William (later Lord) Beveridge in the UK, for example, and paralleled by the social compact drawn up by the architects of the Treaty of Rome, the document that led to the founding of the EEC, have no place in neoliberalism's blueprint for economic success and social peace. A society structured on the basis of neoliberal values, such as 'individualism, personal choice, responsibility and meritocracy', reduces racism to being either a thing of the past, an aberration, merely individual prejudice' or the responsibility of the individual. This undermines the validity of the concept of institutional racism, obscuring racism's systemic and structural nature, which is blamed for encouraging marginalised people, to see themselves as victims, and for fostering a culture of grievance. Unless racism manifests itself as 'illiberal, overt, intentional, violent and the reserve of extremists', neoliberalism disputes whether it is racism at all.

In Israel, the practice of neoliberalism has reinforced the already existing reality of the state not recognising the structural nature of anti-Palestinian/Arab racism, making Palestinians themselves responsible for the social and economic disadvantages they suffer, the high levels of crime they experience, the educational disparities they endure, and so on. Because they refuse to accept Israel as a Jewish state, they engage in violent protest and they promote incitement against Jews. In short: they are accused, explicitly or by implication, of antisemitism. The oft-repeated claim is that Gaza could be an economic success story if the Palestinians there devoted resources to growth, development, entrepreneurship, the education and welfare of their children, etc., rather than on bombs and rockets and missiles. If they put politics aside—as was proposed in the Jared Kushner/Trump peace plan—they will find peace and security. Such a patently dehumanising stereotype can only gain purchase on the back of decades of ongoing, collective racialisation of Palestinians. But what neoliberalism does is provide an additional excuse for the state to believe that, trapped in their antisemitic mindset, Palestinians are destined for underclass status. And as such, they are a 'problem' that requires management rather than any more in the way of equal rights and state support.

The strength of this narrative is evident from the way that key state actors in the region, with which Israel is working to normalise relations, as well as the major powers, barely make any attempt to dispute it. So, when the prosecutors of the 'war' on antisemitism take their 'new antisemitism' concerns to international forums, or raise them bilaterally, they are guaranteed a sympathetic hearing. Is it any wonder then that many observers of the Palestine–Israel conflict reach conclusions such as those expressed by Marta Gonzalez: 'The Palestinian question, already dwarfed by global affairs, will lose its focus of interest owing to the backwardness and lack of political weight of Europe, its sole protector, and will be reduced to a question of Israel's internal security crisis. Its resolution is unlikely'.[23]

Critics of the neoliberal-inspired, dehumanising and racialised discourse about the Palestinians, and the use to which it is put to justify Israeli and Jewish victimhood, understandably argue that Netanyahu, Israel's longest-serving, but now former prime minister, is the principal architect of what the Jewish state has become. In May 2021, one Israeli commentator, Louis Fishman, charged him with '[building] a multidimensional bubble for Jewish Israelis constructed out of a subservient police force, national media, an embrace of neoliberalism and the attempted co-option of select politicians from among the Palestinian citizens of Israel'.[24] Evidence of the authoritarianism he has fostered is seen most starkly perhaps in the increasingly repressive actions of the police, experienced by leftists, Ethiopian Israelis, *haredim* (the strictly orthodox), but most severely by Palestinians. 'We are all witness to the fact that Netanyahu's provision of "normalcy" for most Israeli Jews was no more than an illusion cloaking his quest for sole power', Fishman wrote. 'And, now as we can see that iron fist wrapped in a neoliberal dream, that descent into Netanyahuism, we Israelis need to stare in the mirror. We need to see, really see, what a blatantly racist society we have become'.

Fishman's anger and Lentin's powerful critique make no dent in the broad sympathy many state actors have for both the challenges Israel claims it faces and the measures it feels it has to take to meet them. For many countries, the issues of migration, refugees, fragile or porous borders, who belongs, drawing dividing lines between 'us' and 'them' all loom large, whether they are considered more as problems dealing with potential enemies to nationhood and sovereignty, or more as a humanitarian crisis that could impact on internal group relations but requires cross-border cooperative action to manage. This is a geopolitical phenomenon that, given the certainty of climate disruption, is set only to get worse. Israel has skilfully positioned itself to gain sympathy for, or at the very least the grudging acknowledgement of, its cluster of real or imagined threats of this kind, from both illiberal authoritarian regimes and from states that still claim adherence to liberal democratic values, even if those values are selectively and incompletely applied. The advantage this gives the Jewish state in pursuit of its goals is a more or less guaranteed hearing and acceptance of its presentation of the global antisemitic threat when characterised as principally a threat to the Jewish state.

The neoliberal dimension is especially significant in the Israeli case. First, to quote again from the Global Social Theory entry, in the context of neoliberalism's obscuring of the systemic nature of racism:

citizenship has also been reconstituted as a technology of governance, as opposed to being a 'universal' status that confers rights and protections. In the context of the ongoing Windrush scandal and the refugee crisis, we might think of the way in which the neoliberal goal of 'opening up' borders for the purposes of free trade runs parallel to discourses, policies and the construction of citizenship whereby states are entrusted with the creation of 'waste humans' (Tyler, 2013) both within and at the borders of sovereign territories. Rather than being framed as a result of neoliberal political and economic governance, we live in a time where precarious subjects are both positioned at the centre of social explanation and framed as the cause of social problems.

This is a precise summation of the dual role assigned to the Palestinians by the Israeli state. It did not come about in the wake of Israel's adoption of neoliberal policies. The origins of the image of the 'uncivilised' Palestinians living in unsatisfactory conditions they have brought upon themselves through a hatred of Jews lies in the early days of the development of political Zionism. Up to and beyond Oslo there was an assumption that a political compromise giving the Palestinians some degree of autonomy—a mini-state perhaps, inevitably shackled to assuage Israel's security concerns—would neutralise that antisemitism, and Arafat's decision to surrender and accept a compromise reinforced that notion. Nevertheless, the appropriation of Palestinian land in the cause of ethno-nationalist Zionist settlement continued apace, thereby eating away at any possibility of a Palestinian state worthy of its name. Post-9/11 and the clear evidence from the second intifada that Palestinian opposition to Oslo was strengthening and taking new forms, such as the founding of the BDS movement, but also suicide bombings, it was the Israeli narrative of victimhood, of the Jewish state subjected to 'viral antisemitism' that found a sympathetic hearing geopolitically. At the same time Israel as the high-tech start-up nation-state portrayed itself as a neoliberal project par excellence, of which the expansion of settlement activity was both an economic and political-ideological necessary part. Here, the openly declared 'war' on antisemitism and the de facto 'war' against the Palestinians—the *naqba* that never came to an end—merged. The 'work of surveillance and racialisation' in the service of creeping annexation of the West Bank was mirrored in the growing state-funded and diaspora-supported surveillance and combat strategies deployed against supporters of the BDS campaign and other efforts to reveal the apartheid nature of Israel's treatment and racial governance of the Palestinians. Recent authoritative, fully documented reports exposing the depth and extent of the state's apartheid regime—produced by Israeli and international human rights watchdogs: B'Tselem,[25] Human Rights Watch[26] and Amnesty International[27] (AI)—have only provoked an even more aggressive-defensive Israeli response, rooted in accusations of antisemitism, to yet more evidence of institutionalised injustice. AI's 280-page report on its four-year investigation, launched on 1 February 2022, is (as I write) the most recent document. The Israeli journalist Orly Noy, who hosted the international press conference, commented later:[28] 'Official Israel seems to have gone completely off the rails, disparaging and defiling Jewish historical memory by hysterically waving the antisemitism card at every opportunity.' The IHRA 'working definition' of antisemitism, with its example that 'claiming that the existence of a state of Israel is a racist endeavour' is antisemitic, provides the perfect cover for such a reaction to the AI report.

At a BDS emergency summit organised by Sheldon Adelson in Las Vegas on 4 July 2015, Netanyahu told attendees in a letter read aloud: 'Delegitimisation of Israel must be fought, and you are on the front lines'. 'It's not about this or that Israeli policy', Netanyahu said, 'it's about our right to exist here as a free people'.[29] Concurrently Netanyahu held talks with several officials over the weekend regarding the possible plans of action to combat BDS. They included Strategic Affairs and Information Minister Gilad Erdan, whose office was responsible for fighting BDS, 'as well as other officials from relevant ministries'.

At the event, it emerged that the government was debating ways to improve cooperation between the different government agencies fighting BDS, and Jewish organisations abroad. Erdan mentioned that he is 'flooded with calls from Jewish leaders from across the globe, who want to join the effort against BDS'. Meanwhile, Netanyahu and Erdan agreed that his office would receive at least NIS 100 million, most of which would go to fighting BDS. 'Erdan estimated that the budget can double or triple to NIS 300 million with the help of Jewish and pro-Israel organizations'. He added that 'the campaign against the BDS needs to include government ministries, intelligence agencies and the defence community, as well as increased cooperation with Jewish organizations'.

The budget would be used in part to engender a series of legal initiatives, 'demonstrating yet again', argues Lentin, 'the use of the law in the service of the racial state'. Based on surveillance of both citizens' and visitors' support for boycotting Israel, in January 2017 the Knesset Interior Committee initially approved a bill that would bar issuing entry visas and residency permits in Israel to foreign visitors who knowingly and publicly call for a boycott of Israel or the settlements, and to citizens who represent organisations that call for boycotting Israel, its institutions or territory under its control, namely the Jewish settlements in occupied Palestine.[30]

The second dimension of neoliberalism is the strong thread of religious inspiration behind it, conveyed clearly in the rhetoric of Bush and Blair. This served Israel's interests well, especially in the US, where backing for the Jewish state intensified and solidified among Christian evangelicals and orthodox Jews with very substantial resources, which they have used to fund neoconservative think tanks and educational institutions in Israel, though as Peter Beinart points out, this is an 'enduring [global] network of [such] supporters who endorse Jewish statehood for religious reasons and because they consider it a guarantee against a second Holocaust'.[31] Furthermore, 'In the Democratic Party', Beinart continues, 'this Christian-Jewish Zionist alliance remains hegemonic, though it's being challenged. In the Republican Party, it's not even being challenged ... Today ... many Republicans see Israel as a model for the ethno-state they want in the US. They don't merely oppose boycotting Israel. They want to boycott the boycotters'.

*　*　*

Beinart's final point prompts the question: how can the Jewish state simultaneously market itself as a model and present itself as existentially vulnerable? And how does this seeming contradiction shape the 'war' on antisemitism?

Playing the existential vulnerability card has long been an Israeli strategy, and one which some Israeli leaders have themselves recognised as being somewhat ironic.

> Israeli Prime Minister Levi Eshkol famously described Israel as '*Shimshon der nebechdiker*', Yiddish for 'Samson the weakling'. It perfectly captured the Israeli psyche two decades after the state's founding, on the one hand being confident that the Jewish state was overcoming any and all obstacles in its path and on the other constantly being afraid that annihilation was just around the corner.[32]

Although the 'weakling' image was always, at the very least, an exaggeration and at most even a knowing confection, in the country's early days, it did contain a grain of truth—certainly if you believed that, by quantity alone, hostile propaganda from multiple enemies threatening an Arab military assault, could lead to Israel's destruction. Brian Klug cuts through to the consequences of this Janus-faced Israeli position:

> It is oddly disempowering, casting the Israeli state in the old mould of Jewish victim. More precisely, it combines the old bogey of pre-Israeli-Jewish helplessness with the new mentality of Israeli-Jewish aggressiveness. This combination lends itself to a particular style of politics in Israel, one that is not confined to any single party.[33]

Post-9/11, however, changes in Israeli policy and in the geopolitical environment converged to increase international sympathy for Israel's discourse on Palestinian rejectionism, Islamic extremism, global antisemitism, and Holocaust memorialisation. In addition, its neoliberal economic success, particularly in the military field, security and surveillance, leveraged a great deal in positive attitudes towards the country.

Also working in Israel's favour internationally was what Dov Waxman and Scott Lasensky call 'Jewish foreign policy', which they define as being 'comprised of the external policies and activities of Israeli governments and Jewish organizations (inside and outside Israel) on behalf of the Jewish people or parts of it'.[34] Antisemitism is a 'first order interest' of this policy, which they argue is not implemented by 'two separate actors—Israel and the diaspora', but rather by 'a single corporate actor: the Jewish people or world Jewry'. (In effect, Israel confirmed this linkage or conflation with the passing of the Nation State Law in August 2018 (referred to above), which declared that 'Israel is the state of the Jewish people', emphatically not the state of all its citizens. As Avraham Burg, a former Knesset Speaker, wrote at the time, this means that 'all [Israel's] conflicts, domestic and foreign apply to all the world's Jews. They are vulnerable to our enemies and have no protection from Israel's foolish actions, which often put them at risk'.[35])

The strong state, its rampant ethno-nationalism, its concomitant illiberalism, its weaponisation of diaspora support, its role in implementing a Jewish foreign policy, the core of which is the 'war' on antisemitism, and its position on the front line against militant Islam makes Israel a compatible partner for such countries as China, India, Hungary, Poland, Russia, under their authoritarian, populist, post-politics, post-democratic and post-truth leaders.[36] They admire Israel's disdain for its internal minorities, its characterisation of human rights values as undermining state sovereignty and its determination to use 'lawfare' to suppress free speech that publicly highlights or calls for opposition to human rights abuses. And they willingly heed Israel's concerns about antisemitism representing a genocidal assault on its existence.

As Alain Badiou, Eric Hazan and Ivan Segre argue, Israel is identified

> as an advance outpost of the West. It is 'more one of us than we are ourselves', out there on the front line. If, before the Second World War, Jews were viewed as foreigners without a homeland and incapable of integration now, on the contrary, those established in the Middle East are more European than the Europeans here, as they are defending our values against 'Islamic' barbarism, on an exposed frontier that is also our own.

For this reason, the authors put forward the hypothesis that for the people they are talking about, what matters 'is not the name "Jew"', but rather the 'fate of the west'. 'This is the reason they identify "Jew" with the state of Israel, and so eagerly support this state's war against the Palestinians and other Arabs'.[37]

This is the reality of the significance of the geopolitical strength of Israel's current position: Israel now symbolises the fate of the West, however the West might be defined—which today can be as much about the values a country objects to as about values it shares with others.

Israel's strategic decision to lead the 'war' on antisemitism and to claim for itself pride of place as the main victim of antisemitic assault—'the Jew among the nations'—has only been effective because of that strength. The international public exposure of the 'war' on antisemitism through such initiatives as the IHRA 'working definition' and the media assassination of Jeremy Corbyn would have been far less successful without it. Israeli leaders know that in the post-9/11 world, it engenders sympathy by making the fight against antisemitism a key element of its foreign policy—especially when it can be linked to the Jewish experience of the Holocaust and without consultation with Jewish leaders in communities around the world.

Sympathy, however, should not be conflated with the love of Jews, and Israeli leaders know this. It is transactional: Israel's leadership of the anti-Islam propaganda war; protected status as the US's 'non-negotiable' ally; ability to claim democratic purity at the same time as appealing to authoritarian states; its successful management of 'troublesome' internal others; high-tech edge in surveillance software and hardware, in great part stemming from on-the-ground experience of needing to prevent terror attacks over many years by developing ever-more sophisticated security systems—all of which are beneficial to a diverse range of states. In exchange, Israel more or less gets a free pass to pursue its ethno-nationalist, neo-colonial agenda of settling on land it claims to be its own by biblical promise and ancient history. Very few states are pressing Israel to do anything for the Palestinians, who are constantly characterised as 'never missing an opportunity to miss an opportunity', not simply because they cannot get over or put behind them any injustice they suffered in the past, but increasingly because they are primary conveyors of antisemitism according to the redefinition of antisemitism as primarily hatred of the Jewish state.

While there is no guarantee that Israel's geopolitical strength will endure, at the time of writing, as the Taliban consolidate their control over Afghanistan and the world waits to see, while not holding its breath, whether or not this is a genuinely more conciliatory Islamist dictatorship, it is highly likely that a raft of familiar as well as new destabilising uncertainties will emerge and therefore the elements that give Israel its geopolitical influence will not be diminished. The joint Israel–diaspora 'war' on antisemitism is therefore certain to continue, with the presence of a new force on the world's stage assumed to be as hostile to the Jewish state, probably providing additional impetus to it.

12

'War' Discourse and its Limitations

Before discussing the topic of this chapter, I thought it might be useful to recap and provide an interim answer to the question posed in the title: whatever happened to antisemitism? If any readers assumed that I would argue that antisemitism has gone away, they should know by now that this is not the case.

I begin by briefly summarising the narrative so far.

Confusion is rife about what constitutes antisemitism. Public discussion about the problem is characterised by bitter arguments, *ad hominem* attacks, ignorance, weaponisation for nefarious political motives and the privileging of the opinions of well-known public figures, from peers of the realm to comedians, grandstanding about antisemitism on the basis of precious little knowledge or understanding. Academic debate about contemporary antisemitism is all-too often 'a dialogue of the deaf waged as a battle to the death'. At the core of this clash is a fundamental disagreement over whether anti-Zionism, or serious criticism of Israel, is antisemitic. Those who contend that it is are highly likely to call it 'new antisemitism', a theory or notion that has become, over a period of 30 to 35 years, the dominant narrative about what modern antisemitism is primarily all about. The phrase that most fully expresses this notion is: 'Israel is the "collective Jew" among the nations'. This distinguishes it from so-called 'classical' antisemitism, which targeted the Jews as pariahs and pollutants, whether they lived in tiny *shtetls* or the largest cities.

Ultimately, redefining antisemitism in this way and promoting the new definition became a political project undertaken largely by Jewish organisations, Jewish academics, Israeli governments and their friends and allies. A formal codification of 'new antisemitism', though ostensibly open to discussion, took place under the aegis of the EUMC, and the resulting 'working definition' was posted on its website in 2005. It was then relaunched in almost identical form by the IHRA in 2016.

By the end of the 1990s, the anti-antisemitism organisations, most of the antisemitism research institutes and think tanks, the national and international Jewish representative bodies as well as intergovernmental organisations such as the OSCE functioned to make opposing 'new antisemitism' a transnational field of racial governance. By the end of the first decade of the third millennium, Israel had assumed the role of coordinating this activity. Despite many groups and individual academics and writers critiquing and opposing the use

of the IHRA 'working definition', some of whom produced their own definitions, it became widely referenced internationally. The IHRA and the major
anti-antisemitism Jewish organisations in the US, Europe and Israel encouraged states, international organisations, municipal authorities, educational
institutions, security agencies, anti-racist groups, human rights bodies and so
on not just to formally adopt the 'working definition', but also to treat it as if
it were holy writ and therefore unamendable, making the notion that 'Israel is
the "collective Jew"' among the nations' the essence of this scripture. Although
the 'working definition' is supposed to be non-legally binding and its examples,
most of which relate to various forms of criticism of Israel and Zionism that are
only antisemitic depending on context, neither of these stipulations is respected
by promoters of the 'working definition'. They tend to treat the examples as
antisemitic without question. This makes the 'working definition' a charter
legitimising groundless restrictions on freedom of speech.

The central tenet of 'new antisemitism', that 'Israel is the "collective Jew"'
among the nations' is a myth. A state cannot possibly have the attributes of a
living person. Moreover, there are no grounds in Judaism for deifying the state.
It is a form of idolatry. And by reducing Jews to a singularity, it validates the
antisemitic construct of 'the Jew'. Zionism is a political movement that was
originally in conflict with religious Judaism. Only in recent decades have mainstream orthodox rabbis claimed that Zionism is integral to Judaism.

Beyond Israel's demonisation, delegitimisation and subjection to double
standards, the 'new antisemitism' is alleged primarily to consist in the slew of
accusations that Israel is committing human rights violations in its treatment
of Palestinians in the West Bank and in attacks it mounts on Gaza. These accusations are said to be without foundation and inspired wholly by antisemitic
motives, making human rights culture in general the enemy of the Jewish
people.

Analysts tend to agree that Israel's geopolitical position is very strong, with
little on the horizon likely to alter this situation. Its claim to be first in line facing
the predations of jihadi and Islamist forces, and also at the forefront of international efforts to combat such terrorism, is not contradicted by the major
powers, nor by Arab states whose regimes are targeted by Islamist extremists.
The tendency for many states is therefore to relate to Israel pragmatically, ben-
efitting from the country's hi-tech expertise, its production of security systems
and its arms industry. Israel's treatment of the Palestinians and its occupation
of Palestinian territory is a matter of very low-level concern in its relations with
countries that in the past would have made this issue a firm barrier to normalisation of relations. Many states have thus also responded sympathetically to
Israel's self-designation as being constantly under threat from forces with antisemitic motives.

*   *   *

There is an obvious incongruity arising out of this interim summary. If 'new antisemitism' is such a serious present danger, how is it that its alleged primary target shows no signs of suffering, or being held back in any way, as a result of discrimination, ostracisation and delegitimisation? What does this say about the dire warnings of ever-rising global antisemitism, largely linked to alleged anti-semitism directed at the Jewish state? That Israel presents itself as powerful and successful while at the same time under existential threat from antisemitic forces is surely something that should raise a fundamental question: what precisely *is* the institutional structure of anti-antisemitism that we have identified in the previous chapters? What purpose does it serve? What kind of political, social, cultural phenomenon is it? If, as it appears, its primary effect is to turn specific instances of legitimate speech, the exercise of free speech, into expressions of a redefined antisemitism—one based on a category mistake and notions heretical to Judaism—does this not raise troubling questions about what we are expected to take for granted is a force for good?

Anidjar's premise for responding to the kind of questions I have posed is to describe the anti-antisemitism struggle as a 'war': a 'war' against or on anti-semitism. While not everyone involved in combatting antisemitism necessarily views it as a 'war', very many do. And we can understand why this is so, even though the implications of the use of the word are seriously problematic.

It is not easy to pinpoint when 'war' came to be in common usage as a descrip-tion of the contemporary fight against antisemitism but by 2003, Elyakhim Rubinstein, the former Israeli attorney general and cabinet secretary, who was responsible for the state's first concerted drive to seize the initiative and place Israel at the head of a global Jewish anti-antisemitism campaign when he estab-lished the Israel Government Monitoring Forum on Antisemitism in 1988, was describing the effort to combat antisemitism in these terms.[1] And this is a 'war' in which those who have declared it can never accept any kind of truce. There can be no compromise with an ideology that led to the murder of 6 million Jews. This suggests that, at least metaphorically, like Nazi antisemitism, it must be 'beaten down ... like a dog'.[2] Or so it would seem.

More recently, 'The World Zionist Organisation ... compiled data that reveals a sharp increase in the amount and level of hatred directed towards the Jewish people', the writer, Efraim Ganor reported. 'The state of Israel must be proactive in the face of the surge in global antisemitism. This tidal wave must be stopped before it drowns us all'. Ganor argued that 'The war against antisemitism must be conducted on social media'.[3]

In August 2017 Yedidia Stern declared that 'the whole world must be the arena of the war against antisemitism and the Jewish nation-state must serve as the supreme commander in this universal conflict'.[4] He added: 'As inconceivable as it may seem, the fear of open physical antisemitism of the classic sort has begun to trickle into the hearts of Jews in the Diaspora'.

In 'A war against antisemitism in America', Gilad Katz, Israel's consul general in the southwestern United States, writing in the wake of the Pittsburgh synagogue massacre in which eleven people were murdered, pledged that: 'Just like the state of Israel fought and won, on the battlefield, all our wars against our enemies so, too, we shall fight and beat antisemitism and antisemites. We will defeat them because we have no other option'.[5]

Writing in *Haaretz* in January 2021, Noa Landau argued:

The inauguration of a Democratic president provides an opportunity for Israel to reconsider [promoting the IHRA definition as a supreme diplomatic goal], in light of the fact that its involvement is harming the war on anti-semitism more than it is helping. The politicisation of this issue is clearly an unwise, erroneous step that has also proven counterproductive; it is a battle that has actually served to strengthen the BDS movement.[6]

In May 2021, in the wake of the violent disturbances in Israel and Gaza, Cnaan Lipshitz wrote pessimistically about the subsequent increase in antisemitic incidents in some countries in Europe. The article was headed 'As hate surges, prominent European Jews worry [that the] war against antisemitism is lost'.[7]

We know that 'new antisemitism' has become the dominant narrative and ideological underpinning for this war. But prosecuting a war requires the mobilisation of troops. Writing in 2007, Anidjar's tentatively expressed judgement that, 'As mobilizations go, it *appears* to be a successful one',[8] is correct. At least, I would add, in the sense of giving the *appearance* of being successful. But a successful *mobilization* for war does not guarantee a successful *prosecution* of such. And what or who has been mobilised exactly? Asking such questions is crucial to any serious attempt to understand what has happened to antisemitism, and yet not only is there great reluctance on the part of the leading combatants in this 'war'—if it is a 'war'—to reflect on such matters, they tend to be deeply suspicious of anyone who does and accuse them of antisemitism denial.

Anidjar had concluded that

[there is a] nearly complete lack of public self-reflection on the part of the thinkers, writers, militants, and leaders of WAS [Anidjar's acronym for 'war' on antisemitism]. 'What are we doing? What does it mean? How to explain our achievements and/or successes? Are we, in fact, effective? If not, why not?[9]

Counting himself as a participant in this 'struggle' and recognising its scale, Anidjar nonetheless acknowledged

> the near complete absence (to the best of my knowledge at least) of reflective and indeed concerted gestures on the part of those of us who struggle against antisemitism … We are soldiers of a peculiar army that does not think itself, participants in a war that may know its enemies (or think it does) but hardly its allies.[10]

When he revisited this issue ten years later, he confessed to still being a combatant in the 'war' on antisemitism, but that he was also still plagued by doubts as to what exactly he was involved in.[11] If it is a movement, is it to be understood as 'either religious, social or political'? Can it be a social movement if it 'does not know itself?' Is it concerted? 'What precisely am I in this fight?' he asks. 'What kind of actor does it make me? Am I a rebel or a conformist? Am I an intellectual, an activist or a foot soldier? What exactly is it that I have joined?'[12] As in 2007, he frets over the lack of any serious self-reflection about the nature and history of the struggle against antisemitism. 'The literature on antisemitism is vast and still growing, but it has predictably focused on understanding antisemitism rather than on proposing a reflection on its own genealogy, the conditions of its possibility, its meaning or efficacy.[13] Nevertheless, he still believed, as he concluded in 2007, that

> As mobilizations go it appears to be … a fairly successful one. It seems by now plausible, at any rate, that there is, if not a concerted effort and struggle, at least a multiple and layered deployment of diverse means and interventions, united or not, minimally tactical if not always strategic, all of which gather in pursuit of the same purpose: namely to wage a war against antisemitism.[14]

Anidjar very usefully runs through the 'diverse means and interventions', the range of national and international activities involved: political, legislative, legal, educational, museological, literary, cinematic, press, social media, campus, protest, campaigning and so on. But he still has doubts: 'aside from a heightened awareness (I now know I am in fact part of something larger, a social movement of sorts), what insight does this all-too rapid sketch provide? What knowledge can it contribute? What are its consequences?'[15]

Anidjar's project seems to be fundamentally a personal one. He wants to understand what he is in this struggle and what the 'war' means. But in order to answer the question posed in the title of this book, we must also apply Anidjar's searching interrogatory method to the issue of the achievements, successes and effectiveness of the 'war'—or lack of them. In short, *is* the 'war' on antisemitism being won?

However, we are not quite yet in a position to answer this question. There is still a more fundamental question to be addressed first.

Throughout the book, I have myself occasionally used the word 'war', or some other military-type metaphor to refer to the collective efforts to combat antisemitism over the last 20 years. First, because this is the framing the leaders of the fight use to describe their enterprise, and it is necessary to pay due attention to their mindset. But more significantly, I found Anidjar's descriptive but ultimately questioning and critical framing of the effort as 'WAS' a very useful way of identifying the factors that have contributed to the confusion surrounding our understanding of antisemitism today.

But like so much else in this story, just because it seems natural to take for granted a certain framing of discussion about antisemitism, and especially one that explicitly describes the realisation of a moral imperative—a 'war' against evil: what kind of moral being would oppose such a fight?—does not place it above serious interrogation. Is there, can there be, a 'war' on antisemitism?

Put simply: there cannot.

Some will counter that 'it is only a metaphor'. But the metaphor is nonetheless used to frame the combatting of antisemitism, and more importantly, is the yardstick by which the enterprise is judged. It delineates, and seeks to persuade that a particular course of action is essential, and that its purpose, in all seriousness, is to 'eradicate' or 'eliminate' antisemitism. A critique of the 'war' metaphor cannot therefore simply be dismissed by saying: 'We don't mean it literally'. It therefore requires serious examination.

I interpret Anidjar's characterisation of the twenty-first-century fight against antisemitism as a 'war', like the 'war on terror' or the 'war on drugs', as a missile fired at the heart of this characterisation of the enterprise, as it is portrayed by its generals. Though he does not spell out the arguments as to why calling those efforts 'wars' is an abuse of language, the literature on these issues is extensive.[16]

Given that there is such a close relationship between the declaration of the 'war on terror' and the beginning of the 'war on antisemitism'—a relationship that is of course more than just coincidental—it is hardly surprising that many of the criticisms made of the 'war on terror' apply to the 'war on antisemitism'.

First, in a war there has to be an identifiable enemy, even in the 'confines' of a single country or island. And this is even more the case when it is seen as an international phenomenon. But 'terror' is an abstract noun, and as such cannot be an identifiable enemy.

Second, the governments participating in the 'war on terror'—some on the basis of 'my enemy's enemy is my friend'—have exploited it to pursue often contradictory political and military objectives predating the terror surge, such as reducing civil liberties, chilling freedom of speech and curtailing human rights.[17]

Third, 'terror' is actually a tactic, and plainly, as the evidence suggests, cannot be brought to an end by military means. The author of a 2009 monograph on this issue titled 'The Oddity of Waging War on a Tactic: Reframing the Global War on Terror as a Global Counterinsurgency',[18] a Lieutenant Colonel in the US Army at the School of Advanced Military Studies in Kansas, begins his text with this quote: '[A]part from the oddity of waging war on a tactic, this expression [War on Terrorism] sidesteps the causes, dynamics, and shades of Islamic militancy, with unfortunate consequences for strategy, resources, and results'.[19] When President George W. Bush called it 'a task that does not end' in his speech declaring the 'war on terror' on 20 September 2001,[20] as an indication of America's resolve, it is highly unlikely that he was displaying frankness and foresight, warning the American people to expect as many as 2,372 military deaths.

Much the same can be said about antisemitism, which is also an abstract noun. There are some identifiable enemies in the form of explicitly antisemitic political groups and movements, as well as individual antisemites such as David Duke, but they are few and far between. In most Western countries, those who wish to inculcate or express antisemitic hate in a manner that does not alienate potential supporters know only too well that unvarnished Jew-hate is largely counterproductive. Antisemitism therefore emerges in more diffuse ways, with the internet constituting the most prominent means of communicating the various shades of ambivalent feelings about, animosity towards and dislike and hatred of Jews. Even if it were possible to make clear distinctions as regards the salience of these attitudes, waging a fully coordinated 'war' on social media, or the way it is regulated, or the social media companies themselves, is a fantasy. As with terror, waging 'war' on antisemitism sidesteps its elasticity, its very different national manifestations, the nature of the impact it has on Jews, the disconnect between quantity of antisemitic propaganda and the threat it poses to Jews and Jewish life.

Antisemitism is thought, idea, feeling, emotion. There are ways of influencing people who harbour antisemitic attitudes to think, feel and see differently, but to consider doing what is essentially in depth educational and perhaps psychological work as if it were a war is bound to fail. It is not a crime to think antisemitic thoughts.

In his 'When killers become victims: Antisemitism and its critics', Anidjar argued that 'WAS must be treated as a social and political movement, one that is related and in fact comparable (for obvious reasons having to do with the mimetic dynamism at work in adversarial relations) to that which it has opposed'.[21] This statement seemed to me an appropriate lens through which to examine and understand the dilemmas set out in my introductory chapter. But by 'must be treated as' did he mean 'is'? Whatever the answer, I set myself the task of reaching my own conclusion about what kind of 'movement' the 'war on antisemitism' was by surveying the institutional, political, academic and legal forces engaged in this struggle.

I was also guided by two other Anidjar insights, which he derives from a reading of Hannah Arendt. First, that the 'war' on antisemitism is 'supranational', its 'geographical sweep' is, simply, the entire world, and that this can be demonstrated by identifying with which cultural, institutional, human and educational sectors of society it engages. Second, that as a political and social movement, its social, political and economic dimensions 'must be accounted for'.[22]

Examining the materials relating to the first of these insights, it becomes clear that Anidjar's list of sectors with which the 'war' on antisemitism is engaged is fundamentally accurate: international law and global institutions; non-governmental organisations; museums and memorials; schools, universities and research centres; literature and film; media and entertainment; world-famous personalities; educational materials and more.

But when it comes to Anidjar's second insight, after working through the evidence, it became clear to me that, while the 'war on antisemitism' is political through and through, the forces engaged in it are too diverse and variegated to be called a movement. Its leaders do 'vocally proclaim [its] affinity with, its centrality in, the spread of democracy and freedom', but in reality only lip service is paid to these values. Moreover, it does not 'tend towards realising equality' or towards 'crystallising privilege'—and therefore does not qualify as a social movement, which can be defined as:

a loosely organized but sustained campaign in support of a social goal, typically either the implementation or the prevention of a change in society's structure or values. Although social movements differ in size, they are all essentially collective. That is, they result from the more or less spontaneous coming together of people whose relationships are not defined by rules and procedures but who merely share a common outlook on society.[23]

The 'war on antisemitism' is essentially an elite enterprise. At a pinch, you could say that it arises out of disillusionment with governing structures and official bodies for not taking appropriate action to fight antisemitism, but that some of the disillusioned are themselves governing structures and official bodies. Leaders and members expect to address and influence establishments, security forces, etc. in order to secure protection from antisemitic attacks, incitement, propaganda. There are no grassroots clamouring and mobilising for action. Many of those engaged in the struggle are 'naturally conservative'; they see social and political changes exacerbating antisemitism. Among the forces that make up the loose collective network fighting the battle are new organisations established out of dissatisfaction with older bodies more inclined to non-confrontational forms of action. The new organisations are more assertive, more adept at securing publicity and conveying eye-catching messages about the imminent threat of antisemitism. While some of these bodies have successfully forced older organisations to change and become more vocal and uncompromising, the overall direction of the 'war on antisemitism' is to get as close as possible to 'the powers that be' at national and international levels.

Its sources of funding are not fully transparent. The social make-up of those involved preserves and reproduces stratification. Those engaged in militant activism are from similar, largely privileged social backgrounds and its organisational leaders include, for example, high-level academics, self-made businessmen, Russian Jewish oligarchs, Israeli government officials and former political leaders. In addition to the militant activists and organisational heads, its informal public representatives are often intellectuals and academics, as well as prominent writers, entertainers and columnists. In the global public sphere, those waging the 'war on antisemitism' have secured the highest access to the most prominent platforms to pursue their battles. Through use of the wide variety of mainstream and social media available to all, it reaches a relatively wide audience, but since it is not a movement seeking to mobilise large numbers to engage with this issue at street level, even from the Jewish population, mobi-lisation essentially is only sought at the level of elites, among those who can be effective in international bodies and with governments. Contrary to what some might argue, 'Jews do count'.

An additional important feature, which must be seen as, in one sense, playing a part in the 'war', is what might be called the 'left opposition'. This is made up largely of Jewish people who reject the fundamental thrust of the 'war' to see criticism of Israel as its main target, who insist on drawing attention to the growth and seriousness of far-right antisemitism and who demand that action be taken against the Hungarian and Polish governments, for example, that openly encourage antisemitic elements in their societies and pursue high-profile figures of Jewish origin, singling out them and their Jewish connections for attack.

In Anidjar's rich marshalling of key questions that needed to be addressed to leaders of the 'war', set out in his 2007 *Cosmopolis* article, he made some assump-tions, that, I would argue, no longer apply. First, he speaks of the 'war' as 'today being fought most vocally and adamantly' in Europe. After four years of Trump's green-lighting of white supremacism and neo-fascism, and the growing critique of Israel among Democrats and younger Jews in the US, which the Jewish establishment largely regards as antisemitism, this is probably no longer to be taken for granted. Second, he writes of the West quite suddenly becoming the 'World Headquarters of WAS'. That was at a time when Israel had only recently embarked on its successful quest to make *itself* the 'World Headquarters of

216

WAS'. However, it is certainly true that Israel considered itself as spearheading the effort *on the part of the West*. Although there is little doubt that Israel sets the agenda for fighting antisemitism, it would be wrong to understand its role in terms of concentrated, centralised control. The influential major American Jewish organisations that aim to police the discourse on antisemitism—AJC, ADL, SWC, AIPAC—jealously guard their independence for various reasons: their origins in different sectors of the Jewish immigrant community; organisational rivalry; the competition to finance their operations; and the particular inflexion each brings to the struggle. (Strictly speaking, AIPAC's task is lobbying for Israel, but it is quick to accuse of antisemitism anyone who draws attention to the financial support accruing to lawmakers who are close to AIPAC and support Israel. AIPAC does not give funds directly to candidates standing in congressional elections, but its largely Jewish membership are also members of PACs, which do give funds to pro-Israel candidates and are encouraged to do so by AIPAC personnel.) When the Israeli government first tried putting itself at the head of the fight against antisemitism in the late 1980s and early 1990s, there was polite, though very strong resistance from these bodies. But as anti-antisemitism organisations increasingly coalesced around the discourse of 'new antisemitism', residual objection to Israel asserting its leadership fell away.

The situation in Europe has always been more complex and diverse. Before the collapse of communism, open cooperation on security matters between Jewish communities in European Soviet bloc states and Western European communities was impossible. Even if Europe had not been divided so starkly, the differences between Jewish community structures from country to country, as well as the desire to assert independence, reflecting local history and tradition, would have hampered security cooperation and stymied any attempts by Israel to institute any oversight of the fight against antisemitism. But after 1989, pan-European organisations such as the EJC and the European Council of Jewish Communities (ECJC), which had been pan-European in name only, made the most of optimism about the 'new Europe' and the threat of resurgent antisemitism in former communist countries, to develop pan-communal cooperation. This grew especially in the area of community development in Central and Eastern Europe, but also through efforts to tackle antisemitism. While the three major Jewish communities in Europe—France, the UK and Germany—showed resistance to Israeli efforts to manage the 'war' on antisemitism' in Europe, especially since it came with a strong Zionist message that immigration to Israel—*aliya*—was the long-term solution, both France and the UK were early adopters of 'new antisemitism' theory.[24] (Resistance to Israel's *aliya* solution did not arise out of any objection to Zionism, but rather because Jewish representatives resented the undermining of the physical, spiritual and cultural integrity of their communities, which they were very proud of and jealously guarded.) Opposition to it was also strong, but after 9/11, the message that Israel was 'the "Jew" among the nations' became increasingly popular, opening the way for Jewish bodies to acquiesce in the Israeli government's efforts to exert leadership of the 'war'. This was clearly facilitated by the ongoing impact of the collapse of communism and the growing dominance of powerful Jewish oligarchs from the former Soviet Union, who bought their way into the leadership of the pan-European Jewish organisations, created additional such frameworks and, partly as a means of securing the most power and influence, adopted tougher stances on antisemitism fully in accord with the developing agenda and strategies of the Israeli MSA and MFA. The extent of this influence, and its importance for Prime Minister Netanyahu's government became crystal clear at the Holocaust memorial and opposition to antisemitism gatherings at Auschwitz and in Jerusalem in January 2020.

The fifth World Holocaust Forum was convened by Israel's President Reuven Rivlin in Jerusalem on 23 January 2020. Leaders from more than 40 countries gathered to mark the 75th anniversary of the liberation of Auschwitz. The standfirst of an article on Israel's role in fighting antisemitism by David Weinberg encapsulated the Israeli position: 'As raw antisemitism around the world has risen and morphed into virulent anti-Israel sentiment—making the two phenomena almost indistinguishable—the State of Israel has moved from indifference to active involvement in the struggle against such hate'.

Weinberg continued:[25]

Israel expects world leaders coming to the conference not only to memorialize Holocaust victims. Israel expects world leaders to commit themselves to concretely fighting antisemitic expression and activity in their own countries—in consonance with the IHRA definition of antisemitism, and in a way that protects Israel's place in the world at a time when the very legitimacy of a Jewish state is under assault.

The initiative for these events came from the president of the European Jewish Congress, the Russian Jewish oligarch and Putin ally Moshe Kantor, who lives in Geneva and who also financed the gatherings.

So much of the package of myths, internal contradictions, incompatible expectations and deeply problematic accusations that plague our understanding of antisemitism today made their appearance in those performances, all wrapped in the sanitising, blessed, talismanic, both protective and validating cloak of the Holocaust and the IHRA 'working definition' of antisemitism. And that's before we even speak of the cast of presiding characters whose credentials for protecting and furthering human rights, democracy and anti-racism are hugely underwhelming. In such circuses, the fight against antisemitism is revealed as a messy, even grubby business, rather than the 'never again', solemn, spiritual, memorialising and holy occasion the organisers want the world to see.

This is more like shadowboxing than war: prima facie grounds for challenging the 'war' designation and not simply treating the issue as a matter of semantics. Given the mid-twentieth-century experience of antisemitism and the Holocaust—the impossible to ignore central reference point for our understanding of the consequences of antisemitism, as the Jerusalem 2020 event shows—this is a war, therefore, whose stakes are always life-and-death and in which success can only be total defeat of the enemy. Yet no matter how many times and with whatever vehemence we are told that the aim is total eradication of antisemitism, the fact remains that no amount of troops can destroy an idea. When the enemy is framed in the abstract, total victory is impossible. Conceiving the struggle as a 'war' dooms it to failure. But it could be argued that it suits Zionism because it perpetuates the continuity of complaint—justifying claims of persecution only neutralisable by a secure Jewish state.

*   *   *

After discussing the many ways in which framing anti-antisemitism activity as a 'war' is fundamentally problematic, we must now take a step back and look at the 'war' through the eyes of its generals and its troops, to determine whether they believe their offensive against antisemitism is succeeding.

Judging by statements made by prominent figures in the forefront of the fight, as well as by commentators' assessments, media reports, and the perceptions of anti-antisemitism organisations, the answer must be 'no'.

'Antisemitism continues to exist in a variety of formats and locations around the world and no one seems to be able to prevent its proliferation', said Avner Shalev, chairman of Yad Vashem, in December 2019.[26]

> Over the past weeks, the world has witnessed violent and troubling antisemitic attacks in various countries, including France, Germany, Italy, the United Kingdom and the United States. While these incidents do not represent an increase or significant change from recent months, they do represent the ongoing trend of hate crimes targeting Jews across much of the world.[27]

'We're seeing a perfect storm of antisemitism right now', Professor Deborah Lipstadt, recently nominated by President Biden to be his antisemitism envoy, told The Media Line, 'We're seeing it on the right and we're seeing it on the left. 'We are seeing it because there is a certain nationalism that has arisen. We're seeing it also because of views on the left, often disguised as views on Israel, that are antisemitic in their essence', she said.[28]

Fiamma Nirenstein, a fellow of the Jerusalem Center for Public Affairs, said that the problem, in her view, was the language criminalising the state of Israel, what she describes as 'Israelophobia', a combination of antisemitism and anti-Zionism. 'Institutions [such as the UN and EU] are very responsible for the growth of antisemitism because they build a backing to it', Nirenstein said.[29] 'Any person who follows the news knows that antisemitism is on the rise around the world. As it has spread, so has our insight that this is a hatred with many faces, a many-headed monster fed by myths about Jews that will not die.'[30]

In an interview for Politico headed 'The EU official tackling an antisemitism explosion', Katharina von Schnurbein said:

'There's sometimes little understanding for the enormity of where we are: You are almost 80 years after the Holocaust and we see symptoms in society [where] Jews feel threatened again here. This is of course something incredible', von Schnurbein said. 'When antisemitism is on the rise you know that something bigger is going on.'[31]

What exactly these assessments are based on is rarely made clear. Phrases like 'recent surge', 'surge in global antisemitism', 'tidal wave', 'classic antisemitism trickling into the hearts of Diaspora Jews', and 'antisemitism explosion' serve to dramatise the problem, but they are highly emotive and hardly 'scientific'.

But if we turn to assessments about current antisemitism made by research institutes and antisemitism monitoring bodies, while the language is more circumspect and differentiated, the message is much the same. The Tel Aviv University Kantor Centre's annual report *Antisemitism Worldwide 2019 and the Beginning of 2020* presents a bleak picture of growing antisemitic violence, government responses to antisemitism 'which are overwhelmingly considered inadequate', 'diminishing knowledge of the Holocaust in Germany', 'online antisemitism prov[ing] to be increasingly dangerous', 'a growing discrepancy between on-the-ground reality and government efforts' and 'surveys continuing to raise awareness about the surging antisemitism'.[32] In addition, the report states: 'Despite the adoption of the 2016 IHRA Working Definition of Antisemitism by more than 20 countries and by a host of institutes and organisations, it is still widely under-appreciated and not enough in use in order to identify and define antisemitic incidents'.

A much shorter list, reproduced here in full, highlights 'significant achievements during 2019':

The UN Special Rapporteur on Freedom of Religion or Belief presented a report to the UN General Assembly entitled 'Elimination of All Forms of

Religious Intolerance', warning against growing antisemitism inspired by Nazi and Islamist ideologies.

The EU established a working group to guide Member States in implementing steps against antisemitism.

The German—and Austrian—parliaments defined the BDS as a movement that uses antisemitic tactics, and reached a resolution according to which 'the pattern of argument and methods of the BDS movement are antisemitic'.

The World Holocaust Forum, initiated and supported by Dr Moshe Kantor, President of the European Jewish Congress, held its fifth meeting on January 23, 2020 in Yad Vashem, under the auspices of President Reuven Rivlin, with heads of 52 states coming to declare their commitment to 'Remembering the Holocaust, Fighting Antisemitism'.

To summarise: a UN warning, an EU working group set up, BDS defined as antisemitic, 52 states commit to fighting antisemitism—hardly a persuasive or significant response to the scale of the problems the Kantor report identified or that the media commentators described. (It should be noted that one of the leading promoters of 'new antisemitism', of the IHRA 'working definition' and of the infrastructure of the 'war' against antisemitism, Dina Porat, is head of the Kantor Center.)

The two American Jewish organisations that drove adoption of the 'working definition' of antisemitism through the IHRA, the AJC and SWC—the former acting largely 'behind the scenes', the latter very prominently and publicly— have never been shy of pronouncing on antisemitism, especially in Europe, but also in the US. The 2019 AJC survey of American Jews on antisemitism in the US 'makes clear that American Jews view antisemitism as a significant problem in America—and one that is getting worse'.[33] As for Europe, Rabbi Baker commented in January 2020:

> There has been considerable success in getting European governments and intergovernmental organisations to recognise the problem of antisemitism today. To a degree this is a result of widespread advocacy and educational efforts, which have had considerable support from, among others, the United States Congress in its network of relations and direct meetings with foreign leaders and parliaments. But it has also been a function of the growing severity and lethalness of the problem, which makes it impossible to ignore.[34]

Hardly a ringing endorsement of the way that the 'war' is being waged.

The SWC does not produce research-based assessments or conduct opinion polls. Instead, each year it releases a list of what it judges to be the world's 'top ten worst antisemitic incidents'. In December 2019, before the UK general election, it placed the then Labour Party leader Jeremy Corbyn in this slot. Its press statement proclaimed:

> In a year awash with antisemitism on both sides of the Atlantic, no one has done more to mainstream antisemitism into the political and social life of a democracy than the Jeremy Corbyn-led Labour Party. Chief Rabbi Ephraim Mirvis warned that anti-Jewish racism was a new poison that had taken root in the party.[35]

CST's 2019 UK *Antisemitic Incidents Report*, published on 6 February 2020, shows that it 'received a record high total of 1,805 antisemitic incidents in the UK last year. 2019 was the fourth year in a row to see a record incident total and continues an ongoing trend of rising numbers of antisemitic hate incidents in this country'.[36] In response, the communities secretary, Robert Jenrick MP, said

> Who could have imagined that 75 years after the end of the Holocaust, anti-semitism would be on the rise in the UK and across Europe. There is no place for antisemitism in our society. It is a scourge on us all and the record high number of recorded incidents in 2019 is completely unacceptable.[37]

Shadow policing minister and vice-chair of the All-Party Parliamentary Group Against Antisemitism, Louise Haigh MP, said: 'It is shameful the Jewish community has been subjected to another year of racist abuse'. CST Chief Executive David Delew described 2019 as: 'another difficult year for British Jews'.

In a meeting with Canadian Prime Minister Justin Trudeau, Irwin Cotler, leading protagonist for the existence of 'new antisemitism', among whose more recent interventions was to found and become head of the Montreal-based Raoul Wallenberg Centre for Human Rights (RWCHR),[38] 'stressed that anti-semitism around the world has reached an "intensification that has no parallel since the end of the Second World War and the atmospherics are reminiscent of the 1930s"'.[39] 'Cotler used the starkest terms to describe how grave the situation of Jews in the world, including those in Israel, is today', the report declared.

In a study by JPR, *Young Jewish Europeans: perceptions and experiences of antisemitism: summary of findings*, based on 2018 data and published in July 2019,[40] the authors state:

> The European Union and its Member States are required by law to do everything in their power to combat antisemitism effectively and to safeguard the dignity of the Jewish People. Yet as two recent surveys of discrimination

and hate crime against Jews in the EU, both commissioned by the European Union Agency for Fundamental Rights (FRA), clearly show, the persistence and prevalence of antisemitism hinder people's ability to live openly Jewish lives, free from fears for their security and well-being.

Over the last 30 years or more, Holocaust education has played an increasingly central role in combatting antisemitism. It is no coincidence therefore that the EUMC 'working definition' of antisemitism found a home and a relaunch-pad in the IHRA. Who would dare question a statement about current antisemitism emanating from an 'international' body dedicated to Holocaust commemoration? But there are leading Holocaust historians who do precisely that. Professor Daniel Blatman, a Holocaust-era historian at the Hebrew University of Jerusalem, and chief historian of the Warsaw Ghetto Museum, is trenchant in his critical appraisal of the IHRA: 'an unnecessary, destructive organisation was born—one that has turned Holocaust education and remembrance into a powerful, worldwide concern. Its successes aren't particularly impressive if, after 20 years of activities, discussions and conferences around the world, antisemitism has had a revival today such as it hasn't experienced for years'.[41]

Taken at face value, for all engaged in the fight against antisemitism, these assessments and findings must surely make depressing reading. So much cumulative effort and so little to show for it. Or so it would appear. But like all such snapshots, even though reference is sometimes made to, and comparisons made with, the past, any serious consideration of historical or any other kind of context is effectively absent. And as we have seen, when it comes to some factors held responsible for antisemitism, in this case the alleged actions of one individual, Jeremy Corbyn, the unrestrained hyperbole about his contributions to antisemitism are so far-fetched as to suggest that he came to serve as an all-purpose scapegoat, carrying a degree of responsibility for a congeries of psychological fears, feelings of existential angst, actual instances of antisemitic manifestations for which there is no evidence that he has any responsibility whatsoever. Claims that his alleged 'conscious' or 'subconscious antisemitism' has given licence to numerous others to openly display their unrestrained antisemitism are not substantiated by any actual facts. I will return to interrogate these very important issues of context, apocalyptic language and discourse inflation later. For now, since the combatants in this 'war' are dealing with what they regard as present dangers, and are not engaged in serious reflection on the past, the next obvious question we must ask is: given the intense stress over the last two decades laid on the need to define antisemitism before it can be fought, and the increasingly divisive discussions about the relationship between anti-Zionism and antisemitism that led to it, and the undoubted success of those pressing so hard for the promulgation of such a definition—or to be more accurate, as I argue, a *redef-*

inition—why does it appear not to have made any difference on the ground? Why does antisemitism remain undefeated?

With so much emphasis placed on the belief that anti-Zionism is antisemitism, and the high degree to which this question constitutes the central focus of the interminable bitter debates about antisemitism, it is curious, at the very least, that so little analysis of this phenomenon feeds into these surveys of antisemitism. Could it be that quantifying the exercise of free speech on Israel–Palestine as if it were a category on an antisemitism scale in fact proves to be unworkable?

The leaders of this 'war' themselves tell us, even if only indirectly, that the 'war' is failing. Their relentless message is that antisemitism continues to get worse, particularly in two respects: 'viral antisemitism' directed at the Jewish state (the 'Israelisation of antisemitism') and Islamic hostility to Jews, often just a coded way of speaking of alleged Palestinian and pro-Palestinian antisemitism or anti-Zionism.

It was in Chapter 9—The redefinition project and the myth of the 'collective Jew' exposed—that I introduced a core argument of this book, and it is here that its full relevance applies. If the redefinition of antisemitism as 'new antisemitism', at the heart of which is the concept of 'Israel as the "collective Jew" among the nations', is a category mistake, what has been redefined as today's antisemitism is not antisemitism at all. If, for example, you single out any of the following: questioning Israel's right to exist as a Jewish state; calling Israel an apartheid state; advocating a single secular, democratic state for Jews and Palestinians from the Mediterranean to the Jordan River; campaigning for boycott, divestment and sanctions to pressure Israel to abide by human rights and international law; demanding immediate legislation giving full, equal rights— including national rights—to all who live in Palestine–Israel; replacing the Law of Return, which applies only to Jews, with an immigration policy equitable for Jews and Palestinians; and giving Palestinian refugees the right of return as laid down in UN General Assembly Resolution 3236 in 1974—you are simply denying the right of freedom of speech and peaceful protest, and the practice of legitimate politics, on the wholly false grounds that these demands are antisemitic. As we have seen, however, the bulk of the action initiated by the leaders and activists waging the 'war' relate to these and similar issues, which, they claim, prove that the Jewish state is being persecuted as the individual Jew has been persecuted over the centuries. And the problem for these warriors is that, while they may be having some success with IHRA adoption, pushing back against BDS and preventing apartheid weeks on campuses, those engaging in these political activities will never accept that they are doing anything other than exercising their freedom of speech, and they are and will be supported by free speech guardians. The idea that a war against such expressions of freedom of speech can ever be won is inconceivable.

Presented as targeting classic antisemitism, 'new antisemitism', 'antisemitic anti-Zionism' and so on, the 'war' has, in the form of the IHRA 'working definition' of antisemitism—essentially the codification of 'new antisemitism'—a manifesto that focuses principally on 'Israel, the "collective Jew" among the nations'. That the Israeli MSA, working very closely with the Israeli MFA, managed and directed a worldwide pushback against the principal manifestations of 'new antisemitism' therefore comes as no surprise. Their targets included: BDS; human rights culture; purveyors of charges that Israel manages a system of apartheid both in the occupied territories and within its pre-1967 borders; demands for full, equal rights for Palestinians, which, it is argued, would lead to the destruction of the Jewish state. This effort was undertaken with the close involvement of a panoply of major international and national Jewish organisations, research institutes, think tanks, Jewish community defence groups and monitoring bodies, and campaigning anti-antisemitism organisations, with a significant initiating and supportive role played by Israel lobby organisations, which naturally follow the lead of, and benefit from the services provided— hasbara training, with great emphasis on the use of social media—by the MSA and MFA.

And as is common to the conduct of most wars, attack is the best form of defence. So, rather than simply responding to street protests urging support for BDS, or challenging administrative or legislative measures introducing BDS, the MSA was pre-empting such measures by working with local supporters to have legislation introduced to outlaw even the attempt to bring forward such legal initiatives. This strategy is efficacious because of its success in persuading political and administrative authorities that the principal target of antisemitism is the state of Israel. By its very existence the state is understood as embodying certain fundamental Jewish values, or the very essence of modern Jewishness, which therefore makes any criticism of it a valid reason for apocalyptic prognostications about its future survival and the future survival of Jewish communities globally. Some glorify Jewish sovereignty in Israel as the basis of Jewish strength, power and stability, and contrast that with diaspora Jewish weakness, which is only tolerable because of Israel's strength. So, if threats to Israel's existence are deemed genuine, diaspora Jewry is doomed. Israel is thus framed as being incapable of doing anything that is any more than marginally morally unacceptable, because strong moral censure of its actions is treated as antisemitic discrimination leading to annihilation.

The fallacy is in the principal slogan itself: how do you wage 'war' on opinions and sentiments that people hold and now express in ways that will constantly evade the attacking army by, for example, continuously reinventing the use of social media to spread their views.

It is the reframing of what constitutes antisemitism, its redefinition, that does a great injustice to the many people, Jews and non-Jews, who want to help in

225

tackling Jew-hatred. If you define antisemitism as what it is not, and concentrate most of your attention on that redefinition, you will never successfully combat what is really antisemitism.

*   *   *

The 'war' on antisemitism is indeed a failing project because it is both impossible to wage 'war' against it and the 'antisemitism' it purports to target is not antisemitism as we have understood it since the Holocaust. As demonstrated by the text of the IHRA 'working definition' of antisemitism and its application by those who use it, what the 'war' targets may theoretically include neo-fascism, neo-Nazism, far-right racism, white supremacism and so on, but the energies and primary focus of its warriors are reserved for combatting the perceived assault on Israel's legitimacy.

The generals acknowledge that the 'war' is failing, and yet they present this failure as success. They can do this not solely because the 'myth of the "collective Jew"' is so seductive in itself. But because the consequences of the destruction of the 'collective Jew' would be a catastrophe of such magnitude, any relaxation of vigilance as a result of questioning the strategy of the 'war' could not be contemplated. What is at stake is the future of the entity that is said to embody the existence of the Jewish people, to be the ultimate expression of Jewishness, the guarantor of Jewish life everywhere, the physical manifestation of post-Holocaust redemption, the realisation of Jewish destiny—if you like, all sub-myths made believable if you accept the myth of the 'collective Jew'.

13

'Jewish Power', Medical Analogies and 'Eradication' Discourse

Jewish power

Actively combatting antisemitism was a central feature of the work of the Board of Deputies of British Jews and its defence department in the 1970s and 1980s, but the approach then was very different from what it is now, not least because an independent charity, the Community Security Trust, established in 1994 to handle security matters for the organised Jewish community, pursued a different strategy. The Board's policy was to avoid publicising antisemitic incidents if at all possible, and action and communication with the police was undertaken behind the scenes. It was assumed that bringing incidents to public attention would make matters worse. Rather than alerting the public to these dangers in order to build up support for action, Jewish leaders generally believed that neo-Nazi and neo-fascist groups would be energised by the fact that such acts as desecration of Jewish cemeteries were taking place.

This stance reflected a sense of insecurity, a desire not to rock the boat—not so much out of any genuine reasons to fear mass antisemitic mobilisation, rather because the normalisation of the status of Jews in British society was proceeding rather effectively and that being too visible would disturb that process. There was little discrimination. The image of the Jewish population as largely comprising working-class immigrants from Russia and Eastern Europe was changing rapidly. Increasingly, Jews were highly educated, joining the professions, playing major roles in business and finance. There was, of course, awareness both of an antisemitism ingrained in British culture and a hatred of Jews in continental Europe that had resulted in mass murder. But the British Jewish population had not been directly affected by the Holocaust—a term that only came into common usage from the 1970s—and the trauma experienced by the Jews who remained in continental Europe was felt mostly second-hand. The entire population of Britain had faced disruption during the war, and there had been no aggravated disruption of Jewish life. Safeguarding these post-war gains, which were bolstered by the growing influence of the existence of the state of Israel as a marker of Jewish survival and regeneration, was to be achieved by remaining vigilant in the face of potential threats, but not pursuing enhanced visibility in the public space. Antisemitic tropes about the nefarious exercise of Jewish power were common where antisemitic propaganda circulated, but the organised Jewish community would never have described itself as possessing power.[1]

This was not exactly the case in the United States. Britain still maintained a view of itself as ethnically homogenous—largely white and Christian. The US saw itself as an immigrant society, made up of different groups, each with a perfect right to reach the highest echelons of American society, to achieve success in whatever educational, political, commercial, financial or other endeavours they pursued—a right that in reality was systematically denied to African-Americans and only honoured in the breach for some other Americans of colour. And minorities such as the Irish and the Italians celebrated the power and influence they were able to exert in defending their group interests as well as playing prominent roles in various sectors of American society. The two goals were not seen as incompatible. And certainly, by the 1970s and 1980s, when evidence of antisemitism in America, a force to be reckoned with over many decades, was on the decline, the same applied to the Jewish minority. National Jewish organisations such as the AJC, the ADL and the AJCongress, were proud of the fact that they could lobby politicians as successfully as other groups. Power was celebrated. There was no reticence in displaying it with the understanding that what was good for your minority group was also good for American society. To be referred to as a 'lobby' was not a dirty word.

In contrast, up until the end of the twentieth century, the organisations of British Jewry would have been very reluctant to describe themselves as 'lobbies'. However, there was an awareness of the need for the Jewish community to present its concerns and wishes to the powers that be, especially when communal figures and organisations—pro-Israel and Zionist ones particularly—began to feel that Israel's international position was under attack and required a more robust response on their part.

I recall attending a meeting in the early 1980s where representatives of most of these organisations came together at the IJA in London to discuss how to scale up political work defending Israel. Essentially, the issue was whether to follow the American model and be more upfront in establishing a body with the specific aim of acting as a lobby, or whether to continue with a softly-softly approach of the kind that was followed for antisemitism. There was in fact already a body modelled partially on American practice, the British Israel Political Action Committee (BIPAC), but its lobbying was limp to say the least. It produced material promoting Israel and sought to disseminate it, but there were many who believed it was very ineffective. Some in the discussion wanted to create a fully-fledged lobby group; others preferred the more sedate, less 'vulgar', British approach. One prominent participant, a member of the Liberal

Party as was, quipped that what was required was a cross between a 'lobby' and a '*shammes*'—a Yiddish word for a 'caretaker'. This was immediately countered by another joker who shot down the idea, saying: 'a cross between a lobby and a *shammes* is a *lobos*'—a Yiddish word for a cheeky and rather naughty boy.

Frivolous though this story may sound, it reflects the reality of pro-Israel 'lobbying' in the UK at the time: on the organisational level, even with the involvement of the Israel embassy, it was very amateurish and still wedded to an image of Israel based on the notion that the pioneering kibbutz repre-sented what the country was all about. Even for many centrist or right-of-centre British Zionists, the socialist, communal 'experiment that did not fail', as it was described by the philosopher Martin Buber, epitomised what was 'good' about Israel and Zionism.[2] A more focused and politically motivated lobbying went on at the level of influential individuals who had the ears of government ministers, such as the Sieffs, the principal owners of Marks & Spencer, Lord Rothschild, Lord Goodman and other prominent Jews. Nonetheless, it would have been unthinkable at the time for anyone to speak of Jewish lobbying for Israel or Jewish lobbying on anything for that matter as representing the exercise of Jewish power.

But a word that was once invariably attached to Jews only as an expression of antisemitism has now become a reflection of a reality that many Jews are very happy to acknowledge. From a post-Holocaust position of extreme weakness to one 75 years later of considerable power to decisively influence international public discourse on antisemitism has largely been driven by the very existence of the state of Israel. Whatever else it did or did not achieve, the Zionist movement succeeded in engineering the Jewish emergence from powerlessness—one of the central aims of Zionism—even though the extent of that powerlessness was commonly exaggerated. For the first time since the collapse of the last entity that was an expression of Jewish sovereignty, the country named 'Israel' by the Jewish leader Simon Bar Kochba after he led a revolt against the Romans between 132 and 136 CE, a Jewish collectivity able to act independently came into being. Seen initially as weak and vulnerable, its power to influence the geo-political reality in the Middle East today is fact of life proudly celebrated by Israel's Jewish leaders.

We can see this even more clearly when the question of 'Jewish power' is raised. In any litany of antisemitic tropes, the nefarious, secretive, manipu-lative, world-influencing and corrupt deployment of political and financial 'Jewish power' comes very high up the list. And at one time, let's say a century ago, any mention of Jews and power in the same sentence could have reasona-bly been classed as an antisemitic trope. Of course, matters were always more complex than that. Some Jewish individuals were able to exercise some power in the fields of commerce, banking, culture and politics but no different in kind from that of their non-Jewish counterparts. While as a collective, a community facing demonisation, exclusion, suspicion, persecution, restriction, with little power to neutralise, let alone eradicate, the anti-Jewish racism, Judeophobia and prejudice they experienced, the notion of Jewish 'powerlessness' certainly had some force and validity.

With the establishment of the state of Israel, the collective exercise of Jewish power became a reality. For more than 20 years after the 1948 war, broadly speaking Israel's image in the world—excluding of course Arab countries—was of a vulnerable, endangered, but plucky little state, surviving against the odds. In Jewish-Israeli popular culture, however, the strength derived from nationalist fervour, the heroism of Zionist fighters and the tacit admiration for the Jewish terrorist groups like Lehi and Etzel, revealed a domestic recognition of and pride in what had been achieved by Jews—the new, self-sufficient, physically and mentally strong Jews who, as the Zionist story would have it, had thrown off the debilitating traits of diaspora Jewish life. But after the spectacular victories of the 1967 Six-Day War, despite early fears that the state might be on the verge of being wiped out in a reprise of the Holocaust, the image of plucky little Israel soon gave way to a more realistic appraisal of Jewish military power, which Israeli leaders eventually factored into the way they described and presented the state. If the Israeli Labour Party that dominated the first decades of the state's existence was somewhat circumspect in its attitude to this reality, the incoming right-wing governments, who saw the 1967 developments as validating their expansionist ideology—that Israel had a right to the entire territory of Palestine on both sides of the Jordan river—had no compunction in celebrating Jewish power. There were some military setbacks and for most of the 1967–2000 period international opposition to Israel's policies in the occupied territories meant that Israeli governments were able to maintain and vigorously assert that the state had to exist in an insecure environment. But by the beginning of the twenty-first century, Israel's diplomatic and geopolitical situation became increasingly secure (see Chapter 11). And its readiness to project itself as a major, if not *the* major military and diplomatic power in the region, with global reach by virtue of its highly developed high-tech and arms industry, was clearly evident in the uncompromising way in which it conducted its foreign relations. In short, it now celebrates its power unashamedly.

This transformation came at the expense of Zionism having 'largely dropped its early vision of itself as a fundamental positive force for the world as a whole', a development Adam Sutcliffe draws attention to in writing about 'Jewish purpose'.[3]

The 'light unto the nations' argument, prominent in the speeches and writings of David Ben-Gurion up to the 1960s, has given way to an emphasis on the entitlement of Jews to collective security and an environment free of anti-semitism, and to define for themselves the essential terms of both those two things.

This posture is also adopted by the major Jewish groups in the US, such as AIPAC, ADL, AJC, SWC and the Conference of Presidents of Major American Jewish Organisations. In a country where lobbying for group interests, such as protecting second amendment rights to bear arms, is woven into the political fabric, emphasising your organisation's power, as the National Rifle Association (NRA) does, is standard. AIPAC, which speaks on behalf of a coalition of American Jewish groups, and lobbies lawmakers on behalf of Israel on the grounds that America's and Israel's strategic interests and values are aligned, is regarded as particularly influential and shows no reluctance to celebrate its power. As Peter Beinart, a critic of AIPAC, put it in 2017:

> AIPAC ... does not wrestle with Jewish power. It celebrates it to the point of intoxication. At its conference this week in Washington, it encourages Jews to drink it until they cannot distinguish between 1938 and 2017, between the liquidation of the Warsaw Ghetto and the dismantling of a settlement in the West Bank, between our right to exist and our right to oppress.[4]

When the Democratic congresswoman from Minnesota, Somali-born Ilhan Omar, responded in February 2019 to a Republican threat to punish her and another congresswoman for criticising Israel, she tweeted: 'It's all about the Benjamins baby'—a line about $100 bills from a Puff Daddy song—and sparked a furore.[5] Critics were quick to say Omar was calling up a negative and harmful stereotype or trope of Jewish Americans. In a subsequent tweet she named AIPAC, saying it was funding Republican support for Israel. Both parties then accused her of antisemitic speech. She apologised, but stuck by her criticism of AIPAC's lobbying. The Israeli *Haaretz* journalist Chemi Shalev exposed the hypocrisy of the critical responses to Omar. On 11 February 2019, he tweeted: 'AIPAC has always criticised anyone, especially journalists, who dared label it "Jewish lobby". We are the "pro-Israel lobby", not Jewish. Without condoning her remarks, it's remarkable that when @IlhanMN says AIPAC, everyone, including AIPAC, immediately translates to Jews ...' As for the 'Jews + money' trope, David Ochs, founder of Halev, which helps send young people to AIPAC's annual conference, told the undercover journalist in the Al Jazeera film *Lobby—USA*: 'without sending money ... the pro-Israel lobby isn't able to enact its agenda. "Congressmen and senators don't do anything unless you pressure them. They kick the can down the road, unless you pressure them, and the only way to do that is with money", he explains.[6]

There is no doubt that both power and money are central to the lobbying process in the US, whether you are a Jewish supporter of Israel anxious to ensure your political representative continues to support the Jewish state, or whether you are a Christian believer in the necessity of maintaining gun rights to defend the kingdom of Jesus on earth, as embodied in the United States. To celebrate the first as a Jewish cause and then respond to criticism of this Jewish support by crying 'Foul! Antisemitic trope!' is hypocritical. Carolina Landsmann sets this sleight of hand in the wider context of Israeli government policy. Writing in *Haaretz* she argued:

> Netanyahu's Israel is walking a fine line, swapping the Jewish hat and the Israeli hat according to need. When it's convenient, Netanyahu is the leader of the Jewish world; and when Jews wearing American hats represent Israel's presumed interests with unlimited brazenness, nobody is allowed to say a word because that's antisemitism.[7]

Jewish power is a fact, and yet you would not know it from current debates. Judaken sees the failure to understand this changing reality as one thing that can alter the meanings and potency of what have in the past been seen as tropes, and situates this in the wider context of confusion surrounding what is anti-Jewish hate:

> The word 'antisemitism' is part of the problem. It is used to discuss everything from stereotypes (enduring images or myths about Jews), to prejudice (the internalisation of such views, often unconsciously), to discrimination (calls for social or legal action on the basis of bigoted views), to genocide. These are very different things. If someone reiterates a stereotype about Jews having too much power, for example, this does not make them an antisemite.[8]

Professor Barry Trachtenberg, in evidence he gave to the House Judiciary Committee about proposed speech codes on 7 November 2017, explains the significance of Judaken's somewhat terse, though authoritative, conclusion, for our understanding of what antisemitism is today:[9] 'The root of current debates on antisemitism lies in a seemingly intractable problem of how to critique Jewish collective power in a way that does not immediately resonate with a long history of antisemitism'. Imagined nefarious and secretive Jewish power was central to that history, yet

> in 1948, with the founding of Israel as a solution to antisemitism, the situation changed dramatically. For the first time, a significant number of Jews—identifying as a national group—gained actual, not imaginary, power. Today, the state of Israel has borders, police, courts, a military, a nuclear arsenal, political

parties, and a (mostly) representative and (somewhat) democratic system of government.

Trachtenberg continues:

Like all other states, its actions are—and must be permitted to be—a matter of public debate and discourse both within the Jewish community and outside of it. Yet speech that is critical of Israel still strikes many as inherently antisemitic. The problem, quite simply, is that we still are learning how to talk about Israel's actual political power and repeated claims to represent Jews all over the world in ways that do not immediately echo much older and antisemitic depictions of imaginary Jewish power.

After his testimony was published it seems that some decided Trachtenberg should not have even attempted to talk about 'Israel's actual political power'. He was vilified, called a 'self-hating Jew', subjected to a 'slew of hate mail' which demanded that he be fired, and effectively cast out of the official Jewish community on campus.[10]

This throws up a paradox which, in seeking to explain what happened to antisemitism, has to be brought out into the open and acknowledged. While it is now common for many Jewish leaders to unashamedly present both the main centres of diaspora Jewry and the state of Israel as the subjects and not the objects of history—in other words as influential actors in their diaspora societies and, in the case of Israel, in the Middle East and globally, shaping events rather than being buffeted and controlled by them—any attempts to speak objectively about Jewish power immediately attract the charge of antisemitism. As significant as the abstract idea of the Jewish emergence from powerlessness is, what equals it is the significance of the root idea of the 'new antisemitism'—that 'Israel is the persecuted "collective Jew" among the nations'. It is this narrative of Jewish weakness that pervades the bulk of the text of the IHRA 'working definition' of antisemitism, which essentially seeks to protect Jews from any kind of speech they do not like.

The paradox of presenting Jews as both powerful and weak at the same time is not entirely new. In Chapter 11, I referred to Israel's then prime minister, Levi Eshkol, who coined the phrase characterising his own country as '*Shimshon der nebechdiker*', loosely translated as 'Samson the weakling'.[11] Something of this remains to this day in the psyche of the country's leaders. The agreement to open formal relations between Israel and some of the Gulf states, dubbed the Abraham Accords, has been claimed as a clear sign of Israel's ability to shape the Middle East according to its interests. (And at the time of writing, there are reports that Saudi Arabia may soon follow.) And yet during the Great March of

Return—the Gaza fence protests which began in March 2018—the demonstrations were characterised as a genuine threat to the existence of the state, argues Michael Koplow:

> many Israelis view Palestinian demonstrators and ineffective Hamas tactics as threats of such magnificent proportions that they require the use of live fire, a military build-up in the south, billions of shekels built on a subterranean wall, and describing these demonstrations in apocalyptic terms. Israel looks at what has been taking place in Gaza, and sees itself not as a Samson but as a weakling.[12]

Nonetheless, this mindset manifests itself far more obviously in the Israeli government's politicisation and weaponisation of antisemitism. In part this is because the claim of military or security weakness is so transparently at odds with reality, whereas the abstract nature of antisemitism and Israel's increasing ability to manipulate the narrative around it and portray itself as a victim of it, in concert with diaspora Jewish leaders, more easily captures sympathy from world leaders. It seems that mobilising opposition to BDS around the world, a non-violent form of action that has minimal impact on the Israeli economy, society, academia and cultural life, is far easier than raising awareness and generating action in relation to the meticulously documented repressive Israeli policies that deprive the Palestinians of their rights.

The myth of Jewish powerlessness can no longer be sustained. However, the unequivocal need to distinguish between 'Jewish power' on the one hand as the mythical nefarious exercise of conspiratorial control and manipulation of the media, the banks, political parties and so on, and Jewish power as exercised by an Israel lobby organisation like AIPAC, and on the other by an Israeli government carrying out extra-judicial assassinations of individuals it regards as its mortal enemies, and by the congeries of forces that constitute the 'war' on antisemitism today, must always apply.

Efforts to stigmatise and silence statements of the obvious—that Israel and certain Jewish groups wield considerable clout—create fertile ground for conspiracies: by creating the impression that a secret truth is being suppressed, and by leaving the field to the conspiracy theorists. Those genuinely wishing to reduce the appeal of antisemitic conspiracies should not suppress, but on the contrary promote, sober analyses of Jewish power. But this is just what the crude 'trope' approach to fighting antisemitism prohibits.[13]

Medical analogies and eradication discourse

The use and abuse of language is crucial in the process of bolstering the 'war' on antisemitism. In fact, you could say that language is everything, because in this 'war' action cannot be judged on the success or failure of bombing raids, counterinsurgency initiatives, extra-judicial killing of terrorist leaders, prosecution and jailing of terror operatives, confiscation of funds and assets held by terrorist groups and so on. Even identifying culprits and subjecting them to naming and shaming campaigns is complicated, as we see in the case of Victor Orban, the Hungarian prime minister, who deploys antisemitic propaganda in pursuit of his populist political goals, but is a close ally of the former Israeli prime minister, who saw Orban's main target, George Soros, as his enemy too. So, what the 'war' on antisemitism lacks in terms of metaphorical body bags and brimming jails it makes up for in a discourse which combines a promise of the complete and utter eradication of antisemitism with a descriptive language about antisemitism based heavily on medical analogies.

Surveying the 'war' on antisemitism discourse throws up a range of metaphors and slogans. Metaphors for antisemitism include: 'virus', 'poison', 'disease', 'cesspit', 'reservoir'. Words and phrases for 'curing' people of antisemitism or making it disappear include 'zero tolerance', 'eradication', 'elimination', 'root out', 'enough is enough', 'vaccination'. Neither form of discourse is in any way helpful. They bring the desired total victory over the enemy—nothing less is tolerable to the 'war' on antisemitism's leaders—not one centimetre closer. Indeed, by 'misdiagnosing' the problem and promising the impossible, they make the task of doing what actually works to counter antisemitism even harder.

Some might point to the allies' total victory over the Nazi regime as an example of how antisemitism can be defeated. But this is an unhelpful and inappropriate comparison. As Anidjar explains, it came to an abrupt end, but not through 'protracted struggle' or 'force of persuasion'. 'Rather, on its own territory horror of its consequences made antisemitism a kind of taboo'. It wasn't antisemitism that was 'beaten down like a mad dog', but the stormtroopers who followed the orders to 'exterminate' European Jewry. 'It has not been refuted'. It wasn't antisemitism that was defeated in the Second World War but antisemites, or those who were given the task of implementing the will of antisemites, even if they had no knowledge or understanding of what antisemitism was.

Nevertheless, within a few decades a 'general conversion' was undergone by the same states and populations that tolerated or participated in the murderous violence. A 'radical shift of policies and ideologies … took place and moved individuals and institutions from widespread antisemitism to the struggle against it'. But do we know why this occurred? asks Anidjar:

> Was this a metamorphosis? A temporary reform? A distinct and novel management of populations and issues? A change in the allocation of social energies and knowledge/power practices? For those of us concerned with and fighting against antisemitism, there are as yet no answers available to these questions.[14]

Many of those waging today's 'war' on antisemitism would no doubt dismiss the 'general conversion' as ephemeral. Nevertheless, they are not taking on the unfinished business of refuting the kind of antisemitism that produced the death camps, the antisemitism that has shaped our post-war understanding of what antisemitism is, or at least what it can lead to.

You will not find many respected academic experts on antisemitism using medical analogies to describe the phenomenon. But they nevertheless have a grip on all too many participants in the 'war' on antisemitism. In September 2016, Archbishop Justin Welby contributed a short essay to a compilation called *Lessons Learned? Reflections on Antisemitism and the Holocaust*, assembled by the Holocaust Education Trust and the CST. Archbishop Welby's piece was entitled *Vigilance and Resolution: Living Antidotes to an Ancient Virus*. He likened anti-semitism to a 'virus' that had 'burrowed into' or was 'deeply entrenched in' our culture. It had 'infected the body of the Church' and was continuing to 'seek a host' as it latches onto a variety of different issues, among which he included 'the rights of Israelis and Palestinians and inter faith tensions'.[15] But if Welby means that the virus would infect the quest for justice in the distribution of rights, currently weighted heavily in favour of Israeli Jews, by latching on to the Palestinian host who then introduces antisemitic othering of Jews—their stubbornness, greed, control of media, banks, politicians, etc.—into the demand for full equality, this is surely based on an insupportable assumption of collective Palestinian propensity to be antisemitic.

Turn this around and put Israeli refusal to grant to the Palestinians full, equal national, human and civil rights, implementation of the right of return and so on, down to the anti-Palestinian racist virus that has latched on to Israeli Jews, and the archbishop is likely to see such a notion as viral antisemitism.

The use of 'virus' in this kind of discourse does nothing to expand our understanding of antisemitism.

What are referred to as antisemitic incidents, from tweets, through swastika daubings on Jewish gravestones and buildings, to violent and deadly assaults, are often referred to as 'outbreaks', as if antisemitism were a disease. For example, A documentary was broadcast on PBS television in May 2020 called *Viral: Antisemitism in Four Mutations*.[16] Today, 'the world is experiencing a resurgence of antisemitism not seen since the rise of Hitler and the Nazi Party', reported the *Jerusalem Post* in July 2020,[17] which went on to ask: 'Is there a vaccine for the virus of antisemitism?'

The dangers of this nosological approach to antisemitism are set out by Steven Beller. He is critical of the 'tendency ... to discuss antisemitism with a discourse laden with metaphors of disease'. He says:

Some such metaphors might have originally had a valid purpose, especially for describing the more irrational aspects of antisemitic ideology, yet ... metaphors of mental disease all too easily become conflated in current descriptions of antisemitism with metaphors of disease generally, reifying its subject as something with a will of its own, a contagious 'virus', beyond the capacity of any individual to control or combat.

He continues:

It eerily repeats the same use of metaphors by antisemites to describe the Jewish menace, and by suggesting that antisemitism is a disease, and as such an irrational force of nature, it suggests that the original antisemites who discriminated against, persecuted, and murdered Jews were themselves infected by something, an ideology or a delusion, beyond their power, and hence not really morally responsible for their actions.

'If antisemitism is a disease', Beller concludes:

the product of the diseased discourse of Western civilization, then antisemitic perpetrators were not responsible for their actions, the discourse that led them to do it was to blame. Antisemites become victims rather than perpetrators. This obscures the instrumental rationality often implicated in antisemitism and the moral culpability of those involved.[18]

Once defined as a viral disease globally resurgent in a manner reminiscent of the atmosphere that gave rise to Hitler and the Nazi Party, the demand for nothing less than complete eradication of antisemitism sounds logical. In fact, eradication is the demand in circumstances where antisemitism is claimed to be serious, but not as potentially apocalyptic as those that require comparison with Hitler and the Nazis. For example, following the furore over antisemitism in the Labour Party during Jeremy Corbyn's tenure as leader, all the candidates hoping to become his successor pledged to deal with the issue. During the leadership campaign, the frontrunner and eventual winner, Sir Keir Starmer, pledged to work with the Jewish community 'from day one' to eradicate antisemitism if he became party leader. When he gave this pledge, he also revealed plans for his first family holiday in Israel.[19] Evidently, the columnist Melanie Phillips was sceptical. 'The problem goes much further than the Corbynistas', she wrote. 'For the virus of this bigotry is carried by the cause that serves grotesquely as the international marker of conscience for western progressive circles. The reason the party cannot eradicate its antisemitism is that support for the Palestine cause is the default narrative on the left'.[20] Sceptical, but not about the objective of eradication. For Phillips, eradication of support for the Palestinian cause would be necessary before any total eradication of antisemitism could be achieved.

The discourse of eradication is not new. But it would seem that in the situation of greater Israeli state coordination of the 'war' on antisemitism, the use of such language has become more prevalent. War leaders need slogans and mantras to rally the troops and keep public opinion onside. And for those directing the antisemitism 'war', continually emphasising how dangerous is the threat must go hand-in-hand with holding out the prospect of ridding the world of antisemitism once and for all. And not surprisingly, we find the same preoccupations and discourse in the US.

At a House of Representatives Foreign Affairs sub-committee in 2013, the chairman, Hon. Christopher H. Smith, introduced a session on 'Antisemitism: A Growing Threat to All Faiths', saying: 'It is an ugly reality that won't go away by ignoring it or by wishing it away. It must be defeated. Thus, we gather to enlighten, motivate, and share best practices on how not just to mitigate this centuries-old obsession, but to crush this pernicious form of hate'. Sub-committee member David Cicilline followed: 'considering what actions we can take to respond to this phenomenon, what public policies we can implement, what educational policies we can promote to help to eradicate antisemitism all over the world should be our focus'.[21] This maximalist mindset was evident in the naming of an 'international congress' held in Vienna from 18-22 February 2018, and organised by the University of Vienna, together with the European Jewish Congress, New York University and the University of Tel Aviv titled 'An End to Antisemitism!' In November 2018, five volumes of proceedings were published,[22] running to more than 2,000 pages. The aim of this mammoth publishing project was 'to prevent further Jew-hatred today and in the future'.[23] In other words, to fulfil the promise of the Congress's title. And who would not want to see 'The End of Antisemitism!' Like all eradication discourse, the aspiration is a basic instinct. But in thinking how this congress contributes to the demise of antisemitism, I am left with the absurd image of bludgeoning Jew-hatred to death with thousands and thousands of words of essays, policy ideas and definitions.

In an article for the *Political Quarterly*,[24] three academics, Ben Gidley, Brendan McGeever and David Feldman, gave short shrift to Starmer's eradication aspiration, describing it as

> conceding to demands to achieve the impossible. Thereby paving the way for the continuity of complaint; whatever was being done was never going to be enough—belying the slogan 'Enough Is Enough', prominently displayed on placards held at the 2018 Jewish demonstration in Parliament Square organized by the Board of Deputies of British Jews—since enough would

never be enough when the 'elimination', 'eradication' or 'rooting out' of anti-semitism is the minimum demand.

As Gidley and colleagues affirmed: 'The demand for zero tolerance is almost certainly impossible to meet: while antisemites might be rooted out, antisemitism, flowing through our political culture at large, cannot be'.

Once again, it is important to emphasise that questioning the validity of discourse of this kind is not a matter of quibbling over semantic niceties. The promotors of the IHRA definition insist that there must be clarity as to what constitutes antisemitism. The general public is confused about the issue. And many Jews are too. To argue that the redefinition of antisemitism as primarily treating the Jewish state as 'the "collective Jew" among the nations' provides that clarity and at the same time deploy a discourse that is unwaveringly max-imalist and utterly impossible to achieve when it comes to practical ways of tackling the problem, only leads to confusion worse confounded. To encourage people to believe that antisemitism is a disease for which a complete cure is attainable and at the same time denigrate those who advocate more piecemeal, practical measures predicated on the common-sense idea of pushing racism to the margins of society, is morally dubious at the very least. You cannot eliminate from society all of the social, psychological, cultural, educational, political and economic factors that contribute to the individual expressing antisemitic senti-ments, but it is possible to suppress the negative results they generate.

14

Apocalypticism: Defining the Discourse, Writing the Headlines and Generating Moral Panics

The creation of the organisational and institutional structure of the 'war' on antisemitism was at first largely an organic process, given shape and direction as it emerged. And the individuals who have shaped its discourse and facilitated its growth have come to their views and the roles that they played from diverse starting points. Some, already deeply immersed in researching and analysing contemporary antisemitism from the 1990s or earlier, were either responsible for or instrumental in founding or reorienting research institutes and think tanks dealing with antisemitism. Others tended to operate more independently, often becoming members of the boards of such institutions, and participating in international political initiatives to fight antisemitism. These are not hard and fast distinctions, however. Two examples are the late Robert Wistrich and Irwin Cotler, both mentioned often in this book and, as key figures, who were firmly engaged in dealing with the issue by the 1980s.

Wistrich's early institutional involvement was as director of research at the Institute for Contemporary History and Wiener Library in London. Although he focused on the history of Jews in central Europe and the relationship between Jews and socialism in his early academic career, as editor of the *Wiener Library Bulletin* between 1974 and 1980, a journal that dealt largely with contemporary manifestations of neo-fascism, neo-Nazism, the far right and antisemitism, he also engaged in researching and writing about the politics of current antisemitism, both academically and in opinion pieces for newspapers and magazines. After occupying professorial chairs in Jewish studies at University College London and European and Jewish history at the Hebrew University between 1982 and 2002, he was appointed director of the Sassoon International Centre for the Study of Antisemitism (SICSA), which is located at the Hebrew University. By then he had made his mark arguing that anti-Zionism was effectively a form of antisemitism and that the threat to Jews of antisemitism from Islamic sources in Europe and elsewhere was increasingly dire and was not being taken seriously by Jewish communal leaders, and especially not by political leaders who made calculations that appeasing Muslims was politically necessary. As head of SICSA, he used his position to pursue these themes relentlessly, locating Muslim antisemitism as integral to and related to manifestations of antisemitism stretching back to antiquity. His last major work, *A Lethal Obsession: Antisemitism—From Antiquity to the Global Jihad*, a massive work of 1,184 pages, published in 2010, was his summation of an eternalist theory of antisemitism linking anti-Jewish violence in the decades before Christ to the eliminationist, antisemitic tropes in the manifesto of Hamas and Islamist antisemitism propaganda more widely.

There is no doubt that Wistrich was hugely influential in setting the agenda of the 'war' on antisemitism. A tireless and prolific writer and speaker, he also popularised his views through television and radio. Although he was initially sometimes cautious in endorsing the notion of 'new antisemitism', as the third millennium began he effectively came to support the notion in full. And those who have vociferously promoted 'new antisemitism' theory regard his work as integral to their outlook.

Nevertheless, *A Lethal Obsession* was not universally well received. Wistrich put this down to political bias among reviewers and, especially in the UK, institutional unwillingness to accept the unvarnished truth about Muslims that he claimed to be revealing. Reviews appearing in UK publications were based on the US edition of the book. Wistrich claimed that the publisher decided against publishing in Britain. Another story is that Wistrich himself insisted it not be published in the UK because it would not get a fair hearing.

Despite the reverence in which he is held in some circles, particularly by the political leadership of the 'war' on antisemitism, many prominent historians of antisemitism were severely critical of his direction of travel and the highly politicised positions he took in the last 20 years of his life.[1] His reaction to the book's reception reflected his inability to tolerate criticism even from people who were not unsympathetic to his preoccupations. And even though he addressed parliamentary committees, major international organisations like the OSCE, practically all of the major international and national Jewish organisations, not to mention numerous high-level conferences around the world, he seemed to become increasingly obsessed that his apocalyptic warnings about the fate facing Jews were not being heeded, a condition that applied to many of the prominent historians, commentators and researchers engaged in waging the 'war'.

In a review of *A Lethal Obsession*, published in the *Journal of Modern History*, Thomas Weber wrote:[2] 'The book's central argument is that the villains and fools are responsible for—or at least have inadvertently facilitated—a recent global revival of antisemitism no less dangerous than the genocidal antisemitism of the 1940s'. The 'villains and fools' include political leaders such as Barack Obama, Bill Clinton, Yitzhak Rabin, Helmut Schmidt and Javier Solana; academics such as Tony Judt and Tariq Ramadan; and Mahmoud Ahmadinejad, Mahmoud Abbas 'and almost every single Muslim mentioned on any of the close to 1,200 pages'. There are very few heroes standing up to these characters, 'men like Silvio Berlusconi and Donald Tusk'.

Weber sums up Wistrich's apocalyptic views:

[T]he same antisemitism has been around for two millennia [and] has recently mutated into an almost constant and worldwide vilification of Israel. According to Wistrich, this gathering antisemitic storm has evolved since 9/11 into the early phases of a genocidal perfect storm that might well bring about an anti-Jewish Armageddon (938). For Wistrich, this new attempt at an extermination of world Jewry is fueled by the Muslim world. However, Europeans supposedly are little better, as they are caught up in 'cynical double-talk, political correctness, and multicultural illusions in the face of creeping domestic Islamicization' (932) and as they try to overcompensate or rechannel their 'latent and often unavowed guilty feelings about the Jews' (631).

Irwin Cotler has never held an academic position running an institution dealing specifically with antisemitism. He is neither a historian nor a political scientist, but came to the problem of antisemitism from his position, from 1973, as professor of law at McGill University and the director of its Human Rights Programme until his election as a Member of Parliament in 1999 for the Liberal Party of Canada. He was Minister of Justice and Attorney General of Canada from 2003–2006. Specialising in international and human rights law, from early in his career he combined academic work with political activism both in the field of counselling prominent figures—political prisoners and dissidents—subjected to human rights abuses and, in his role as Jewish community activist, on the issue of antisemitism and human rights. He has had a successful career in the human rights field and has used his national and international profile to develop a consistent, trenchant, uncompromising and extensive charge sheet against international institutions with responsibility for upholding international human rights law, especially the UN and its agencies, for conducting an anti-semitic hate campaign against Israel under the guise of calling the country to account for alleged human rights abuses.

I have quoted extensively above from his written and spoken remarks and drawn attention to his primary role in popularising the central tenet of 'new antisemitism'—Israel is the 'collective Jew' among the nations. In November 2020, the former Canadian justice minister was chosen by Prime Minister Justin Trudeau as the nation's first envoy to combat antisemitism and to head the Canadian delegation to the IHRA.[3] As a supporter of the IHRA 'working definition', which the Canadian government adopted in June 2019, he will no doubt play a role in further extending awareness and adoption of the controversial codification of the 'new antisemitism'.[4] The Canadian Centre for Israel and Jewish Affairs (CIJA) applauded Cotler's appointment. Jeffrey Rosenthal, co-chair of the organisation's board of directors, said there is 'no one more qualified' than him to lead the fight against anti-Jewish racism on the international stage. Joel Reitman, also a co-chair of the CIJA board, called Cotler 'a Canadian icon who has been tirelessly advocating for human rights for decades'.

B'nai Brith Canada also applauded the announcement, saying the organisation has called for the creation of the position for many years and that Cotler is an 'excellent choice'. But Independent Jewish Voices Canada issued a statement saying it is 'deeply troubled' by the appointment, arguing that it further aligns the government with the IHRA's definition of antisemitism and that the definition is being 'weaponised' to portray supporters of Palestinian human rights as antisemitic and to shield Israel from criticism.

'Following Cotler's appointment to this post, it is critical that provincial and municipal governments, university administrations and other institutions take a firm stand against the IHRA definition now', said Corey Balsam, the group's national coordinator. 'Antisemitism must be fought, but it cannot be done at the expense of legitimate criticism and protest of Israeli human rights violations'.

'Today', the *Canadian Jewish News* reported,

> Cotler, though retired from academia and politics, is hardly retired from the pursuit of justice. At nearly 80, but indefatigable as ever, he dedicates himself to his Montreal-based Raoul Wallenberg Centre for Human Rights, an organisation dedicated to the idea that 'one person with the compassion to care and the courage to act can confront evil, prevail and transform history'.[5]

'In the past', Nora Barrows-Friedman wrote, 'Trudeau has acknowledged Cotler's influence on the Canadian government's extreme pro-Israel policies, including its smear campaign against the nonviolent boycott, divestment and sanctions (BDS) movement for Palestinian rights'.[6]

In a meeting with Trudeau in December 2019, Cotler 'stressed that antisemitism around the world has reached an "intensification that has no parallel since the end of the Second World War and the atmospherics are reminiscent of the 1930s"'. Very strong language, reminiscent of the warning Wistrich issues in his *A Lethal Obsession*, quoted above. And echoed in much of the discourse of the most vocal anti-antisemitism warriors. So much so that it is, understandably, the apocalyptic warnings that are remembered, rather than any empirical evidence or analysis provided to substantiate these claims, if indeed it is provided. There are key words and phrases in these jeremiads that convey the message that to doubt them is antisemitism denial, which is but one step away from toleration of antisemitism or even worse.

But should it not be *de rigueur* to subject the Holocaust parallels, the Kristalnacht comparisons, the prophesy of a coming anti-Jewish Armageddon and the predicted genocidal assault fuelled by Muslims to searching critique? Should we not be concerned about the shelf-life of such forecasts? 'Never Again' is one of the main slogans of anti-antisemitism activism, especially antisemitism seen as something that inevitably led to the Holocaust. But how are we to judge whether that 'again' is truly on the horizon if our assessment of whether it is likely to occur is unreliable, faulty and driven by factors other than the objective analysis of current conditions and an understanding of change over time? If we are asking 'Whatever happened to antisemitism?' these issues are central. And the well-documented views of Cotler are a good place to start.

Tracking back from what he told Trudeau in 2019, after participating in the first-ever UN General Assembly forum on global antisemitism, in January 2015, Cotler wrote: 'The underlying thesis of my remarks at the UN was this: We are witnessing a new, sophisticated, global, virulent, and even lethal antisemitism, reminiscent of the atmospherics of the 1930s, and without parallel or precedent since the end of the Second World War'.[7]

This is what he wrote in 2002:

What we are witnessing today—which has been developing incrementally, almost imperceptibly, and sometimes indulgently, for some thirty years now—is a new, virulent, globalizing and even lethal anti-Jewishness reminiscent of the atmospherics of the 1930s, and without parallel or precedent since the end of the Second World War. This new anti-Jewishness overlaps with classical antisemitism, but is distinguishable from it. Anchored in the 'Zionism is Racism' resolution, but going beyond it, the new anti-Jewishness almost requires a new vocabulary to define it. It can best be defined as the discrimination against, denial of, or assault upon, national particularity and peoplehood anywhere, whenever that national particularity and peoplehood happens to be Jewish.[8]

And this is what he said and wrote in 1992, quoted in Chapter 10:

[I]n a world in which human rights has emerged as the new secular religion, the portrayal of Israel as the metaphor for a human rights violator in our time exposes Israel as the 'new anti-Christ', with all the 'teaching of contempt' for this 'Jew among the nations' that this new antisemitism implies ... human rights becomes the mask under which this 'teaching of contempt' is carried out.[9]

The indictment continues:

> the problem ... is not that Israel as the 'Jew among the nations' seeks to be above the law, but that it has been systematically denied equality before the law; not that Israel must respect human rights—which she should—but that the human rights of Israel have not been respected; or that human rights standards should be applied to Israel—which they must—but that these standards have not been applied equally to anyone else.

There is a remarkable level of consistency here over almost 40 years. As for Robert Wistrich's views, how have they developed over this period?

In an interview in 2007 Wistrich spoke of the storm of Muslim extremism, an increasingly anti-Zionist Europe and 'irresponsible levels' of Jewish and Israeli self-flagellation, caused by 'apocalyptic antisemitism' espoused by Iran and introduced into the Arab world, according to which 'the annihilation of Israel is a necessary prologue to the redemption of all humanity through Islam'.

> Whenever I enter [an internet] chat room relating to antisemitism, I am shocked to see the mind-boggling level of ignorance and prejudice, particularly about Israel. This is the new antisemitism ...
>
> Europeans are reluctant to accept and admit that, despite all the Holocaust education and commemoration that's taking place—and all the solemn declarations about having thoroughly learned the lessons of the past—antisemitism has returned in such strength ...
>
> For decades, Israel has been discriminated against internationally in the most obvious and palpable way. It is a singling-out mechanism, which is even worse than applying a double standard. Double standards are automatically applied to anything Israel does. But it is only when Israel is deemed to violate human rights that there is a major international scandal.[10]

In 2003, he wrote:

> For Muslim radicals ... [t]heir opposition to [Israel's] existence is total, visceral and existential. In terms of its ideology and long-term goals, Muslim radicalism essentially exploits and uses the 'Palestinian cause' as the revolutionary prologue to global jihad. Anti-Zionism (and antisemitism), viewed from this perspective, are the Trojan Horse by means of which it will be easier to sap and undermine the moral foundations of Israel, the status of Diaspora Jewry and the will of the West to defend its most basic values.[11]

In a paper he wrote in 1998, he pointed to an antisemitism continuously poised to unleash mass mayhem and havoc: 'Neither Western not Eastern Europe is immune from the spectre of economic disintegration, chronic political instability, moral nihilism and despair in which both fascism and antisemitism have traditionally flourished.[12] These comments echo his conclusion in an article for the *American Jewish Year Book* in 1993:

> The virus of antisemitism is embedded, as it were, in the heart and the very bloodstream of European society and culture, ready to be activated at the first major crisis—whether it be war, revolution, the fall of empire, economic depression, or the unleashing of ethnic conflict. With the end of the Communist era, many of these conditions are now in place—a not very encouraging prospect.[13]

There are some slight variations in Wistrich's views over 30 years, but not much. As with Cotler, consistency seems to be the key. However, there is something deeply worrying about two such influential figures, both of whom, in their academic work, must have displayed some awareness of the significance of change over time, adhering religiously to understandings of antisemitism that seem to allow for no other variations except that of the arrival of 'new antisemitism', which, for both of them, only validates the eternal nature of the phenomenon. This is a consistency rather more like the rigidity of fundamentalist clerics.

What we see here in their work over a period of 30 to 40 years is the repetition of key phrases describing circumstances that only ever get worse, never better; warnings and predictions of imminent apocalyptic disaster, most often centred on the annihilation of Israel, but also often encompassing diaspora Jewish populations principally in the Nazi killing fields of Europe, and beyond that to the demise of 'Western civilisation' itself. The alleged Muslim 'exterminatory' threat to Jews has been ramped up over these years as jihadi terrorism intensified, but anti-antisemitism warriors such as Wistrich and Cotler clearly regard this as the true voice of Islam and the contemporary manifestation of Islam's fundamental hatred of Jews. It easily slots into their eternalist view of antisemitism.

We can trace the same, repetitive discourse in the writings of numerous prominent commentators. But equally, if not more significant, is the reception and treatment of their prognostications by major media outlets. A random selection of headlines that reflect the voices and data on antisemitism throws up the following:

- '[President] Says Antisemitism Is at Worst Level Since World War Two' CNN *21 February 2019*
- 'The threat of rising antisemitism', BBC News US and Canada, *2 November 2018*
- 'Antisemitism is so bad in Britain that some Jews are planning to leave' CNN *17 August 2018*

- 'Antisemitism on rise across Europe "in worst times since the Nazis"' *Guardian 2014*
- 'A dramatic rise in global antisemitism' *The Conversation* (website) *2014*
- 'Why Europe's Jews are fleeing once again' *Newsweek 2014*
- 'Antisemitism in the Twenty-First Century is a Ticking Time-Bomb' Bernard Henri-Levy, *New Republic 2014*
- 'The threat to the safety and security of the Jewish people [is] as great, if not greater, than what was faced in the thirties' Abe Foxman, *January 2004*
- The 'new' antisemitism: is Europe in grip of worst bout of hatred since the Holocaust' *Guardian, 25 November 2003*
- Antisemitism is 'the real, ultimately murderous thing' Jonathan Sacks, *Guardian 28 February 2002*
- 'An anti-Jewish atmosphere has pervaded the entire world [since the outbreak of the second intifada]' *Maariv June 2001*

With close to 20 years separating the earliest and latest of these headlines, no serious student of modern antisemitism could avoid asking such a basic question as: How often can a phrase like 'the worst time since the Nazis' or 'the worst bout of hatred since the Holocaust' be repeated every few years, as if there were a constant rising curve of increasingly lethal antisemitic manifestations, and have any credibility when Israel is militarily, economically and geopolitically strong and dominant, and notwithstanding the persistence of antisemitism in the US, Europe, the former Soviet Union and elsewhere, Jewish communities are active and vibrant, and suffering from racism far less than are Muslims and other minorities of colour?

How often do we need to read that antisemitism is now worse than the last time we read it was worse than the time before that we read it was worse than the time before that we read it was worse than … at any time since the Holocaust— before we begin to wonder whether or not we're reading from a metafictional novel by Flann O'Brien? Journalism might still cling on to some semblance of being the first draft of history, but whatever journalists and their editors publish as that 'first draft' is invariably a snapshot in time and cannot be relied upon to contain an appreciation of context let alone even short-term historical perspective. This is perhaps especially so when it comes to the issue of antisemitism, a subject on which few journalists are expert and who therefore rely to a great extent on Jewish reflections on antisemitic manifestations and on the lazy, but clearly understandable immediate urge to connect anything to do with antisemitism, from a swastika scrappily daubed on a wall, to the desecration of a Jewish cemetery, to a terrorist attack or suicide bombing of Israelis in Tel Aviv, to the Holocaust. The often-repeated apocalyptic prognostications of Wistrich, Cotler and others serve to feed the headlines, and the headlines reinforce the prognosticators' sense of the validity of their apocalyptic predictions, *ad infinitum*.

Such is the material for the recruiting posters of the 'war' on antisemitism. But it is also what demands interrogation and questioning.

Simcha Epstein, a former lead researcher at SICSA, is one of few scholars who have devoted attention to this issue. He specialised in subjecting comparisons of bouts of post-1945 antisemitism to searching critique.

When the Al-Aqsa intifada began at the end of September 2000, it generated a wave of anti-Jewish incidents aimed at synagogues and community centres throughout the world, especially in Europe, Epstein wrote in 2001.[14] Anti-Israel, anti-Zionist and anti-Jewish discourse accompanied it, and media reporting—Jewish, Israeli and general—amplified and increased the sense of anxiety felt by Jews. A seasoned observer of such developments, Epstein wrote:

> As is natural, all these gloomy factors stimulated in Jewish ranks a dramatic upsurge of verbosity: words adjusted to feelings, theories conforming to emotions, reactions demonstrating fear. Some orators went so far as to claim that the number of synagogues 'hit' by desecrators in October 2000 was as great as the number of synagogues 'hit' during the Kristallnacht pogroms of November 1938. Declarations such as this are unacceptable for obvious reasons.[15]

'The main idea', Epstein continued, 'propagated by numerous officials and commentators, was that we were confronted with "the highest wave of antisemitism since the Second World War"'. Turning his critical eye on this judgement, Epstein compared data, especially antisemitic incidents, from three other periods of high antisemitic activity in Western societies: the 'Swastika epidemic' 1959–1960; the wave of the late 1970s and early 1980s, which experienced the fallout from the siege of Beirut and the Sabra and Chatilla massacres; and the late 1980s and early 1990s. He concluded that 'there is no way of becoming convinced that fall 2000 was more "anti-Jewish" than summer 1982.'

He says this was true on two levels. 'First, the attacks in 1982 combined vandalism and desecrations with shooting, bombing, and killing, whereas in 2000 there were only ... aggressive acts of the first category. From this point of view, the October 2000 incidents were less lethal than what we saw in 1982'.

Epstein added: 'Secondly, no objective and scientific research has yet established that there is more anti-Jewish rhetoric today than there was in 1982, or that this rhetoric is any more ferocious than it was formerly'.

Epstein concluded that his research on comparisons strengthened the argument for seeing 'waves' of antisemitism as cyclical, with each cycle sometimes more or less serious than the last. Evidence of an irresistible rise was absent. As was evidence of a consistent decline. Although there were claims made, throughout the 1990s and into 2000, of 'an end to antisemitism', Epstein remained unconvinced.

Whether the cyclical theory tells us that much more about changes in anti-semitism than any other explanation of what has happened, or is happening, to antisemitism, is doubtful. It depends on what vectors of antisemitism are taken into account. A cyclical theory is compatible with eternalism and all the problems associated with it. Kenneth L. Marcus, for example, embraces 'new antisemitism' theory, seeing anti-Zionism, BDS, apartheid accusations and so on as 'nothing but the latest repetitions of an eternal cycle that has perpetually plagued Jews, triggered by the same set of causes'.[16] It may seem incongruous or counterintuitive that an eternalist understanding of antisemitism is compat-ible with what is called the 'new antisemitism'. But we should not fixate on the 'new'; it is the fundamental features of 'new antisemitism', especially the 'Israel is the "collective Jew" among the nations' mantra, that constitutes our starting point. For once this becomes the new definition of antisemitism, one is no longer looking for the *cause* of a certain perception of, or behaviour towards, Jews, rather the task seems to be explicating the *purposes they serve* in the light of the basic, unassailable 'truth' that 'Israel is the "Jew" among the nations'. If that is the *fons et origo* of today's antisemitism, it follows that anything which allegedly harms Israel—anti-Zionism, determining that Jewish settlements in occupied territory contravene international law, BDS, accusations of apartheid, charges of human rights violations, holding Israel responsible for the Naqba— is *a priori* antisemitic. This teleological approach undermines the possibility of open-minded research into the nature of current antisemitism.

The nature of the threat is so enormous, the demand for total defeat—as in complete 'eradication' of 'a social virus/disease', but in reality, with the defeat of Nazism as the real-world model, beating it to death like a rabid dog—is the goal that brooks no compromise. Even so, like the 'war on terror', or the 'war on drugs', in the writings, lectures, speeches of Wistrich, Cotler, Phillips, Sacks, Sharansky, Rosenfeld, Small, Wisse, Chesler and many more, a distinct sense is conveyed that the 'war' on antisemitism can have no end (see Chapter 12). For the prophets of doom, at root this is a civilisational struggle, Manichean in character. All the easier, therefore, to treat Jews who refuse to accept this narrative as traitors, self-haters, deserving of vilifying censure of special virulence.

Wistrich was particularly explicit on this subject. He appears to concede that the stereotype of Jews as a 'hypercritical people' has validity, and that this 'critical faculty', when 'turned with particular intensity and vehemence against co-religionists or co-nationals' is due, 'in some cases ... to a genuine sense of indignation'.[17] But, in the interview from which I am quoting, by laughingly invoking the 'two Jews, three opinions' stereotype, he sets the scene for characterising this as a fatal weakness:

> [The indignation] often appears to have no rational limits—[as] if these 'critics' are neither aware of, nor interested in, the wider implications of their accusations. If you are part of a society whose very survival is threatened, and your opinions—as legitimate an expression of free speech as they may be—are feeding into hostility that could produce *genocidal results*, I think a little responsibility is called for [emphasis added].

Wistrich struggles to hang on to the concessions he makes as regards 'free speech' and the exercise of a 'critical faculty', shifting his ground to psychological categories:

> This doesn't necessarily mean self-censorship or being false to your beliefs. But it does mean the application of a minimum amount of sanity. After all, the critics of Israel are always one-sided. They always seem—despite their claims for caring about Palestinian rights and so on—to be totally, *autistically*, focused on Israel. It's as if the human consequences of so much of what goes on in the Arab world is a matter of absolutely no concern to them.

For such a lauded historian of antisemitism, who must surely have understood the power and relevance of prejudicial stereotypes, his cavalier, prejudiced stereotyping of critical Jews and Israelis is highly revealing. (And the oft-repeated accusation that critics of Israel reveal their anti-Jewish animus by ignoring human rights abuses in the Arab world, or further afield in Africa and South-East Asia, a claim of preciously little substance.[18]) Once again, he nods to liberal values, only to clear the way to his damning conclusion:

> Now, I'm as critical as the next person about what's going on in this country [Israel]. But being critical doesn't mean you can embrace cheap and empty slogans, such as claims that Israel is an apartheid state. When such blatant falsehoods are uttered by intellectuals, one not only has to question their self-proclaimed status, but to wonder what it is they are trying to achieve. My conclusion is that this is an incurable pathology. I'm against heavy-handed responses to it. But people who hold such views should not be given excessive importance, which is what they crave. They have to be put in their proper place as a footnote in the long and sad saga of Jewish self-hatred.

I suspect that the solid evidence of apartheid in Israel and the occupied Palestinian territories produced by Amnesty International,[19] Human Rights Watch[20] and B'Tselem[21] would not have shifted Wistrich's views in the slightest.

Why is it that we poked fun at, and regarded as benignly unhinged, the harbingers of doom who walked the streets clad in billboards pronouncing that 'The End of the World is Nigh!'? and yet, when professors, public intellectuals, leading columnists, community leaders, politicians do the same when it comes to contemporary antisemitism, they are taken deadly seriously. Antisemitism certainly remains a potent force, but as I have demonstrated in this book, to construe current conditions as conducive to the predicted imminent apocalypse is the fantasy it has always been. And why are we likely to see no contrition, no retreat even, on the part of the prophets who so earnestly and solemnly predicted an antisemitic apocalypse?

The second question can be answered far more easily than the first. Apocalyptic prophesy about antisemitism rests on belief, not rational thinking.[22] Central to that belief is the conviction that all antisemitism is genocidal. The essence of antisemitic thinking must be elimination of the Jews. The fact that awareness of the Holocaust did not rid the world of antisemitic sentiment means that its persistence is ever a prelude to genocide. In reality, just as there was non-genocidal antisemitism before the Holocaust, so there is non-genocidal antisemitism today. The notion that every swastika daubing, attack on a synagogue or the holding aloft of a placard with the words 'From the river to the sea, Palestine will be free' are mere preludes to mass murder is ahistorical nonsense. But the protagonists and their believers are predisposed to resist scrutiny from critical interrogation and being faced with the fact that the prophesies of doom that some have been making for two or three decades have not materialised. These prophets will simply insist that disaster is still on its way, and will be helped to sustain their belief by the numbers of people who continue to believe in the prophesy. It is just taking longer to arrive. And as a belief which has more than just the semblance of a religion about it, moral condemnation by those who contest what they see as false prophesies and who themselves adhere to the views that give rise to the apocalyptic predictions, is integral to it. It took a serious degree of insensitivity, a loss of moral compass and absence of self-awareness for Wistrich to use a medical condition of great complexity, one that presents challenges to both those who have it and their parents and carers, to illustrate the moral guilt of critics of Israel, especially Jews, with the phrase: '*autistically* focused on Israel'. The charge sheet reeks of a 'holier-than-thou' mindset: 'blatant falsehoods', 'incurable pathology', 'opinions ... feeding into hostility that could produce genocidal results ... I think a little responsibility is called for'.

Wistrich is by no means alone in using this discourse. For example, another prolific writer on antisemitism, Edward Alexander, professor emeritus of English at the University of Washington, believes

Most of the world averts its eyes from the genocidal intentions and capacity of the Iranian theocracy; antisemitism, briefly given a bad name by the Holocaust, is again emerging as the 'default' ideology of Europe, which may become *judenrein* within a decade; the angelic sociology of liberals, including Jewish ones, is invoked to 'explain' suicide bombing as the inevitable result and measure of Israeli oppression. So let's talk about something pleasant, like the explosive power of boredom in activist university professors.[23]

(Alexander said this in 2012. As I write, in February 2022, an estimated 1.3 million Jews live in Europe.) Nevertheless, without the institutional structures of the 'war' on antisemitism, which serve to encourage, amplify, repackage and communicate both the apocalyptic and less extreme warnings about the antisemitic threat on a global/geopolitical level, to audiences receptive and pre-disposed to accept them—because it is couched in the language of international diplomatic and political discourse—the prophets would be far less influential. The leaders of the 'war' on antisemitism, who have successfully cultivated the global audience of political decision-makers, are very skilful in crafting the content and style of their concerns to lawmakers with many interests and not necessarily long attention spans. Their 'frank' reports delivered at congressional hearings and parliamentary select committees consistently say that things are not getting any better. On the contrary, they are getting worse. This message is positively received because, as I have argued, it slots into a geopolitical consensus about wider threats to the 'West': jihadi terrorism, predominantly Muslim migration to Europe and North America—all of which are said to impact on Israel disproportionately. As I write, former Labour prime minister Tony Blair has issued a warning, in the wake of the American withdrawal from Afghanistan, that 'Islamism remains the first order security threat to the West'.[24] So, when representatives of Jewish groups demand the increased tightening of structures of racial governance to combat antisemitism, politicians are only too ready to oblige.

The first question—why do we take seriously those who make apocalyptic predictions bordering on guaranteeing that another Holocaust is just around the corner—takes us uncomfortably back to the anti-Zionism/antisemitism question. Even so, there is no straightforward answer.

There are two aspects of apocalyptic discourse about antisemitism that appeal to the commentariat, the literati and performers of various kinds. News reports of antisemitic violence, desecration of synagogues, surveys of opinion purportedly showing high levels of antisemitic sentiment and so on are very often laced with some reference to the Holocaust. We are therefore predisposed to fear the worst—a condition that seems to be borne out by surveys of Jewish opinion.[25] However, in a country like the UK, that is probably the safest for Jews anywhere in the world, the absence of forces or figures responsible for antisemitic incidents that can plausibly be regarded as capable of igniting an antisemitic conflagration minimises the likelihood of seeing anything that borders on panic. When an added element of comment by a well-known public figure, whether that be a Lord Winston, a Maureen Lipman, a David Baddiel, a Chief Rabbi Mirvis, or a Margaret Hodge—types favoured by the media especially because they are known to see any antisemitism story through a particularly dark lens—ratchets up the fear level, it is likely that the degree of concern among Jews intensifies, especially among those who rely a great deal on news and comment communicated through their social media bubbles that affirm fears rather than calm them. This picture suggests that many Jews engaged in Jewish communal life across the secular-religious spectrum have, over the last two decades, been primed to expect the atmosphere of insecurity, which Jewish communal leaders have consciously fostered, to morph into a major crisis of some kind.

The second aspect of the apocalyptic discourse that resonates is that while, quite understandably, Holocaust fear may well be the psychological trauma that underpins Jewish responses to stories of antisemitism, it was always likely, given the relentless shift towards validation of the idea that criticism of Israel and antisemitism are one and the same, that any crisis would be triggered by some incident related to the vexed issue of Israel and the Palestinians. And it was precisely this scenario that was made real when Jeremy Corbyn was elected leader of the Labour Party and the sorry saga of Labour and antisemitism, began, based largely on the perception that Corbyn's commitment to the cause of justice for Palestinians was not just evidence of his alleged hatred of Jews, but also antisemitic in itself. This was the essence of the accusation made by Marie Van der Zyl, President of the Board of Deputies of British Jews, in August 2018, that Jeremy Corbyn had 'declared war on the Jews' in the UK and that his 'hatred of Israel and Zionism runs so deep he cannot separate that from antisemitism'.[26] Jewish establishment organisations, already having a track record of attacks on Jeremy Corbyn, did virtually nothing to reassure the Jewish population, to dial down the rhetoric, or calm fears. A month earlier the three British Jewish newspapers published the same front-page editorial warning that Corbyn would pose an 'existential threat to Jewish life' in the UK if he became prime minister.[27] A survey in September 2018 purported to show that 40 per cent of British Jews would 'seriously consider' leaving the country if Corbyn became prime minister. Contrast this with a poll in January 2015, before Corbyn became leader, that revealed 88 per cent had not considered leaving. The Chief Rabbi of the mainstream orthodox United Synagogue denomination, Ephraim Mirvis, wrote in *The Times* in November 2019, shortly before the general election: 'A new poison—sanctioned from the very top—has taken root in the Labour Party'.

Tracking of the media during the Corbyn years 2015–2019 confirms that there was a constant drumbeat of allegations of Corbyn's antisemitism, none of which were ever proven, but all of which were taken to be true in the mainstream media. While there were many who questioned this discourse and took on the accusations and the accusers, very few had access to the major media outlets and were therefore confined to news websites, online periodicals and blogs.

Although attended only by approximately 2,000 people, the demonstration against Labour antisemitism organised by Jewish communal bodies outside Labour headquarters in March 2018 set the seal on the impression that British Jewry had mobilised in force, with the support of parliamentarians, brandishing placards saying 'Zero Tolerance', 'Enough is Enough', to do whatever it could to compel Corbyn to take action or it would seek to turn the entire community against him and Labour.

Hardly a week seemed to pass without some new allegation against Corbyn, or the reheating of an existing allegation by another public figure who had yet to have their say on the matter. As the furore mounted, some were quick to reverse their views about him. In March 2018, Labour MP Margaret Hodge said 'Jeremy is not himself antisemitic'.[28] In the House of Commons chamber in July 2018, with other MPs nearby, she reportedly called Corbyn a 'fucking racist and antisemite'. (She later denied that she had used the f-word.) It became hard to exclude the possibility of an organised campaign against Corbyn by some party members and MPs, and anti-antisemitism Jewish communal bodies.

Indeed, the Labour antisemitism controversy had all the hallmarks of a moral panic,[29] the sociological concept most closely associated with the work of the late Professor Stanley Cohen, who described it as happening when 'a condition, episode, person or group of persons emerges to become defined as a threat to societal values and interests'. It is a view shared by various writers.[30] Seeing the Labour and antisemitism furore in this light does not imply that antisemitism is not a real problem in our society or that Labour, or any political party for that matter, is free of it.

What may well be the most disturbing feature of the Labour antisemitism crisis, and one that is a central building block in the respectability achieved by apocalyptic warnings of imminent antisemitic conflagration, came to light in a seven-minute video made direct to camera by Joe Glasman who describes himself as 'a volunteer at Campaign Against Antisemitism [CAA] where I head the political investigations team which, among other things was responsible for our successful submission to the EHRC'. (In fact, the CAA's complaint that Labour was institutionally antisemitic was not upheld by the EHRC.) Made in the privacy of his home and misleadingly low-tech, it was scripted and then 'enhanced' with on-screen comments and emojis. A composer and music producer, he founded his company, Hum, in 1989, which creates 'music for global commercials campaigns and audio branding for the world's biggest brands, TV On-screen identities and worldwide news stations, as well as incidental TV and film music'. It was posted on 25 December 2019 as a private Vimeo page by Hum titled 'Joe's Chrismukah thank-you'. The opening caption reads: 'A rambling outburst of personal gratitude to all activists who fought the antisemitism of Corb ... more'.

Glasman's claims are set in the context of his interpretation of the symbolic meaning of the Jewish festival of Hannukah, which always takes place close to Christmas. He expresses his pride in the successful effort to bring about the electoral defeat of Corbyn and the antisemitic forces he allegedly unleashed as leader within the Labour Party:

> I'm just speaking in [sic] as one more person who volunteered like you because, a Hanukkah miracle has happened. The beast is slain, and I have an urge to express my love and personal gratitude to every single person, some of whom I've never met, who've played their part, and wish them a Hanukkah, or maybe Chrismukkah *semeach* [happy].

In colourful language he continues by outlining the extent of this collective endeavour:

> By word and deed, by protest and Tweet, by our spies and intel, by our fab celebrities and our anonymous volunteers, by pleading, by rigorous research and gathering of evidence, by incredible video making, by interminable hours combing through tweets, by prayer, by dramatic speeches and street protests, by lorries carrying huge billboards, by writing and shouting and taking the mick out of the most humourless bunch of people ... this country's politics have ever made us suffer, and—[mocking Jeremy Corbyn] Can I finish? ... by sheer bloody-mindedness we metaphorically took the temple back. And if Jerusalem is builded here in England's green and pleasant land, then just for now at least, we have our Jerusalem back.

Glasman intended the video to be seen only by the people who were part of the effort he describes, but it was posted online and he tweeted about it on Christmas Day 2019. It was soon set to private. Left-wing Labour activists managed to download a copy and posted it on the Barnet Momentum Facebook page. He then claimed copyright as a way of removing it from the public domain, but YouTube rejected the claim and it has remained available to all.[31]

Glasman's video received remarkably little attention.[32] Tellingly, however, no Jewish communal organisation refuted Glasman's claims. It seemed that something like an 'official silence' had been imposed. But this silence felt like a message that said: 'We are satisfied that we achieved this result, but we have no more to say on the matter'.

For most Jews marking the festival in the present, the central ritual of the event is the lighting of eight candles which recalls the story of the Jewish sect, the Maccabees, who led a revolt, commencing in 168 BCE, against Antiochus IV, King of Syria, to whom the Jews were subject. When they sealed their victory in 164 BCE, by recovering control of Jerusalem and the Jewish Temple—which had been defiled with the blood of swine and robbed of all its sacred furniture and treasures as part of Antiochus's draconian decree forbidding the Jews from following their own customs and religion—they cleansed and restored it, dedicating it anew on the 25th of the Jewish month of Kislev, having rekindled the *ner tamid*, the eternal light, in a ceremony that lasted eight days. The Great Council of the Maccabees decided that the Jews should keep the eight days from 25 Kislev as a festival celebrating victory over the Syrian army.

Legend has it that the Jews found only enough oil to keep the *ner tamid* alight for one day, but that it lasted, miraculously, for eight. On the first night, one candle is lit, on the second night two candles, and so on, finishing with all eight candles, plus a ninth, which is used throughout to light the eight main candles.

Glasman interprets the story as a 'two-millennium-old celebration of a Jewish military victory to reestablish Jewish national and religious sovereignty in Jerusalem'—in essence, Zionism *avant la lettre*. In his version, the left-wing Jewish supporters of Corbyn were like the Hellenised Jews who, it is alleged, tried to reverse their circumcisions in order to adopt Hellenic culture: 'de-circumcisers' in his words. He and his friends were true, liberal-minded Jews, like the Maccabees, defeating the Greeks and the Hellenised Jews.

While not all the historical facts are known, Glasman's version is self-serving myth-making. Many of the Jews at the time were trying to adjust to diasporic existence, and adopting elements of Hellenic culture was part of that process. And history is clear: Judaism, a product of diaspora life, was positively influenced by Hellenism and would not be what it is today without that influence.

Some scholars see the Maccabean revolt more as a Jewish civil war than purely an uprising against the Greeks. The Maccabees forced Hellenic Jews to return to following the strict letter of Jewish law, and if they didn't, they were killed. Some therefore regard the Maccabees as being more like a Jewish al Qaida than centrist, neoliberal freedom fighters defending Jews and especially Israel. (The Maccabees would have been appalled by the modern political Zionism that produced the state of Israel given its fundamentally secular character. It copied both the ethno-nationalisms of the late and early twentieth century and the 'civilising' settler colonialism of states with imperial ambitions.)

Glasman and his associates emerge from this more like uncompromising zealots, the ideal warriors in the 'war' on antisemitism.

It seems reasonable to assume that many of those who spread fear of a Corbyn-inspired antisemitic apocalypse were directly or indirectly involved in the Glasman project, and would feel vindicated that their prophesies of doom played some part in bringing down the Labour leader. But we should not be fooled into thinking that the downfall of Corbyn, the success of Glasman and his cohorts and the purge of left-wing pro-Palestinian Jews from the Labour Party instigated by Starmer and his General Secretary David Evans will have any effect on the continuing dissemination of the myth of the 'collective Jew' through pressure to make the IHRA 'working definition' the only acceptable definition of antisemitism.

15
Against Typological Thinking:
Summary and Conclusions

> One prod to the nerve of nationalism and the intellectual decencies can vanish, the past can be altered, and the plainest facts can be denied.
>
> George Orwell, *Notes on Nationalism*

Abraham Joshua Heschel, cited in Chapter 8, bears quoting again. The Polish-American Conservative Jewish theologian, who marched with Martin Luther King Jr at Selma in 1965, warned against worshipping the two fundamentals of Zionism: 'Judaism is not a religion of space and does not worship the soil', he wrote. 'So too, the state of Israel is not the climax of Jewish history'.[1]

But these are strictures not heeded by the leaders of the 'war' on antisemitism. Indeed, they would probably conclude that Heschel was guilty of contravening the IHRA 'working definition' of antisemitism. For them, the existence of the Jewish state is not just the basis of Jewish security worldwide; it is the beating heart of the Jewish people, its spiritual centre. Yet they also tell us that Israel's existence is in mortal danger from 'viral delegitimisation'. There is no longer a 'Jewish question', they say. It has been replaced by the 'Israel question', or the 'Israelisation of antisemitism'.

This is but one of a number of contradictions I have encountered in the diverse material I have examined in my attempt to explain in this book what has happened to antisemitism. I hope that the conclusions I have reached are clear, although I confess that there are many twists and turns on the paths I have gone down to seek answers. Nevertheless, from the very beginning I have been quite frank about where I would end up, as the book's subtitle conveyed the essentials: antisemitism has been redefined as 'new antisemitism', ostensibly to account for the hostility to the Jewish state and the ideology upon which it was founded. And that redefinition is based on the myth that 'Israel is the persecuted "collective Jew" among the nations', which is the bedrock concept of the 'new antisemitism'.

This hostility, allegedly antisemitic in character, would certainly have been chronologically new since it could only have come fully into being after the state was founded in 1948. Zionism, whether seen as the political ideology on which the national liberation movement of the Jewish people was based, or as a form of settler colonialism, or a combination of the two, was subject to criticism from its inception, and was rejected by most Jews right up until the Second World War and the Holocaust. The Zionist movement fought ferociously to secure its place and ideology within the Jewish world. Zionists had to compete with assimilated Jews, converts, the orthodox, Bundists, communists, reformists, and more, and they were not always very choosy about how they did this. Before 1914, 2.5 million Jews emigrated to North and South America, whereas only tens of thousands emigrated to Palestine. Whatever one calls hostility to Israel today, at first it was seen there by the Zionist political parties and observers as largely political. When Yehoshafat Harkabi challenged the Zionist narrative of the time—that antisemitism was an ever-present hatred regardless of Jewish conduct or political status—by concluding from his research that Arab attitudes towards Israel were by then suffused with antisemitic tropes and sentiment, he was roundly condemned and attacked.

But pressure mounted, mainly from Zionist organisations, some pro-Zionist Jewish academics and public intellectuals to label anti-Israel hostility a new form of antisemitism, which they called 'new antisemitism'. The main trigger for this was an increase in criticism of and animosity towards the Jewish state and Zionism after the Six-Day War in 1967. And the main conversation was around whether antisemitism and anti-Zionism were one and the same, whether the latter was a cloak for disguising the former or whether there was a clear distinction between the two.

This largely intra-Jewish debate on the nature of hostility to the Jewish state intensified during the 1990s, while at the same time many commentators were noting a decrease in antisemitism generally, with some even arguing that serious antisemitism had ceased to exist. But after the outbreak of the second intifada, the UN anti-racism conference in Durban and 9/11, a dramatic shift to support for the 'new antisemitism' argument occurred, centred on growing concern about alleged Muslim antisemitism. The weight of Zionist and Jewish opinion came down increasingly firmly on the side of the argument that anti-Zionism was antisemitism.

While there was no formal agreement about what constituted 'new antisemitism', the equation of anti-Zionism and antisemitism was undoubtedly integral to it. It was explained by the argument that while classical antisemitism was persecution of Jews, however, they chose to live and organise themselves, the 'new antisemitism' was discrimination against, denial of or assault upon the right of the Jewish people to live as an equal member of the family of nations, making Israel 'the persecuted "collective Jew" among the nations'.

Even as 'new antisemitism' theory became the dominant narrative about antisemitism, objection to the idea was increasingly vocal. Those who opposed it regarded it as largely a way of deflecting criticism of the state's policies towards the Palestinians and the human rights abuses it was perpetrating against them on the West Bank and in Gaza, and a product of Islamophobic attitudes to Muslims; and as a means of defending an extreme form of ethno-nationalist, messianically inspired Zionism.

The 'new antisemitism' proponents won a major victory when, in 2005, the EUMC produced a 'working definition' of antisemitism, which largely consisted of deeming as antisemitic a whole range of forms of critical speech about Israel and Zionism, depending on context. Formulation of the EUMC 'working definition' was an almost entirely Jewish affair and was justified on the grounds that no formal definition of antisemitism existed that included extreme animosity towards Israel especially among Muslims, which made antisemitism difficult to combat. In fact, in my experience, antisemitism researchers had no difficulty in using existing consensus understandings of antisemitism to accommodate instances of anti-Israel hostility that were of an antisemitic character, whether that hostility came from Islamic or non-Islamic sources. There never was a clamour for a new definition.

Meanwhile, a transformation in the way antisemitism was being fought was taking place. Israeli governments, after blowing hot and cold about heading the antisemitism fight, from initial attempts to do so during the late 1980s and early 1990s, and acting inconsistently into the mid-2000s, finally took up the cause in earnest, projecting the fight as a 'war' and working closely with major Jewish and Zionist organisations around the world, but especially in the USA and Europe.

A complex field of anti-'new antisemitism', transnational racial governance came into being—partly organically and partly by design—with the cooperation of international organisations, national governments, many civil society organisations, research institutes, think tanks, monitoring bodies, national Jewish leadership organisations and anti-antisemitism organisations supporting the 'war' and policing discourse about antisemitism. Left-wing Jewish groups, pro-Palestinian organisations, international human rights bodies as well as radical and human rights groups in Israel and the occupied Palestinian territories continued to reject the 'new antisemitism' thesis, but on the political front, this was a losing battle. The narrative of Israel as the 'persecuted "collective Jew" among the nations' and the 'anti-Zionism is antisemitism' position were becoming ever-more deeply embedded in Jewish and Zionist thinking. For a brief period after the 2008–2009 Israeli offensive on Gaza, called by Israel 'Operation Cast Lead', revulsion at Israel's disproportionate use of force reached such a level that a new wave of Jewish protest looked as if it might turn the tide of Jewish opinion.[2] But that optimism did not last. In great part this was due to Israel's strengthening geopolitical status, a dramatic reduction in the number of states that would normally criticise Israel severely for what it was doing, its role as a key player in the Western 'coalition of the willing' fighting jihadi terrorism, the fallout from the 2007–2008 financial crash and an increasing willingness for many states to acquiesce in Israel's presentation of itself as chief victim of 'new antisemitism'.

But what the 'war' on antisemitism was increasingly targeting was non-violent political activities such as BDS, Israel apartheid weeks on campuses, discourse critical of Zionism, teaching about the *naqba*, accusing Israel of ethnic cleansing and so on.

Notwithstanding the expanding, influential and diverse coalition of forces accepting the premises of the 'war' on antisemitism, assembled through close cooperation between the Israeli government and major Jewish organisations, according to reports antisemitism continued to worsen, a situation that leading figures in the 'war' on antisemitism were eager to publicise. It justified the need to continue and intensify what they were doing.

Nevertheless, during the 2010s, evidence from surveys suggested that the general public and many Jews too were increasingly confused as to what anti-semitism was. Among some involved in fighting the 'war' and in writing about antisemitism, so as to influence thinking about the objectives of the 'war', there were those arguing that vilification and demonisation of Israel had become *the* principal global form of antisemitism, a position increasingly adopted by the state itself.

As politics in many countries took a turn towards illiberal populism, some governments, in Europe particularly, but not only, were openly encouraging the spread of classic antisemitic propaganda. This did not prevent the Israeli gov-ernment from developing close relations with these governments and turning a blind eye to their tolerance of antisemitism on the grounds of close affinity as regards illiberal domestic policies, opposition to migration (except from their ethno-national diasporic communities), Islamophobia, denigration of human rights organisations and general authoritarian governance. And par-ticularly because these governments never offered more than token criticism of Israel's treatment of the Palestinians and barely raised any objection to the creeping annexation of Palestinian land in the occupied Palestinian territories. The Palestinian issue was parked in the lot marked 'Two state solution at some unspecified date in the future'.

Jewish and non-Jewish bodies monitoring racism and antisemitism were not unaware of a growth in far-right white supremacist extremism, a development particularly marked in the US and increasingly visible worldwide with Donald Trump's campaign to become president. Here was the world's most powerful leader, openly encouraging white supremacy and organised groups spreading antisemitic propaganda, often repeating antisemitic tropes himself, but portray-ing himself as acting as Israel's best friend. Material here for confusion about antisemitism was plentiful.

Divisions among Jews on these issues, already deep and bitter, were aggravated further as some found no fault in Trumpism, because he put Israel first in a world allegedly still hostile to the Jewish state, while others were alienated by his antisemitism, misogyny, support for Zionist ethno-nationalism and the expansion of Jewish settlement.

Meanwhile, the Israeli government, from the early 2010s, was allocating increasing resources to combat what they defined as antisemitism but was in fact political action and speech opposing Israel's policies towards the Palestinians. Hundreds of millions of shekels were being devoted to fighting BDS campaigns, supporting attempts to introduce laws outlawing boycott actions and apartheid weeks on campuses, as well as strengthening Jewish support and lobbying for Israel in communities worldwide, training young Jews to use social media to defend Israel and shut down anti-Israel activity by pro-Palestinian groups.

A step change in the 'war' on antisemitism came in 2016 when the IHRA adopted a slightly modified form of the EUMC 'working definition' of anti-semitism, and the principal figures in anti-'new antisemitism' circles worked assiduously to persuade national and state governments, local authorities, international governmental and non-governmental organisations (which had briefs to cover racism and antisemitism), states, universities, trade unions, political parties and so on to 'adopt' the IHRA 'working definition', with some considerable success.

Strong criticism of the document on the part of many experts on antisemi-tism—Jewish and non-Jewish—did not prevent it from becoming ubiquitous, even though, from early on, there was confusion and controversy over what exactly constituted the definition—whether it was the short definition plus the eleven examples, most of which concerned Israel and Zionism, or the short definition alone.[3] This did not seem to have any effect on the rapid spread of the influence of the 'working definition'. But as Stern-Weiner conclusively proves, IHRA's decision-making body decided to exclude all the examples from its definition. Nonetheless, pro-Israel campaigners and even senior IHRA officials systematically misled the public about the examples. The entire text was presented as unamendable and sacrosanct, thereby seeming to confer on it the status of holy writ. Nonetheless, some countries and bodies quietly took a pick-and-mix approach: recognising only the short opening paragraph as the definition, treating the examples as purely advisory, amending the examples or treating the examples as unequivocally antisemitic. When critics raised this inconsistency with the IHRA, the body stonewalled and doubled down, insisting that the definition was the entire text, and that any amendments or omissions rendered the resulting text no longer the IHRA 'working definition'.

As a means of spreading the 'collective Jew' among the nations redefinition of antisemitism, and its use in suppressing free speech on Palestinian rights and their experience of ethnic cleansing, the 2016 text has been highly successful. But scrutiny as to how this has come about and increasing evidence that the redefinition of antisemitism has done nothing to reduce genuine antisemitism, let alone critical speech on Israel, has made even more intense the bitter divisions among Jews and among academics studying antisemitism as to what constitutes antisemitism. The attempt to reduce the influence of the IHRA working definition by offering an alternative definition in the form of what was called the Jerusalem Declaration on Antisemitism (JDA), published in March 2021, and signed by more than 200 prominent, mostly Jewish academics, was viciously attacked.[4]

In the UK, reverberations continue to be felt from the accusations of antisemitism levelled at Jeremy Corbyn, which, after he stepped down as leader at the end of 2019, led to his successor, Kier Starmer, finding an excuse to suspend him from the party, with expulsion possibly to follow. With hardly a word from the mainstream media, Starmer has been carrying out a purge of left-wing, pro-Palestinian Jews from the party, on the grounds of expressions of antisemitism and making the party safe for Jews.

It is a curious 'war' on antisemitism waged by Starmer that has so many Jews in its sights. Make no mistake, Jews can be antisemites too. But it would be reasonable to expect a certain degree of caution to be exercised before making such an allegation about a Jewish person, especially a Jewish person who, in their own way, values their Jewish identity, of which there are many varieties. If it is the right of Jews to be allowed to define racism against themselves—a key element of how 'new antisemitism' theory was arrived at, as well as the 'Israel is the "Jew"', or the '"collective Jew" among the nations' notion—this right must surely apply also to dissident, left-wing Jews. Not so. Compared with all Labour members, the relative risk of facing actioned complaints about antisemitism was at least 30x as great for members of Jewish Voice for Labour (JVL) and over 200x for their leaders.[5]

Attacking non- and anti-Zionist Jews is a feature of the 'war' on antisemitism not only in the UK but also in the US, France, Germany, Australia and other countries even with rather small Jewish populations. The groundwork for Starmer's exercise was laid by various writers and commentators who felt they knew something about antisemitism. Adam Sutcliffe highlights the 2010 history of English antisemitism written by the prominent lawyer Anthony Julius and titled *Trials of the Diaspora: A History of Antisemitism in England*, in which Julius 'devoted over a quarter of his history since the medieval period to contemporary anti-Zionism, dedicating more pages to his critique of Jewish anti-Zionism than to either the Muslim or the Christian variants of the phenomenon.'[6] Julius described these Jews as 'fellow travellers' of antisemitism.

In Israel, the new foreign minister, Yair Lapid, the politician responsible for putting together the coalition government that took power in May 2021, has signalled that the country must take a 'new' approach to antisemitism. A careful scrutiny of his remarks suggests only a further intensification of Israel's particularist approach to the problem—and to the Jewish organisations across the world engaged in the struggle against 'new antisemitism'—dressed up as the Jewish state taking the 'moral' lead in the 'war' based on renewed emphasis on the lessons of the Holocaust.

There is continuity and consistency here—of a very negative kind. There is no sign of any reflection by leaders of the 'war' on the fundamental questions about the nature of the 'war' that Anidjar insistently argued needed answering:

> what are we doing? What does it mean? How to explain our achievements and/or successes? Are we, in fact, effective? If not why not? … We are soldiers of a peculiar army that does not think itself, participants in a war that may know its enemies (or think it does) but hardly its allies.

Many of those very questions have guided me in my analysis of how we have reached this current predicament.

This led me to conclude that, like the 'war on terror' and the 'war on drugs', framed as a 'war' on 'new antisemitism', the real task of countering, dismantling, educating about and refuting antisemitism, in close cooperation with anti-racist allies, is made very difficult and is largely avoided. A 'war' aimed at eliminating antisemitism is an impossible and unwinnable enterprise. Driven by endlessly repeated apocalyptic predictions about the consequences of hating the Jewish state; by the unachievable goal of nothing less than total eradication of antisemitism, falsely described as a disease, a virus; by Jewish exceptionalism that ranks antisemitism as racism's principal form and definable only by Jews themselves; by 'values' that are anti-democratic and anti-human rights in that Jewish rights in Israel–Palestine are assumed to trump Palestinian rights and justify apartheid and ongoing ethnic cleansing—framed as a 'war', anti-antisemitism action perpetuates injustice and is failing in its stated quest.

But the weaponisation of antisemitism by Israeli governments over the last 15 to 20 years has proved immensely valuable as an arm of the country's foreign policy, a policy that is a joint Israel–diaspora enterprise. Other countries, including increasing numbers of Arab states, seem to have no problem in either accepting or tolerating the way Israel presents itself as a hi-tech, globalised powerhouse, militarily unmatched in the region, geopolitically strong, while at the same time existentially vulnerable to political criticism of its actions, which it sees as the harbinger of a second genocide of Jews.

There are so many seemingly irreconcilable internal contradictions in this story, is it any wonder that confusion about what constitutes antisemitism continues to prevail? And while much as I have tried to explain how the confusion has come about and why it persists, I cannot hold out much hope that the confusion will be resolved in a satisfactory way any time soon. The confusion does not in any way restrict what Israel does. Nor does it have any negative impact on the claim of the leaders of the 'war' on antisemitism to be leading the fight against hatred of Jews. On the contrary. The confusion adds to the difficulty that critics of the 'war' have in building a movement based on unified anti-racism action, tackling antisemitism and other forms of race and ethnic hate, and thereby undermine the IHRA 'working definition' and the Jewish exceptionalism built into it and into the 'war' on antisemitism. The emphasis on antisemitism in recent years, and the tendency for authorities to accept the 'canary in the mine' narrative about antisemitism, sucks the oxygen out of work to combat other forms of racism that have far more severe impacts on their victims today.

Let us be clear, the promoters of the notion of the 'new antisemitism', of 'Israel is the "collective Jew" among the nations', and of the 'war' on antisemitism are not confused at all. They are in thrall to a dangerously narrow version of Jewish particularism. They endorse the 'principle' that only Jews can define the nature of the racism they experience. They believe 'Jews are the canary in the mine'— when there is rising antisemitism and Jews are attacked, that is the sign of a society sliding into moral and political collapse. They see the Holocaust as the worst evil human beings can inflict upon each other, and a lesson never to allow such a thing to happen again—the 'never again' mantra that, in the light of the many attempted genocides since the Holocaust, seems to have taken on the narrow meaning of '*never again* will Germans attempt to inflict mass murder on Jews in Europe'. They see no distinction between the state of Israel and Jews anywhere else in the world. 'If you attack me as a Zionist', they say, 'you attack me as a Jew'. This was the reaction in Israel to the UN 'Zionism is racism' resolution of 1975. Particularist then and even more so now. This is because orthodox Judaism, in the last few decades, has produced more than enough rabbis who are ready to use Jewish teaching to justify Jewish supremacy over the Palestinians, to legitimise the taking of extreme measures to ensure that there will always be a Jewish majority in Palestine–Israel, to justify segregation and discrimination, and even to admit that if denying Palestinians their civil rights is to be called apartheid, then so be it. And as Adam Sutcliffe shows, especially influential in this development has been Habad Hasidism. Although they have 'sustained in their messianic theology [the] tradition of universalistic utopianism … in political terms Habad has fully supported, and unabashedly underpinned with theological reasoning, an uncompromisingly inward-oriented emphasis on Jewish collective interests.[7]

The potent intertwining of myth and history in Zionist thinking and practice that Turgeman and Hadari identified as being so influential in the debate around Arab antisemitism and Resolution 3379 is probably even more significant today, with project 'Greater Israel' both more transparent and substantially realised. But we see this not only in Israeli state-funded organisation and deployment of the powerful weaponisation of 'new antisemitism' (which makes for a highly effective, pre-emptive system, bolstered by, and constituting part of, the transnational field of racial governance, for neutralising any threat—real or imagined—faced by the Jewish state), but in a further particularist conceptualising of the Jewish state's current position.

Yossi Shain, the prominent Tel Aviv University professor, and now member of Knesset for Avigdor Lieberman's Yisrael Beiteinu (Israel Our Home) Party, whose academic work on the foundations of Israel's policies on antisemitism I have cited above (see Chapter 5), and who advises governments around the world on diaspora issues, seeks to contextualise, sanitise and justify ethno-nationalist Zionism—far-right, messianically inspired, religiously influenced—on the grounds of what was necessary for the liberation of the Jewish people. He argued that the continuous cycles of Jewish instability that are a central feature of diasporic Jewish history have been brought to an end with Israel's attainment of sovereignty.[8] It 'broke the paradigm' of an existence that was always 'arbitrary'. The semblance of 'an age of stability' existed in the past but was always short-lived. And for diaspora Jews 'arbitrariness' still exists.

Nonetheless, Shain maintains, 'the Jewish Question is dead—today it's the Israel Question'. By the latter he means 'the viral delegitimisation of Israel', which he and others now call 'the Israelisation of antisemitism',[9] which seeks 'genocide'. By 'Jewish Question' he means antisemitic opposition to Jewish life wherever it is outside Israel. He believes that Jews have never been in a better position. But he is not saying there is no antisemitism, rather that the antisemitism experienced by diaspora Jews does not threaten Jewish diaspora existence because no attacks on Jews are sanctioned from above by state authorities. And second, Shain says, Israel is 'a strong state', able to protect Jews since 'Israel's penal code states that if a Jew is attacked, Israel won't stand by—it will send Mossad operatives to protect and save Jewish lives'.

Such action would not solve the underlying problem facing diaspora Jews, whom he describes as 'the soft belly of Israeli security'. Their biggest challenge, he claims, is whether they can say, of the countries where they live, 'I am at home here'. This is 'no longer a *fait accompli*. In Israel, we Zionists say "we told you so"'. To be at home in the diaspora, you have to hide your Jewishness—but this is incompatible with 'multiculturalism'. In Israel, sovereignty means a Jew *can* say 'I am at home here'. Nevertheless, Shain regards the 'come here now' message Netanyahu and his ministers convey to diaspora Jews when a violent attack occurs as 'triumphant stupidity'. On the other hand, diaspora Jews also demonstrate 'triumphant stupidity' when they are too apologetic when 'Israel does something the world doesn't like'. 'Don't apologise', he tells them. 'You are part of the voice of the Jewish people, successful today only because of [Israeli] sovereignty'.

In Shain's views there are loud echoes of Turgeman and Hadari's findings from 1975 of the extreme Zionist reaction to Resolution 3379. 'Every Jew who comes to Israel belongs. You may feel uneasy, but you belong', Shain urges.[10] 'Having a personal Jewish identity without Israel is becoming more and more difficult', says Shain. 'On what would you draw, if not on your religiosity—if you are secular—or your ethnicity (if you are an assimilated American, among which there are 70 per cent intermarriages)'.[11]

Looking back from the 1980s, Harkabi believed that the antisemitism of Resolution 3379 'was different from the antisemitism of the past, because of its main object, hatred of Israel, with Jew-hatred coming second, if it exists at all'. In 2021 Shain said: The 'Jewish Question ... the antisemitism of the past, is dead. What matters today is the "viral delegitimisation of Israel ... the Israelization of antisemitism",[12] which seeks "genocide".[13]

The leaders of the 'war' on antisemitism are clearly fortunate in having thinkers like Shain unabashedly ready to find increasingly outrageous ways of reinforcing the myth of the 'collective Jew', and in an almost matter-of-fact way placing the genocide bomb on the table. If Jews turn their faces away from Israel they confront insecurity, loss of identity, no sense of belonging, reliance on the Mossad for their safety. In other words, diaspora Jews may think they can live an autonomous Jewish life outside of Israel, but they are only kidding themselves. Having a sense of Jewish peoplehood today is only possible because of 'Israeli sovereignty'. You cannot be at home in diaspora without it. It is as if even the antisemitism a diaspora Jew experiences is a derivative of and less consequential than the effects of the 'Israelisation' of antisemitism—which is just another way of referring to the 'new antisemitism'.

This discourse is a gift to the 'war's' leaders, making it ever easier to get away with portraying failure as success. 'We have so much expertise and know racism against us better than anyone else', they seem to believe, 'that there is no alternative, no better way of conducting this fight. Every report indicating worsening antisemitism means we must redouble our efforts and continue the fight'. But failure is built into the combatting of antisemitism because it has been defined as what it is not.

The human instinct to pursue justice, not to be cowed into accepting the curtailment of freedom of speech, not to be suppressed by forces far stronger than you are, is a powerful one. This makes critical speech about Israel, as with any other country—however harsh and sometimes exaggerated it might become—legitimate. To impose sanctions on this only perpetuates injustice. To treat the narration of Palestinian experience of Zionism, which is objectively about dispossession, ethnic cleansing, apartheid and the suppression of Palestinian culture and identity, as unacceptable hate speech when it isn't, and attempt to outlaw it, can only ever be temporarily successful, as the history of the last 74 years has shown.

The state of Israel is not like an individual Jew. It is a category mistake to compare a state to a person. A state does not have a will of its own. It cannot think, feel or see. It has no agency that does not derive from human action. But based on this seductive mistake, a theory of antisemitism has been conceived that is an open invitation to attack freedom of speech.

There cannot be a 'war' on antisemitism, but there can be a war on freedom of speech. And if you have convinced yourself that the legitimate speech you are attacking is antisemitism, real antisemitism gets a free pass and false antisemitism will not be defeated. Not only that, others will line up to defend it. And so, you will claim that antisemitism is rising, that civilisation is losing the fight against it, but you must redouble your efforts to eliminate it: another impossibility. In this way you present failure as success. And while you vocally proclaim your 'war's' 'affinity with, its centrality in, the spread of democracy and freedom',[14] you are actually aligning yourself with anti-democratic forces.

'New antisemitism' is effectively predicated on the notion that the state can do no wrong. But the deification of the Jewish state is a heresy, tantamount to idolatry. This does not seem to disturb religious Jews who increasingly see the state doing God's work by 'repossessing' the 'land of Israel', working to formally annex the West Bank, denying equal rights to Palestinians and making them strangers in their own land in order to secure a Jewish majority in perpetuity and hasten the coming of the Messiah.

I would like to think that anyone brought up in the tradition of mainstream orthodoxy in the immediate post-war period would recognise this fetishisation of the state as a corruption of Judaism. But judging by many people of my generation who had this upbringing and who express themselves on the issues I discuss in this book, sadly that is not the case.

I cannot think of any modern-day figure who fulfils the false messiah role of a Sabbatai Zevi (1626–1676). But there seems to me something in the now-so-prominent element of the messianic in Zionism and its inextricable link to the deification of the state that has the feel of Sabbatianism about it. Is this far-fetched? Sutcliffe, in discussing Gershom Scholem's study of Sabbatianism, reveals that Scholem argued that it 'was a crucial stage ... in the history of Jewish "activist messianism", which he traced forward to modern Zionism'.[15]

Sabbatianism and Frankism (the beliefs of those who followed the Polish messianic leader Jacob Frank, 1726–1761) have passed into history, but the experiences of Jews who followed false messiahs are perhaps not so alien to us as we might think, living as we still do in the huge shadow of the greatest disaster in diaspora Jewish history. The schisms dividing Jews today are deep; existentially, politically and theologically fundamental. To a degree, there has already been a fragmentation in different societies in the Jewish world. Diaspora Jewish and Israeli-Jewish leaders bullishly insist that the symbols of Jewish unity—the Holocaust, the Jewish state and the 'war' on antisemitism—still bind Jews together. But if Jewish tragedy, an apartheid state and a war on freedom of speech masquerading as a 'war' on antisemitism are all that can be offered as a basis of common purpose—if that is what you want—who would dare confidently claim that an even more severe fragmentation will not happen. This is the lachrymose in modern Jewish history served up as a best scenario for Jewish destiny.

It does not help when non-Jews reinforce this trend and seek to determine what Jews should feel about these matters. For example, Lord Pickles, the head of the UK Delegation to the IHRA and special government envoy for post-Holocaust issues, attacked the Bristol University Jewish academic Rebecca Ruth Gould in 2017 for what she wrote in an article on antisemitism as 'one of the worst cases of Holocaust denial' he had seen in recent years.[16] Her 'offence' was to say that the Holocaust was available for 'manipulation by [Israeli] governmental elites, aiming to promote the narrative most likely to underwrite their claims to sovereignty'. 'Claiming the Holocaust as a holy event sanctifies the state of Israel and whitewashes its crimes', Gould added. People should stop 'privileging the Holocaust'. The 'offence' belongs to Pickles for revealing his ignorance of the fact that Gould's remarks echo those of many Jewish academics and commentators in Israel and beyond.

A similar 'holier-than-thou' attitude was clearly evident in December 2020 in a heated exchange between Lord Mann, whom Prime Minister Theresa May in July 2019 appointed as the British government's independent advisor on antisemitism—dubbed the 'Antisemitism Tsar'—and Birkbeck antisemitism research institute head David Feldman, who is Jewish, over the pros and cons of the IHRA 'working definition'.[17] In measured terms, Feldman has authoritatively exposed its weaknesses, not least how it is used to chill free speech. Mann, who has little expertise on antisemitism and in 2016 was himself accused of racism against travellers and Roma,[18] dismissed Feldman's criticisms out of hand.

There is a glaring, almost theological absolutism in this rigid policing of what Jews can say about antisemitism, Zionism, anti-Zionism, Israel, the Holocaust and Jewish identity. And while this varies from country to country, there are strong parallels between this policing in the USA and the UK—and in Germany, where, A. Dirk Moses, the Professor of Human Rights history at the University of North Carolina at Chapel Hill, writes in an article titled 'The German Catechism': 'The moral hubris leads to the remarkable situation of Gentile Germans lecturing American and Israeli Jews with accusing finger about the correct form of remembrance and loyalty to Israel'.[19] This manifestation of racial governance has been alarmingly toxic in Germany and is summed up in the Catechism's five articles of faith:

1. The Holocaust is unique because it was the unlimited *annihilation of the Jews for the sake of annihilation* (exterminating the Jews for the sake of extermination itself) distinguished from the limited and pragmatic aims of other genocides. It is the first time in history that a state had set out to destroy a people solely on ideological grounds.
2. It was thus a civilisational *rupture and the moral foundation of the nation.*
3. Germany has a special responsibility to Jews in Germany, and a special loyalty to Israel: 'Israel's security is part of Germany's reason of *state*'.
4. Antisemitism is a distinct prejudice—and was a distinctly German one. It should not be confused with racism.
5. Anti-Zionism is antisemitism.

Moses argues that 'We are witnessing, I believe, nothing less than a public exorcism performed by the self-appointed high priests of the *Catechism of the Germans*'. He concludes: 'The time has come to set it aside'.

Of these articles, 2 and 3 are specific to Germany. The threads of the other three are interlaced with the broader story of the redefinition of antisemitism as 'new antisemitism' and its fundamental assumption—but more like an article of faith—that 'Israel is the "collective Jew" among the nations', which have been the central focus of this book. I have therefore respectfully chosen to follow Moses's deliberately provocative, but revealing, Catechism framing, which has generated fierce debate in Germany, to compile a Global Catechism, drawn from my narrative, that similarly should be consigned to the dustbin of history:

1. Israel is the persecuted 'collective Jew' among the nations.
2. The founding of the state of Israel is God's redemptive response to the Holocaust.
3. The consequence of the Holocaust was to reveal that Zionism is integral to Judaism.
4. Therefore, the state of Israel is the climax of Jewish history, the fulfilment of Jewish destiny, the realisation of Jewish values, the personification of the post-Holocaust Jew—and as such is above criticism.

5. As the realisation of God's purpose for the Jews, the state should be worshipped.
6. Antisemitism is a unique prejudice and Jews alone are allowed to define it.
7. The IHRA working definition of antisemitism is the Gold Standard definition and is holy writ.
8. New antisemitism is now the dominant variant of the antisemitism virus.
9. Anti-Zionism is antisemitism.
10. The Palestinians are the main disseminators of the eternal hatred of Jews, and therefore can never be entitled to equal rights in the Jewish state or in any territories controlled by Israel.
11. Only complete eradication is an acceptable outcome in the war on antisemitism.

I am tempted to add to this Catechism one more article of faith, which was only recently (January 2022) given prominence by the actress Maureen Lipman and comedian David Baddiel:[20] 'Only Jews can play Jewish characters in plays, films, sitcoms, operas, etc. It is antisemitism when a non-Jew is chosen for such roles'. But I fear some readers would think this was not for real and that I was being ironic.

All the same, irony is certainly one means of exposing the bankruptcy of the lachrymose conception of Jewish history,[21] which legitimises and perpetuates the myth of Israel as the persecuted 'collective Jew' among the nations and feels like constant repetition of a self-inflicted wound. By reducing Jewishness to a singularity, Zionism is endorsing an antisemitic construction of the 'Jew'. If this alliance between antisemitic figuring and pro-Zionism seems incongruous and unlikely, the history of the relationship between Zionism and antisemitism tells a different story.

Antisemitism nurtured and empowered Zionism. It was mobilised for the sake of the Zionist project. Herzl wrote in his diary: 'The antisemites will become our most loyal friends, the antisemitic nations will become our allies'.[22] In the 1930s, Ben-Gurion said that 'le malheur of the Jews was the chance of Zionism'.[23] In a talk in London in 2008, the historian Idit Zertal described the diaspora Jew as the first 'other' of Zionism, against which Zionism defined itself.

The relationship between Zionism and the Holocaust or Shoah is also deeply problematic since both terms implied sinners who had to be absolved of their sins through the catastrophe, a dangerous blurring of the meaning of what happened. It has been ideologised, simplified and politicised by Israel for the sake of the Zionist cause.

The affinity in the outlook of antisemites and Zionists is undoubtedly disturbing, and the fact that it is not just historical but has contemporary relevance through the antisemitic resonances of the myth of 'Israel as the "collective Jew" among the nations' does not bode well for the future.

This is a stark conclusion. Challenging the promotion of the concept of 'new antisemitism' and revealing the bankruptcy of the myth of Israel being 'the "collective Jew" among the nations' is an uphill struggle to say the least. But things never stay the same and resistance is not just an option but a necessity. This book is intended as a contribution to that resistance and to encourage others to do the same.

Appendix: The IHRA Working Definition of Antisemitism*

In the spirit of the Stockholm Declaration that states: "With humanity still scarred by … antisemitism and xenophobia the international community shares a solemn responsibility to fight those evils" the committee on Antisemitism and Holocaust Denial called the IHRA Plenary in Budapest 2015 to adopt the following working definition of antisemitism.

On 26 May 2016, the Plenary in Bucharest decided to:

> Adopt the following non-legally binding working definition of antisemitism:
>
> "Antisemitism is a certain perception of Jews, which may be expressed as hatred toward Jews. Rhetorical and physical manifestations of antisem-itism are directed toward Jewish or non-Jewish individuals and/or their property, toward Jewish community institutions and religious facilities."

To guide IHRA in its work, the following examples may serve as illustrations:

Manifestations might include the targeting of the state of Israel, conceived as a Jewish collectivity. However, criticism of Israel similar to that leveled against any other country cannot be regarded as antisemitic. Antisemitism frequently charges Jews with conspiring to harm humanity, and it is often used to blame Jews for "why things go wrong." It is expressed in speech, writing, visual forms and action, and employs sinister stereotypes and negative character traits.

Contemporary examples of antisemitism in public life, the media, schools, the workplace, and in the religious sphere could, taking into account the overall context, include, but are not limited to:

- Calling for, aiding, or justifying the killing or harming of Jews in the name of a radical ideology or an extremist view of religion.
- Making mendacious, dehumanizing, demonizing, or stereotypical allegations about Jews as such or the power of Jews as collective — such as, especially but not exclusively, the myth about a world Jewish conspiracy

---

* Taken from www.holocaustremembrance.com/resources/working-definitions-charters/working-definition-antisemitism

273

or of Jews controlling the media, economy, government or other societal institutions.

- Accusing Jews as a people of being responsible for real or imagined wrong-doing committed by a single Jewish person or group, or even for acts committed by non-Jews.
- Denying the fact, scope, mechanisms (e.g. gas chambers) or intentional-ity of the genocide of the Jewish people at the hands of National Socialist Germany and its supporters and accomplices during World War II (the Holocaust).
- Accusing the Jews as a people, or Israel as a state, of inventing or exaggerat-ing the Holocaust.
- Accusing Jewish citizens of being more loyal to Israel, or to the alleged pri-orities of Jews worldwide, than to the interests of their own nations.
- Denying the Jewish people their right to self-determination, e.g., by claiming that the existence of a State of Israel is a racist endeavor.
- Applying double standards by requiring of it a behavior not expected or demanded of any other democratic nation.
- Using the symbols and images associated with classic antisemitism (e.g., claims of Jews killing Jesus or blood libel) to characterize Israel or Israelis.
- Drawing comparisons of contemporary Israeli policy to that of the Nazis.
- Holding Jews collectively responsible for actions of the state of Israel.

Antisemitic acts are criminal when they are so defined by law (for example, denial of the Holocaust or distribution of antisemitic materials in some countries).

Criminal acts are antisemitic when the targets of attacks, whether they are people or property – such as buildings, schools, places of worship and ceme-teries – are selected because they are, or are perceived to be, Jewish or linked to Jews.

Antisemitic discrimination is the denial to Jews of opportunities or services available to others and is illegal in many countries.

Notes

Introduction

1. Yair Lapid, 'Is antisemitism racism?', *Haaretz*, 26 July 2021.
2. www.wiesenthal.com/assets/pdf/global_antisemitism_2021_top_ten.pdf
3. Walter Reich, 'Seventy-five years after Auschwitz, antisemitism is on the rise', Brookings, Washington DC, 28 January 2020, www.brookings. edu/blog/order-from-chaos/2020/01/28/75 Brookings-years-after-auschwitz-antisemitism-is-on-the-rise/
4. David Feldman, 'The meanings of antisemitism', 13 February 2017, Birkbeck University podcast, https://backdoorbroadcasting.net/2017/02/david-feldman-the-meanings-of-antisemitism/
5. See Irwin Cotler, 'Defining the new antisemitism', *National Post*, 9 November 2010, https://nationalpost.com/full-comment/irwin-cotler-defining-the-new-antisemitism
6. A tweet by Greenblatt on 13 December 2018, https://twitter.com/jgreenblattadl/status/1073229821768028160?lang=en
7. Zack Beauchamp, 'The fall of Jeremy Corbyn: Why Labour lost and what it means for Britain', *Vox*, 13 December 2019, www.vox.com/world/2019/12/13/21004755/uk-election-2019-jeremy-corbyn-labour-defeat
8. Jonathan Judaken, 'Ten Commandments for thinking about modern antisemitism', *Forward*, 5 January 2018.
9. Anthony Julius, *Trials of the Diaspora: A History of Antisemitism in England* (Oxford: OUP, 2010), 523–525, 554.
10. For the text of the 'working definition', see the appendix.
11. Antisemitism in historical perspective, *American Historical Review*, nos. 123–124, October 2018, cited as *AHR* 2018, www.historians.org/publications-and-directories/perspectives-on-history/october-2018/antisemitism-in-historical-perspective-in-the-october-issue-of-the-emamerican-historical-review/em
12. The other authors: Scott Ury, Maurice Samuels, Bryan Cheyette, David Feldman, Daniel Schroeter, Stefanie Schuler-Springorum, Ethan B Katz.
13. Introduction to the *American Historical Review*'s Round Table on Antisemitism in historical perspective, October 2018, www.historians.org/publications-and-directories/perspectives-on-history/october-2018/antisemitism-in-historical-perspective-in-the-october-issue-of-the-emamerican-historical-review/em, 1123.
14. Ibid., 1124.
15. Ibid., 1124–1125.
16. Gil Anidjar, 'When killers become victims: antisemitism and its critics', *Cosmopolis: A Review of Cosmopolitics*, no. 3, 2007.

17. Gil Anidjar, 'Antisemitism and its critics' in J. Renton and B. Gidley, eds., *Antisemitism and Islamophobia in Europe: A Shared History?* (London: Palgrave Macmillan, 2017).

18. Renton and Gidley, eds., 2017, 187.

19. Ibid., 190.

20. Ibid., 191.

21. Ibid., 196.

22. Ibid., 199–200.

23. Ibid., 200.

24. Esther Romeyn, '(Anti) "new antisemitism" as a transnational field of racial governance', *Patterns of Prejudice* vol. 54, nos. 1–2, February–May 2020. Doi: 10.1080/0031322X.2019.1696048

25. No reliable source exists proving he said this, but when answering this question in an interview for *Theory Culture and Society* (22 December 2010) 'to what extent [do] you think the liquidity of your own life experiences has influenced (as Martin Jay suggests in his TCS article) your interpretation of (liquid) modernity? Do you recognise yourself, for example, as an "ambivalent outsider" who has "learned to walk on quicksand"?' he said 'Having been in that story a bird rather than an ornithologist (and birds, as we all know, being not particularly prominent in the annals of ornithology', https://www.theoryculturesociety.org/interview-with-zygmunt-bauman

26. '"As a Jew" explained', CAMERA UK, 23 June 2011, https://camera-uk.org/2011/06/23/as-a-jew-explained/

1. Varieties of Confusion in Understandings of Antisemitism

1. Steven Beller, *Antisemitism: A Very Short Introduction* (Oxford: OUP 2015), 1.

2. Kenneth L. Marcus, *The Definition of Antisemitism* (Oxford: OUP 2015), 5, 6.

3. Allison Kaplan Sommer, *Haaretz*, 19 March 2018.

4. www.jta.org/2018/01/02/news-opinion/opinion/how-do-you-define-antisemitism-its-complicated#.Wk_phpHgdcY.email

5. Dov Waxman, 'Who gets to define antisemitism?', *Times of Israel*, 2 August 2018, https://blogs.timesofisrael.com/who-gets-to-define-antisemitism/

6. Birkbeck University podcast, www.pearsinstitute.bbk.ac.uk/events/past-events/2017-events/the-meanings-of-antisemitism/

7. Populus *Sub-Report commissioned to assist the All-Party Parliamentary Inquiry into Antisemitism: Antisemitism Poll Survey.* All Party Parliamentary Group Against Antisemitism, January 2015, https://archive.jpr.org.uk/object-uk177

8. www.populus.com/techpapers

9. Fundamental Rights Agency (FRA), *Discrimination and Hate Crime Against Jews in EU Member States: Experiences and Perceptions of Antisemitism*, https://fra.europa.eu/sites/default/files/fra-2013-discrimination-hate-crime-against-jews-eu-member-states-0_en.pdf

10. *Second Survey on Discrimination and Hate Crime Against Jews in EU Member States Technical Report*, https://fra.europa.eu/sites/default/files/fra_uploads/fra-2018-experiences-and-perceptions-of-antisemitism-technical-report_en.pdf

11. 'Conceptualising Contemporary Antisemitism: How Debates About Immigration Have Shaped the Understanding of Jew-Hatred in Germany and Britain

since 1945', Royal Holloway University 2015, https://pure.royalholloway.ac.uk/ws/files/29001133/2015LetzmannDMPhil.pdf

12. Jonathan Boyd, 'Reflections on the European Union Agency for Fundamental Rights (FRA) survey of Jewish people's experiences and perceptions of antisemitism' *JPR/Analysis*, December 2018, www.jpr.org.uk/documents/JPR.2018.Reflections_on_the_FRA_antisemitism_survey.pdf

13. Rosa Doherty, 'Exclusive: Fewer than half of British adults know what "antisemitism" means, poll reveals' *Jewish Chronicle*, 14 March 2019, www.thejc.com/news/uk/fewer-than-half-of-british-adults-know-what-antisemitism-means-poll-reveals-1.481476

14. Simon Rocker, 'Leading Holocaust educator: Drop the word "antisemitism" because students do not understand it', *Jewish Chronicle*, 20 March 2019, www.thejc.com/education/education-news/leading-holocaust-educator-drop-the-word-antisemitism-because-students-do-not-understand-it-1.481754

15. Greg Philo et al., *Bad News for Labour: Antisemitism, the Party and Public Belief* (London: Pluto Press, 2019), 3–7.

16. David Graham and Jonathan Boyd, 'The apartheid contention and calls for a boycott', *JPR/Analysis*, January 2019, www.jpr.org.uk/documents/JPR_2019._Apartheid_briefing_paper.pdf

17. *Labour, Antisemitism and the News: A Disinformation Paradigm*, 27 September 2018, www.mediareform.org.uk/blog/new-mrc-research-finds-inaccuracies-and-distortions-in-media-coverage-of-antisemitism-and-the-labour-party

18. www.adl.org/news/press-releases/anti-semitic-stereotypes-persist-in-america-survey-shows

19. 'US antisemitism worst since 1930s, ADL leader says', Jewish Telegraphic Agency (JTA) 17 November 2016, www.timesofisrael.com/us-antisemitism-worst-since-1930s-adl-leader-says/

20. Richard Allen Greene, 'CNN poll reveals depth of antisemitism in Europe', https://edition.cnn.com/interactive/2018/11/europe/antisemitism-poll-2018-intl/?ref=hvper.com&utm_source=hvper.com&utm_medium=website

21. Netanyahu reacts to CNN poll on antisemitism, https://edition.cnn.com/videos/tv/2018/11/27/exp-netanyahu-reaction-to-antisemitism-poll.cnn

22. Judy Maltz, 'Naftali Bennett seeks to tie synagogue shooting to Palestinians', *Forward*, 29 October 2018, https://forward.com/fast-forward/412975/naftali-bennett-seeks-to-tie-synagogue-shooting-to-palestinians/

23. Ibid.

24. Shlomo Fischer, 'Israelis are divided over whether they are "Jewish" or "Israeli"', 25 October 2015, https://forward.com/opinion/412732/israelis-are-conflicted-about-whether-they-are-jewish-or-israeli-heres/

25. Twitter, https://twitter.com/dpjhodges/status/634960993764909056

26. 'John Mann MP leaves Labour to become No 10's Antisemitism "Tsar"', *The Times*, 8 September 2019, www.thetimes.co.uk/article/labour-mp-is-no-10-antisemitism-tsar-77stzrl57

27. Twitter, https://twitter.com/michaelrosenyes/status/1211976225675251712

28. Noam Pianko, *Jewish Peoplehood: An American Innovation. Key Words in Jewish Studies* (Rutgers: Rutgers University Press, 2015), Introduction, 1.

29. See Cynthia Baker, *Jew. Key Words in Jewish Studies* Rutgers: (Rutgers University Press, 2017).

30. See Idit Zertal, *Israel's Holocaust and the Politics of Nationhood* (Cambridge: Cambridge University Press, 2005), Ela Shohat, *On the Arab-Jew, Palestine, and Other Displacements: Selected Writings of Ella Shohat* (London: Pluto Press, 2017), and Tom Segev, *The Seventh Million: Israelis and the Holocaust* (London: Picador, 2000).

31. See Ian S. Lustick, 'The Holocaust in Israeli political culture. Four constructions and their consequences', *Contemporary Jewry*, vol. 37, no. 1, April 2017, 125–170. Doi: 0.1007/s12397-017-9208-7

32. www.telegraph.co.uk/politics/2019/11/02/jewish-families-will-leave-uk-jeremy-corbyn-wins-general-election/

33. See Jonathan Karp and Adam Sutcliffe, eds., *Philosemitism in History* (Cambridge: Cambridge University Press, 2011).

34. Zygmunt Bauman, 'Allosemitism: premodern, modern, postmodern' in Bryan Cheyette and Laura Marcus, eds., *Modernity, Culture, and 'the Jew'* (Cambridge: Polity Press, 1998).

35. Bryan Cheyette in dialogue with Professor Michael Rothberg, Lernen aus der Geschichte, Relational Thinking: A Dialogue on the Theory and Politics of Research on Antisemitism and Racism, 27 November 2019, http://lernen-aus-der-geschichte.de/Lernen-und-Lehren/content/14651

36. *AHR* 2018, 1124.

37. See Patricia Cohen, 'Essay linking liberal Jews and antisemitism sparks a furor', *New York Times*, 31 January 2007.

38. Alvin H. Rosenfeld ed., 'Introduction', *Anti-Zionism and Antisemitism: The Dynamics of Delegitimization* (Bloomington: Indiana University Press, 219), ix–x.

39. Ibid., x–xii.

40. Alan Johnson, 'Introduction: seeing the IHRA plain', *Fathom*, February 2021, https://fathomjournal.org/wp-content/uploads/2021/02/Fathom-eBook-In-Defence-of-the-IHRA-Working-Definition-of-Antisemitism.pdf

41. Richard Landes, review of Gerstenfeld (Jerusalem: Jerusalem Center for Public Affairs 2015) in *Jewish Political Studies Review*, vol. 26, nos. 3–4, Fall 2014, www.jstor.org/stable/43922008

42. Scott Ury, 'Strange Bedfellows? Antisemitism, Zionism, and the Fate of "the Jews"', *AHR* 2018, 1152.

43. Ibid., 1164.

44. Ibid., 1167.

45. Ibid., 1169.

46. Jonathan Judaken, 'So what's new? Rethinking "new antisemitism" in a global age today', *Patterns of Prejudice*, vol. 42, nos. 4–5, 2008, 531.

47. Ibid., 559–560.

48. *AHR* 2018, 1124.

49. The group subsequently changed its acronym to JJP.

50. Rosenfeld 2006, 9.

51. Ibid., 12.

52. Ibid.

53. Shulamit Reinharz, 'Fighting Jewish antisemitism', *Jewish Advocate* (Boston), 21 December 2006.

2. The Use and Abuse of Antisemitic Stereotypes and Tropes

1. 'An idiot's guide to antisemitic tropes', 19 February 2019, www.jta. org/2019/02/19/opinion/an-idiots-guide-to-anti-semitic-tropes-2
2. Brian Klug, 'Interrogating new antisemitism', *Ethnic and Racial Studies* (2012), 8.
3. Ron Kampeas, 'That Trump ad: is it antisemitic? An analysis', *JTA*, 7 November 2016, www.jta.org/2016/11/07/politics/that-trump-ad-is-it-anti-semitic-an-analysis
4. Shimon Stein and Moshe Zimmerman, *Haaretz*, 13 July 2017, www.haaretz. com/opinion/the-laughing-jew-the-nazi-backstory-of-hungary-s-anti-soros-poster-campaign-1.5493827
5. https://labour.org.uk/wp-content/uploads/2017/10/Chakrabarti-Inquiry-Report-30June16.pdf
6. Tom Marshall, 'Labour MP Ruth Smeeth storms out of antisemitism report launch "in tears"', *Evening Standard*, 30 June 2016, www.standard.co.uk/ news/politics/labour-mp-ruth-smeeth-storms-out-of-antisemitism-report-launch-a3285106.html
7. Media Reform Coalition, *Labour, Antisemitism and the News: A Disinformation Paradigm*, 27 September 2018, www.mediareform.org.uk/blog/ new-mrc-research-finds-inaccuracies-and-distortions-in-media-coverage-of-antisemitism-and-the-labour-party
8. Michiel Willems, 'Jewish Chronicle newspaper to compensate expelled Labour activist after false accusations', *CITYA.M.*, 22 July 2021, www.cityam.com/ jewish-chronicle-newspaper-to-compensate-expelled-labour-activist-after-false-accusations/
9. Paper on 'Postcolonialism, theory, and antisemitism', at 'Jews, the Left, and Antisemitism: International Perspectives', International Workshop, Pears Institute for the Study of Antisemitism Birkbeck University of London Seminar, 5 December 2018.
10. *AHR* 2018, 1125.
11. Ibid., 1137.
12. John Mann, 'The antisemitism report gives a route out of this mess', *Labour List*, 1 July 2016, www.labourlist.org
13. Jeremy Diamond, 'Trump to Republican Jewish Coalition: "I'm a negotiator like you"', 3 December 2015, https://edition.cnn.com/2015/12/03/politics/donald-trump-rjc-negotiator/index.html
14. Hannah Roberts, 'Banking protest mural resembling Nazi anti-Semitic propaganda to be removed from East End', *Daily Mail*, 5 October 2012, www. dailymail.co.uk/news/article-2213536/Banking-protest-mural-resembling-Nazi-anti-Semitic-propaganda-removed-East-End.html
15. www.thejc.com/news/uk/mayor-tower-hamlets-mural-to-be-removed-1.36785
16. 'Jeremy Corbyn regrets comments about "antisemitic" mural', *BBC News*, https://www.bbc.co.uk/news/uk-politics-43523445
17. http://qern.org/robert-fisk-on-anonymous-internet-cowards-like-david-toube/
18. www.hurryupharry.org/2012/10/05
19. www.thejc.com/news/uk/mayor-tower-hamlets-mural-to-be-removed-1.36785
20. https://medium.com/@pitt_bob/antisemitism-the-brick-lane-mural-and-the-stitch-up-of-jeremy-corbyn-6656b77cc941

21. Marcus Dysch, 'Did Jeremy Corbyn back artist whose mural was condemned as antisemitic?', *Jewish Chronicle*, 6 November 2015.
22. Rob Merrick, 'Jeremy Corbyn forced to backtrack over apparent support for antisemitic mural', *Independent*, 23 March 2018, www.independent.co.uk/news/uk/politics/jeremy-corbyn-anti-semitic-mural-mear-one-luciana-berger-east-end-a8271111.html
23 Executive summary (pdf), www.mediareform.org.uk/blog/new-mrc-research-finds-inaccuracies-and-distortions-in-media-coverage-of-antisemitism-and-the-labour-party
24 Jonathan Judaken, 'So what's new? Rethinking the "new antisemitism" in a global age', *Patterns of Prejudice*, 42:4–5, 531–560. Doi: 10.1080/00313220802377453
25. Jessica Elgott, 'Dozens of rabbis say Labour chooses to ignore UK Jewish community' *Guardian*, 16 July 2018, www.theguardian.com/politics/2018/jul/16/68-rabbis-labour-chooses-ignore-uk-jewish-community
26. Pippa Crerar, 'Labour under pressure over Peter Willsman's antisemitism remarks', *Guardian*, 31 July 2018, www.theguardian.com/politics/2018/jul/31/labour-under-pressure-peter-willsman-antisemitism-remarks
27. https://cst.org.uk/news/blog/2019/08/04/engine-of-hate-the-online-networks-behind-the-labour-partys-antisemitism-crisis
28. Jonny Paul, 'Palestinian envoy to Britain dismisses two-state solution', *Jerusalem Post*, 20 January 2013.
29. www.israellycool.com/2019/11/20/watch-jeremy-corbyn-engages-in-antisemitic-trope/

3. Motivated by Antisemitism? Challenges to Zionism 1975–1989

1. www.americanrhetoric.com/speeches/danielpatrickmoynihanun3379.htm
2. www.americanrhetoric.com/speeches/chaimherzogunitednationszionism notracism.htm
3. Abba Eban, *American Jewish Congress*, vol. 40, Issues 2–14, 1973, xxv.
4. Pierre-André Taguieff, *La nouvelle judéophobie* (Paris:1001 NUITS, 2002).
5. Pierre-André Taguieff, *Rising From the Muck: The New Antisemitism in Europe* (Chicago: Ivan R. Dee, 2004), 62.
6. Quoted in Kahn-Harris and Gidley 2010, 138.
7. Ibid.
8. A Forster and B R Epstein, *The New Antisemitism* (San Francisco: McGraw-Hill, 1974).
9. *Theology Today*, *Sage Journals*, vol. 31, issue 4, 373–377.
10. Asaf Turgeman and Gal Hadari, '"Arab antisemitism debate": the birth of new antisemitism in public and academic discourse in Israel', *Journal of Modern Jewish Studies*, vol. 14, no. 3, November 2015, 502.
11. Turgeman and Hadari, 2015, 512.
12. Ibid.
13. Ibid., 511.
14. Ibid., 515. Emphasis added.
15. See Lapid, 2021.
16. Brian Klug, 'The collective Jew: Israel and the new antisemitism', *Patterns of Prejudice*, vol. 37, no. 2, June 2003 (London: Routledge).

17. For a fuller exposition of this Zionist argument see Julius Gould, 'Impugning Israel's legitimacy: anti-Zionism and antisemitism', jn William Frankel ed., *Survey of Jewish Affairs 1985* (Cranbury, NJ: Associated University Presses, 1985), 197–213.

18. https://en.wikipedia.org/wiki/Institute_for_Jewish_Policy_Research

19. www.worldjewishcongress.org/en/about

20. The paper is in the possession of the author.

21. Moshe Davis, ed., *Zionism in Transition* (New York: Arno Press, 1980).

22. See www.americanrhetoric.com/speeches/danielpatrickmoynihanun3379.htm

23. Ibid., xi.

24. Ibid., xiv.

25. Ibid., 100.

26. Ibid., 109.

27. Ibid., 338.

28. Ibid., 344.

29. Ibid., 256.

30. Ibid., 259.

31. Ibid., 313.

32. Amir Oren 'With Ariel Sharon gone, Israel reveals the truth About the 1982 Lebanon War', *Haaretz*, 17 September 2017, www.haaretz.com/israel-news/with-sharon-gone-israel-reveals-the-truth-about-the-lebanon-war-1.5451086

33. See, for example, Fergal Keane, 'Sabra and Shatila: dealing with facts', *Panorama* (n.d.), http://news.bbc.co.uk/1/hi/programmes/panorama/1390979.stm

34. London: Weidenfeld and Nicolson, 1981.

35. Ibid., 75.

36. Paper in the personal possession of the author.

37. Robert Wistrich, *Anti-Zionism and Antisemitism in the Contemporary* World (London: Macmillan in association with the IJA, 1990). In Keith Kahn-Harris and Ben Gidley, *Turbulent Times: The British Jewish Community Today* (London: Continuum, 2010), the authors refer to the book, describing it rather generously as 'the first sustained analysis of what was coming to be called the "new antisemitism"', 139. Full disclosure: I worked very closely with Wistrich and edited most of the volume.

38. Yehuda Bauer, 'Antisemitism in 1983—two evaluations: ii A real threat?' in William Frankel, ed., *Survey of Jewish Affairs 1983* (New Jersey: Associated University Presses, 1985), 214.

39. Kahn-Harris and Gidley 2010, 31.

40. Frankel 1983, 223–224.

41. *Ein Wort über unser Judenthum* (A Word about Our Jews), January 1880.

42. 'Antisemitism in 1983—two evaluations. (i) The centrality of Israel' in William Frankel, ed., *Survey of Jewish Affairs 1983* (New Jersey: Associated University Presses, 1985), 210.

43. Frankel, 1985, 213.

44. Yehuda Bauer, ed., *Present-Day Antisemitism: Proceedings of the Eighth International Seminar of the Study Circle on World Jewry under the auspices of the President of Israel, Chaim Herzog, Jerusalem, 29–31 December 1985* (Jerusalem: Vidal Sassoon International Center for the Study of Antisemitism, 1988), ix.

45. Ibid., 5.

46. Ibid., 341.

47. Ibid., 44.
48. Ibid., 176.
49. Ibid., 178.
50. Ibid., 33–34.
51. Ibid., 168.
52. Ibid., 129.
53. Ibid., 60.
54. Ibid., 65–66.
55. Bernard Lewis, 'The new antisemitism', *New York Review of Books*, 10 April 1986, www.nybooks.com/articles/1986/04/10/the-new-antisemitism/
56. Bauer, 1998, 329.
57. Ibid., 330.
58. Ibid., 331.

4. 'New Antisemitism': Competing Narratives and the Consequences of Politicisation

1. Wistrich, 1990, 3.
2. Ibid., 6.
3. Ibid., 81.
4. Ibid., 87–88.
5. Ibid., 206.
6. Ibid., 207.
7. Volume 25, no. 2, 3–78. Full disclosure: I was editor of the journal at the time and contributed to the symposium.
8. Ibid., 23.
9. Ibid., 15.
10. Ibid., 26.
11. Ibid., 39.
12. Ibid., 40–41.
13. Ibid., 62.
14. Ibid., 76–77.
15. Ibid., 77.
16. Ibid., 78.
17. Ibid., 47–48.
18. Ibid., 44.
19. Shmuel Almog, 'Between Zionism and antisemitism', *Patterns of Prejudice*, vol. 28, no. 2, 1994, 59.
20. Yehuda Bauer, 'Antisemitism as a European and world problem', *Patterns of Prejudice*, vol. 27, no. 1, 1993, 23.
21. Jewish Telegraphic Agency, https://www.jta.org/1992/07/08/archive/jesse-jackson-urges-reconciliation-in-speech-to-antisemitism-conference. See also MS 241/7/157 IJA 10, Anglo-Jewish Archives, Parkes Collections, Hartley Library, Southampton University.
22. David E. Lowe, *Touched With Fire: Morris B. Abram and the Battle Against Racial and Religious Discrimination* (Nebraska: University of Nebraska Press, 2019). I was there, and recall that the large lecture theatre where the event was held was full.

23. Irwin Cotler, 'Jewish NGOs and religious human rights: a case study' in J. Witte and J. D. Van der Vyver eds., *Religious Human Rights in Global Perspective: Religious Perspectives* (The Hagjue: Martinus Nijhoff Publishers/Kluwer Law International, 1996), 235–294.

24. Ibid., 285–286.

25. Ibid., 286–287.

26. Ibid., 287–288.

27. Bauer, 1988, 43.

28. Cotler in Witte and Van der Vyver, 286.

29. Arthur Herzberg, 'Is antisemitism dying out?', *New York Review of Books*, 24 June 1993, 51–57.

30. Ibid., 57.

31. Ibid., 54.

32. Ibid., 56.

33. Ibid., 52.

34. Ibid., 56.

35. Ibid., 57.

36. 'The meaning of antisemitism', *Jewish Quarterly*, vol. 38, no. 1, 1991, 33–44.

37. Raymond Kalman, 'The meaning of antisemitism', 1991, 38–39.

38. Robert Wistrich, 'Antisemitism in Europe since the Holocaust' in *Working Papers on Contemporary Antisemitism* (New York: American Jewish Committee, 1993), 21.

39. Statement at the hearing 'Global dimensions of antisemitism' before the House of Representatives Sub-committee on International Security, International Organizations, and Human Rights: Committee on Foreign Affairs, 103rd Congress, 2nd session, 8 February 1994, published as 'Antisemitism is an international problem' in Laura K. Egendorf, *Antisemitism* (San Diego: Greenhaven Press, 1999), 11.

40. Daniel Pipes, 'The new antisemitism', in proceedings of the Brussels conference, www.danielpipes.org/226/the-new-antisemitism

41. Jerome Chanes, ed., *Antisemitism in America Today:Outspoken Experts Explode the Myths* (New York: Birch Lane Press, 1995), 23.

42. Daniel Pipes, 'The new antisemitism', *Jewish Exponent*, 16 October 1997, www.danielpipes.org/article/288

43. Jonathan Sacks, 'From integration to survival to continuity: the third great era of modern Jewry' in Jonathan Webber, ed., *Jewish Identities in the New Europe* (London: Littman Library of Jewish Civilization, 1994), 110.

44. Diana Pinto, 'The new Jewish Europe: challenges and responsibilities', 3–15, *European Judaism*, vol. 31, no. 2, European Jewry Between Past and Future, Autumn 1998, 3 and 6.

45. Franklin Foer, 'In the circles of influence', 29 December 1996, www.washingtonpost.com/wp-srv/style/longterm/books/chap1/jewishpower.htm

46. 'Crise au Proche Orient: un nouvel antisémitisme', *La Croix*, 20 October 2000, cited in Timothy Peace, 'Un antisémitisme nouveau? The debate about a "new antisemitism" in France', *Patterns of Prejudice*, vol. 43, no. 2, 2009, 110.

47. Brian Klug, 'Interrogating "new antisemitism"', *Ethnic and Racial Studies*, November 2012, 1.

48. Kahn-Harris and Gidley 2010, 136–162.

5. The Development of Institutions Combatting Antisemitism
1970s–2000

1. Antony Lerman, 'Sense on antisemitism', *Prospect*, August 2002, 34.
2. www.ngo-monitor.org/reports/ngo_forum_at_durban_conference_/
3. Michael Whine, 'International organizations: combating antisemitism in Europe', *Jewish Political Studies Review*, vol. 16, nos. 3–4, Autumn 2004, www.jcpa.org
4. See Larissa Allwork, *Holocaust Remembrance Between the National and Transnational* (London: Bloomsbury Academic, 2015). One of the questions Allwork asks is: 'How far did the legacies of the SIF [Stockholm International Forum on the Holocaust] 2000 encourage, in the words of the Stockholm Declaration, the contemporary prevention of "genocide, ethnic cleansing, racism, antisemitism and xenophobia"?'
5. https://powerbase.info/index.php/British-Israel_Public_Affairs_Committee
6. Notes of the meeting in the possession of the author.
7. Shai ben Ari, 'The housewives who took on the USSR to help Soviet Jewry', 3 November 2019, https://blog.nli.org.il/en/the-35s/
8. Flooh Perlot, 'Waldheim Affair: Austrian political controversy', *Britannica*, www.britannica.com/event/Waldheim-Affair
9. David Weinberg, 'Politics of antisemitism', *Jerusalem Post*, 16 November 1997.
10. Yossi Shain and Barry Bristman, 'Diaspora, kinship and loyalty: the renewal of Jewish national security', *International Affairs*, vol. 78, no. 1, 2002, 78.
11. Cited in Giora Goldberg, 'Ben-Gurion and Jewish foreign policy', *Jewish Political Studies Review*, vol. 3, nos. 1–2, Spring 1991, 92, quoted in Shain and Bristman 2002, 79.
12. Gili Cohen, 'Argentine-Israelis urge Israel to disclose past junta ties', 21 March 2016 (updated 10 April 2018), www.haaretz.com/jewish/argentine-israelis-disclose-jerusalems-junta-ties-1.5419863
13. See Yitzchak Mualem. 'Between a Jewish and an Israeli foreign policy: Israel-Argentina relations and the issue of Jewish disappeared persons and detainees under the military junta, 1976–1983'. *Jewish Political Studies Review*, vol. 16, nos. 1–2, 2004, 51–79.
14. See Jane Hunter, *Israeli Foreign Policy* (Boston: South End Press, 1987).
15. Chris Greal, 'Brothers in arms—Israel's secret pact with Pretoria', www.theguardian.com/world/2006/feb/07/southafrica.israel
16. Shain and Bristman, 2001, 71.
17. Dov Waxman and Scott Lasensky, 'Jewish foreign policy: Israel, world Jewry and the defence of Jewish interests', *Journal of Modern Jewish Studies*, 2013, 4. Doi: 10.1080/14725886.2013.796153
18. Weinberg 1997; but see also David Weinberg, 'Israel's role in the struggle against antisemitism', *Jewish News Syndicate* (*JNS*), 19 January 2020, www.jns.org/opinion/israels-role-in-the-struggle-against-antisemitism/
19. Elyakim Rubinstein, 'The Israeli government's role in the struggle against antisemitism', *Justice, journal of the International Association of Jewish Lawyers and Jurists*, no. 6, August 1995, 36.
20. Ibid.
21. Ibid.

22. Jacques Julliard, 'Paris: the bomb in rue Copernic', *Washington Quarterly*, vol. 4, no. 1, 1984, www.tandfonline.com/doi/abs/10.1080/01636608109451506?journalCode=rwaq20

23. Weinberg, 1997.

24. Ibid.

25. Ibid.

26. Shain and Bristman, 2002, 78.

27. Yossi Melman. 'What is the Mossad's role?', *Haaretz*, 6 April 2004.

28. Shain and Bristman, 2002, 88.

29. Ibid., 81.

30. Gabriel Sheffer, 'The elusive question: Jews and Jewry in Israeli foreign policy', *Jerusalem Quarterly*, no. 46, spring 1988, 107, cited in Shain and Bristman, 2002, 81.

31. Shain and Bristman, 2002, 87. The sources they give for this—a reference to Howard M. Sachar's *Israel and Europe: An Appraisal in History* and a discussion Shain had with Yossi Melman on 13 August 2001—provide little in the way of substance to authenticate their judgement.

32. My text from this point on draws on my own experience with the Forum and the Mossad while I was Director of the Institute of Jewish Affairs (1991–1996) and its successor body, which I founded, the Institute for Jewish Policy Research (1996–1999). Some of my recollections are already in the public domain, principally in my book, *The Making and Unmaking of a Zionist: A Personal and Political Journey* (London: Pluto Press, 2012), 98–99; 'Antisemitism redefined: Israel's imagined national narrative of endless external threat' in Jewish Voice for Peace, *On Antisemitism: Solidarity and the Struggle for Justice* (Chicago: Haymarket Books, 2017), 11–13; and see also my blog, www.antonylerman.com

33. Weinberg, 1997.

34. 'The politics of antisemitism', *Jewish Quarterly*, London, vol. 31, nos. 3–4, 1984, 1.

35. 1994: Israel's London Embassy bombed, BBC News, 26 July 1994, http://news.bbc.co.uk/onthisday/hi/dates/stories/july/26/newsid_2499000/2499619.stm

36. https://en.wikipedia.org/wiki/Oslo_Accords

37. Shain and Bristman, 2002, 78.

38. Waxman and Lasesnky, 2013, 3.

39. Beilin outlined his views on this in Yossi Beilin, 'On unity and continuity: a new framework for Jewish life in Israel and the diaspora', *Policy Forum*, Institute of the World Jewish Congress, no. 20, 2000.

40. Stephen Miller, Marlena Schmool and Antony Lerman, 'Social and political attitudes of British Jews: some key findings of the JPR survey', *JPR Report*, no. 1, February 1996, 2.

41. Barry Kosmin, Antony Lerman and Jacqueline Goldberg, 'The attachment of British Jews to Israel', *JPR Report*, no. 5, November 1997.

42. Ibid., 22.

43. Ibid., 21.

44. Ibid., 21–22.

45. Michael Whine, 'At issue: devising unified criteria and methods of monitoring antisemitism', *Jewish Political Studies Review*, vol. 21, no. 1/2, spring 2009), 63.

46. Michael Whine, 'International organizations: combating antisemitism in Europe', *Jewish Political Studies Review*, vol. 16, nos. 3–4, autumn 2004, www.jcpa.org

47. Ibid., 68.

48. Jerome A. Chanes, *A Primer on the American Jewish Community* (New York: American Jewish Committee, January 2000), 24–25.

49. Alan M Dershowitz, *The Vanishing American Jew: In Search of Jewish Identity for the Next Century* (New York: Touchstone, 1997), 12–13.

50. Neil Somers, 'Germans grapple with rule of law as tools of oppression, democracy', *Jewish Telegraphic Agency*, 10 June 1999, www.jta.org/1999/06/10/lifestyle/focus-on-issues-germans-grapple-with-rule-of-law-as-tools-of-oppression-democracy

51. The Runnymede Trust Commission on the Future of Multi-Ethnic Britain, *The Future of Multi-Ethnic Britain: The Parekh Report*, named after the commission's chair, Professor Bhikhu (now Lord) Parekh (London: Profile Books, 2000), 60.

52. Full disclosure: I was a member of the commission.

53. Ibid.

54. Ibid., 60–61.

55. Robert Wistrich, 'Nationalist challenges in the new Europe', *Antisemitism Worldwide 1997/8* (Tel Aviv: The Stephen Roth Institute for the Study of Contemporary Antisemitism and Racism, 1998).

56. Robert Wistrich, 'Is antisemitism dead or just sleeping', *Jewish Chronicle*, 12 November 1999.

6. The Turning Point: 'New Antisemitism' and the New Millennium

1. Dina Porat 'On several definitions of antisemitism', Coordination Forum for Countering Antisemitism, 23 December 2010, https://antisemitism.org.il/en/50971/. This article was written following the publication of Professor Shmuel Almog's book '*The Jewish Viewpoint: Jews in Their Own Eyes and the Eyes of Others, Essays and Researches* (Tel Aviv: Sifriat Hapo'alim Publishing Company, 2002).

2. For the concept of 'transnational racial governance' see Esther Romeyn, '(Anti) "new antisemitism" as a transnational field of racial governance', *Patterns of Prejudice* published online 29 April 2020. Doi: 10.1080/0031322X.2019.1696048

3. See Kahn-Harris and Gidley, 2010, 143–149, *passim*.

4. See Robert Fine, 'Fighting with phantoms: a contribution to the debate on antisemitism in Europe', *Patterns of Prejudice*, vol. 43, no. 5, 2009.

5. Anidjar, 2007, 9; see also Romeyn, 2020.

6. Briefing to the Foreign Press by Deputy Foreign Minister Rabbi Michael Melchior, Durban: UN World Conference Against Racism, Jerusalem, 9 August 2001, https://mfa.gov.il/mfa/pressroom/2001/pages/briefing%20to%20the%20foreign%20press%20by%20dep%20fm%20melchior%20-.aspx

7. Jonathan Sacks, 'Let us pray for a world free of hate', *London Jewish News*, 28 September 2001, 8.

8   Jonathan Sacks, 'The hatred that won't die', *Guardian*, 28 February 2002, www.theguardian.com/world/2002/feb/28/comment

9. Stuart Schoffman, 'Deconstructing Durban', *Jerusalem Report*, 8 October 2001, 36.

10. Peter Beaumont, 'The new antisemitism?', *Observer*, 17 February 2002.

11. Gordon, 2002, 1.

12. Ibid., 16.

13. www.cbsnews.com/news/battling-antisemitism-in-europe/23 April 2002

14. Charles Krauthammer, *Washington Post*, 26 April 2002.

15. Melanie Phillips, 'As a Jew, I have never felt such a sense of foreboding', *Daily Mail*, 6 March 2002.

16. David Goldberg, 'Let's have a sense of proportion', *Guardian*, 26 January 2002, www.theguardian.com/world/2002/jan/26/religion.uk1

17. Eliahu Salpeter, 'The new antisemitism is not so new', *Haaretz*, 12 March 2003.

18. Brian Klug, 'The collective Jew: Israel and the new antisemitism', *Patterns of Prejudice*, vol. 37, no. 2, 2003, 17.

19. Leon Wieseltier, 'Against ethnic panic. Hitler is dead', *New Republic*, 27 May 2002.

20. Anthony Julius, 'Don't panic', *Guardian*, 1 February 2002, www.theguardian.com/uk/2002/feb/01/britishidentity.features11

21. Paul Iganski and Barry Kosmin, *A New Antisemitism? Debating Judeophobia in 21st Century Britain* (London: Profile Books for the Institute for Jewish Policy Research, 2003; full disclosure: my article 'Sense on antisemitism', *Prospect*, August 2002, was reproduced in the book, under the same title, with some small amendments).

22. Iganski and Kosmin, 2003, 8.

23. Ibid., 275.

24. Ibid., 284-5.

25. Ibid., 291.

26. Ibid., 293.

27. Ibid., 296.

28. Weinberg, 2020.

29. About us page, www.antisemitism.org.il/

30. Yossi Melman, 'Mossad steps up its monitoring of global antisemitic violence', *Haaretz*, 22 May 2002, www.haaretz.com/1.5187964

31. Press conference marking the establishment of the International Commission to Combat Antisemitism, 6 January 2002, https://mfa.gov.il/MFA/Foreign Policy/AntiSemitism/Pages/Press%20conference%20marking%20the%20 establishment%20of%20the.aspx

32. CFCA Press Release, 'Israeli government reaction on the growing antisemitism in Europe', 23 March 2003.

33. CFCA Press Release, 'Forum agrees upon definition of "new" antisemitism', 2 February 2004.

34. List from 2 Feb 2004 press release.

35. Information Department, Israel Foreign Ministry, Jerusalem, 'January 27: Israel's national day to combat antisemitism', 22 January 2004.

36. David Weinberg, 'Israel's role in the struggle against antisemitism', Jewish News Syndicate, 19 January 2020, https://davidmweinberg.com/2020/01/19/ israels-role-in-the-struggle-against-antisemitism-2/

37. Editorial, 'Mutual responsibility', *Haaretz*, 22 January 2002.

38. Michael Whine, 'International organizations: combatting antisemitism in Europe', *Jewish Political Studies Review*, vol. 16, nos. 3–4, Fall 2004, 73.

39. Shlomo Shamir, 'Catholic Church equates anti-Zionism with antisemitism', *Haaretz*, 9 July 2004, www.haaretz.com/1.4753221

40. Abe Foxman, 'Blurring the line', *Haaretz*, 4 April 2004, www.haaretz.com/life/books/1.4773075

41. Max Hastings, 'A grotesque choice', *Guardian*, 13 March 2004, www.theguardian.com/world/2004/mar/11/race.pressandpublishing

42. BBC News Online, 'Viewpoints: antisemitism and Europe', http://news.bbc.co.uk/1/hi/world/europe/3234264.stm

43. Martin Jay, 'Ariel Sharon and the rise of the new antisemitism', *Salmagundi*, nos. 137/138, 17, winter-spring, 2003, www.jstor.org/stable/40549457

44. Edward Alexander, 'Blaming the Jews 101', *FrontpageMagazine.com*, 11 November 2003.

7. The Codification of 'New Antisemitism': The EUMC 'Working Definition'

1. Dina Porat, 'Defining antisemitism', in *Antisemitism Worldwide* 2003/2004, Dina Porat and Roni Stauber eds. (Tel Aviv: Stephen Roth Institute, Tel Aviv University, 2005), 5–17.

2. Natan Sharansky, 'Foreword: emerging antisemitic themes', *Jewish Political Studies Review*, Autumn 2004, 5–8, www.jstor.org/stable/25834600

3. CFCA Press Release, 'Forum agrees upon definition of "new" antisemitism', 2 February 2004.

4. David Feldman, Sub-Report commissioned to assist the All-Party Parliamentary Inquiry into Antisemitism, January 2015, https://archive.jpr.org.uk/object-uk176

5. In Dina Porat and Esther Webman, eds., *The Working Definition of Antisemitism—Six Years After: Unedited Proceedings of the 10th Biennial Seminar on Antisemitism* (Tel Aviv: Kantor Center for the Study of Contemporary European Jewry, 2012), https://en-humanities.tau.ac.il/sites/humanities_en.tau.ac.il/files/media_server/0001/unedited.pdf

6. Ken Stern, 'The working definition of antisemitism—a reappraisal' in Porat and Webman, 2012, 2. Also. 'I drafted the definition of antisemitism. Right wing Jews are weaponizing it', *Guardian*, 13 December 2019, www.theguardian.com/commentisfree/2019/dec/13/antisemitism-executive-order-trump-chilling-effect

7. Ibid.

8. Kenneth S. Stern, 'Proposal for a Redefinition of Antisemitism', in *Antisemitism Worldwide. 2003/4* (Tel Aviv: Roth Institute, 2005), pp. 18–25.

9. The Stephen Roth Institute for the Study of Antisemitism and Racism at Tel Aviv University held a conference on '*The Protocols of the Elders of Zion*: The One Hundred Year Myth and Its Impact' from 22–24 October 2004, https://en-humanities.tau.ac.il/roth/events/past

10. EUMC, 2004, 226–241.

11. I supplement the documentary evidence supporting this account with what Baker told me personally when we met in London a year or two after the 'working definition' was published.

12. Stern, 2012, 2.

13. Reuters, 'EU Racism watchdog shelves antisemitism report', *Haaretz*, 2 November 2003, https://www.haaretz.com/1.4767650; Liz Fekete, 'Controversy over EUMC antisemitism report', Institute of Race Relations, 28 November 2003.

14. Stern, 2012, 2–3.

15. Manifestations of Antisemitism in the EU 2002–2003, 3 May 2004, 27,https://fra.europa.eu/en/publication/2010/manifestations-antisemitism-eu-2002-2003

16. The author was initially invited to the EUMC discussion of the draft by the head of a body that worked closely with the EUMC and Jewish organisations, Pascal Charon, director of Centre European Juif d'Information (CEJI). I believe she was given some freedom to invite a few people she thought could contribute to the discussion, but the invitation to me was withdrawn without formal explanation.

17. Dina Porat, 'The international working definition of antisemitism and its detractors', *Israel Journal of Foreign Affairs*, vol. 5, no. 3, 2011, 96.

18. The RAXEN network (Racism and Xenophobia Network) is composed of National Focal Points (NFPs) in each EU member state. Through the RAXEN network the EUMC each year drew (and its successor the FRA still draws) together from the member states a collection of data on the phenomena and manifestations of racism, xenophobia, Islamophobia and antisemitism.

19. Michael Whine, 'Two steps forward, one step back: diplomatic progress in combating antisemitism', *Israel Journal of Foreign Affairs*, vol. 4, no. 3, 2010, 95, www.thecst.org/docs/michaelwhine.pdf

20. Porat, 2011, 93: the definition is only 'one page' if printed in very small type.

21. In January 2021, three of those involved in the process of finalising the working definition penned an 'Open Letter' claiming to put right what they said was Stern's incorrect claim that he was its main author. This was in response to Stern's increasingly open and public campaign against what he called 'misuse of the WD' to chill free speech on Israel-Palestine issues such as BDS, and enshrine its successor, the IHRA WD, in law. The Open Letter from Baker, Berger and Whine was published on the website of Engage, https://engageonline.wordpress.com/2021/01/20/ken-stern-isnt-the-only-author-the-ihra-working-definition-of-antisemitism/

22. Kenneth Stern, 'Proposal for a redefinition of antisemitism', in Dina Porat and Roni Stauber eds, *Antisemitism Worldwide 2003/4* (Tel Aviv: Stephen Roth Institute, Tel Aviv University, 2005), 18–28. Although this reference appears in Dina Porat, 'The struggle over the international working definition of antisemitism' in Mikael Shainkman, ed., *Antisemitism Today and Tomorrow: Global Perspectives on the Many Faces of Contemporary Antisemitism* (Academic Studies Press, 2018), no online version of it seems to exist.

23 Michael Whine, 'Progress in the struggle against antisemitism in Europe', in *Post-Holocaust and Antisemitism*, no. 41, 1 February 2006, http://jcpa.org/phas/phas-041-whine.htm

24. Ibid.

25. There is no verifiable evidence that substantiates this assertion, though the general point that it attracted a great deal of favourable attention is correct, as is the fact that criticism of it was also being voiced.

26. Porat, 2011, 98.

27. Michael Whine, 'Two steps forward, one step back: diplomatic progress in combating antisemitism', *Israel Journal of Foreign Affairs*, vol. 4, no. 3, 2010, 97–99.
28. Ibid.
29. The tree-week offensive by Israel on Gaza from 27 December 2008 to 18 January 2009.
30. Eve Garrard, 'A lesson in logic', Normblog, 27 May 2011, https://normblog. typepad.com/normblog/2011/05/a-lesson-in-logic-by-eve-garrard.html. Credit to Ben White for some of the examples here and below. See his 'Israel lobby uses discredited antisemitism definition to muzzle debate', *Electronic Intifada*, 28 September 2012, https://electronicintifada.net/content/ israel-lobby-uses-discredited-antisemitism-definition-muzzle-debate/11716
31. A working group on 'Combating Antisemitism' at the Israeli government's 2009 Global Forum gathering, chaired by the Community Security Trust's Michael Whine, described the draft definition as 'the European Union's own definition of antisemitism'.
32. Manfred Gerstenfeld, 'Anti-Israelism and antisemitism: common characteristics and motives', *Jewish Political Studies Review*, vol. 19, nos. 1/2, 2007, 91–92.
33. Jonathan Hoffman, 'Is Jeremy Corbyn an antisemite?', 20 September 2016, https://blogs.timesofisrael.com/is-jeremy-corbyn-an-antisemite/
34. Dina Porat, 'What makes an antisemite?', *Haaretz*, 27 January 2007, www. haaretz.com/1.4955384
35. Sarit Catz, 'Harvard to host conference promoting Israel's destruction', CAMERA, 17 February 2012, www.camera.org/article/harvard-to-host-conference-promoting-israel-s-destruction/
36. 'Protestors rebuffed in bid to get pension manager to boycott Israel', *NGO Monitor*, 20 July 2011, www.ngo-monitor.org/in-the-media/protestors_ rebuffed_in_bid_to_get_pension_manager_to_boycott_israel/
37. Cary Nelson and Kenneth Stern pen open letter on campus antisemitism, American Association of University Professors, AAUP Updates, 20 April 2011, www.aaup.org/news/cary-nelson-and-kenneth-stern-pen-open-letter-campus-antisemitism#.Xx_f5FTdvMw
38. Whine, 2010.
39. CST, *Antisemitic Discourse in Britain 2008* (London 2009), 41.
40. Report of the All-Party Parliamentary Inquiry into Antisemitism: Government Response, 29 March 2007, Cm 7059, 3, www.gov.uk/government/publications/ report-of-the-all-party-parliamentary-inquiry-into-antisemitism-government-response
41. EJJP, Correspondence with EUMC 2005 https://jfjfp.com/ejjp-correspondence-with-eumc-2005/
42. Richard Kuper, 'Antisemitism and delegitimisation', *JNews*, 22 February 2011, www.jnews.org.uk/commentary/antisemitism-and-delegitimisation/
43. See White 2012 and 'All-Party Inquiry into Antisemitism: Government Response, One Year On Progress Report' (United Kingdom government, 12 May 2008 [PDF]).
44. Richard Kuper, 'Antisemitism and delegitimisation', *JNews*, 22 February 2011, www.jnews.org.uk/commentary/antisemitism-and-delegitimisation/
45. As told to Brian Klug in correspondence with Ioannis N. Dimitrakopoulos, 16 February 2011.

46. Whine, 2010. See collection of papers presented at a conference at Tel Aviv University's Kantor Center for the Study of Contemporary European Jewry.

47. As noted above, the EUMC did not 'adopt' the 'working definition'.

48. Andrew Baker, testimony given at Combating Antisemitism in The OSCE Region: Taking Stock of the Situation Today. Hearing before The Commission On Security and Cooperation in Europe, One Hundred Twelfth Congress First Session, 2 December 2011.

49. White, 2012.

50. Irwin Cotler, *The New Anti-Jewishness* (Jerusalem: JPPPI, 2002), reprinted 2004.

51. David Sheen, interview, 'Canadian MP Cotler: Calling Israel an Apartheid state can be legitimate free speech', *Haaretz*, 1 July 2011, www.haaretz.com/1.5024562

52. Remarks at the 2011 B'nai B'rith International Policy Conference, 5 December 2011,https://web.archive.org/web/20130112222340/http://www.state.gov/j/drl/rls/rm/2011/178448.htm

53. Kenneth L. Marcus, *Jewish Identity and Civil Rights in America* (Cambridge: Cambridge University Press, 2010).

8. Responding to 'New Antisemitism': A Transnational Field of Racial Governance

1. Yehonatan Tommer and Tzvi Fleischer, 'What's new about the "New Antisemitism"?', interviews with Dina Porat, Robert Wistrich and Yehuda Bauer, 6 May 2007, Canadian Institute for the Study of Antisemitism (CISA), Scholars for Peace in the Middle East (SPME), https://spme.org/boycotts-divestments-sanctions-bds/boycotts-divestments-and-sanctions-bds-news/dina-porat-robert-wistrich-and-yehuda-bauer-hates-revival/3049/

2. Robert Wistrich, 'The new antisemitism', *Standpoint*, 19 November 2008, https://standpointmag.co.uk/issues/october-2008/the-new-antisemitism-october/

3. Obituary, 'Robert S. Wistrich, Scholar of Antisemitism, dies at 70', *New York Times*, 28 May 2015, www.nytimes.com/2015/05/28/world/europe/robert-s-wistrich-scholar-of-antisemitism-dies-at-70.html

4. Tommer and Fleischer, 2007.

5. Dina Porat quoted in https://mondoweiss.net/2018/09/netanyahus-secret-semitism/

6. https://kantorcenter.tau.ac.il/ Current head, Professor Uriya Shavit.

7. Austin Smith, 'Yale's latest gift to antisemitism', *New York Post*, 7 June 2011, https://nypost.com/2011/06/07/yales-latest-gift-to-antisemitism/

8. Editorial, 'Yale project is the victim of a menacing zeitgeist', *Jewish Chronicle*, 24 November 2016, www.thejc.com/comment/analysis/yale-project-is-the-victim-of-a-menacing-zeitgeist-1.23970

9. Antony Lerman, 'Antisemitism research just improved: Yale's "initiative" for studying antisemitism is axed', https://antonylerman.com/2011/06/10/antisemitism-research-just-improved-yale%E2%80%99s-initiative-for-studying-antisemitism-is-axed/

10. Jeremiah Haber, 'Boola! Boola! Yale decides that it's curtains for the Yale Initiative for the Study of Antisemitism', 9 June 2011, www.jeremiahhaber.com/2011/06/boola-boola-yale-decides-that-its.html

11. https://ypsa.yale.edu/
12. A 2020 Forward investigation found that in 2018 ISGAP received 80 per cent of its funding from the Ministry of Strategic Affairs.
13. 4 February 2020, https://isgap.org/flashpoint/officially-sanctioned-hate-at-the-university-of-michigan/
14. Clemens Heni, 'Grass and the Sueddeutsche', *Algemeine.com*, 11 April 2012, www.clemensheni.net/tag/what-must-be-said/
15. https://journals.academicstudiespress.com/index.php/JCA
16. https://networks.h-net.org/h-antisemitism
17. An incomplete and not entirely reliable blogpost by Clemens Heni gives a picture of the range of journals that either wholly or in part focus on contemporary antisemitism, https://blogs.timesofisrael.com/journals-in-research-in-antisemitism/
18. https://www.academicstudiespress.com/journals/jca
19. BICOM, www.bicom.org.uk/about-us/ https://fathomjournal.org/about-us/
20. https://isca.indiana.edu/index.html
21. Alvin H. Rosenfeld, *Progressive Jewish Thought and the New Antisemitism*, New York, American Jewish Committee, December 2006, 9.
22. About the Brandeis Center, https://brandeiscenter.com/about/
23. http://canisa.org/index.html
24. https://bisa.bbk.ac.uk/about/overview/
25. www.tu-berlin.de/fakultaet_i/center_for_research_on_antisemitism/menue/about_us/history_and_organization/parameter/en/maxhilfe/
26. https://engageonline.wordpress.com/
27. Nick Cohen, *New Statesman*, vol. 18, iss. 880, 10 October 2005.
28. https://engageonline.wordpress.com/
29. www.ngo-monitor.org/
30. https://unwatch.org/about-us/mission-history/
31. www.amazon.co.uk/dp/toc/0253040027/ref=dp_toc?_encoding=UTF8&n=266239
32. Michael Galchinsky, 'Jewish non-governmental organizations' in Thomas Cushman, ed., *Routledge Handbook of Human Rights* (pp. 560–569), (New York: Routledge 2011), open access, https://core.ac.uk/reader/214043794, 17–18
33. Jane Jackman, 'Advocating occupation: outsourcing Zionist propaganda in the UK', *eSharp* (University of Glasgow), vol. 1, no. 25, June 2017 (pdf), www.gla.ac.uk/research/az/esharp/issues/25vol1spring2017-riseandfall/
34. See Schleifer and Snapper, 2015.
35. Berlin declaration (pdf), www.osce.org/cio/56259
36. Amiram Barkat, 'Members of the tribe/Who should deal with antisemitism?' *Haaretz*, 16 February 2007, www.haaretz.com/1.4806248
37. Yossi Melman, 'Why the Mossad must remain an intelligence service for all Jews', *Haaretz*, 4 November 2010, www.haaretz.com/1.5134754
38. Barkat, 2007.
39. Whine, *JPSR*, 2004.
40. Weinberg, 'Israel's role in the struggle against antisemitism', *JNS*, 19 January 2020, https://davidmweinberg.com/2020/01/19/israels-role-in-the-struggle-against-antisemitism-2/
41. Barkat, 2007.

42. Neve Gordon, 'The new antisemitism', *London Review of Books*, 4 January 2018, www.lrb.co.uk/the-paper/v40/no1/neve-gordon/the-new-anti-semitism

43. Avner Golov, *The Israeli Community in the United States: A Public Diplomacy Asset for Israel*, The Institute for National Security Studies Memorandum 181, August 2018, 34.

44. Ibid., 34, quoting State Comptroller's Officer, *Annual Report of the State Comptroller 66C* (2016): 866 [in Hebrew].

45. See Ben White, *Cracks in the Wall: Beyond Apartheid in Palestine/Israel* (London: Pluto Press, 2018).

46. Ibid., 34, quoting *Annual Report* 2016, 863.

47. Ibid., 35, quoting *Annual Report* 2016, 862.

48. Noa Landau, 'Mossad involved in anti-Boycott activity, Israeli Minister's Datebooks reveal', *Haaretz*, 12 June 2019, www.haaretz.com/israel-news/. premium-mossad-involved-in-anti-boycottactivity-israeli-minister-s-diaries-reveal-1.7360253

49. This section draws on the comprehensive work of Jane Jackman in her article 'Advocating occupation: outsourcing Zionist propaganda in the UK', *eSharp* Issue 25:1, 'Rise and Fall', www.gla.ac.uk/media/Media_816593_smxx.pdf

50. Golov, 2018, 37–38.

51. Joshua Leifer, 'Israel's one-state reality is sowing chaos in American politics', +972 *Magazine*, 26 August 2019, www.972mag.com/one-state-israel-trump-netanyahu/

52. Ben White, 'Delegitimizing solidarity: Israel smears Palestine advocacy as antisemitic', *Journal of Palestine Studies*, vol. 39, no. 2, Winter 2020, 68–69.

53. Ibid. From here, the account of weaponising antisemitism allegations targeted at BDS and Palestine advocacy groups is drawn from this thoroughly researched article.

54. Stuart Winer, 'Israel Seen as a "Pariah State", Says Top Strategy Official', *Times of Israel*, 7 August 2016, www.timesofisrael.com/israel-seen-as-a-pariah-state-says-top-strategy-official/ quoted in White 2020, 70.

55. These statements were made on 7 August 2018 in a written response the government had filed to the Israeli Supreme Court relating to the petition against the Settlement Regularization Law filed by Adalah—The Legal Center for Arab Minority Rights in Israel, Jerusalem Legal Aid and Human Rights Center (JLAC), and Al Mezan Center for Human Rights (Gaza) on behalf of 17 local Palestinian authorities in the West Bank, www.adalah.org/en/content/view/9585

56. White, 2019, 70.

57. Asa Winstanley, 'Israel running campaign against Jeremy Corbyn', Electronic Intifada, 7 August 2018, https://electronicintifada.net/blogs/asa-winstanley/israel-running-campaign-against-jeremy-corbyn

58. Jeremy Corbyn backs boycott of Israeli universities involved in arms research, www.bdsmovement.net, 2 August 2015 (Electronic Intifada).

59. White, 2020, 65.

60. Ibid.

61. Joseph Nasr, Riham Alkousaa, 'Germany designates BDS Israel boycott movement as anti-Semitic', *Reuters*, 17 May 2019, www.reuters.com/article/us-germany-bds-israel-idUSKCN1SN204

62. https://www.timesofisrael.com/czech-lawmakers-pass-resolution-condemning-bds-movement/

63. Stav Shafir, 'Israel's Ministry of Strategic Failure', *Haaretz*, 22 July 2021, www.haaretz.com/opinion/.premium-israel-s-ministry-of-strategic-failure-1.10021187

64. Lahav Harkov, 'Flawed, unfairly maligned Strategic Affairs Ministry shutters – analysis', *JPost*, 19 July 2021, www.jpost.com/israel-news/flawed-unfairly-maligned-strategic-affairs-ministry-shutters-analysis-674326

9. The Redefinition Project and the Myth of the 'Collective Jew' Exposed

1. Roni Stauber, 'The academic and public debate over the meaning of the "new antisemitism"' in Charles Small ed., *The Yale Papers: Antisemitism in Historical Perspective* (New York: ISGAP, 2015), https://isgap.org/post/2016/01/new-publication-the-yale-papers-antisemitism-in-comparative-perspective/

2. Mark Weitzman, 'The IHRA working definition of antisemitism', in Armin Lange, Kerstin Mayerhofer, Dina Porat and Lawrence H. Schiffman eds., *An End to Antisemitism! Volume 1: Comprehending and Confronting Antisemitism. A Multifaceted Approach* (Berlin: de Gruyter, 2019), 465.

3. In Small, 2015, 431.

4. Ibid.

5. Andrew Baker, 'To fight antisemitism, first define it', Times of Israel blog, 1 December 2016, https://blogs.timesofisrael.com/to-fight-antisemitism-first-define-it/

6. http://www.knessetnow.co.il/%D7%95%D7%A2%D7%93%D7%95%D7%AA/%D7%A4%D7%A8%D7%95%D7%98%D7%95%D7%A7%D7%95%D7%9C/45074/%D7%94%D7%9E%D7%90%D7%91%D7%A7-%D7%91%D7%90%D7%A0%D7%98%D7%99%D7%A9%D7%9E%D7%99%D7%95%D7%AA-%D7%95%D7%91%D7%93%D7%94-%D7%9C%D7%92%D7%99%D7%98%D7%99%D7%9E%D7%A6%D7%99%D7%94-%D7%A9%D7%9C-%D7%9E%D7%93%D7%99%D7%A0%D7%AA-%D7%99%D7%A9%D7%A8%D7%90%D7%9C

7. www.holocaustremembrance.com/about-us

8. www.holocaustremembrance.com/news-archive/statement-experts-uk-delegation-ihra-working-definition-antisemitism. See also Dina Porat, 'What makes an antisemite?', *Haaretz*, 27 January 2007, www.haaretz.com/1.4955384

9. AWR 1994 (London: Institute of Jewish Affairs), xxxv, and also xvi–xvii.

10. Brian Klug, 'Interrogating "new antisemitism"', *Ethnic and Racial Studies*, vol. 36, no. 3, 2013, 8. Doi: 10.1080/01419870.2013.734385.

11. Ibid., 13.

12. See: EUMC, *Manifestations of Antisemitism in the EU 2002-2003* (2004) https://fra.europa.eu/sites/default/files/fra_uploads/184-AS-Main-report.pdf

13. *AHR*, 2018, 1124. It is highly significant, however, that the ICRAR consortium responsible for the AHR round-table on re-thinking antisemitism firmly rejects the eternalist approach to the subject.

14. Ibid.

15. See Robert Wistrich, *The Longest Hatred* (London: Pantheon Books, 1992).

16. See the Review by the Runnymede Commission on Antisemitism, *A Very Light Sleeper: The Persistence and Dangers of Antisemitism* (Runnymede Trust, London, January 1994).

17. Robert Wistrich, *A Lethal Obsession: Antisemitism from Antiquity to the Global Jihad* (New York: Random House, 2010).

18. See 'Antisemitism today', *Patterns of Prejudice*, vol. 16, no. 4, 1982, 3, www.tandfonline.com/doi/abs/10.1080/0031322X.1982.9969684

19. See 'Antisemitism in the 1990s', *Patterns of Prejudice*, vol. 25, no. 2, 1991, 3, www.tandfonline.com/doi/abs/10.1080/0031322X.1991.9970073

20. Phyllis Chesler, *The New Antisemitism: The Current Crisis and What We Must Do About It* (San Francisco: Jossey-Bass, 2003).

21. Pierre-André Taguieff, *La nouvelle judéophobie* (Paris: 1001 Nuits, 2002).

22. David Matz, 'Trying to understand the Taba talks', *Palestine-Israel Journal*, vol. 10, no. 3, 2003, www.pij.org/articles/32/trying-to-understand-the-taba-talks

23. See Jamie Stern-Weiner, 'The Politics of a Definition: How the IHRA Working Definition of Antisemitism Was Manufactured, Misused and Misrepresented' April 2021, https://freespeechonisrael.org.uk/ihra-politics

24. Antony Lerman, 'Sense on antisemitism', *Prospect*, August 2002, 34–38.

25. Ibid., 34–35.

26. Pre-amble to lecture delivered by Chief Rabbi Dr Jonathan Sacks to the Parliamentary Committee Against Antisemitism, January 2002, quoted in Written Evidence, Memorandum submitted by the Parliamentary Committee Against Antisemitism to the Select Committee on Home Affairs September 2004, https://publications.parliament.uk/pa/cm200405/cmselect/cmhaff/165/165we32.htm

27. Ibid., 36.

28. Ibid.

29. www.judiciary.uk/wp-content/uploads/JCO/Documents/Judgments/eemployment-trib-fraser-v-uni-college-union-judgment.pdf

30. See Wikipedia entry for category mistake, https://en.wikipedia.org/wiki/Category_mistake

31. Weber, 'Politics as a Vocation', 1919.

32. Locke, *Second Treatise on Government* (1690).

33. David Biale ed., *Cultures of the Jews* (New York: Schocken Books, 2002).

34. Shlomo Fischer, 'Israelis are divided over whether they are "Jewish" or "Israeli"', *Forward*, 25 October 2018, https://forward.com/opinion/412732/israelis-are-conflicted-about-whether-they-are-jewish-or-israeli-heres/

35. Thanks to JS-W for this insight.

36. Martin Buber, 'Nationalism' (1921), in *Israel and the world: Essays in a Time of Crisis* (New York: Schocken Books, 1963), 219.

37. Abraham Joshua Heschel, *Israel: Echo of Eternity* (New York: Jewish Lights Publishing, 1969).

38. Natasha Roth-Rowland, 'The danger of false accusations of antisemitism', *+972 Magazine*, 7 January 2022, www.972mag.com/edition/emma-watson-antisemitism-danon/

39. Brian Klug, 'The myth of the new antisemitism', *Nation*, 15 January 2004.

40. *AHR*, 2018, 1134.

41. Ibid., 1135.

42. *Left in Dark Times: A Stand Against the New Barbarism* (New York: Random House, 2010), 147–166.

43. See Ivan Kalmar, 'Islamophobia and antisemitism: the case of Hungary and the "Soros Plot"', *Patterns of Prejudice*, vol. 54, nos. 1–2, 2020.
44. https://jerusalemdeclaration.org/
45. www.holocaustremembrance.com/news-archive/statement-experts-uk-delegation-ihra-working-definition-antisemitism
46. Campaign Against Antisemitism, https://antisemitism.org/definition/

10. Human Rights: The 'Mask Under Which the Teaching of Antisemitic Contempt for Israel is Carried Out'

1. Michael Galchinsky, 'Jewish non-governmental organizations' in Thomas Cushman, ed., *Routledge Handbook of Human Rights* (New York: Routledge, 2011), 560–569.
2. Irwin Cotler, 'Jewish NGOs and religious human rights: a case study' in van der Vyver and Witte, 1996, 287.
3. Ibid., 287–288.
4. Michael Galchinsky, *Jews and Human Rights: Dancing at Three Weddings* (Lanham, MD: Rowman & Littlefield, 2008), 119–120.
5. Ibid., 121–122.
6. Diana Pinto, 'The new Jewish Europe: challenges and responsibilities', European Jewry between past and future, *European Judaism*, vol. 31, no. 2, Autumn 1998, 11–12.
7. https://publications.parliament.uk/pa/cm200405/cmselect/cmhaff/165/165we32.htm
8. Elie Wiesel, *A Jew Today* (New York: Random House, 1978).
9. Josh Kaplan, 'Contesting antisemitism: human rights, Israel-bashing and the making of a non-problem', *Anthropological Quarterly*, vol. 83, no. 2, 2010, 437.
10. Gould, 2020, 7.
11. David M. Weinberg, 'Israel has a role in fighting antisemitism', *JNS*, 4 November 2018, www.jns.org/opinion/israel-has-role-in-fighting-antisemitism/
12. Elan S. Carr, MFA Press Release, 25 September 2019, cited by Ben White, 'Delegitimizing solidarity: Israel smears Palestine advocacy as antisemitic', *Journal of Palestine Studies*, vol. 49, no. 2, Winter 2020, 65.
13. Kaplan, 2010, 437.
14. Ibid.
15. Ibid., 445.
16. Ibid., 435.
17. Galchinsky, 2008, 167–171.
18. See Victoria Clark, *Allies for Armageddon: The Rise of Christian Zionism* (New Haven and London: Yale University Press, 2007).
19. See 'Pompeo accused of appeasing Christian Zionists with speech from occupied Jerusalem', MEMO, 26, August 2020, www.middleeastmonitor.com/20200826-pompeo-accused-of-appeasing-christian-zionists-with-speech-from-occupied-jerusalem/
20. See Paul Rogers, 'Trump, Pence and Jerusalem: the Christian Zionism connection', openDemocracy, December 2017, www.opendemocracy.net/en/trump-pence-jerusalem-christian-zionism-connection/

21. See e.g. ISCR Team, *The New Philosemitism: Exploring a Changing Relationship Between Jews and the Far Right*, Department of War Studies, Kings College University of London, 2020, https://icsr.info/2020/11/10/the-new-philosemitism-exploring-a-changing-relationship-between-jews-and-the-far-right/

22. Eric H. Yoffie, 'What on earth is the problem with a Jewish majority in Israel', *Haaretz*, 18 July 2021, www.haaretz.com/israel-news/.premium-what-on-earth-is-the-problem-with-a-jewish-majority-in-israel-1.10009667

23. Neil Levi and Michael Rothberg, Guest Editors' introduction: 'Trump and the "Jewish question"', *Studies in American Jewish Literature*, special issue, vol. 31, no. 1, 2020, 4–16.

24. Michael Rothberg and Bryan Cheyette, 'Lernen aus der Geschichte: relational thinking: a dialogue on the theory and politics of research on antisemitism and racism, Im gesprach', http://lernen-aus-der-geschichte.de/Lernen-und-Lehren/content/14651

25. Ibid.

26. See the judgment of the Employment Tribunal in the case brought by Ronnie Fraser against the Universities and Colleges Union and the demands of Jewish groups such as the CAA that the EHRC declare the Labour Party institutionally antisemitic under the terms of the 2010 Equality Act.

27. See the report at https://assets.publishing.service.gov.uk/government/uploads/system/uploads/attachment_data/file/277111/4262.pdf and Antony Lerman https://www.opendemocracy.net/en/racism-or-racist-incident-whats-difference-ucu-and-eumc-working-definition-of-antise/

28. www.timesofisrael.com/netanyahu-an-icc-investigation-of-israel-would-be-pure-antisemitism/

29. apnews.com/article/israel-west-bank-palestinian-territories-courts-crime-19117d4265f5d564256ea7fe75854aa6

30. Yoffie, 2021.

31. See Bernard Avishai and Sam Bahour, 'Want Israeli-Palestinian peace? Try confederation', *New York Times*, 12 February 2021, www.nytimes.com/2021/02/12/opinion/israel-palestinian-confederation.html

32. Yair Lapid, 'Is antisemitism racism?', *Haaretz*, 26 July 2021, www.haaretz.com/opinion/.premium.HIGHLIGHT-is-antisemitism-racism-1.10033287

33. https://en.wikipedia.org/wiki/Alexandrian_riots_(38)#:~:text=The%20Alexandrian%20pogrom%2C%20or%20Alexandrian,of%20Egypt%2C%20Aulus%20Avilius%20Flaccus.

34. Galchinsky, 2010, 14.

35. See Haim Cohn, *Human Rights in Jewish Law* (New York: Ktav Publishing House, 1984).

36. Antony Lerman, 'What can religion offer politics?' *Guardian*, 26 June 2009, www.theguardian.com/commentisfree/2009/jun/26/religion-politics-britain-public

37. Quoted in a blogpost by Eliott Abrans, www.cfr.org/blog/understanding-human-rights-assaults-israel

38. Galchinsky, 2010, 170–171.

39. Galchinsky, 2008, 10.

40. Jonathan Neumann, *To Heal the World? How the Jewish Left Corrupts Judaism and Endangers Israel* (London: St Martin's Press, 2018).

41. Sutcliffe, 2020, 278–279.

11. Geopolitics, Israel and the Authentication of 'New Antisemitism'

1. Yehuda Bauer, 'Antisemitism and anti-Zionism—new and old' in Wistrich, 1990, 204.
2. Seymour M. Finger and Ziva Flamhaft, 'The issue of "Zionism and racism" in the United Nations', *Middle East Review*, vol. 18, no. 3, Spring 1986, 55–58.
3. See Chapter 16.
4. Natan Sachs and Kevin Huggard, 'Israel in the Middle East: the next two decades', November 2020, Center for Middle East Policy, Brookings.
5. Marta Gonzalez, *Atalayar*, 28 October 2020, https://atalayar.com/en/blog/israel-and-geopolitics-middle-east
6. Elie Podeh, 'Secret histories: Israel's road to normalization', *Jewish Quarterly*, August 2021, 58.
7. Ibid., 58–59.
8. White, 2020, 71.
9. Lapid, 'Is antisemitism racism?' *Haaretz*, 26 July 2021, www.haaretz.com/opinion/.premium.HIGHLIGHT-is-antisemitism-racism-1.10033287
10. Yakov M. Rabkin, *What Is Modern Israel?* (London: Pluto Press, 2016), 175.
11. Ibid., 178.
12. See, for example, Ben Weinberg, 'The rise of neo-conservative think tanks in Israel: the brief history of a peculiar context', *Public Seminar*, 29 October 2018, https://publicseminar.org/2018/10/the-rise-of-neo-conservative-think-tanks-in-israel/
13. Podeh, 2021, 59.
14. Yakir Adelman, 'Yitzhak Rabin never wanted Palestinian statehood', *+972 magazine*, 27 October 2015, www.972mag.com/yitzhak-rabin-never-supported-palestinian-statehood/
15. See Francis Fukuyama, *The End of History and the Last Man* (London: Free Press 1992).
16. Kim Ghattas, *Black Wave: Saudi Arabia, Iran and the Rivalry that Unravelled the Middle East* (London: Wildfire, Headline Publishing Group, 2020), 332.
17. Rabkin, 2016, 173.
18. Ibid., 174.
19. It further revokes Arabic as an official language, though 'its speakers have the right to language-accessible state services. See Jonathan Lis, 'Israeli lawmakers back contentious Jewish nation-state Bill in heated preliminary vote', *Haaretz*, 10 May 2017, www.haaretz.com/israel-news/knesset-backs-contentious-nation-state-bill-in-preliminary-vote-1.5470464
20. Ronit Lentin, 'Race and surveillance in the settler colony: the case of Israeli rule over Palestine'. *Palgrave Communications*, 3: 17056 Doi: 10.1057/palcomms.2017.56.
21. Efraim Davidi, 'Neo-colonialism—a Palestinian nightmare', MR, 23 October 2005, https://mronline.org/2005/10/23/neo-colonialism-a-palestinian-nightmare/
22. https://globalsocialtheory.org/topics/racial-neoliberalism/?utm_source=rss&utm_medium=rss&utm_campaign=racial-neoliberalism
23. Gonzalez, 2020.
24. Louis Fishman, 'Netanyahu Is leading Israel into civil war between Jews and Palestinians', *Haaretz*, 12 May 2021, www.haaretz.com/israel-news/.premium.

HIGHLIGHT-netanyahu-is-leading-israel-into-civil-war-between-jews-and-palestinians-1.9797672?lts=1629495687220

25. B'Tselem, *A regime of Jewish supremacy from the Jordan River to the Mediterranean Sea: This is Apartheid*, 12 January 2021, www.btselem.org/publications/fulltext/202101_this_is_apartheid

26. Human Rights Watch, *A Threshold Crossed: Israeli Authorities and the Crimes of Apartheid and Persecution*, 27 April 2021, www.hrw.org/report/2021/04/27/threshold-crossed/israeli-authorities-and-crimes-apartheid-and-persecution

27. Amnesty International, *Israel's Apartheid Against Palestinians: A Cruel System of Domination and a Crime Against Humanity*, 1 February 2022, www.amnesty.org/en/latest/news/2022/02/israels-apartheid-against-palestinians-a-cruel-system-of-domination-and-a-crime-against-humanity/

28. Orly Noy, 'Israelis mustn't fear Amnesty's apartheid report', +972 *Magazine*, www.972mag.com/edition/israel-apartheid-report/

29. Itamar Eichner, 'Israel to allocate NIS 100 million for BDS battle', Ynetnews.com, 6 July 2015, www.ynetnews.com/Ext/Comp/ArticleLayout/CdaArticlePrintPreview/0,2506,L-4665676,00.html

30. Jonathan Lis, 'Israeli bill would cut funds to universities with lecturers backing boycott', *Haaretz* 24 April 2018, www.haaretz.com/israel-news/.premium-bill-would-cut-funds-to-universities-with-lecturers-backing-boycott-1.5493726

31. Peter Beinart, 'Israel's lunatic response to Ben and Jerry's', 26 July 2021, https://peterbeinart.substack.com/p/israels-lunatic-response-to-ben-and?token=eyJ1c2VyX2lkIjoyMjcyODQwNCwicG9zdF9pZCI6MzkyMTUxMTIsIl8iOiJKRVddJTCIsImlhdCI6MTYyNzMzMDI3NiwiZXhwIjoxNjI3MzMzODc2LCJpc3MiOiJwdWItMTA1MjYwIiwic3ViIjoicG9zdC1yZWFjdGlvbiJ9.Ifk3cMRqRk6hgWKryUlGool65eWMktDjk9YNAVAJ7XQ

32. Michael J. Koplow, 'Samson the weakling', 17 May 2018, https://israelpolicyforum.org/2018/05/17/samson-the-weakling/

33. Klug, 2003, 17.

34. Dov Waxman and Scott Lasensky, 'Jewish foreign policy: Israel, world Jewry and the defence of "Jewish interests"', *Journal of Modern Jewish Studies*, 6 August 2013. See also Michael Galchinsky, 'Is there a global Jewish politics?' *JPR /Policy Debate*, Institute for Jewish Policy Research, January 2009.

35. Avraham Burg, 'Israel is the nation-state of the Israelis', *Haaretz*, 2 August 2018.

36. Jan-Werner Muller, 'Populism and the people', *London Review of Books*, 23 May 2019, www.lrb.co.uk/the-paper/v41/n10/jan-werner-mueller/populism-and-the-people

37. Alain Badiou, Eric Hazan and Ivan Segre, *Reflections on Antisemitism* (London: Verso Books, 2013).

12. 'War' Discourse and its Limitations

1. Elyakim Rubinstein, 'Al ha-antishemiyut: Mekomah ve-tafkidah shel Yisrael ba-milharnah baantishemiyut' (On antisemitism: Israel's place and role in the war on antisemitism), *Massuah* 31 (2003): 55–66.

2. Anidjar, 2007, 8.

3. Efraim Ganor, 'The war against antisemitism must be conducted on social media', *Jerusalem Post*, 4 March 2019, www.jpost.com/opinion/the-war-against-antisemitism-must-be-conducted-on-social-media-582351

4. Yedidia Z. Stern, 'The voice of our brothers' blood', Israel Democracy Institute, 31 August 2017, https://en.idi.org.il/articles/18657 (accessed 31 August 2020).

5. Gilad Katz, 'A war against antisemitism in America', *Jewish Herald Voice* (Greater Houston), 8 November 2018, https://jhvonline.com/a-war-against-antisemitism-in-america-p25151-159.htm

6. Noa Landau, 'How Israel is harming the war on antisemitism', *Haaretz*, 18 January 2021, www.haaretz.com/opinion/.premium-how-israel-is-harming-the-war-on-antisemitism-1.9459655

7. Cnaan Lipshitz, 'As hate surges, "prominent European Jews worry war against antisemitism is lost"', www.timesofisrael.com/as-hate-surges-prominent-european-jews-worry-war-against-antisemitism-is-lost/

8. Anidjar, 2007, 2.

9. Ibid., 5.

10. Ibid.

11. Gil Anidjar, 'Antisemitism and its critics' in James Renton and Ben Gidley, eds., *Antisemitism and Islamophobia in Europe: A Shared Story?* (London: Palgrave Macmillan, 2017), 191.

12. Ibid., 191.

13. Ibid., 194.

14. Ibid., 198.

15. Ibid., 199–200.

16. See for example Gilles Andreani, 'The "War on terror": good cause, wrong concept', *Survival: Global Politics and Strategy*, vol 46, no. 4, 2004 and Nick Schou, 'America's war on drugs was designed to fail. So why is it being revived now?' history.com, 31 August 2018, www.history.com/news/americas-war-on-drugs-was-designed-to-fail-so-why-is-it-being-revived-now

17. George Monbiot, www.monbiot.com/2003/03/11/a-wilful-blindness/

18. Lieutenant Colonel Judson P. Nelson Jr United States Army, 'The oddity of waging war on a tactic: reframing the global war on terror as a global counterinsurgency' (School of Advanced Military Studies, United States Army Command and General Staff College Fort Leavenworth, Kansas, 2009).

19. David C. Gompert and John Gordon, *War by Other Means: Building Complete and Balanced Capabilities for Counterinsurgency* (Santa Monica, CA: National Defense Research Institute, RAND Corp, 2008), 6.

20. https://georgewbush-whitehouse.archives.gov/infocus/bushrecord/documents/Selected_Speeches_George_W_Bush.pdf

21. Anidjar, 2007, 4.

22. Ibid.

23. www.britannica.com/topic/social-movement

24. See Haim Bresheeth, 'The Israel lobby, islamophobia and judeophobia in contemporary Europe and beyond: myths and realities', *Journal of Holy Land and Palestine Studies*, vol. 17, no. 2, 2018.

25. David M. Weinberg, 'Israel's role in the struggle against antisemitism', https://davidmweinberg.com/2020/01/19/israels-role-in-the-struggle-against-antisemitism-2/

26. Maayan Jaffe-Hoffman, 'Holocaust awareness is essential for our war on antisemitism', *Jerusalem Post*, 28 December 2019, www.jpost.com/israel-news/yad-vashem-educating-on-the-holocaust-fighting-against-antisemitism-612288

27. Ibid.
28. www.jpost.com/diaspora/antisemitism/vaccinating-against-the-virus-of-antisemitism-636253
29. Ibid.
30. Ibid.
31. www.politico.eu/newsletter/brussels-playbook/brussels-playbook-out-of-afghanistan-us-travel-ban-eus-antisemitism-czar/?utm_source=POLITICO. EU&utm_campaign=3de801dac8-EMAIL_CAMPAIGN_2021_08_31_05_04&utm_medium=email&utm_term=0_10959edeb5-3de801dac8-190248089
32. Esther Webman, editor in chief, *Antisemitism Worldwide 2019 and the Beginning of 2020*, Kantor Center for the Study of Contemporary European Jewry, Tel Aviv University 2020, 5–6, https://en-humanities.tau.ac.il/kantor
33. www.ajc.org/Antisemitism-Survey-2019
34. Personal Representative of the OSCE Chairperson-in-Office on Combating Antisemitism, Testimony, Committee on Foreign Affairs, Subcommittee on Europe, Eurasia, Energy and the Environment 'Resisting Antisemitism and Xenophobia in Europe' 29 January 2020, www.ajc.org/news/rabbi-andrew-baker-on-europe-eurasia-energy-and-the-environment-resisting-antisemitism-and
35. www.wiesenthal.com/about/news/top-ten-worst-antisemitic.html
36. https://cst.org.uk/news/blog/2020/02/06/antisemitic-incidents-report-2019
37. Ibid.
38. www.raoulwallenbergcentre.org/en/
39. Janice Arnold, 'Cotler urges Trudeau to name antisemitism envoy', *Canadian Jewish News*, 12 December 2019, https://www.cjnews.com/news/canada/cotler-urges-trudeau-to-name-antisemitism-envoy
40. https://www.jpr.org.uk/publication?id=16933 2
41. Daniel Blatman, 'Maybe, when it comes to antisemitism, no different Germany exists?', *Haaretz*, 3 July 2019, www.haaretz.com/opinion/.premium-maybe-when-it-comes-to-antisemitism-no-different-germany-exists-1.7434793

13. 'Jewish Power', Medical Analogies and 'Eradication' Discourse

1. See David Biale, *Power and Powerlessness in Jewish History* (New York: Schocken Books, 1986).
2. See, e.g. Alison M. Bowes, 'The experiment that did not fail: image and reality in the Israeli kibbutz', *International Journal of Middle East Studies*, vol. 22, no. 1, 1990.
3. Adam Sutcliffe, *What Are Jews For? History, Peoplehood, and Purpose* (Princeton and Oxford: Princeton University Press, 2020), 282–283.
4. Peter Beinart, 'Aipac reflects heroism of Jewish power—and its perils', *Forward*, 28 March 2017.
5. Cody Nelson, 'Minnesota congresswoman ignites debate on Israel and antisemitism', 7 March 2019, www.npr.org
6. The intercept.com
7. Carolina Landsmann, 'Israel is giving Palestinians the Jewish finger'. *Haaretz*, 23 March 2018, www.haaretz.com/opinion/israel-is-giving-palestinians-the-jewish-finger-1.5936932
8. Jonathan Judaken, '10 Commandments for thinking about antisemitism, *Forward*, 5 January 2018.

9. https://forward.com/opinion/387016/expanding-the-definition-of-antisemitism-hurts-jews-testimony-before-the-h/

10. Barry Trachtenberg, 'The New Kherem, or "Barry Trachtenberg does not represent us!": On speaking for and against Jewish self-interests', *Mondoweiss*, 4 May 2020, https://mondoweiss.net/2020/05/the-new-kherem-or-barry-trachtenberg-does-not-represent-us-on-speaking-for-and-against-jewish-self-interests/

11. Michael J. Koplow, 'Samson the weakling', 17 May 2018, https://israelpolicyforum.org/2018/05/17/samson-the-weakling/#

12. Ibid.

13. H/t to JS-W for this insight.

14. Anidjar, 2007, 8.

15. Justin Welby, *Vigilance and Resolution: Living Antidotes to an Ancient Virus* in Holocaust Education Trust and CST, *Lessons Learned? Reflections on Antisemitism and the Holocaust* (London, 2016), 10, https://cst.org.uk/data/file/0/c/Lessons%20Learned.1474879309.pdf

16. www.jta.org/2020/05/26/culture/antisemitism-examined-as-a-social-virus-in-new-pbs-documentary

17. www.jpost.com/diaspora/antisemitism/vaccinating-against-the-virus-of-antisemitism-636253

18. Steven Beller, *Antisemitism: A Very Short Introduction* (Oxford: OUP, 2007) 5–6.

19. https://jewishnews.timesofisrael.com/keir-starmer-interview-i-will-work-to-eradicate-antisemitism-from-day-one/

20. www.thejc.com/comment/columnists/labour-will-never-eradicate-its-antisemitism-until-the-left-acknowledges-racism-elsewhere-1.480754

21. House of Representatives, Subcommittee on Africa, Global Health, Global Human Rights, and International Organizations, Committee on Foreign Affairs, Washington, DC, 27 February 2013, www.govinfo.gov/content/pkg/CHRG-113hhrg79580/html/CHRG-113hhrg79580.htm

22. Conference Proceedings published, 1 November 2021, https://anendto antisemitism.univie.ac.at/home-news/news/news/conference-proceedings-published/?tx_news_pi1%5Bcontroller%5D=News&tx_news_pi1%5Baction%5D=detail&cHash=fc901a9c90c9be719b3ccc491f4cebe0

23. Press Release on release of conference proceedings, https://anendtoantisemitism.univie.ac.at/fileadmin/user_upload/p_anendtoantisemitism/PDF/Release2021_Pressrelease.pdf

24. https://onlinelibrary.wiley.com/doi/epdf/10.1111/1467-923X.12854

14. Apocalypticism: Defining the Discourse, Writing the Headlines and Generating Moral Panics

1. Full disclosure: I was among writers and researchers who engaged critically with his work over this period.

2. Thomas Weber, *Journal of Modern History*, vol. 84, no. 3, 2012, www.journals.uchicago.edu/doi/10.1086/666037

3. www.timesofisrael.com/human-rights-activist-irwin-cotler-named-as-canadas-first-antisemitism-envoy/

4. www.theglobeandmail.com/politics/article-former-justice-minister-irwin-cotler-named-canadas-envoy-for/

5. www.cjnews.com/perspectives/opinions/shinewald-the-diverging-careers-of-irwin-cotler-and-alan-dershowitz

6. https://electronicintifada.net/blogs/nora-barrows-friedman/justin-trudeau-taps-top-israel-lobbyist-police-speech-canada

7. https://blogs.timesofisrael.com/antisemitism-old-and-new/

8. Irwin Cotler, *Human Rights and the New Anti-Jewishness*, JPPI, November 2002, http://jppi.org.il/uploads/Alert%201%20New%20Anti%20Jewishness.pdf

9. Irwin Cotler, 'Jewish NGOs and religious human rights: a case study'.

10. Ruthie Blum, 'One on one: back to the future', *Jerusalem Post*, 28 February 2007.

11. Robert Wistrich, 'Muslims, Jews and September 11: the British case' in Iganski and Kosmin, 2003, 188–189.

12. Robert Wistrich, 'Nationalist challenges in the new Europe', *Antisemitism Worldwide 1997/8* (Tel Aviv: The Stephen Roth Institute for the Study of Contemporary Antisemitism and Racism, 1998).

13. Robert Wistrich, 'Antisemitism in Europe. Since the Holocaust' in *Working Papers on Contemporary Antisemitism* (New York: American Jewish Committee, 1993), 21.

14. Simcha Epstein, 'The "highest wave of antisemitism since 1945"—is it so?', *SICSA Annual Report 2001* (Jerusalem), 7–8.

15. On 9 November 1938, 91 Jews were killed, more than 30,000 were arrested (1,000 of whom were later murdered) and 191 synagogues were set on fire. No one died in the 2000 upsurge.

16. Marcus, 2015.

17. Ruthie Blum, 'One on one: back to the future', *Jerusalem Post*, 28 February 2007.

18. See for example a debunking of this allegation by Jonathan Cook in relation to its use in the propaganda war over the Israel-Hamas violent confrontation in May 2021.

19. Amnesty International, *Israel's Apartheid Against Palestinians: A Cruel System of Domination and a Crime Against Humanity*, 1 February 2022, www.amnesty.org/en/latest/news/2022/02/israels-apartheid-against-palestinians-a-cruel-system-of-domination-and-a-crime-against-humanity/

20. Human Rights Watch, *A Threshold Crossed: Israeli Authorities and the Crimes of Apartheid and Persecution*, 27 April 2021, www.hrw.org/report/2021/04/27/threshold-crossed/israeli-authorities-and-crimes-apartheid-and-persecution

21. B'Tselem, *A Regime of Jewish Supremacy from the Jordan River to the Mediterranean Sea: This is Apartheid*, 12 January 2021, https://www.btselem.org/publications/fulltext/202101_this_is_apartheid

22. See Leon Festinger, Henry Riecken, Stanley Schachter, *When Prophesy Fails: A Social and Psychological Study of a Modern Group That Predicted the Destruction of the World* (New York: Harper Torch-Books, 1956).

23. Peter Kelly, interviewing Edward Alexander, 'Jewish condition, "new" antisemitism observed in Edward Alexander's "The State of the Jews"', UW News, 14 December 2012, www.washington.edu/news/2012/12/14/jewish-condition-new-antisemitism-observed-in-edward-alexanders-the-state-of-the-jews/

24. www.theguardian.com/politics/2021/sep/06/islamism-remains-first-order-security-threat-to-west-says-tony-blair

25. *Experiences and Perceptions of Antisemitism: Second Survey on Discrimination and Hate Crime Against Jews in the EU*, EU Fundamental Rights Agency, 10 September 2018, https://fra.europa.eu/en/video/2018/video-blog-michael-oflaherty-antisemitism

26. Lee Harpin, 'Board president: "It's like Jeremy Corbyn has declared war on the Jews"', *Jewish Chronicle*, 22 August 2018.

27. 'Jewish papers take unprecedented step of publishing the same page on Labour', *Jewish Chronicle*, 27 July 2018, www.thejc.com/comment/leaders/three-jewish-papers-take-the-unprecedented-step-of-publishing-the-same-page-on-labour-antisemitism-1.467641

28. Estelle Shirbon, 'British Jews protest against Labour's Corbyn over antisemitism', 26 March 2018, https://mobile.reuters.com/article/amp/idUSKBN1H21H1

29. See Antony Lerman, 'Weapons in the Labour antisemitism wars?' in Greg Philo et al., *Bad News for Labour: Antisemitism, the Party and Public Belief* (London: Pluto Press, 2019), 160–161.

30. For example, Gavin Lewis in *Arena*, in 'Antisemitism moral panics', November 2017, Jonathan Cook, in 'More than bad faith about antisemitism matters', 4 March 2019, and Bob Pitt in 'Has the Labour left subjected Luciana Berger to hatespeak and death threats?', 2019, https://bobpitt.org.uk/has-the-labour-left-subjected-luciana-berger-to-hatespeak-and-death-threats

31. Link to the video: www.youtube.com/watch?v=evSj4S4AC4Q

32. See Asa Winstanley, 'We "slaughtered" Jeremy Corbyn says Israel lobbyist', *Electronic Intifada*, 19 January 2020.

15. Against Typological Thinking: Summary and Conclusions

1. Heschel, 1969.

2. A reflection of that atmosphere was the publication in 2008 of *A Time to Speak Out: Independent Jewish Voices on Israel, Zionism and Jewish Identity*, edited by Anne Karpf, Brian Klug, Jacqueline Rose and Barbara Rosenbaum, published by Verso in London in 2008.

3. For a comprehensive analysis of the deliberate obfuscation of the process of adoption of the 'working definition' by the IHRA itself, see Jamie Stern-Weiner, *IHRA: The Politics of a Definition* (London: Free Speech on Israel, 24 April 2021), https://freespeechonisrael.org.uk/ihra-politics/#sthash.4NkmBvk1.dpbs

4. For example see Dr Dana Barnett, 'The Jerusalem Declaration on Antisemitism is itself antisemitic', 3 October 2021, Begin-Sadat Center for Strategic Studies, Bar Ilan University, Perspectives Paper No. 2,166, https://besacenter.org/the-jerusalem-declaration-on-antisemitism-is-itself-antisemitic/

5. Supplementary Submission by JVL to the EHRC and the Forde Inquiry, August 2021, www.jewishvoiceforlabour.org.uk/app/uploads/2021/08/How-Labours-Claim-of-Countering-Antisemitism-Has-Resulted-in-a-Purge-of-Jews-Supplementary-submission.pdf

6. Sutcliffe, 2020, 279.

7. Ibid., 287.

8. See Yossi Shain, 'The Israelization of antisemitism' in Shain, Erez Kasif and Michal Shwartz, 'The Israeli century and the Israelization of Judaism', *Ha-meah ha-yisraelit ve-ha-yisraelizaziyah shelha-yahadut* (Tel Aviv: Chemed Books,

2019); Yossi Shain, lecture at the ISGAP Oxford Summer Institute 2018, Day 6, YouTube.

9. See M Schwarz-Friesel and J Reinharz, 'The Israelization of antisemitism', *Jerusalem Post*, 16 February 2017.

10. https://blogs.timesofisrael.com/interview-with-mk-yossi-shain/

11. Ibid.

12. Friesel and Reinharz, 2017.

13. Interview with Yossi Shain, *The Times of Israel*, 20 August 2021, https://blogs.timesofisrael.com/interview-with-mk-yossi-shain/

14. Anidjar, 2007, 4.

15. Sutcliffe, 2020, 49.

16. Jasmin Gray, 'Student behind letter accusing Bristol University lecturer of antisemitism leads calls against her sacking', *Huffpost*, 21 February 2022, www.huffingtonpost.co.uk/entry/student-behind-letter-accusing-bristol-university-lecturer-of-anti-semitism-leads-calls-against-her-sacking_uk_58ac429de4b0f077b3eddbf1

17. Jenni Fraser, 'Lord Mann and David Feldman clash over IHRA antisemitism definition', *JC*, 29 December 2020, www.thejc.com/news/uk/government-adviser-lord-mann-and-antisemitism-expert-david-feldman-clash-over-ihra-definition-1.510171

18. 'Antisemitism Tsar', JVL, 9 December 2019, www.jewishvoiceforlabour.org.uk/article/antisemitism-tsar/

19. A. Dirk Moses, 'The German Catechism', *Geschichte der Gegenwart*, 23 May 2022, https://geschichtedergegenwart.ch/the-german-catechism/

20. Jonathan Myerson, 'Of course Dame Helen can play a Jew, darling. It's called acting!' Maureen Lipman once played an Anglican vicar—but she complains that Helen Mirren is the wrong religion to be cast as Golda Meir, *Daily Mail*, 6 January 2022, www.dailymail.co.uk/news/article-10373419/Of-course-Dame-Helen-play-Jew-darling-called-acting-Writes-JONATHAN-MYERSON.html

21. For a sympathetic re-working of Salo Baron's critique of the 'lachrymose conception' of Jewish history see Adam Teller, 'Revisiting Baron's "lachrymose conception": the meanings of violence in Jewish history', *AJS Review*, vol. 38, no. 2, 2014, www.cambridge.org/core/journals/ajs-review/article/revisiting-barons-lachrymose-conception-the-meanings-of-violence-in-jewish-history/2ACA85264350A0E96FD8CEEA19351151

22. Quoted in Klug, 2003, fn. 50.

23. Antony Lerman, '9/11 and the destruction of the shared understanding of antisemitism', openDemocracy, 14 September 2011, www.opendemocracy.net/en/911-and-destruction-of-shared-understanding-of-antisemitism/

Index

Thanks to our Patreon subscribers:

Andrew Perry
Ciaran Kane

Who have shown generosity and
comradeship in support of our publishing.

Check out the other perks you get by subscribing
to our Patreon – visit patreon.com/plutopress.

Subscriptions start from £3 a month.

The Pluto Press Newsletter

Hello friend of Pluto!

Want to stay on top of the best radical books
we publish?

Then sign up to be the first to hear about our
new books, as well as special events,
podcasts and videos.

You'll also get 50% off your first order with us
when you sign up.

Come and join us!

Go to bit.ly/PlutoNewsletter